D0759528

Trade Like an O'Neil Disciple

Founded in 1807, John Wiley & Sons is the oldest independent publishing company in the United States. With offices in North America, Europe, Australia and Asia, Wiley is globally committed to developing and marketing print and electronic products and services for our customers' professional and personal knowledge and understanding.

The Wiley Trading series features books by traders who have survived the market's ever changing temperament and have prospered—some by reinventing systems, others by getting back to basics. Whether a novice trader, professional or somewhere in-between, these books will provide the advice and strategies needed to prosper today and well into the future.

For a list of available titles, visit our Web site at www.WileyFinance.com.

Trade Like an O'Neil Disciple

How We Made Over 18,000% in
the Stock Market

GIL MORALES
AND DR. CHRIS KACHER

WILEY

John Wiley & Sons, Inc.

Published by John Wiley & Sons, Inc., Hoboken, New Jersey.
Published simultaneously in Canada.

Charts provided courtesy of eSignal. Copyright 2010 by eSignal.

For general information on our other products and services or for technical support, please contact our Customer Care Department within the United States at (800) 762-2974, outside the United States at (317) 572-3993 or fax (317) 572-4002.

Wiley also publishes its books in a variety of electronic formats. Some content that appears in print may not be available in electronic books. For more information about Wiley products, visit our web site at www.wiley.com.

Library of Congress Cataloging-in-Publication Data:

Morales, Gil, 1959–
  Trade like an O'Neil disciple : how we made over 18,000% in the stock market /
Gil Morales, Chris Kacher.
      p. cm. – (Wiley trading series)
  Includes index.
  ISBN 978-0-470-61653-6
  1. Stocks. 2. Speculation. 3. Portfolio management. I. Kacher, Chris. II. Title.
  HG4661.M597 2010
  332.63'22–dc22

                                                    2010013522

Printed in the United States of America.

10 9 8 7 6 5 4

It is said that dedicating a book is one of the most exquisite acts of love one can perform. I love all who seek out and find their passion in life and in spirit, which include those closest to me, you know who you are.
—Chris Kacher

For the other riders in my bumper car of life: Linda, Claire, and Alex, and for the two people who are responsible for setting me off on this bumper car ride:
my parents, Bob and Irene.
—Gil Morales

Contents

Foreword

B ill O'Neil is a passionate student of the markets and one of the most successful traders of the modern era. From our days at SMU and later during his time in Alaska, Bill was studying charts and developing his vast understanding of the markets. Based upon his historical studies back into the nineteenth century, Bill has always tried to help the investor improve their success ratios.

His commitment to bringing that knowledge to the average and/or professional investment community has cost him millions of dollars through the subsidization of *Investor's Business Daily*® and other O'Neil projects.

It has been my privilege to have known Bill for almost sixty years and while my own investment style is not exactly O'Neil's, it is built upon the same building blocks. When I first went to Wall Street in June 1962 (ten years after meeting WON almost to the day), William T. Golden, the New York partner in Cornell, Linder & Co., a member of the NYSE, told me: "We mostly invest in stocks and convertibles with increasing sales and increasing earnings. Go find them, keep your losses under control and everything will work out."

Luckily for me, those few words of wisdom have been the basis of my investment style during the past fifty years.

Stripped to its core values that is also basically O 'Neil's CAN SLIM®.

O'Neil is often accused of being only a technician, but that is not true. His investment style builds heavily upon fundamentals, chart patterns, market trends, sector rotation, and economic strength. O'Neil is also not a fan of modern portfolio theory and often concentrates his portfolio in only a few stocks. Performance, not diversity, is the key to O'Neil's long-term success. There have been times when O'Neil's investment portfolio could be 100 percent in cash or concentrated in just one or two positions.

Gil Morales and Chris Kacher learned from O'Neil while working as successful portfolio managers at William J. O'Neil + Co., Inc. In this book, they help the investor understand how the CAN SLIM investment system works and have added a few tweaks to the O'Neil strategies that they have developed.

It is evident that they are highly indebted to O'Neil's philosophy and trading principles. However, like all traders that are constantly seeking an edge, they have also developed some of their own unique indicators and rules that they disclose in the book.

It is all here, the gains, the losses, both at the O'Neil firm and later on their own, the changes in the O'Neil system as market conditions dictate. Wall Street is a big casino and black swans do occur to upset the best laid plans.

Dr. K and Gil make it quite evident that there is a lot to learn from O'Neil and the CAN SLIM investment system and they are deeply indebted to WON as are his many legions of admirers for providing the tools to improve investment success ratios.

But most important, they also demonstrate that it is impossible to trade like Bill O'Neil because it is simply impossible to have his unique feel for the markets. But by understanding O'Neil's principles, investors can improve their success ratios.

Trade Like an O'Neil Disciple fascinated me and I will read it time and time again to improve my results!

Fred Richards
www.adrich.com
www.stratinv.net

Preface

As a successful investor, William J. O'Neil has touched the lives of individual and institutional investors around the globe whom he has taught to make money in stocks. How many we cannot know for sure, but rest assured that it is likely in the hundreds of thousands, if not far more. His methods and the investment tools he and his firm have developed for individual and institutional investors alike have empowered many to find financial freedom in their lives. We are two of those investors, and we can vouch for the fact that Bill O'Neil is responsible for helping to create many new millionaires in this world. As former internal portfolio managers at William O'Neil + Company, Inc. we met many individual and institutional investors who benefitted from O'Neil's strategies and expertise, so we know this from first-hand experience. We've also made lots of money in the markets, thanks to learning and executing O'Neil's methodologies.

This book is our attempt to articulate what we learned from Bill O'Neil, working directly with him under fire in real-time while trading the markets. But first a disclaimer: this book is not sanctioned by or approved by Bill O'Neil or William O'Neil + Co., Inc. Our interpretation and views may not be those of Bill or the company. This book explains how we trade based on our learning experience as proprietary traders at William O'Neil + Co., Inc. This book is also not about the CAN SLIM® methodology. Readers are encouraged to read Bill's seminal work (and all his other books), *How to Make Money in Stocks*, and to refer to *Investor's Business Daily* and investors.com. Between Bill's excellent books, the reporting in the paper, and the web site, there is a plethora of tutorials and educational materials that detail O'Neil's methods. We encourage you to make good use of these books and tools.

Trade Like an O'Neil Disciple is our unique experience with this man who we feel is likely the world's greatest investor. In this book we provide insights into O'Neil's genius as we saw it. We track the markets of the late 1990s and early 2000s with real-time excerpts from our trading diaries that bear witness to O'Neil's incredible investment genius. In real-time, O'Neil embodies the Latin term *speculari*, which means "to spy out or examine" as he perceives subtle shifts in the market, almost by osmosis. In this book we hope to provide insight into some of his thought processes, as we saw them unfold, using real-time market examples. The O'Neil methodologies primarily represent a dynamic approach to the stock market, and this dynamism is entirely correct and appropriate since the stock market is itself a dynamic beast. The brutal bear markets of 2000–2002, and 2008 have proven that "static" buy-and-hold strategies are a fantastic way to lose a lot of money. The markets are dynamic and O'Neil's methods are likewise dynamic, yet we are still human beings with our foibles and quirks. O'Neil advises making up "little rules" along the way as you observe your own trading and recognize these little "quirks" in yourself. These little rules may be sub-systems or rules that establish boundaries for containing weaknesses or are put in place to capitalize on strengths. We ourselves, as longterm, experienced practitioners of O'Neil methodologies, have come up with many over the years. It's not as if we are turning the system upside down, or using it in piecemeal fashion as we pick and choose what rules we choose to use. Instead, what we have done over time is to use the market as an effective feedback system with respect to our own trading to come up with small rules and sub-systems that enhance our own approach to O'Neil's methods. One of our "quirks" is that we like to buy stocks earlier in bases, and not just when they stage an obvious new-high base-breakout. Another "quirk" of ours is that we like to buy gap-ups, particularly in a strong leader as it is breaking the "line of least resistance" to the upside and potentially embarking on a sharp price run. In this book we share with you trading rules that have worked well for us, and how we buy stocks and short stocks using refined "sub-methods" that we have tested both statistically and in practice, and have found to be effective enhancements to our investing.

We've also made a lot of mistakes, and in this book we discuss those mistakes in order to help prevent you from making the same mistakes, hopefully saving you time, money, and misery in the process.

Trading for us has been as much a spiritual journey as it has been an investing journey, and in the process has provided each of us with a microcosm of life itself. The return of +18,241.2 percent works out to +110.5 percent on an annualized basis over the seven-year period from January 1996 to December 2002. But to achieve such a result, a couple of sizeable drawdowns did occur including one that was nearly −50% during the second and third quarter of 1999. As well, we would point out that the returns we discuss in Chapters 2 and 3 were achieved in our personal accounts, and not in the accounts we managed for William O'Neil + Company, Inc.

While the dollars in our trading accounts and the returns are the way we track our success and performance, trading is ultimately not so much about making money as it is about understanding what Eckhard Tolle referred to as "The Power of Now." Like athletes and thrill-seekers who engage in activities that seem extremely dangerous, almost to the point of the unthinkable to those who live more normal lives, we as traders seek the "rush" that comes not from a successful trade, but from the experience of being entirely in the present as we operate "in the zone" and a certain fluidity and calmness pervades our actions as we engage the markets in real-time. Ocean wave surfers experience this as the intensity of riding a powerful wave-form that forces them to focus on the matter at hand as a matter of sheer survival. Focusing on the matter at hand forces one to operate entirely in the present—there is no worrying about yesterday's problems, or tomorrow's challenges, there is only the "now." If you cannot understand why someone would seek to ride a 50-foot-high "death wall" of ocean water then you likely have never ridden one. Riding such a wave is the rush—what we call being "in the zone"—and it applies to trading as much as it applies to surfing, hang-gliding, rock-climbing or any other dangerous yet exhilarating endeavor that humans are drawn to like moths to a porch light. As traders we both share an appreciation for the spiritual aspects of this phenomenon, which is really nothing more than the simple, spiritual act of "becoming one" with the present moment; nothing more, nothing less. This is the essence of successful trading.

Gil Morales
Dr. Chris Kacher
June 2, 2010

Acknowledgments

W hile it is always important to acknowledge those who assisted in the production of a book such as this, we feel it is just as important to acknowledge that this book was written and produced with absolutely no assistance, endorsement, or cooperation from William J. O'Neil or any of the O'Neil organizations. This is an independent work. However, there were many people who are responsible in some way, large or small, for this book that you now hold in your hands. Among these, we would like to thank Mike Scott, who provided invaluable technical assistance in creating the charts for this book, the folks at eSignal, who let us use their excellent charts and data, Rachel Hain, who helped on several fronts during the writing of the book, and Kevin Marder.

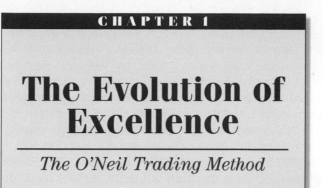

CHAPTER 1

The Evolution of Excellence

The O'Neil Trading Method

A s portfolio managers who once ran money for William J. O'Neil, we have observed that a meaningful portion of the O'Neil "body of thought" is derived from the philosophies of those who preceded him, particularly the works of Richard Wyckoff and Jesse Livermore. When it comes to market thought, you can never entirely understand Bill O'Neil until you have read and understood these two gentlemen. Obviously, the techniques and philosophies of the famous trader Jesse Livermore, as presented in the classic *Reminiscences of a Stock Operator*, by Edwin Lefèvre and Livermore's own *How to Trade in Stocks*, figure heavily in the underlying pulse that governs the way Bill O'Neil and his stable of portfolio managers trade. Richard Wyckoff, as one of the first to write about Jesse Livermore in his original work, *Jesse Livermore's Methods of Trading Stocks*, espoused much of the common sense investment philosophies and maxims that have found their way into the writings and investment thought of William J. O'Neil. Even Nicolas Darvas, in his famous book, *How I Made $2 Million in the Stock Market* (Carol Publishing Group, 1998), laid the foundation for O'Neil's "chart bases" with his own "boxes," which he described as simply normal consolidation channels within which a stock's action was judged to be normal or abnormal.

The themes that echo from Wyckoff, Livermore, Darvas, and others weave the essential fabric from which "O'Neil–style" investment methodologies are cut. These methodologies utilized the work of O'Neil's predecessors by bringing into play the time-tested characteristics of winning stocks that O'Neil painstakingly identified, analyzed, catalogued, and verified in his numerous Model Book Studies, some of which your authors had the privilege of producing and contributing to. By sifting through the best-performing, institutional-quality leading stocks in each and every type of market cycle, O'Neil identified their key common characteristics, the most basic of which provided the genesis for O'Neil's unique stock-selection template, commonly known to the investing public as CAN SLIM. Certainly, O'Neil owes a debt to the thinking of Livermore, Wyckoff, and others, and the roots of the O'Neil investment methodologies run deep in this regard. However, as former portfolio managers for William O'Neil + Company, Inc., we can vouch for the fact that such roots do not imply that O'Neil simply copied his predecessors. That would be a gross oversimplification, since the truth is that the O'Neil methodologies took the thinking of these outstanding stock market investors from the past to a much higher level by bringing greater clarity to the process as he formulated a concrete, concise, and practical approach to making money in the stock market.

The parallels between O'Neil and his predecessors provide an overarching backdrop to a general philosophy, a certain ethos, if you will, toward the market that is more than just Livermore's, or Wyckoff's, or even O'Neil's. As O'Neil himself used to tell us, "It's not MY system. It's the market's, because it is based on how the market actually works." In this manner, O'Neil simply sees his own work as furthering the basic process of understanding the market through observation and the application of common sense rules gained thereby. It is nothing more or less than understanding all the small realities that make up the stock market. Reviewing how O'Neil has taken and expanded upon the works of his predecessors is a useful exercise, and sets the backdrop for much of the research we have done to further our approach to the O'Neil/Livermore/Wyckoff approach to the market, and which is one of the main topics of this book.

PREPARATION, STUDY, AND PRACTICE

Don't dabble in stocks. Dig in and do some detective work.
—William O'Neil, *How to Make Money in Stocks*,
2nd ed. (New York: McGraw-Hill, 1995), 34

This the essential premise of O'Neil methodologies: They are in no way, shape, or form intended as a panacea for making money in the market. Human beings are complex organisms, and so represent the greatest variable in the implementation of any investment methodology, whether of "O'Neilian" origin or otherwise. This is why O'Neil insists that one must put in the time, effort, and work required if one intends to become a successful stock market investor: "Human nature being what it is, 90 percent of the people in the stock market, professionals and amateurs alike, simply haven't done enough homework."

O'Neil laments the fact that so many investors are looking for some magic formula that enables them to produce an optimal result in the stock market with little or no effort. In *The Successful Investor*, he laments the "rise of the individual investor" during the dot-com bubble market of 1999. "Most people, both investors and advisors, got hurt in the 2000 to 2002 downturn because they never took the time to learn sound investment rules and principles. In the 90s they thought they'd found a way to make money without doing much homework. They just bought tips, touts, and stories" (William J. O'Neil, *The Successful Investor* [New York: McGraw-Hill, 2004], xii).

While most investors do not hesitate to dabble in the markets, they would rarely dabble in medical or legal practice, or even in playing professional baseball. O'Neil reminds us, however, "Outstanding stockbrokers or advisory services are no more frequent than are outstanding doctors, lawyers, or baseball players" (William O'Neil, *How to Make Money in Stocks*, 2nd ed. [New York: McGraw-Hill, 1995], 256). This is not too far off from Richard Wyckoff's astute observation that "A person becomes competent in other fields because he has generally gone through a long period of practice and preparation. A physician, for example, goes to college, attends medical clinics, rides in an ambulance, serves in hospitals, and after some years of preparatory work, hangs out a sign. In Wall Street, the same M.D. would hang his sign first; then proceed to practice" (Richard Wyckoff, *How I Trade and Invest in Stocks & Bonds* [New York: The Magazine of Wall Street, 1924], 159–160).

Investing is hard work, and an investor requires no less preparation and expertise than any other white shoe professionals practicing their craft, whether it be law, medicine, software design, moviemaking, or otherwise. Jesse Livermore became annoyed when he was approached by friends or acquaintances who would ask him how they, too, could make money in the market. Biting his tongue, Livermore's answer eventually evolved into a curt, "I don't know," as he found it difficult "to exercise patience with such people. In the first place, the inquiry is not a compliment to a man who has made a scientific study of investment and speculation. It would be as fair for the layman to ask an attorney or a surgeon: 'How can I make some quick money in law or surgery?'" (Jesse Livermore, *How to Trade in Stocks* [Greenville: Traders Press, 1991], 15).

While reminding investors that success can only be achieved by hard work and persistence, O'Neil, always the optimist, makes it plain that success is within the reach of anyone willing to make the effort, and in his book, *How to Make Money in Stocks* (2009, 9), he urges us all on with a touch of self-sufficient idealism, "The American dream can be yours if you have the drive and desire and make up your mind to never give up on yourself." But O'Neil insists from the start that, as Wyckoff wrote, ". . . anybody who thinks he knows of a short-cut that will not involve 'sweat of the brow' is sadly mistaken" (*How I Trade and Invest in Stocks & Bonds* [New York: The Magazine of Wall Street, 1924], 93).

BUY EXPENSIVE—NOT CHEAP—STOCKS

Like Livermore, O'Neil despises a lazy approach to the market because it results in one trying to take what is perceived as the easy route to stock market riches. Nowhere else is this more embodied than in the idea of buying stocks that are "cheap." This age-old trap is easy to fall into, since most novice investors approach the market with an incorrigibly ingrained consumer mentality that views anything selling today at a lower price than it was yesterday as a "bargain." This is perhaps because the individual investor views herself as a consumer endpoint, when in fact the investor should act like a business that purchases raw or finished goods and intends to turn around and sell them at a higher price. Hence, O'Neil's story about red dresses and yellow dresses, where the slower-selling yellow dresses are marked down by the store owner to get them out of the "portfolio," otherwise known as the store inventory, so that more of the hotter-selling red dresses can be purchased and resold at higher prices.

O'Neil advocates buying stocks that are "red dresses" selling "like hotcakes" at all-time high prices. The reason for this is simple: ". . . real leaders start their big moves by selling at new price highs, not near new lows or off a good amount from their highs" (*How to Make Money in Stocks*, 4th ed. [New York: McGraw-Hill, 2009], 426). In a contrarian sense, this is what makes the concept of buying stocks at new highs so effective. It is simply not obvious to the crowd, who fear buying a stock that looks to be selling at such a high price, because, as O'Neil points outs, "What seems too high in price and risky to the majority usually goes higher eventually, and what seems low and cheap usually goes lower" (2009, 174). The market tries to fool the majority of investors the majority of the time, so if new high prices in a particular stock make the crowd timid about buying it, then that is likely the precise time to be buying the stock.

Like O'Neil, Jesse Livermore appreciated higher-priced stocks far more than "cheap" stocks, advising, "One should never sell a stock, because it seems high-priced. . . . Conversely, never buy a stock because it has had a big decline from its previous high. The likelihood is that the decline is based on a very good reason. That stock may still be selling at an extremely high price relative to its value—even if the current level seems low" (Jesse Livermore, *How to Trade in Stocks* [Greenville: Traders Press, 1991], 25).

AVERAGING DOWN

Trying to buy cheap stocks is but one frequent sin committed by novice or lazy investors. Another lazy man's sin eschewed by O'Neil and his predecessors is the concept of "averaging down." Richard Wyckoff observed, "A great deal of money is lost or tied up by people who make a practice of averaging. Their theory is that if they buy a security at 100 and it goes to 90, it is that much cheaper, and the lower it goes the cheaper it grows."

Retail stock brokers, when in need of a way to avoid taking responsibility for a bad recommendation, often try to use "averaging down" as a way to justify the initial decision to purchase a stock at higher prices. To some extent, this evolved as a convenient corollary to the retail investment concept of "dollar-cost averaging" when purchasing mutual funds, about which we're sure many readers are only too familiar. To O'Neil, this is shameful: "About the only thing that's worse is for brokers to take themselves off the hook by advising customers to 'average down.' If I were advised to do this, I'd close my account and look for a smarter broker" (*How to Make Money in Stocks*, 4th ed. [New York: McGraw-Hill, 2009], 247).

Jesse Livermore was no less harsh in his assessment of the averaging-down technique when he said, "It is foolhardy to make a second trade, if your first trade shows you a loss. Never average losses. Let that thought be written indelibly upon your mind" (*How to Trade in Stocks* [Greenville: Traders Press, 1991], 26). Richard Wyckoff took the concept just a little bit further by adding, "It is better to 'average up' than to 'average down'" (*Stock Market Technique Number 1* [New York: Richard D. Wyckoff, 1933], 50). And as we know, O'Neil contrasts his sermons against averaging down by strongly advocating "averaging up" on one's winning stocks.

CUTTING LOSSES QUICKLY

Jesse Livermore wrote in *How to Trade in Stocks*, "You should have a clear target where to sell if the market moves against you. And you must obey your rules! Never sustain a loss of more than 10 percent of your capital. Losses are twice as expensive to make up. I always established a stop before making a trade" (*How to Trade in Stocks* [Greenville: Traders Press, 1991], 171). O'Neil advises a 7 to 8 percent automatic stop-loss policy on all stock purchases, and the main reason for this is to keep oneself out of danger. Huge losses in the market can be debilitating, and O'Neil views a strict stop-loss policy, whether at his threshold of 6 to 7 percent or Livermore's 10 percent, as absolutely necessary for survival in the stock market. Livermore observed, "Taking the first small loss is wise . . . profits take care of themselves but losses never do" (1991, 7).

Richard Wyckoff in *Stock Market Technique Number 1* advised: "Your first line of defense is a stop order—placed when you make the trade, or immediately thereafter. If you fail to limit your risk at inception, make a practice of looking over your commitments every day, or twice every week and selling out, at the market, all showing a loss. That will keep your sheet clean and allow your profitable trades to run until the time comes to close them out" (1933, 96). This concept of using a stop-loss as a "line of defense" runs parallel to O'Neil's thinking that "letting your losses run is the most serious mistake made by almost all investors" (*How to Make Money in Stocks*, 2nd ed. [New York: McGraw-Hill, 1995], 93) simply because "[i]f you don't sell to cut your losses when you get into trouble, you can easily lose the confidence you'll need to make buy and sell decisions in the future" (1995, 252). Not only do losses cut into the capital an investor has available to capitalize on potential opportunities in the stock market, they also take their toll on an investor's psychological capital, their all-important self-confidence.

To O'Neil, Livermore, and Wyckoff, losses are just part of the process, and it is always better to take a little pain now rather than a lot of pain later, because, as O'Neil reveals, "The whole secret to winning big in the stock market is not to be right all the time, but to lose the least amount possible when you're wrong" (1995, 240).

TAKING PROFITS TOO SOON—LETTING YOUR WINNERS RUN

The O'Neil methodology is essentially a trend-following system—you want to be in the market when the trend is in your favor, and you want to capture a large portion of any trend by riding with it for as long as possible. To O'Neil, buying a winning stock is only half the problem, because the key to capitalizing on a big price move in any potential, big, winning stock is in how you handle the stock once you have bought it. As Livermore said, it is the uncommon man who can "sit tight and be right," so sitting with and properly handling a meaningful position in a big, winning stock through the bulk of its upside price move is a big part of how O'Neil makes big money in the stock market. This necessitates adhering to a basic principle that Livermore stipulated when he said, "As long as a stock is acting right, and the market is right, do not be in a hurry to take a profit" (*How to Trade in Stocks* [Greenville: Traders Press, 1991], 21). You can't make big money in stocks if you don't give them a chance to make big money for you.

O'Neil recommends "take your losses quickly and your profits slowly," because "your objective is not just to be right but to make big money when you are right" (*How to Make Money in Stocks*, 4th ed. [New York: McGraw-Hill, 2009], 247–272). Trading for quick profits requires that one be constantly active and thinking about the next trade. It is a notoriously busy way to approach the market, and is entirely out of sync with the ideal that O'Neil–style investing tends toward. In our experience, there is nothing easier than making big money in the market once you have latched onto a big winner, because at that point all you are doing is sitting more and thinking less. When your stocks are trending nicely to the upside and you are fully invested, there is, from a practical standpoint, very little to do. You are simply letting your winners run. This is what we like to call "being in the zone," a mental space that derives from Livermore's principle: "It never is your thinking that makes big money. It's the sitting" (Edwin Lefèvre, *Reminiscences of a Stock Operator* [New York: John Wiley & Sons, 1994], 68).

Richard Wyckoff had his own unique perspective on the idea of cutting losses quickly and letting winners run when he wrote in *Stock Market Technique Number 1*, "Are you getting rich backwards? Then you are taking two points profit on your speculative trades and letting your losses run. Why not reverse this rule? Limit your risk to one, two or three points and let your profits run" (1933, 52).

POSITION CONCENTRATION

A big part of handling a winning stock correctly is properly scaling one's position size. If you only want to make average market returns, then scale your positions to a very small size, and your portfolio will act very much like a market index. Having scores of positions is nothing more than "closet indexing." Most mutual fund managers take positions that make up 1 to 2 percent of their portfolio equity or less, and they may have 100 to 200 positions or more. To O'Neil, this is anathema. If you want to make big returns, then you absolutely must concentrate your capital in a strongly-trending stock, and position sizes of 1 to 2 percent of one's total portfolio equity are, to put it bluntly, quite wimpy from an O'Neil perspective. The O'Neil method of pyramiding into strongly acting positions while weeding out weaker ones generally gets an investor concentrated in the right stocks during a bull market cycle. At times, your authors have been fully invested in as few as two stocks, using full, 200 percent margin, so that each position represents 100 percent of the account's gross equity. This is how you make big money in the market, and it is the essence of handling one's stocks properly to achieve maximum effect.

For this reason, O'Neil eschews "diversification" and cites the wisdom of Gerald Loeb, who declared that diversification was a "hedge for ignorance." O'Neil's solution was to be very specific about what stocks one owned in any bull market cycle, suggesting, "The more you diversify, the less you know about any one area. Many investors overdiversify. The best results are achieved through concentration: putting all your eggs in just a few baskets that you know a great deal about and continuing to watch those baskets very carefully" (*How to Make Money in Stocks*, 4th ed. [New York: McGraw-Hill, 2009], 274).

The purpose of position concentration from an O'Neil perspective is two-fold. On the one hand it allows an investor to fully capitalize on a big price move in a winning stock, while on the other it allows the investor to focus his or her attention on "fewer eggs," which O'Neil views as a safer mental approach than trying to keep track of too many positions at once. Even Livermore himself thought ". . . that it is dangerous to start spreading out all over the market. By this I mean, do not have an interest in too many stocks at one time. It is much easier to watch a few than many" (*How to Trade in Stocks* [Greenville: Traders Press, 1991], 33).

To O'Neil, it is not necessary to own every stock in the market; to have a need to "kiss all the babies," as he is fond of saying. He whittles it all down to one basic concept: "The winning investor's objective should be to have one or two big winners rather than dozens of very small profits" (*How to Make Money in Stocks*, 4th ed. [New York: McGraw-Hill, 2009], 274).

DEALING IN BIG STOCKS AND INSTITUTIONAL SPONSORSHIP

Owning the biggest winners in the market means owning the stocks that institutions are piling into, and O'Neil sees modern-day mutual funds, hedge funds, and pension funds, and other members of the "institutional investor zoo," as akin to the "pools" and "trusts" of Jesse Livermore's and Richard Wyckoff's era. It is the accumulation of stock by large institutions that produces the huge price moves upon which O'Neil methodologies seek to capitalize. And the smart institutions, such as those with the better research and stock selection skills, are the ones in whose footsteps you want to follow. O'Neil asserts, "It takes big demand to push up prices, and by far the biggest source of demand for stocks is institutional investors, such as mutual funds, pension funds, hedge funds, insurance companies, [etc]. A winning stock doesn't need a huge number of institutional owners, but it should have several at a minimum." O'Neil continues, "[Diligent investors] look for stocks that are held by at least one or two of the more savvy portfolio managers who have the best performance records" (*How to Make Money in Stocks*, 4th ed. [New York: McGraw-Hill, 2009], 193–194).

Knowing where the smart money is moving is central to O'Neil's methodology, and understanding the quality of institutional sponsorship coming into a stock is no different from what Richard Wyckoff advised when he wrote, "It is important to know whether large operators, inside interests, pools, or the public dominate the market for a certain security or group." Wyckoff went on to explain, "The reason this is so important is as follows: A combination of bankers will seldom be found on the long side of the market unless they expect a pronounced change in security market conditions in the near future. Their own purchases, therefore, are an indication of probable betterment. When a pool takes hold, it is usually in a certain one or a few issues which are likely to be favorably affected by developments known to a few but not generally known" (*How I Trade and Invest in Stocks & Bonds* [New York: The Magazine of Wall Street, 1924], 183).

O'Neil's unique and deep understanding of the institutional investor and the implications of institutional sponsorship is founded in the experience he has had advising some of the largest and most successful institutional investors on the planet. It is this understanding that generates what we have dubbed The Big Stock Principle that drove O'Neil's thinking in any market cycle. Knowing which stocks represented the cutting edge of developments driving any particular economic, and hence market, cycle means knowing where institutional investors "have to be" with respect to positioning their portfolios. When institutional investors start shoveling money into stocks that they "have to be" invested in, this fuels tremendous upside price moves in those stocks, and it is what makes them "Big Stocks." It is a central tenet of O'Neil-style investing.

CHART PATTERNS

Books like *How I Made $2 Million in the Stock Market*, by the famous ballroom dancer Nicolas Darvas, figure into O'Neil's concepts of "bases," which Darvas termed "boxes." O'Neil, however, took it quite a bit further with his colorful, descriptive cataloguing of consolidation patterns or bases that he termed "ascending," "cup-with-handle," "double-bottom," "square box," "flat base," and "high, tight flag," among others—the chart patterns from which, as O'Neil observed, big, winning stocks emerged as they started their huge upside price romps. As well, these patterns represented the "continuation" that patterns hugely performing stocks form on the way up as they naturally and normally pause and digest their gains during an overall intermediate to longer-term price run before proceeding higher.

Like O'Neil and his bases, Darvas's "box theory" emerged from his own direct observation and study of stock charts and tables: "I started to realize that stock movements were not completely haphazard. Stocks did not fly like balloons in any direction. As if attracted by a magnet, they had a defined upward or downward trend which, once established, tended to continue. Within this trend stocks moved in a series of frames, or what I began to call boxes. They would oscillate fairly consistently between a low and a high point. The area which enclosed this up-and-down movement represented the box or frame. These boxes began to exist very clearly for me" (Nicolas Darvas, *How I Made $2 Million in the Stock Market* [New York: Carol Publishing Group, 1998], 51).

O'Neil is far more specific, however, about the precise structure of these "boxes" or "bases," and his work goes into much detail about the exact shapes, durations, and magnitudes of these various price consolidation structures. But, like Darvas, O'Neil recognizes: "Chart patterns are simply areas of price correction and consolidation, usually after an earlier price advance. The primary challenge in analyzing price consolidation structures is to diagnose if the price and volume movements are normal or, instead, signal significant weakness or distribution" (*How to Make Money in Stocks*, 2nd ed. [New York: McGraw-Hill, 1995], 161).

It is, however, important to understand that Darvas's "box theory" is nothing more than a very rudimentary, initial version of O'Neil's chart pattern zoo. Darvas never bothered to measure the minimum durations for his boxes to determine whether a longer duration was preferable to a shorter one, nor did he measure the magnitude, or range, of these boxes to determine any meaningful characteristics thereby. As he puts it, "I found that a stock sometimes stayed for weeks in one box. I did not care how long it stayed in its box as long as it did—and did not fall below the lower frame figure" (*How I Made $2 Million in the Stock Market* [New York: Carol Publishing Group, 1998], 52).

O'Neil also went way beyond the simplistic "box theory" by recognizing the importance of applying historical precedent in his work. O'Neil observed that the chart patterns formed by market-leading stocks in one market cycle often repeated themselves in the market leaders of a later cycle. As an example, O'Neil has discussed in public forums how a big pullback by America Online (AOL) to its 50-day moving average back in 1998 reminded him of another big winner he played, Syntex Corp., in 1965. In this manner, Syntex served as a "historical precedent" for AOL in 1998, and served as an invaluable guide in helping O'Neil handle the position for what turned out to be massive gains. We know—we were there when it happened.

The idea of historical precedence, of course, can be seen as derived from Jesse Livermore, who declared in *How to Trade in Stocks*, "I absolutely believe that price movement patterns are being repeated. They are recurring patterns that appear over and over, with slight variations. This is because markets are driven by humans—and human nature never changes" (Greenville: Traders Press, 1991, 96). And, as O'Neil says, "It's just history repeating itself over and over again, human nature continually on parade" (*The Successful Investor*, 3rd ed. [New York: McGraw-Hill, 2004], 84). Wyckoff also observed that, "In a certain sense, reading charts is like reading music, in which both endeavor to interpret correctly the composer's ideas and the expression of his art. Just so a chart of the averages, or of a single stock, reflects the ideas, hopes, ambitions, and purposes of the mass mind operating in the market, or of a manipulator handling a single stock" (*Stock Market Technique Number 2* [New York: Richard D. Wyckoff, 1933], 136).

O'Neil is often pejoratively dismissed as a "chartist," as if this is proof that he should be written off as some sort of investment pariah. But we should not forget that while he was a pioneer in figuring out how to automate the production of printed stock charts, he was not the first to recognize the usefulness of charts in stock forecasting. In *Stock Market Technique 2*, Richard Wyckoff devoted a short chapter to answering Why You Should Choose Charts and summed up his assessment of the usefulness of consulting stock price charts by writing, "The ticker records stock market history on a long strip of tape. The charts record the same history transposed into another form, more convenient, more valuable for the purpose of studying past performance as an aid in forecasting—I should say *invaluable*" (1933, 66).

For O'Neil, technical analysis and the use of charts is all about determining the actions of institutional investors as they set about systematically accumulating stocks. In this way O'Neil does not approach the use of charts in a mechanical way, without incorporating any aspects of judgment, but rather as a tool to determine what the big players, the institutions, are doing. In this manner he is similar to Wyckoff, who advised that investors study charts in order to uncover the "motives behind the market action to interpret the behavior of stocks" (*Charting the Stock Market, The Wyckoff Method*, ed. Jack K. Huston [Seattle: Technical Analysis, Inc., 1948], 13, 16).

PIVOTAL POINTS VERSUS PIVOT POINTS

Buying at the exact right point is a key mechanic in the O'Neil methodology, and O'Neil's concept of a "pivot point" is drawn from Livermore's "pivotal point," of which Livermore had a "reversal pivotal point" and a "continuation pivotal point." We might consider O'Neil's pivot point buy points in stocks, generally defined by breakouts to new price highs, as more in keeping with Livermore's concept of a "continuation pivot point," whereas O'Neil's concept of a "follow-through day" as confirming an upturn in the market after a prior correction or bear market to be similar to Livermore's "reversal pivotal point" since it indicates a reversal in the market's trend from bear to bull phase. In *How to Trade in Stocks* by Jesse Livermore and *How to Make Money in Stocks* by William O'Neil, both writers share a common regard for such a "pivot" or "pivotal" buy point as the exact point where the risk/reward equation is most in the investor's favor, where the ducks are lined up in a row, so to speak, and so the stock should be bought once the price reaches this key pivot/pivotal point.

Waiting for the pivotal point to present itself requires patience, and Livermore would do his best to avoid taking action until and unless the correct pivotal point signal was given, because this assured his success, as he puts it, "Whenever I had the patience to wait for the market to arrive at what I call a 'Pivotal Point' before I started to trade, I have always made money in my operations. Why? Because I then commenced my play just at the psychological time at the beginning of a move" (*How to Trade in Stocks* [Greenville: Traders Press, 1991], 43). O'Neil says, "The winning individual investor can afford to wait and begin buying at these precise pivot points. This is where the real move starts and all the exciting action originates" (*How to Make Money in Stocks*, 2nd ed. [New York: McGraw-Hill, 1995], 164). The correct buy point lies at what both O'Neil and Livermore saw as a "line of least resistance," where the stock was "in the clear" and able to launch higher with little to no impediment.

The point of buying right is to enter a stock right at the point where the real move begins, so that if a stock is trading at 50, but the correct pivotal point is at 55, one must still wait for the stock to trade at the higher price if it is determined that this is where the line of least resistance lies. In this way, neither O'Neil nor Livermore were interested in capturing the movement between 50 and 55 as the stock approached the 55 pivotal point, but rather the "big move" from 55 to 100. As O'Neil says in *How to Make Money in Stocks*, second edition, "Your object is never to buy at the cheapest price or near the low but to begin buying at exactly the right time. This means you have to learn to wait for a stock to move up and trade at your buy point before making an initial commitment" (p. 165). In Chapter 6, we take the concept of pivot and pivotal points further.

TIMING THE MARKET: WHEN TO BE IN, WHEN TO BE OUT

From the O'Neil/Livermore perspective, waiting for the "pivotal point," or the exact right time to enter the markets means only being in the market when it is ripe for making money. Wait for the trend to develop and then jump on. A line with which we are all familiar came from something Jesse Livermore wrote in *How to Trade in Stocks*, "Successful traders always follow the line of least resistance. Follow the trend. The trend is your friend" (Greenville: Traders Press, 1991, 69).

O'Neil and Livermore both maintain that there is a time to be in the market and a time to be out of the market, even though common investment wisdom dictates that one cannot time the market and therefore should always be fully invested in the market so as not to miss a bull phase and fail to keep up with the market indexes. O'Neil vigorously disagrees with such mindless orthodoxy when he writes, "Don't ever let anyone tell you that you can't time the market. This is a giant myth passed on mainly by Wall Street, the media, and those who have never been able to do it, so they think it's impossible." According to O'Neil, "The erroneous belief that you can't time the market—that it's simply impossible, that no one can do it—evolved more than 40 years ago after a few mutual fund managers tried it unsuccessfully. They relied on personal judgments and feelings to determine when the market finally hit bottom and turned up for real. At the bottom, the news is all negative. So these managers, being human, hesitated to act" (*How to Make Money in Stocks*, 4th ed. [New York: McGraw-Hill, 2009], 200).

Indeed, opinions have no place when it comes to stock selection or market timing, and we have sought to implement objectivity to our methods. The "Dr. K Market Direction Model," which is discussed in detail in Chapter 7, is a statistical formalization of the price/volume action of the NASDAQ Composite and S&P 500 Indexes. The timing model, from its earlier forms to its most evolved form of today, has guided our trading with success since 1991. It was inspired by the "M" in O'Neil's "CAN SLIM" investment system. More about Dr. K's Market Direction Model and the current market timing signal can be found at the following web site: www.virtueofselfishinvesting.com, and Gil Morales's work with respect to market trend timing can be found at www.gilmoreport.com.

EMOTIONS AND PREDICTIONS

Trading the market is a very "Zen" activity, where you stay in the now, not worrying about what the market will do in the future, and not getting upset about a bad trade you may have made in the past. Instead one should stay focused in the present, reacting in real time to the evidence that the market is constantly presenting. No one has ever been able to predict market direction with any consistent reliability, but that is wholly unnecessary to being a successful investor. Successful investing is about watching the market day-to-day and acting accordingly. In fact, attempting to predict the market often leads to over-intellectualization, which is usually a recipe for losing money in the market. When the market goes against your own intellectualized "conclusions," you may be less likely to reverse your position, even in the face of factual price/volume action that is telling you that you are wrong. Pay less attention to what you think the market should be doing, and more to what the market is actually doing. As Livermore wrote, "Don't try and anticipate what the market will do next—simply go with the evidence of what the market is telling you—presenting you." (Richard Smitten, *Trade Like Jesse Livermore* [Hoboken, NJ: John Wiley & Sons, 2005], 13).

In the same vein as Livermore, O'Neil preaches that an investor does not need to know what the market is ***going to do***, but only what it is ***doing right now***. O'Neil wrote in *How to Make Money in Stocks*, third edition, "The key to staying on top of the stock market is not predicting or knowing what the market is going to do. It's knowing and understanding what the market has actually done in the past several weeks and what it is currently doing now" (2002, 75). Even Wyckoff adhered to this concept of remaining in the present at all times as he evaluated fresh evidence from the market in real time. He declared, "I am not one of the many who form opinions as to the future course of the stock market and then insist that the market justify their predictions.... It is enough to know that the market tells me what it is probably going to do today and in the near future. I do not expect to be informed very far in advance, because the market often changes its course. I must change my position accordingly" (*Stock Market Technique Number 1* [New York: Richard D. Wyckoff, 1933], 53).

This entire line of thought speaks to the concept of keeping one's emotions out of the equation. To Livermore, the twin evils of fear and hope were the undoing of most investors who operated heavily in the realm of emotion. Perhaps it is not so much that investors fear and then hope, but that they rarely fear or hope at the right time, as Livermore observed, "... when you inject hope and fear into the business of speculation ... you are apt to get the two confused and in reverse positions" (*How to Trade in Stocks* [Greenville: Traders Press, 1991], 20). On the other hand, when it comes to operating without fear, and keeping one's emotions in check when taking losses in the market, O'Neil borrows a bit of advice that comes from Richard Wyckoff suggesting one "sell down to the sleeping point."

LISTENING TO OPINIONS, NEWS, AND TIPS

When someone asks for a tip, it is best to tell them this: "Take no tips." Much money is lost by those who listen to tips. The person giving the tip may have an underlying motive. Or he just may not have all the facts even though he thinks he does. As Jesse Livermore wrote in *How to Trade in Stocks*, "Markets are never wrong—opinions often are" (1991, 18).

Markets are the final arbiter of all news known up to that point in time. At least that is what the big auction known as the stock market does. It prices the stock relative to its peers, so it is best to believe the market's assessment.

O'Neil wrote in *How to Make Money in Stocks*, fourth edition, "Many people are too willing to risk their hard-earned money on the basis of what someone else says, rather than taking the time to study, learn, and know for sure what they're doing. As a result, they risk losing a lot of money. Most rumors and tips you hear simply aren't true" (2009, 305). The same could be said of opinions by experts. O'Neil continued, "Maybe this explains why virtually every analyst appearing on CNBC after September 2000 continually recommended buying high-tech stocks as they were on their way to 80–90 percent declines." To paraphrase Livermore, opinions are often wrong, but markets never are.

Yet much of the investing public prefers the lazy way out. Wyckoff wrote, "Depending on the advice of others is a widespread public weakness" (quoted in William O'Neil *How to Make Money in Stocks*, 3rd ed. [New York: McGraw-Hill, 2002], 253). Many prefer to be handed the answers. Over the years, the question we have heard most frequently is "What are you buying?" The person asking the question usually has little understanding of the market and even less confidence in her own judgment, since she has not done the necessary preparation. Diligent study is the antidote. Wyckoff wrote, "When you understand stock market science you have no concern about important developments in your morning newspaper, because the news is not a factor in your operations. An experienced judge of the market regards the whole story that appears on the tape as though it were the expression of a single mind; that is, the composite mind of all traders, investors, bankers, pools, institutions, and others who are participating in the transactions" (*Stock Market Technique Number 2* [New York: Richard D. Wyckoff], 139).

OVERTRADING

Once an investor becomes seasoned and has developed a winning strategy that he has executed successfully for a number of years, he is still not immune to overtrading. Overtrading seems to plague both novice and expert alike, both in terms of trading when one should just be sitting in cash, and in terms of selling a position too soon, only to buy it back a few days later, then repeating this pattern of buying and selling.

Jesse Livermore wrote of an investor who lived in the mountains and received quotes that were three days old. Only a few times a year would this investor call his broker to place trades. This man was quite detached from the markets, so it came as a total surprise when people learned of his remarkable long-term success in the markets. When asked about his success, the man replied, "Well, I make speculation a business. I would be a failure if I were in the confusion of things and let myself be distracted by minor changes. I like to be away where I can think. Real movements do not end the day they start. It takes time to complete the end of a genuine movement. By being up in the mountains I am in a position to give these movements all the time they need" (*How to Trade in Stocks* [Greenville: Traders Press, 1991], 32).

Wyckoff echoed this sentiment when he wrote, "When in doubt do nothing. Don't enter the market on half convictions; wait till the convictions are fully matured." Wyckoff continued, "And so, whenever we feel these elements of uncertainty, either in our conclusions or in the positions we hold, let us clean house and become observers until, as that eminent trader Dickson G. Watts wrote, 'The mind is clear; the judgment trustworthy'" (*Stock Market Technique Number 1* [New York: Richard D. Wyckoff, 1933], 51, 108).

O'Neil acknowledges that there is a time when doing nothing is the best thing to do, and he is more specific about the symptoms: "It isn't that bases, breakouts, or the method isn't working anymore; it's that the timing and the stocks are simply all wrong. The price and volume patterns are phony, faulty, and unsound. The general market is turning negative . . . Be patient, keep studying, and be 100 percent prepared" (*How to Make Money in Stocks*, 4th ed. [New York: McGraw-Hill, 2009], 151). Indeed, patience exercised wisely by staying out of the market when conditions are not right can save an investor a huge sum of money.

THE O'NEIL APPROACH: TECHNO-FUNDAMENTALISM

O'Neil is often chided for being a "technician," but anyone who truly understands the O'Neil methodology understands that it is in reality a "techno-fundamental" approach that combines the use of technical analysis to determine when a stock is under accumulation within a chart pattern and where the proper pivot buy point is on the one hand with essential fundamental characteristics of historically big, winning stocks on the other hand. Nicholas Darvas coined the term "techno-fundamental" to describe his system for investing in stocks, which combined monitoring the price action of a stock to determine that it was acting correctly within its "boxes" as well as to define buy points as a stock emerged from the top of a "box" with earnings growth as Darvas describes, "I saw that it is true that stocks are the slaves of earning power. Consequently I decided that while there may be many reasons behind any stock movement, I would look only for one: improving earnings power or anticipation of it. To do that, I would marry my technical approach to the fundamental one. I would select stocks on their technical action in the market, but I would only buy them when I could give improving earnings power as my fundamental reason for doing so" (*How I Made $2 Million in the Stock Market* [New York: Carol Publishing Group, 1998], 79).

O'Neil doesn't just buy a stock just because it has a pretty chart—it must also exhibit the proper fundamental characteristics typical of winning stocks throughout history, according to O'Neil's own studies of historical precedent.

CONCLUSION

After intensive study of multitudes of market cycles spanning over one hundred years, it is clear that O'Neil carries on and refines the conversation that Jesse Livermore, Richard Wyckoff, and Nicholas Darvas started. Human nature does not change, so we carry on the conversation, voicing our successes, failures, and findings—all of which carry deep learning both on analytical and psychological levels. This is not rocket science, and almost anyone can apply these methodologies to become successful in their own right, but the technique does require long-term focus and dedication. While we do not pretend to be equal to the stature of any of these gentlemen, we do believe that as former O'Neil portfolio managers and as successful investors in our own right, using the O'Neil methodologies, we have something of value to add to the conversation. Certainly, as the markets continue to evolve, certain mechanics and applications of O'Neil methodologies will evolve as well, and it will be left up to traders like us to continue to evolve and improve our methods, but the basic philosophical foundation, the "ethos," of the O'Neil methodologies will remain the same.

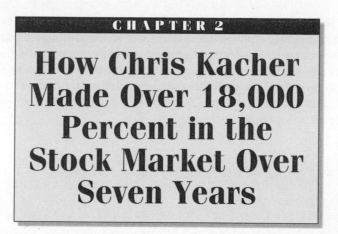

CHAPTER 2

How Chris Kacher Made Over 18,000 Percent in the Stock Market Over Seven Years

I t's one thing to learn an investment system with the idea that you should be able to use it to make reasonable profits in the stock market over time, perhaps having a triple-digit annual gain from time to time, but it's another thing to see how it is all put into practice. It's also interesting to hear how some individuals have made big money in the stock market, achieving unheard of gains in excess of, say, 1,000 percent in a single year, or some other ridiculous number like 18,000 percent over seven years. Most investors, however, have not seen what it looks like from the driver's seat, and when they hear of someone who has produced such performance numbers, it begs the question, "Exactly HOW was that done?" In this chapter and the next, we will give some insight into how we achieved big gains in the stock market—the stocks we bought, the market conditions under which they were bought, and our thought processes and decisions as we maneuvered through it all in real time.

By following along with us as we go through the experience of making big gains in the market, you may find that it is not as complicated as you might think. In the end, it is about working hard to put yourself in the position of being in the right place at the right time; that is, when a leading stock is just starting a huge upside price run. There is skill involved, and there is also some luck, but it is luck that you have to create for yourself by being in the right place at the right time. Once a position in a big leader has been taken and fully sized within your portfolio, the process becomes even simpler as you think less and sit more. Find the wave, catch the wave, and ride the wave for as long as it will take you. In this manner, investing is a lot like surfing, and when done properly, it can be just as exhilarating.

The rest of this chapter and the next will take the reader through periods in our separate trading careers where we made our biggest gains. Using annotated charts to illustrate what we were experiencing and thinking at the time, we get as close as we can to giving the reader a sense of what it was like to operate in real time during significant bull markets and windows of opportunity and to come away with huge profits that enabled us to achieve financial independence.

GAINING A FOOTHOLD IN THE BUSINESS

A journey of a thousand miles begins with a single step.
—Lao-tzu, Chinese philosopher (604 B.C.–531 B.C.),
The Way of Lao-tzu

I had always wanted to work for William O'Neil after learning that he and his protégé David Ryan had produced exceptional long-term investment track records that outperformed the markets over multiple market cycles. When I read William O'Neil's book, *How to Make Money in Stocks* back in 1989, it revolutionized my way of thinking about the market. O'Neil's hybrid method of applying both fundamental and technical analysis, as well as the "M" in CAN SLIM—a technique that enables one to stay on the right side of the market—resonated deeply within me.

So began my journey. From 1989 onward, I devoted many hours to the pursuit of making sense of the markets. In these early years, I created all sorts of econometric timing models based on a myriad of economic indicators that seemed to have predictive value. However, I later found that most of these indicators only worked over a period of less than 15 years; thus should markets change, these indicators would lose their ability to predict. I realized that studying 15 years worth of data was insufficient. Not surprisingly, in the years ahead, my market direction model kept returning to the purity of price/volume action of the major indices. As I developed my skills at reading charts, price/volume action in timing the markets eventually became the most important variable. I also spent much time poring over individual stock and stock market data so that I could learn what variables and situations drove stocks higher.

All these research studies not only put my trading account on track, but years later when I was hired at William O'Neil + Co, Inc., O'Neil noticed the breadth and depth of my market knowledge, so during the six years I was at O'Neil's firm, I was given the freedom to use all of the company's resources to carry out my studies. In some cases, I worked directly with O'Neil, and took the helm of some of his pet research projects including the *1998 Model Book* study. Naturally, being his right-hand stock market research man, I shared my research findings with him, sometimes calling him late at night, as he said I could call him anytime no matter how late it was if I felt I had made a significant discovery. Here was someone who clearly shared my passion for the markets. My decision to switch out of nuclear physics into the world of investments had been exactly the right thing to do. I always say once one finds one's true passion in life and takes the necessary steps to make the dream a reality, circumstances tend to align in one's favor.

The *1998 Model Book* project examined top performing stocks from 1992 to 1998, and to date, I have gone through nearly 20 market cycles going all the way back to the 1920s to study the stocks that made huge gains in each cycle. I have carefully studied each stock in detail to determine which fundamental and technical variables predicted success with the highest probability, and I came up with a set of variables that the winning stocks shared.

I also created and then refined a market direction model, discussed in full in Chapter 7, so that I would be on the right side of the market whether we were in an uptrend or a downtrend. The model has never missed a bull or bear market, and I have used it under fire and in real time since 1991, my first successful year in the market. In back tests, it has well outperformed the major averages returning an average of +33.1 percent per year since 1974, the first year of thorough back testing. To ensure the robust nature of the model, I have also spot tested the model in the 1920s and 1930s, which produced results that handily outperformed the leading market averages. The systematic portion of the model is a statistical formalization of price/volume action within the major indices. The discretionary portion of the model observes other factors such as behavior of leading stocks, sentiment/psychological indicators, and involves exchange-traded fund (ETF) selection, position sizing, and degree of leverage, depending on the strength of the signal.

Years after I had formulated my model, a salesperson who was retiring in 1999 and had been with William O'Neil + Company, Inc. since the late 1960s came to my office and gave me a large stack of original William O'Neil + Company, Inc. market calls that were dated from 1968 to 1999. I went carefully through each one and charted William O'Neil's buy and sell signals on the market. I saw that O'Neil never missed a bull or bear market. This further confirmed the validity of O'Neil's method in using price/volume of the major indices to time markets, and further underscored the importance of my statistically formalizing price/volume action of the major indices.

Prudent market timing by moving to the sidelines when the market was weak and buying leading stocks in leading industry groups when the market was in an uptrend resulted in a return of 18,241.2 percent, which works out to 110.5 percent on an annualized basis over the seven-year period from January 1996 to December 2002.* The rules I formulated are not my rules nor Wall Street's rules, but rules that are based on how the market actually works and how top stocks actually behave. Let's delve deeper by examining each year up close.

1996—"Y2K" STOCKS PUT ME OVER THE TOP

I made only minor headway with my personal account (PA) during the first quarter of 1996 as the market was what we might call "sideways" or mostly trendless. Over the years, I have found such trendless, choppy, and sideways markets to be the most challenging because it is easy to get nickeled and dimed as the market whips you in and out, forcing you to take many small losses that begin to add up over time. While getting nickeled and dimed, one must avoid being drawn and quartered.

In mid-March of 1996, I noticed a few high-quality stocks breaking out such as Iomega Corp. (IOM), shown in Figure 2.1. IOM had a natural monopoly on portable storage in the form of portable hard drives. They were the first company to effectively market the portability of their hard drives and so enjoyed this first-mover advantage in a space that had little competition at the time. At the time of the breakout, IOM had a 700 percent increase in earnings to 16 cents per share in its most recent quarter and a 287 percent increase in sales. In the prior quarter of September 1995, they had shown only 3 cents of profit per share so 16 cents represented a huge acceleration into profitability. Additionally, sales accelerated over the prior 6 quarters from –2 percent, 2 percent, 16 percent, 60 percent, 138 percent, to 287 percent.

IOM's base served as a beautiful launch pad for the stock. I put the usual 25 percent of my trading account into IOM on March 18 as it gapped up to new highs, even though very few stocks were still consolidating due to the sideways action in the general market.

When buying a stock breaking out of a base, you want the base to have strong, constructive and proper characteristics to help ensure that your stock possesses the best chance of a successful breakout. I used to carry around a hard copy of the William O'Neil + Company, Inc. Daily graphs®,

---

*Account verified by big-four auditor KPMG. KPMG, using normal accounting standards, could not account for the substantial tax earmarked funds that were sitting in my account but not traded, thus returns would have been significantly larger had I removed these funds at the beginning of each new year instead of letting them sit in the account.

FIGURE 2.1 Iomega Corp. (IOM) daily chart, breakout 1996.
Chart courtesy of eSignal, Copyright 2010.

so that I could mark it up and learn the difference between constructive and defective bases, and I recommend this old-fashioned technique to anyone who wishes to improve his chart reading abilities. General market action was a key variable. For example, in a weak, downtrending market, the strongest stocks would often form the left-hand side of what would eventually become a constructive cup-and-handle or double-bottom base. The strongest stocks act like springs. Once the weight of the market comes off, they spring forward, breaking out of sound bases they had formed during the market correction and doing what they wanted to do all along—go higher.

As more leading stocks broke out of sound bases in April, I began to increase the number of positions I had. I quickly found myself on full margin by mid-April, enjoying the rally from late March into June and sitting in my typical 12 to 18 positions. Incidentally, I've noticed that my trading style in terms of position sizing, number of positions, and risk levels has not changed over the years. It is independent of account size, such that whether I was running a small account in 1996 or running big money for Bill O'Neil in 1999 onward, I still tend to hold 12 to 18 positions in any uptrending market. I will typically put 15 to 25 percent of my trading account into each stock, then either add to the initial position a second, third, and even a fourth time provided the stock sets up logical buy points

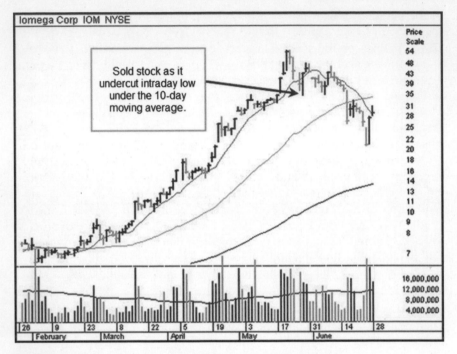

FIGURE 2.2   Iomega Corp. (IOM) daily chart, 1996: the top.
Chart courtesy of eSignal, Copyright 2010.

as it presses higher. Otherwise, I will sell at least half the position if the stock hits my mental sell alert, or will sell to free up capital for new buys in fundamentally strong and potentially faster stocks breaking out of sound bases.

In June 1996, my account peaked at +72 percent, year-to-date, by the time the market topped that summer. Over the next several days, each stock I owned then began to hit my sell alerts, so I sold. With IOM, I used the 10-day moving average to guide my mental sell alert, as Figure 2.2 shows, and thus placed my mental stop slightly under the 10-day. After IOM peaked on May 22, it sliced through the 10-day moving average on big volume on May 28. I put my mental stop $^1/_{16}$th under the low of that trading day, or 36.31, and so I sold my position the next day as the stock reached my mental sell stop. That said, it could be argued that a climax top occurred in those three up days on high volume at the peak. Back in 1996, I did not understand climax tops well enough to sell into them and found that I preferred to sell on weakness instead of strength as it more suited my trading personality.

Incidentally, I use the 10-day as a sell guide for the fastest names, as they tend to get support around the 10 day as they move higher. For slower stocks, or for stocks that trade with more volatility, I use the 50-day moving average as my guide on where to sell. Should the stock penetrate the 50-day, I will then put the stock on standby sell to see whether it should be sold or held. We cover this selling strategy in detail in Chapter 6.

I eventually found myself 100 percent in cash by mid-June. I had no idea the market was going to have a mini-crash but I always stick to my rules. Here is a key but obvious point that ensures that you will not fall in love with your stock and hold it past its prime. Buy based on both fundamentals and technicals, but sell purely on technicals. Technical action should always be the final judge when selling a stock.

The NASDAQ Composite proceeded to drop −19.6 percent from its peak set on June 6, as Figure 2.3 shows. Many of the high-growth stocks I owned suffered far more severe corrections since such stocks tend to be more volatile. But I was protected, because I was in cash.

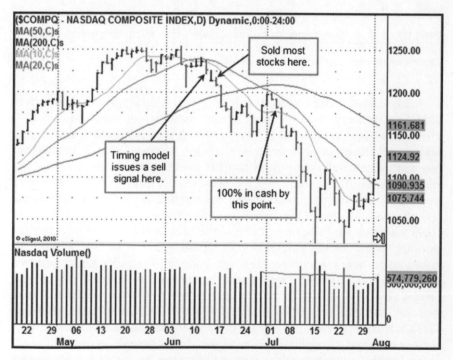

FIGURE 2.3 NASDAQ Composite Index daily chart, 1996. The NASDAQ breaks down and trends lower before finding a bottom in July 1996.
Chart courtesy of eSignal, Copyright 2010.

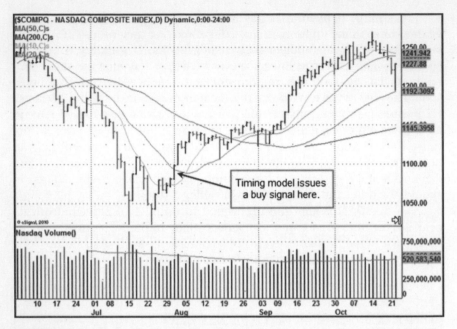

FIGURE 2.4 NASDAQ Composite Index daily chart, 1996. The timing model issues a buy signal on August 1, 1996.
Chart courtesy of eSignal, Copyright 2010.

The market continued its correction until it finally found a bottom in July. Shortly thereafter my timing model issued a buy signal on August 1, 1996, as we see in Figure 2.4. I also noticed stronger leading names just starting to break out of sound bases, always a good sign as it signals that a potential new bull phase in the market is emerging. Stronger names are often the first to break out, and when this occurs in synchronicity with a buy signal, it is highly constructive. So, listening to these stocks shouting to be bought, I began to buy in earnest once again.

By December 1996, one of the big buzzes in the market was the impending year 2000 or "Y2K" crisis. Companies that were coming up with solutions to help computer systems to cope with the date change from a "19" prefix to a "20" prefix were garnering interest from investors. It is one thing to buy into a big story on the basis of the buzz alone, but in this case certain "Y2K" stocks like the year 2000 stocks TSR Inc. (TSRI), Zitel Inc. (ZITL), and Accelerate Inc. (ACLY) had been discussed at length on how they could avert potential disaster as the clocks ticked over to January 1, 2000. I took notice of these stocks, which were the major players in this subsector as they broke out of proper bases. So I bought. The buys put me over the 100 percent mark in my personal account, and I finished the year up +121.57 percent. All it takes is one or two good homeruns in any given year to make up for all the small losses. As a general rule, following the method of buying fundamentally strong stocks at the right pivot points, then moving to cash when the market is weak puts the odds greatly in your favor so that you will achieve that golden 100 percent return in a given year, provided you are in a bull market environment. If you are in a bearish environment, you still might be able to hit one or two homeruns, which will counteract any small losses.

1997—KEEPING PROFITS DURING THE ASIAN CONTAGION

During the first quarter of 1997, the market was in a downtrend. By April, some portfolio managers with whom I was speaking were ready to throw in the towel for the year as frustration ran high. I had stayed mostly in cash during this period as my timing model had been on a sell signal, and there were almost no stocks worth buying. Then on April 22, my timing model gave a buy signal, shown in Figure 2.5—the first buy signal since

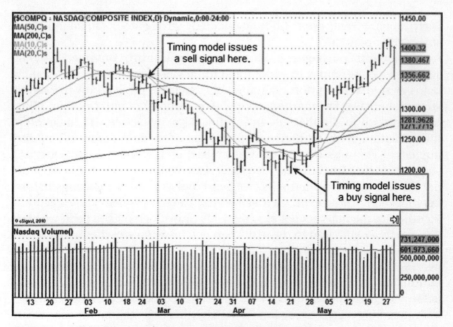

FIGURE 2.5 NASDAQ Composite Index daily chart, 1997.
Chart courtesy of eSignal, Copyright 2010.

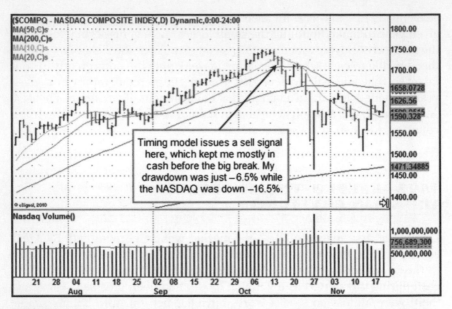

FIGURE 2.6 NASDAQ Composite Index daily chart 1997. The Asian Contagion. Chart courtesy of eSignal, Copyright 2010.

early January—and I noticed fundamentally strong stocks in sound bases starting to break out.

I bought the strongest of stocks, then as the rally continued, I would sell the weakest names to make room for any new strong names breaking out. I was effectively force feeding any available buying power into the strongest names. The market continued on its uptrend into October. I then was surprised to see that just over a few days, by October 17, most all of my stocks suddenly hit their sell alerts, just a few days before the market imploded. The massive sell-off was caused by the Asian currency crisis, shown in Figure 2.6. I had no idea this crisis was going to occur when it did nor that the market would sell off so hard. But as I had always done before, I sold when my stocks hit their sell alerts. Thus, I was safely in cash a few days before the markets got slammed. My drawdown off the peak was just –6.5 percent compared to the –16.2 percent drawdown in the NASDAQ.

Incidentally, my success-to-failure rate in 1997 was one of the lowest ever, with the number of my losing trades outnumbering my winning trades by roughly 4:1, or a success rate of just over 20 percent. Yet I was able to achieve a triple digit return, just barely (102 percent according to my accounting, 98 percent according to KPMG) because the home runs made all the difference. I point this out to illustrate that the number of profitable trades is perhaps the least important variable with this investment methodology. The percent gained on a trade is a far more important variable. That said, in other bull market years, my success rate is usually closer to 50 percent.

1998—DEMORALIZATION SETS IN JUST BEFORE THE MARKET TAKES OFF

While the first quarter of 1998 was highly profitable, the months from July through early October were some of the most challenging. Shortly after the market peaked in mid-July, my stocks hit their sell alerts so I ended up back in cash just several days after the peak. The market then staged a feeble rally in September. Very few high-quality stocks were breaking out of sound bases; thus there was little to buy that month. I remember, however, many investors buying that month eager to assume the rally was continuing. But when October came around, the markets sold off very hard, absolutely demoralizing many investors. Many had year-to-date losses by that point. Figure 2.7 shows the big market bounce on October 8 that led a few days later to my timing model issuing a buy signal on October 14. I also noticed a few high-quality stocks breaking out of sound bases in the ensuing days such as eBay Inc. (EBAY). EBAY was a most interesting IPO.

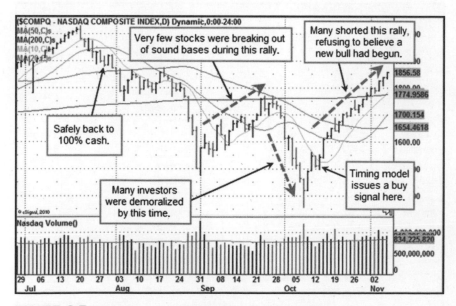

FIGURE 2.7 NASDAQ Composite Index daily chart, 1998 lows. Chart courtesy of eSignal, Copyright 2010.

It had one of the best business models and had first-mover advantage in its space much like Yahoo! Inc. (YHOO) for search engines and Amazon.com (AMZN) for online retail. EBAY came public on September 24, but despite its brilliant business model proceeded to lose more than half of its value due to the nasty bear market that caused the NASDAQ to lose –33.1 percent. So even though EBAY had one of the strongest business models, it sold off hard with the rest of the market, thus neatly illustrating why fundamentals are only half the story. No matter how great a stock's fundamentals, a serious bear market will usually drag a stock down.

When my timing model signaled a buy shortly after the market bottomed, it only took a few days for EBAY to hit its buy alert. On October 26, EBAY gapped up out of what I call a U-pattern or what Gil Morales refers to as an "IPO U-Turn" as we see in Figure 2.8. These rare U-patterns can be seen in the strongest of stocks. The stock is so strong that it is not going to wait to form a handle, and the length of the base is often four weeks or less. I bought my first position in EBAY on the gap up, and then bought a second position as the stock bounced off its 10-day moving average. I have found that the strongest stocks often constructively trade around their 10-day moving average, using it as support to rest briefly before continuing their move higher.

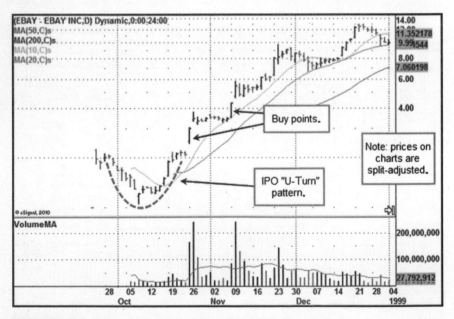

FIGURE 2.8   eBay, Inc. (EBAY), daily chart, 1998. The "IPO U-Turn."
Chart courtesy of eSignal, Copyright 2010.

Meanwhile, many investors had been so demoralized by the brutal bear market that began in July and thus were skeptical as the market bounced in October. I remember some stayed short the market into November as the market rose like a rocket. And as the market continued to rally, it forced those who were reluctant to buy, to either cover their short positions or admit their error and start buying. However, they were late buyers, and so they missed some of the most compelling breakouts. The best stocks are sometimes the first ones to break out shortly after a new uptrend begins as they often offer the best gains. EBAY was an excellent example of this.

The fourth quarter of 1998 turned out to be a highly profitable quarter. As the technology sector led the way higher, stocks that had first-mover advantages in their space often well outperformed their peers, making them true market leaders. I screened for stocks with top fundamentals, which included having great business models and then investigated whether any had a first-mover advantage. I then pruned the list further by investigating each stock in detail. Of the few stocks that made the cut, I put mental buy alerts on each, so that when the stock traded through its buy alert, my software would immediately alert me.

The fourth quarter of 1998 presented what I call a high-class problem. So many great stocks were breaking out of sound bases that buying power quickly became exhausted and it became a challenge to figure out which stock or stocks to sell out of my roughly 14 to 17 positions during this period to make room for potentially faster stocks breaking out. I reduced the weakest positions by half or sold them in full on the basis that their relative strength was not as high and/or their fundamentals were not quite as strong. I was then able to force-feed capital into the strongest names at all times while the market was advancing, which gave me a huge edge. This insured that, being fully on margin, 200 percent of my capital was being deployed strategically.

1999—THE BUBBLE EXPANDS

Part of successful investing is knowing when a fundamental part of the market changes, even though the market may have never behaved this way in the past. In the late 1990s, it was the earnings metric. Some Internet stocks that made huge gains had little to no earnings. While earnings are one of the most important variables I use to gauge the potential of a stock, I realized that sales growth was a useful metric for stocks with no earnings. Understanding the fundamental story behind the stock together with understanding how Wall Street perceived the story behind the stock proved beneficial because it is the institutional money from mutual, hedge, and pension funds that cause a stock to make huge advances. Because of this fundamental change in the market, I learned that markets sometimes change in subtle and not-so-subtle ways. While certain key fundamental and technical variables continue to work cycle after cycle and form the core of my strategy, other variables have a limited life. It is up to investors to follow the markets closely so they can see when new variables can be used to enhance profits as well as when such variables lose their predictive value. Be wary of black box methodologies that claim to be profitable without having to be fine-tuned. They may work for one or two market cycles but must be fine-tuned to keep up with changes in the markets.

In the first quarter of 1999, most of the stocks that triggered buy alerts were technology stocks since the Internet was touching so many aspects of technology. I always do what the stocks and general markets tell me to do, so I was fully margined during the uptrend that led to the April 13 reversal day in the CBOE Internet Index (INX), shown in Figure 2.9, an index that is a good measure of performance in the Internet space. I noticed many Internet stocks had staged or were staging reversals after making huge gains. Also, the day before, on April 12, some stocks announced they were going to attach ".com" to their name. Some more than doubled in price on the announcement. This extreme buying struck me as some sort of temporary climax top for the Internet group. Then on April 14, before the market opened, I noticed many of the stocks in my portfolio were going to gap slightly down from the prior close they had set the day before. After the first few minutes of trade, they were unable to rally from their lower opening price. Noticing this and taking into account the prior action that led up to this day, I gave my trader a "shopping list" of stocks to sell just several minutes after the market opened. This "shopping list" was 14 out of the 16 stocks that I held, thus I was effectively reducing my market exposure from 200 percent down to about 35 percent. The CBOE Internet Index (Figure 2.9) proceeded to tank about 20 minutes after I gave my sell orders, taking the stocks down with it that I had finished selling only minutes earlier. The CBOE Internet Index overall finished the day down –9.6 percent.

That day, some of the best-performing stocks were down twice the decline in the CBOE Internet Index. Infospace, Inc. (INSP) in Figure 2.10 gives a sense of just how fast some of these stocks fell. It took just six days for INSP to get sawed in half, as it fell almost 50 percent from peak to trough.

Timing is everything, especially when it comes to handling high octane names. Like dynamite, they must be handled with care, especially if you decide to concentrate your portfolio in one sector. Had I not acted quickly when I saw the warning signs, I would have given back a much larger portion of the profits I had made during the first quarter of 1999. Being able to sell most of my positions within 20 minutes was also key. I had a rule

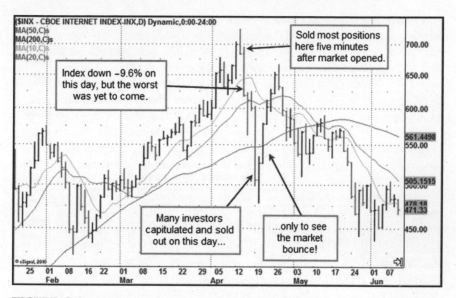

FIGURE 2.9 CBOE Internet Index (INX) daily chart, 1999.
Chart courtesy of eSignal, Copyright 2010.

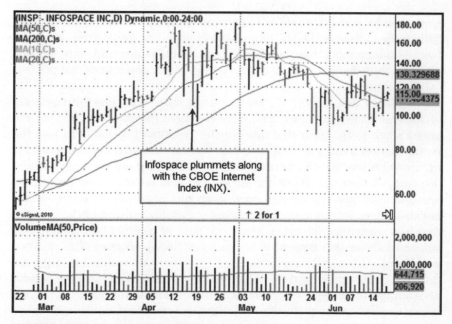

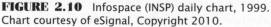

FIGURE 2.10 Infospace (INSP) daily chart, 1999.
Chart courtesy of eSignal, Copyright 2010.

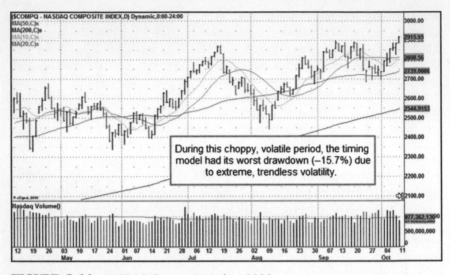

During this choppy, volatile period, the timing model had its worst drawdown (−15.7%) due to extreme, trendless volatility.

FIGURE 2.11 NASDAQ Composite Index, 1999.
Chart courtesy of eSignal, Copyright 2010.

back then by which I would hold no more than 10 percent of the average daily trade in a stock. Today, times have changed, so here in the year 2010, I would put no more than 5 percent of the average daily trade into any one position, and also focus more on the mid-to-larger-cap names that are less subject to noise.

While the first quarter of 1999 was a gift, the second and third quarters of 1999, as shown in Figure 2.11, were the most treacherous I had experienced since 1991, a year that marked the first time I was able to beat the major market averages: 1999 also represented the largest drawdown for my timing model of −15.7 percent and the largest for my personal account of nearly −50 percent. While the KPMG verification shows my drawdown was about −30 percent, my real drawdown was larger at nearly −50 percent because I was intentionally not trading a sizeable portion of the account that was earmarked for taxes. Thus, the base of capital I was trading was substantially smaller than what was actually in my account. This resulted in larger drawdowns than reported by KPMG, but also resulted in larger annualized gains than reported by KPMG. Of course, KPMG follows regular accounting standards, so it had no way of accounting for this.

At any rate, the high level of volatility in a trendless market exhausted many traders. It was not until October that the market resumed its uptrend in earnest. I'm glad to say that periods such as the second and third quarters of 1999 are rare.

That said, it is important to stick with a winning strategy, in good times and bad. I have lived with my strategy since 1991. This gave me the confidence to stick with it even during the treacherous second and third quarters of 1999. I never lost sleep during this period, nor have I ever lost sleep over the market. The key is to always understand why one is making or losing money. My timing model sheds much light on the character of the market. If the model is struggling to make profits, such as it did during the second and third quarters of 1999, it helps me realize that we are in an unusual environment. In this case, the market was both volatile and relatively trendless, the Achilles' heel of trend following. Fortunately, as demonstrated clearly in Michael Covel's book *Trend Following*, which I highly recommend to any investor, markets tend to trend more often than not; thus highly successful portfolio managers such as Bill Dunn and John Henry can remain successfully in business with exemplary 25+ year long-term track records and continue to thrive to this day. That said, periods of steep drawdowns are part and parcel of trend following. It is critical to stick with the strategy in both good times and bad. As shown by Dunn, Henry, O'Neil, and other successful trend followers, the profits made during the good times more than make up for the losses during difficult, trendless periods.

2000—THE BUBBLE BURSTS

Celera Genomics (CRA), shown in Figure 2.12, had made a critical announcement about their mapping of the human genome in late 1999, sending biotechnology stocks soaring. The group continued to make huge price advances in early 2000. As with the Internet sector, many of which had no earnings, market perception played an important role in the bio-techs, many of which not only had no earnings but also had no revenues. So, with none of the classic fundamental variables on which to measure the company, I applied to the biotechnology sector what I had learned about market perception with the Internet sector. If market perception was highly positive due to a belief held by institutional funds that the company had huge potential, this could be seen in the price/volume action of the stock, as it was the signature of significant, big money institutional buying. This was key to my making a triple-digit return in 2000 on the long side, a year when the market averages such as the NASDAQ Composite were down nearly –40 percent.

The biotechnology sector topped in late February, shortly before the general market topped. The general market then put in a top on March 10 as shown in Figure 2.13. I was quick to take my account off margin and move into cash as each one of my stocks hit its sell alert in the ensuing days. For

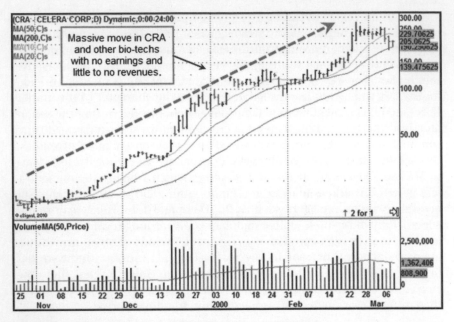

FIGURE 2.12 Celera Corp (CRA) daily chart, 1999–2000.
Chart courtesy of eSignal, Copyright 2010.

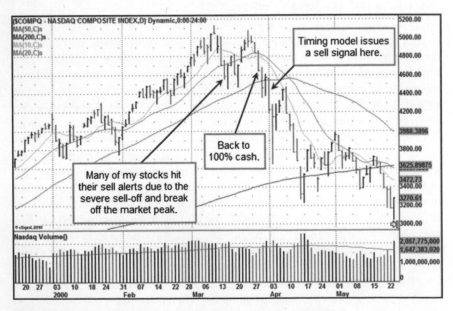

FIGURE 2.13 NASDAQ Composite Index daily chart, 2000.
Chart courtesy of eSignal, Copyright 2010.

the rest of the year, I did some infrequent, light buying, and so I was able to preserve most of the profits I had made that first quarter. It is critical not to overtrade, and perhaps it is often best to do nothing, and just sit in cash when the market is not acting right. That said, overtrading is one of the most difficult issues to overcome even for the most seasoned investors. The market will tempt the trader to jump back in by making things look almost right. And most traders would rather remain active than dormant. But it is often best just to sit and do nothing if the market is not acting just right. In my experience, I have observed that this is easier said than done.

Here is another argument for staying on the sidelines if the market is not acting just right. If one only trades 10 optimal buy situations in a given year, and makes an average of 10 percent on each trade, one's entire account would be up 159 percent in that year if one invested one's whole account each time such an optimal buy point arose. In practice, due to risk management reasons, even if one invested 25 percent of one's account in each trade, one's whole account would still be up about 40 percent for the year. Of course, ample experience is required to know that the odds are greatly on your side, and that there are no guarantees. However, if we take the period of 2006–2009 as one example, the latter part of 2006 and 2007 were just right for buying, and big money could be made during such windows of opportunity. Then in early September 2009, GLD had a perfect setup and gold stocks could be bought, as they correlate highly with GLD. Of course, there were other picture-perfect plays during these years, giving one further opportunity to do well. I am not saying this in hindsight but am basing this on my actual profits during these picture-perfect, albeit brief, periods. My mistake was overtrading during the less optimal periods.

Incidentally, I noticed that O'Neil does little when the market is not acting right. You can make a fortune just by being long the right stocks at the right times when the window of opportunity is open. My market direction model is almost always on a buy signal during such times, and, if not, it has always switched to a buy signal within days after the first few leading stocks break out of sound bases. You can further enhance your performance by learning short selling techniques, which are discussed in Chapter 6.

2001—A LESSON IN SHORTING

In February, I pyramided a short position in the Powershares QQQ Trust (QQQQ). I remember as profits were building, I started calling this my "Modena trade." A Ferrari Modena back then was the hottest new model and cost about $250,000 with the mark-up. Thus, a profit of $500,000 on a trade would pay for the car, after federal, state, and miscellaneous taxes were paid. I finished the trade at a profit of over $600,000, but I never bought the car. I learned that even though I had always wanted to own a Ferrari, I did not buy it because it was not the act of possessing the car that was important. Psychologically, it was the idea that I could easily possess it. So buying it became unnecessary. It brought me greater pleasure to keep the capital on hand to invest in the markets. As I learned from O'Neil in the years I worked with him, one should never make the market pay for one's luxuries.

Then in March, I re-shorted my QQQQ position. I pyramided the position as before, and profits eventually amounted to over $1,000,000. The problem was that greed got the best of me and I thought the market was going to crack wide open, and my profit of over $1,000,000 would turn into $2,000,000 or more in the event of a market crash. I was heavily leveraged on the short side and failed to consider the more likely outcome that the market could bounce big after having sold off so hard. On April 5, the market gapped up fiercely and rallied the rest of the day (Figure 2.14). I finally closed my position at the end of the day. I lost just over a cool million in one day. My profits on the trade shrank from over $1,000,000 to about $100,000. Gil Morales came into my office, shook my hand, and told me "that's one

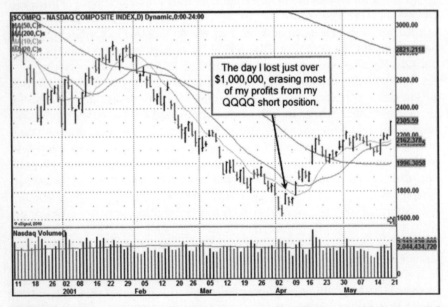

FIGURE 2.14 NASDAQ Composite Index daily chart, 2001. The "Modena trade" goes awry!
Chart courtesy of eSignal, Copyright 2010.

hell of a ride," and that he had enjoyed the vicarious thrill by watching me make the trade. I then recalled the Victor Sperandeo interview in Jack Schwager's book, *Market Wizards*, where he talks about going into a bar and telling the bartender, "I just made $100,000 today. I really need a drink." So the bartender asks, "Why the down face? Shouldn't you be celebrating?" Sperandeo replied, "The problem is, I was up $800,000 earlier today."

The rest of 2001 was uneventful with just a few losing trades. The window of opportunity was clearly shut, so I stayed mostly on the sidelines as my timing model was usually either on a sell or a neutral signal.

2002 TO PRESENT—CHOPPY, SIDEWAYS MARKETS AND THE BIRTH OF THE POCKET PIVOT

The year 2002 was also uneventful, and I stayed mostly in cash. I remember many funds closing their doors. While 2001 was a massacre, 2002 was equally brutal. Few were left standing. Once the NASDAQ Composite was off more than 70 percent, the market seemed to be excessively oversold. So I decided to take a small position in the QQQQs for a long-term play. I reasoned that the market could go lower but historically, had always resumed a strong rally after being so oversold. This was true after the panic of 1907, after the Great Depression when the market lost almost 90 percent of its value, and after other serious market setbacks dating back to the nineteenth century.

So 2002 was profitable by a hair due to this one trade, which reversed my small losses. My losses had been small because I remained mostly on the sidelines, safely in cash. That said, I would have been nicely profitable had I shorted indices on any sell signals issued by my timing model. This was also true in other years. Thus, this bias I had toward staying in cash during bear markets was replaced starting in 2009 with the action of shorting major indices on sell signals; 2008 was a wake-up call to start shorting the major indices as 2008 was a good year for my timing model, as shown in Figure 2.15, due to the collapse in the general markets. The return of +31.1 percent is good, but under the model's long-term average annualized returns of +33.1 percent. But when accounting for optimization of the follow-through day threshold, which I discuss in Chapter 7, the return increases to +38.8 percent for 2008. I prefer to err on the side of absolute caution, so I show the "worst-case" situation of +31.1 percent.

Note, the timing model's back-tested historical average of +33.1 percent/year from 1974 to 2006 was achieved by going 100 percent long the NASDAQ Composite on a buy signal (B), 100 percent short the NASDAQ

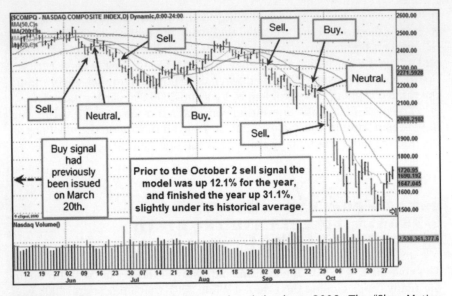

FIGURE 2.15 NASDAQ Composite Index daily chart, 2008. The "Slow Motion Crash" of late 2008.
Chart courtesy of eSignal, Copyright 2010.

Composite on a sell signal (S), and 100 percent cash on a neutral signal (N). In working with my model in real time since 1991, the returns in my personal and institutional accounts were larger because I was buying individual stocks during periods when my model was on a buy signal.

The toughest year for my model was 2007, as it was one of the only two years when the model was down in its entire 36-year run. Its negative return of 10.9 percent was due to a large number of false price/volume signals. That year, distribution day clusters often did not lead to a falling market, as the market continued to grind higher. This may have been due to the many one-time confluences of cross-currents including the end of the housing bubble, the early stages of a breakdown of financials as seen in the XLF index, and the beginning of the recession. Fortunately, years such as 2007 are extremely rare. On balance, my timing model continues to keep me on the right side of the market cycle after cycle. For historical interest, Figure 2.16 shows my timing model in action during the crash of 1987 and its aftermath.

In the current decade, the compressed, sideways markets observed from January 2004 to August 2006 brought new trading challenges, as shown in Figure 2.17, and my market direction model's returns, while still ahead of the major averages, have been under its historical returns of +33.1 percent/year.

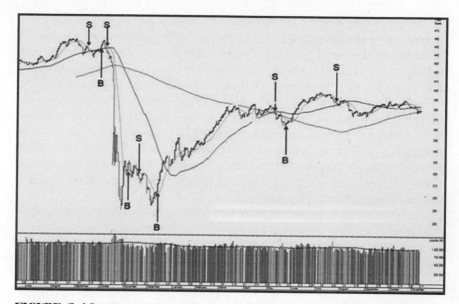

FIGURE 2.16 The timing model during the 1987 market crash clearly outperformed.
Chart courtesy of eSignal, Copyright 2010.

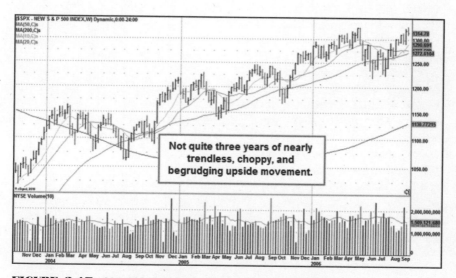

FIGURE 2.17 S&P 500 weekly chart. Three years of difficulty.
Chart courtesy of eSignal, Copyright 2010.

But whatever doesn't kill you makes you stronger. In late 2005, I came up with a major refinement to my strategy, which enabled me to make my initial buy in a stock's base just before it broke out, a method I call buying "in the pocket," which will be discussed in detail in Chapter 6. Not only does this refinement work today but also worked beautifully in prior 1970s, 1980s, and 1990s markets. Those of you who subscribe to The Gilmo Report will note that we have discussed them in some detail in prior reports, which can be found at www.gilmoreport.com. This technique will improve your investment performance should the market encounter choppy, sideways action that grinds higher, such as during much of 2004–2007 or during windows of opportunity such as the brief uptrends of September to November 2006 and September to October 2007.

Looking back, as the saying goes, if I only had known in the 1990s what I know now, my returns would have been higher. We are all students of the market, always learning, always optimizing, and hopefully always evolving. It certainly keeps the journey alive and well.

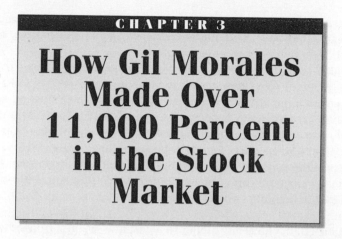

CHAPTER 3

How Gil Morales Made Over 11,000 Percent in the Stock Market

Do not be concerned with the fruit of your action—just give attention to the action itself. The fruit will come of its own accord. This is a powerful spiritual practice.
—Eckhard Tolle, *Practicing the Power of Now*

I didn't get into the investment business until June of 1991, when I got a job as a Financial Consultant trainee at Merrill Lynch's Beverly Hills branch. At the time I was making $2,000 a month, which wasn't enough to live anywhere in Los Angeles where you didn't risk getting hit by stray bullets. So I had to suck it up and live with my parents while I gave my nascent brokerage career a chance to gain traction. In the end it wasn't so bad. Living with my parents as an adult was not much different from living with other adult housemates, which I had done many times before during my post-college existence, except that these housemates didn't stay up all night partying and they didn't stick you with the phone bill.

Beverly Hills is also a surreal place to work. Where else can you, while driving your 1991 Dodge Colt, almost end up running over the actress Jamie Lee Curtis as she jaywalks across Rodeo Drive? Even better, the Beverly Hills Merrill Lynch office occupied the top two floors of a building that housed a Sharper Image store on the ground floor. One afternoon I headed down six floors to the third and bottom level of the building's underground parking garage only to find my car blocked by a large limousine. I went up to the limo door, which was ajar, to ask the occupant(s) if they could move only to find that the occupant was Michael Jackson, who had sent a small entourage up to the Sharper Image to buy some items. He could not move the limo, he said in his trademark soft, plaintive tone. I went back upstairs, a bit disgruntled that I couldn't get my car free, whereupon my assistant inquired, "I thought you were leaving."

I said, "I would, but Michael Jackson's limo is blocking my car." At that point, a gaggle of office assistants ran screaming downstairs to harass Mr. Jackson, which did not help my cause with respect to getting my car out of the parking garage. In any case, such was life working in Beverly Hills, and it added an entertaining aspect to my early days as a stockbroker. I could not complain however, as I found the business fascinating and I was having fun, despite the grueling task of enduring life as a rookie broker trying to drum up new accounts and obtain a foothold in the business. Most trainees didn't survive their first two years, but fortunately I was not going to be one of them.

In 1991 I didn't have any money to invest myself, but I remember having some initial success with the O'Neil methodologies when I bought stocks like Solectron (SLR) in 1991 and Pyxis (PYXS) in 1993 for some of my clients. At that time, I was just getting my feet wet, and I was so green that I can remember my hands shaking when I wrote out my first buy ticket for a client order of 200 shares of SLR stock at the market. It wasn't until 1993, when my maternal grandmother passed on and left me $3,000, that I finally had my grub stake. Over the next couple of years I grew it a little bit, and added to it through savings and bonuses I made as a broker when I moved over to PaineWebber, Inc. in mid-1994. By 1995 I had a few more thousands to play with, and I began investing when the market began to turn in late 1994, specifically when it staged a textbook O'Neil "follow-through" day to confirm a new market uptrend on December 14, 1994.

A ROCKY START TURNS GOLDEN

Despite the new market uptrend, I got off to a wretched start. By April 1995 I was down over 30 percent in my account, and the market had been in a "confirmed rally" that had been in force for nearly five months! I could see the river running before me, but every time I got into it with my boat it promptly tipped over, and I was starting to get frustrated. Fortunately for me, I tend to focus most when I am ticked off, and so I began working harder, going through my weekly printed Daily Graphs® books with an even more discerning eye. To this day I can still smell the fresh ink on those books when I used to go directly down to the O'Neil offices in Marina del Rey (where I would later be employed in 1997) to pick up my books every Saturday morning when they came off the press. To me, it was pure aromatherapy.

My intensified efforts were soon rewarded when I came across a company that was developing mpeg encoder, decoder, and codec products that enabled video to be compressed so that it could be viewed on computers and transmitted over the newly emerging Internet. At the time, this was a key enabling technology, and the company producing it was C-Cube Microsystems (CUBE) in 1995. At the time CUBE was showing three big quarters of earnings growth at 700 percent, 1,100 percent, and 375 percent, respectively. Sales were up 101 percent in the most recent quarter, and after-tax quarterly margins were at a peak of 18.6 percent. CUBE's return on equity was a healthy, peak number of 15.7 percent, and its group rank was a strong #13. From a fundamental perspective, the stock fit the characteristics that I was looking for.

Back in those days I was not very picky about my buy points. If a stock came out of a big consolidation to new highs I would simply buy it, as I did with CUBE as it moved to new highs on May 16, 1995. Figure 3.1 shows CUBE's weekly chart from 1995 to 1996, and you can see that the base formation was a bit unclear in this particular time frame. In Figure 3.2, the daily chart of CUBE from that period, you can make out a cup-with-handle formation, but this is not evident on the weekly chart. However, since I was using O'Neil's Daily Graphs® product every week, I was looking at

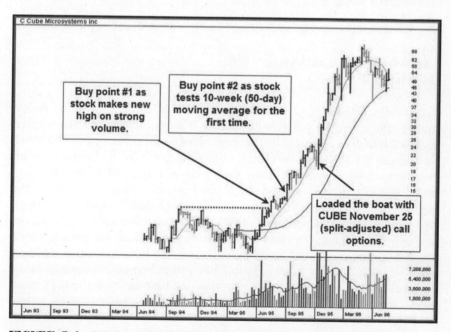

FIGURE 3.1 C-Cube Microsystems (CUBE) weekly chart, 1995, split-adjusted. Chart courtesy of eSignal, Copyright 2010.

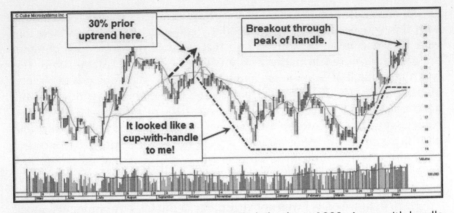

FIGURE 3.2 C-Cube Microsystems (CUBE) daily chart, 1999. A cup-with-handle base formation?
Chart courtesy of eSignal, Copyright 2010.

nothing but daily charts at the time, so I bought what I thought was a cup-with-handle breakout. Once the stock cleared what I saw as the peak of the handle at around 24 and change, I assumed I was buying a proper cup-with-handle pivot point.

CLIMBING ON BOARD THE ROCKET RIDE

If you refer to Figure 3.2 and Figure 3.3 simultaneously, you can follow the buy points in the pattern. On Figure 3.3, we see the initial breakout to new highs that I bought at the cup-with-handle pivot point. The stock then spent the next five weeks or so pulling back to the breakout point and the inching up before it launched again at Buy point #2 on the chart. In hindsight, this was also a test of the 10-week moving average as the weekly chart of Figure 3.1 shows. At the time I didn't see that because I was looking exclusively at daily charts, but to me it looked like a breakout from a miniature cup-with-handle formation and so I considered the stock buyable at that point, and today I now know that in fact the action at Buy point #2 constituted a "pocket pivot" buy point, something we will cover in detail in Chapter 4. CUBE then stair-stepped its way to around 49 (note on the weekly chart, Figure 3.1, the prices are split-adjusted 2-for-1, hence are halved) before it pulled back sharply toward its 50-day moving average in late September into early October. I remember my clients calling me, upset that I hadn't sold them out of their CUBE close to the 49 high. But as

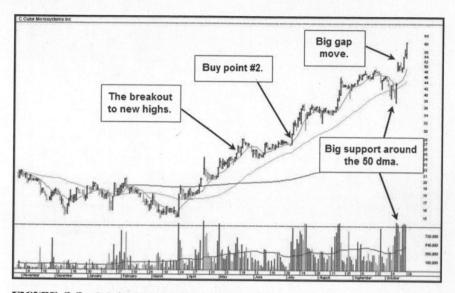

FIGURE 3.3 C-Cube Microsystems (CUBE), 1995 daily chart.
Chart courtesy of eSignal, Copyright 2010.

I saw it, the stock was pulling right back to its 50-day moving average for the first time since it originally broke out in mid-May, and this was a place to add! We had to buy, I told my clients. At this point, I was running low on funds in my account since I was already loaded up with CUBE stock, so I bought a bunch of November 50 calls at about 1½, or about $1.50 in today's decimalized terms, when the stock was at around 37.

From that point, as Figure 3.3 shows, the stock rocketed higher as it went parabolic, and by November the stock was at a split-adjusted 95, and the calls were worth $45. I had sold the calls on the way up, as the profits were getting to be ridiculous and I didn't want to be a pig. But I made enough to be up over 500 percent at that point in my personal account. Instead of a few tens of thousands of dollars, I had a few hundreds of thousands, and with just one stock I had turned my account around from being down over 30 percent to being up over 500 percent by year-end.

Getting out of CUBE wasn't all that difficult, since it started to act very erratically as it moved into the end of the year, and while I did not sell at the exact top, I sold close enough to make big money in the stock. Ultimately, CUBE went on to form a classic head & shoulders topping formation with a neckline as I've drawn in on Figure 3.4, from which it broke down in earnest in the summer of 1996, but we'll save that topic for a more detailed discussion in Chapter 4. When I look back at this first love of mine, at least in the stock market, I wonder if I would have played it so well today. Back

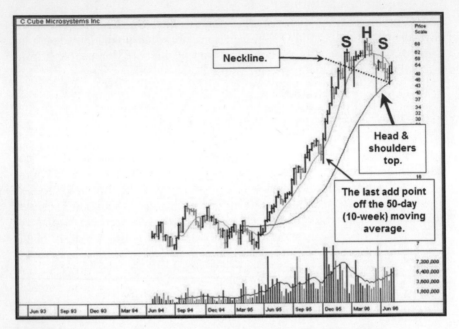

FIGURE 3.4 C-Cube Microsystems (CUBE) weekly chart, 1995–1996.
Chart courtesy of eSignal, Copyright 2010.

then I knew enough about chart patterns to "think" I knew when I was
looking at a cup-with-handle in CUBE, at least enough to buy the stock on
that breakout. By following some simple rules, and keeping my cool when
the stock made that hectic break from a peak of 49 down to 37, just below
its 50-day moving average, I stepped up and loaded up on CUBE calls and
stock. In a way, given my relative inexperience, I was fearless, and this is
what allowed me to capitalize on CUBE's huge move. As well, I became
very acquainted with the stock's business story, and I considered the fact
that CUBE had critical enabling technology for transmitting and viewing
videos on PCs and the Internet to be a big reason to own the stock. One of
the lessons I take away from my CUBE experience is that companies that
have such key, enabling technologies for an area that was experiencing
rapid growth such as personal computers and the Internet were in 1999,
often have the key ingredient for a big price move.

Another critical lesson—something that has a very visceral meaning
for me—is the fact that by remaining persistent and not giving up, even
when I was down over 30 percent in 1995, I eventually achieved a result in
excess of 500 percent by year-end. This gave me the confidence that came
from knowing that I had the ability to recover from any short-term setback
in the market, and has served me well since then. All traders will, from

time to time, experience cold spells when they feel as though they can't do anything right, and as Bill O'Neil once told me, what makes a trader great is not the positive results she achieves, but the ability to bounce back from difficult times when one has been "kicked around pretty good."

JOINING THE 1,000 PERCENT CLUB

When you hear about the great "dot-com bubble market" of 1999 you get the idea that it was just one big, year-long party for stock investors. Nothing could be further from the truth. As Figure 3.5 shows, the first nine months of the year saw the NASDAQ Index chop and slop its way higher in a slow, grinding rally that took the market to new highs in early October 1999. During these difficult months of 1999, the NASDAQ would consistently make new highs and then promptly roll over again. It was very difficult to make progress, and every time a stock began to work it would just as quickly reverse course and shake you out. By mid-October of 1999, the market was not looking all that promising.

While the NASDAQ was at least floundering its way higher in broken stair-step fashion, the Dow Jones Industrials were, by September 1999, making lower lows as they struggled to hold their 200-day moving average in October 1999, as Figure 3.6 reveals. Both Chris Kacher and I had our share of difficulties during that whipsaw environment, and it would be an understatement to say that we had become fairly exasperated with the

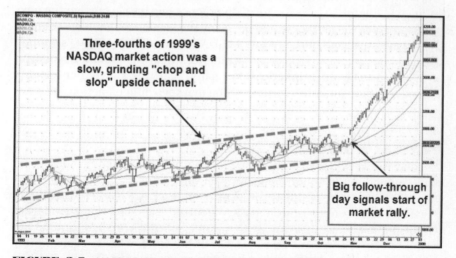

FIGURE 3.5 NASDAQ Composite Index daily chart, 1999.
Chart courtesy of eSignal, Copyright 2010.

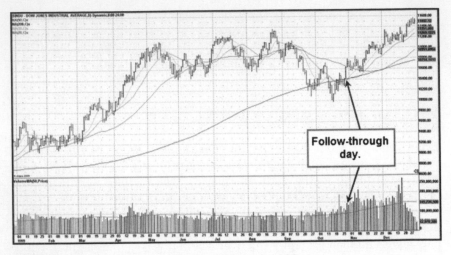

FIGURE 3.6 Dow Jones Industrials daily chart, 1999.
Chart courtesy of eSignal, Copyright 2010.

market by that point. Because of this our tendency was to think that it was likely headed lower. Given the level of frustration we were experiencing as we had been whipsawed to death since early February, it was not hard to take a discouraged point of view. However, if you compare the chart of the NASDAQ (Figure 3.5) to that of the Dow Jones Industrials (Figure 3.6), you will notice the interesting divergence between the two. The steady upside progress of the NASDAQ Index, as evident in the grinding uptrend channel outlined in Figure 3.5, was a critical divergence and a key clue that the next upside move in the market would be led by the smaller technology-oriented stocks, the bread and butter of the NASDAQ Index. The NASDAQ's choppy uptrend divergence in 1999 was nothing less than the bubbling cauldron of the soon-to-be-unleashed dot-com mania that was slowly but steadily coming to a boil under the surface of the market's difficult action.

ORACLE BUBBLES UP

Sure, enough, on October 28, just seven days after we had thought that big-cap stocks were about to be destroyed, and the market with them, a massive upside follow-through day occurred, signaling that the market was beginning a new uptrend. At that point, whatever we had thought before about the market was tossed right out the window as we immediately shifted into buy mode. There were no ifs, ands, or buts. The market had given its verdict with the follow-through day, and when the market turned,

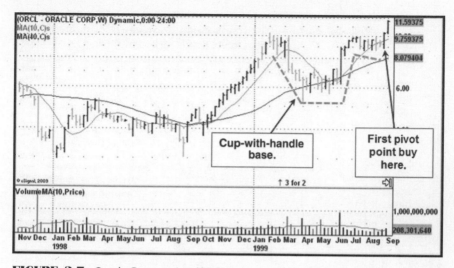

FIGURE 3.7 Oracle Corporation (ORCL) attempted breakout from initial cup-with-handle base formation.
Chart courtesy of eSignal, Copyright 2010.

we turned with it. Of course, at the time, we had no idea that we were about to get the bullish tidal wave ride of our careers, a literal rocket ride that Figure 3.5 shows in all its upside glory. My buy watch list had already been simmering on the stove for several weeks, and I was ready to act. One of the stocks I had been watching was Oracle Corp. (ORCL), which had already broken out of a cup-with-handle base in September 1999, well before the late October general market follow-through, as Figure 3.7 shows. Note that in all these charts ORCL's price is split-adjusted, so that $10 on the charts I'm using here is actually $40 in 1999 pre-split terms.

The daily chart of ORCL (Figure 3.8) gives better detail of this early breakout, which was, for all practical purposes, a clear textbook "pivot point" buy signal as it came popping up out of the top of the six-week consolidation that was in fact the handle within the overall cup-with-handle formation. Volume was brisk and above average, which is what you would want to see on this type of breakout. While I saw ORCL break out at the time, I took no action since I was negatively fixated on ORCL's quarterly earnings numbers, which showed that earnings growth was actually decelerating. The sequence over the immediately prior four quarters was 58 percent, 43 percent, 33 percent, and the most current quarter's earnings growth at the time of 23 percent. Sales growth during the most recent quarter was 13 percent. Normally you would want to see sales growth of 20 percent or more with respect to a more orthodox "CAN SLIM" type of stock. For these reasons as well as the fact that the general market was

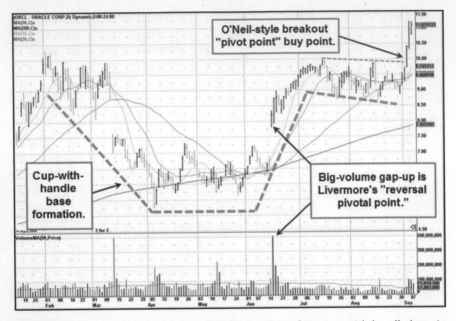

FIGURE 3.8 Oracle Corporation's (ORCL) breakout from cup-with-handle base in September 1999 gives the first hint of strength.
Chart courtesy of eSignal, Copyright 2010.

still correcting and had not yet signaled a follow-through day to the upside, I initially ignored this breakout in ORCL. But there was more going on here than met the eye.

Oracle's CEO, Larry Ellison, had first come up with the idea of "net computing" in 1995, and in 1997 Oracle created Network Computer, Inc. as a wholly-owned subsidiary. Ellison was a big advocate of web-based applications, which users accessed via the Web from a central network server rather than having the applications installed and housed on their own personal computers. What Ellison and Oracle were onto was an early idea of an "information appliance." This was a radical idea at the time, but one that the rapidly growing Internet was making more and more feasible. Today, we see the offshoots of Oracle's original concept in things like "cloud computing" as well as in handheld "Internet appliances" like Apple Inc.'s iPhone and Research in Motion's Blackberry devices. Conceptually, Oracle was considered a leader in the development of applications based on the facility provided by the emergence of the Internet. The 1999 bull market was a highly liquidity-driven market thanks to the Fed's easy money policy that arose to address the Long-Term Capital Crisis in 1998 as well as the upcoming "Y2K Crisis" that was allegedly set to turn the world's computer systems on their heads when they would all have to deal with a year that started with "20" instead of the "19" that they had all originally been created to handle. Institutions were awash in liquidity, and this money had to be put to work. Liquidity often seeks liquidity, and so a lot of it was put right into liquid, high-quality large-cap names that were perceived as potentially huge beneficiaries of the rapidly growing Internet. Oracle was one of these, and while the earnings growth was decelerating the company was still a very profitable enterprise showing a very high return on equity of 38.8 percent. Institutional investors often favor established companies with a long-term record of strong profitability, of which return on equity is a strong measure, as it is generally a sign of a well-managed company capable of producing steady, dependable, and material earnings growth. In this sense, Oracle fit the bill perfectly, but it took me nearly two months to slowly evolve my view of the company within a more accurate big picture context to the point where I was comfortable buying it.

PATIENCE AND A WATCHFUL EYE

Because Oracle had originally broken out in early September 1999, well before the market had bottomed and turned to the upside again in late October, it was too early to buy the stock on that first breakout, and so it ended up backing and filling for another six weeks as it formed another consolidation or base on top of the prior handle from which it broke out in early September. I considered this lack of upside thrust as confirmation of my earlier assessment that the stock just wasn't showing the kind of earnings acceleration that I considered optimal at the time. Nevertheless, I kept the stock on my watch list as it built this second six-week base on top of the prior handle consolidation, essentially forming a very powerful base-on-base formation.

A base-on-base formation is often a powerful formation because it is visually showing you a stock that has broken out and really wants to move higher, but because the general market environment is not ready yet, for instance, is not in an up-trending bull phase, the stock simply goes about its business setting up in another consolidation or base just above the prior breakout point, as you can see in Figure 3.9, as it "coils" in anticipation of springing higher once the weight of the general market lifts. Oracle also flashed a volume clue in this second base as it pulled back sharply right after breaking out of the first base in early September. As I've labeled on the chart, you can see that this sharp pullback was very much like a little shakeout that saw volume pick up sharply as the stock bounced right off the top of the prior base and closed that day in the upper part of its daily

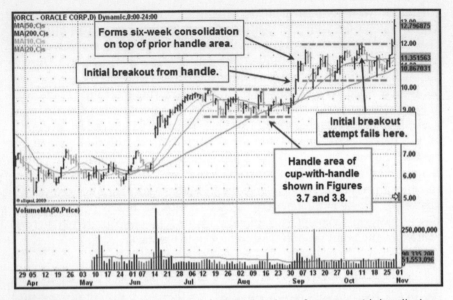

FIGURE 3.9 Oracle Corporation's (ORCL) breakout from cup-with-handle base pauses to build a six-week base to complete what ultimately becomes a base-on-base formation as it waits for the general market to turn bullish.
Chart courtesy of eSignal, Copyright 2010.

trading range, a clear sign of support on the pullback. This was a critical clue that institutions used that pullback as a clear opportunity to accumulate Oracle stock in size. Oracle then spent the next six weeks for the most part moving sideways, even attempting to make one early breakout through the $12 price level that resulted in the stock backing down again and retesting its 50-day moving average. There was nothing wrong with Oracle stock on this initial breakout attempt that failed—it was simply that the market was not ready. This illustrates a strong concept of Livermore's that one must wait for the "line of least resistance" to be penetrated, and in Oracle's case it meant that not only did the stock itself need to be set up properly but also that Oracle had to be "cleared for takeoff" by the general market environment.

CLEARED FOR TAKE-OFF

Once the general market followed through in late October, Oracle broke out of this second base, as Figure 3.9 shows, and this was the correct time to make the trade. All the conditions had lined up properly so that the "line

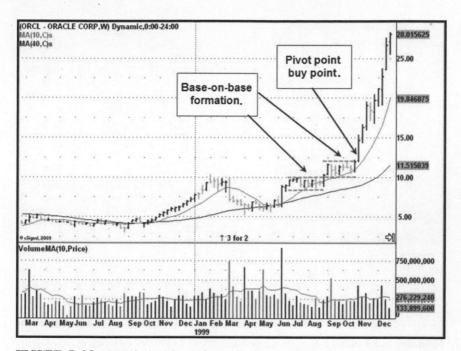

FIGURE 3.10 ORCL's breakout from the base-on-base formation results in a sharp upside move into the end of 1999.
Chart courtesy of eSignal, Copyright 2010.

of least resistance" was properly penetrated, and the stock was free to begin its price climb.

The weekly chart of Oracle in Figure 3.10 shows the volume support on the first week down in the second base of the base-on-base formation, as I've labeled. This is the type of volume support clue that can show up on the weekly and daily charts and which should always be watched for. This clue, combined with the strong base-on-base formation that essentially "hugged" the 10-week or 50-day moving average was highly constructive as I saw it, and I began taking a partial position as the stock was working on the sixth week of this second base. When the market followed through and Oracle broke out through the top of this second base the stock was off to the races.

By mid-November 1999, Oracle had just about doubled, and I was riding a nice wave at the time. The daily candlestick chart of Oracle in Figure 3.11 shows this move in November. The small black triangles that start showing up on the chart indicate days where the stock was, at those points, trading up 12 out of 15 days in a row, and you will notice that Oracle showed this indicator for 12 days in a row before it finally started its first decent pullback and consolidation. The key here is that when a stock is

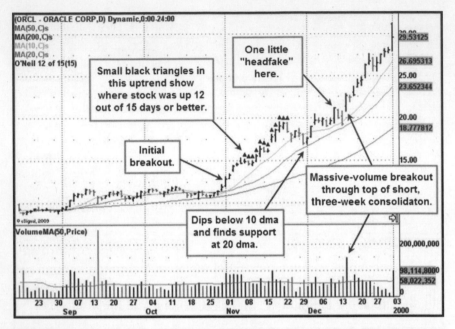

FIGURE 3.11 Oracle Corporation (ORCL) daily candlestick chart gives a buy signal on a key pullback during the stock's price run in late 1999.
Chart courtesy of eSignal, Copyright 2010.

up 12 out of 15 days in a row or better, it is showing exceptional upside thrust, and once the stock begins to consolidate this sharp upside move after breaking out of a proper base, it must be watched for another move and "breakout" to new highs, as this is a point where one should be willing to add to the position aggressively. In addition to the 12 out of 15 days in a row or better in the initial uptrend off the late October breakout, the stock had also dipped below its 10-day moving average where it found support at its 20-day moving average. When Oracle cleared this little three-week consolidation it flashed a second major buy point and so at this point it was possible to add stock aggressively, which enabled me to ride the ensuing move through December right up into the year-end peak.

VERISIGN: THE "SPICE IN THE SOUP"

We see in the Oracle example the idea that stocks that try to break out before the general market has finished correcting and turned back to the upside are often your strongest buy candidates once the market actually does begin a new uptrend. Given that I was long a quality big-cap name in Oracle, I wanted to balance my portfolio with a hotter, newer name that I felt had huge potential given its exposure to the rapidly-growing Internet.

One thing that Chris Kacher and I had picked up on in 1999 is that earnings were becoming less a driver of stock price movement in an entire raft of recent new issues with business related to the Internet, and many stocks with little to no earnings had been showing strength throughout the year. We discovered that the key metric in most of the sounder cases was not earnings growth, but sales growth. In a sense, this seemed logical since the Internet was a rapidly emerging phenomenon, and the market accurately sensed that this would likely change the entire paradigm of how business was done, how society's vast libraries and sources of data and information would become easily accessible and hence readily integrated into the day-to-day activities of the average citizen, and how individuals would then conduct their personal lives and business with respect to online banking, shopping, networking, and more. In a sense, the market was trying to find a metric with which to measure those companies with the best potential to capitalize on this emerging phenomenon, and since many of these had very little to offer in the way of earnings growth, sales growth became the "default" metric.

Among the stocks that had been trying to move higher before the market turned in late October 1999, Verisign (VRSN) was one I was watching closely. In late August it had shown signs of strong upside thrust and strength as it had cleared to new highs, and it subsequently began showing the little black triangles that indicate the stock is up 12 out of 15 days up or better as it was making those new highs, as we see in Figure 3.12.

Verisign offered a very compelling Internet-related concept as a company that offered electronic verification and security products that enabled safe, secure online transactions to take place. This was a basic enabling technology of the coming wave of e-commerce stocks that were coming public and from which "big stock" leaders like Amazon.com (AMZN) and Priceline.com (PCLN) emerged as survivors and de facto e-commerce industry group leaders. While Verisign was barely profitable, given that it wasn't until the September 1999 that the company finally reported a profit of 2 cents a share after losing money since inception, it had logged 11 straight quarters of at least triple-digit sales growth. Here we find the sales growth metric coming into play over earnings. Verisign was a "dot-com mania" play, no doubt about it, but institutional money was flowing into stocks like Verisign, which appeared to me to be the leader in the brand-new and rapidly growing field of online e-commerce security. Annual estimates for VRSN in 2000 called for earnings of 25 cents a share, which gave the stock a forward P/E ratio somewhere around 240, and by the time VRSN topped out in March of 2000, it was trading over 963 times 2000 estimates! This may

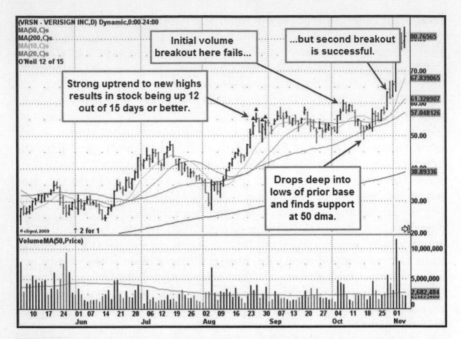

FIGURE 3.12 Verisign, Inc. (VRSN) daily chart, 1999 (note the small black triangles indicating the stock was up 12 out of 15 days or better as it moved to new highs in late August 1999, a sign of initial power and strength).
Chart courtesy of eSignal, Copyright 2010.

appear nonsensical based on the 2000 annual earnings estimate of 25 cents, but when all the beans were finally counted after 2000 ended, Verisign had earned 72 cents a share in 2000, nearly twice as much as analysts were diligently figuring in 1999.

Verisign's first breakout actually occurred in early October 1999, as Figure 3.12 shows, and the stock immediately sold off down to its 50-day moving average, where it found support and held. Obviously, if you had bought the stock on the first breakout you would have been stopped out fairly quickly, but the key point here is that the first breakout on the chart occurred BEFORE the general market had logged a follow-through day and commenced a technical upturn and new market uptrend.

The second breakout, which occurred in sync with the general market follow-through on October 28th shown in Figure 3.13, was the one to buy, because Livermore's "line of least resistance" had finally been pierced; not only was Verisign breaking out again through the 60 price level, but this time volume was even higher, and the general market was also moving into a "confirmed rally" so that the market's tide was with Verisign. Again,

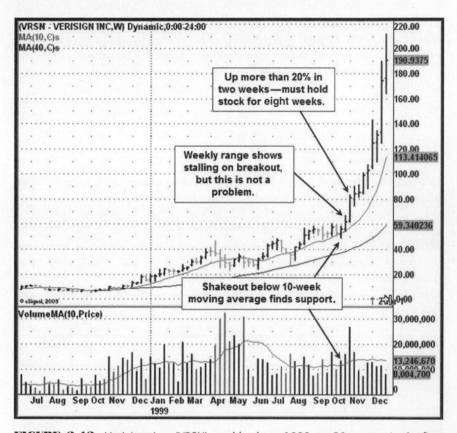

FIGURE 3.13 Verisign, Inc. (VRSN) weekly chart, 1999, up 20 percent in the first two weeks.
Chart courtesy of eSignal, Copyright 2010.

we see that the line of least resistance is not necessarily a rote technical concept relating to stocks breaking out to new highs, but also one of having all the conditions in place to raise the odds of success. We might say this is nothing more than waiting for all the ducks to be lined up in a row, and the general market turning to the upside was one such "duck" that was lining up in Verisign's favor.

Verisign ran up very quickly, and like Oracle, was up over 20 percent in the first two weeks since breaking out in late October. This made things rather simple, since we operated on a basic rule taught by O'Neil that if you buy a stock as it breaks out at the pivot point and it moves up 20 percent in three weeks or less, then it must be held for eight weeks unless you are stopped out. Essentially, this meant that I was holding Verisign for the rest of the year. I could breathe easy, because the only thing that could push me out of Verisign at that point would have been a total and complete breakdown back through its original buy point at around the 60 price level. There was nothing left to do but sit and not think at the time, as I tried to live up to Livermore's idea of the "uncommon man" who can "sit tight and be right."

SITTING NOT THINKING

At this point I more or less let the trend run its course as Verisign climbed higher, hugging its 10-day moving average all the way up until it made a sharp move higher up toward the 140 price level as we see in Figure 3.14, a daily chart of Verisign showing the insane move from a split-adjusted $60 at the initial breakout to over $200 in two months! While Verisign held its 10-day moving average throughout its uptrend, and not that in some strongly acting stocks it is possible to consistently add bits to your position as the stock trends up along the 10-day line, it did have one short "spin

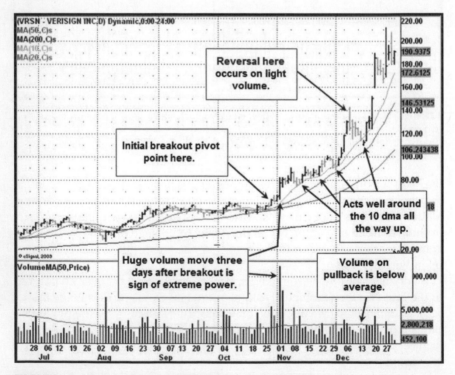

FIGURE 3.14 Verisign, Inc. (VRSN) daily chart, 1999.
Chart courtesy of eSignal, Copyright 2010.

out" that occurred after the stock rapidly ran up from just below 100 to 140, a move of over 40 percent, in five days. Note the reversal off the 140 price level, which occurs on less than average weekly volume. Given that Verisign had started its move at 60, it was logical that this sort of short-term climax type of move would result in at least what Livermore would call a "normal reaction" and pullback. Perhaps most investors would have considered a move from 60 to 140 as "enough" and thereby taken their profits, not wanting to be pigs. The situation here was not that Verisign had gone up "enough," but that it had done so in only about five weeks, and I was still holding the stock based on the eight-week rule for stocks that go up 20 percent in three weeks or less of breaking out! My rules said that the stock had to be held until at least year-end; to be, for lack of a better term, simply "dumb and long."

I've long been a fan of candlestick charts, simply because they represent another tool from which one can garner critical clues. In the case of Verisign's pullback in the first half of December 1999 shown in Figure 3.15, we can see that the stock, after reversing off the 140 price peak, then continued to pullback down for the next four days. On the fifth day down, the

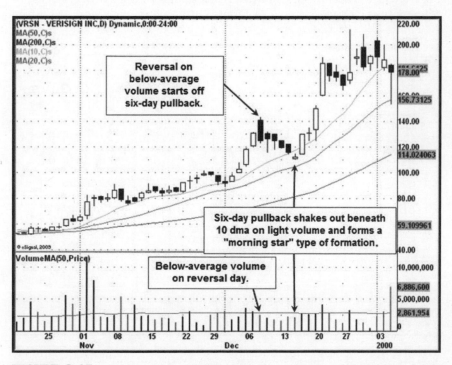

FIGURE 3.15 Verisign Corp. (VRSN), daily chart, 1999, a "morning star" buy signal.
Chart courtesy of eSignal, Copyright 2010.

stock gapped lower on the opening, breaching the 10-day moving average for the first time since its late October breakout at the 60 price level. Note, however, that the stock held well above its 20-day moving average. The very next day, Verisign gapped up on the open, completing what was quite clearly a "morning star" formation where the tiny little candle on the fifth day down represented the "star" in the pattern, and the long upside candle on the sixth day completed and confirmed the formation. The "morning star" set-up is a very bullish candlestick pattern, and in a strongly trending stock like Verisign was a clear point at which to add to the stock, even aggressively so. From there it was simply a matter of letting the stock run right up to its year-end closing high.

CLOSING IN ON THE TOP

Verisign and Oracle continued to move higher in the first quarter of 2000, but there were enough warning signs to signal that it was perhaps time to exit the stocks, particularly as we moved into March 2000 when many big leaders were showing climactic types of upside price action typical of "climax tops." Oracle, shown in Figure 3.16, built a short double-bottom

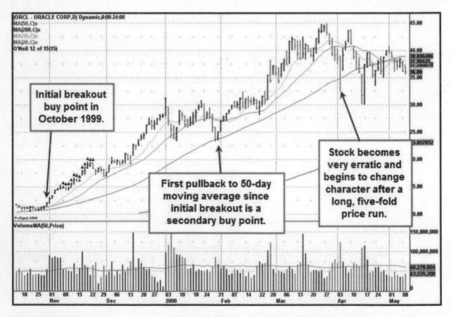

FIGURE 3.16 Oracle Corp. (ORCL), daily chart, 1999–2000, the last run to the top in March 2000.
Chart courtesy of eSignal, Copyright 2010.

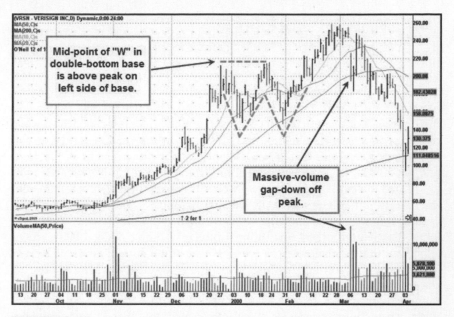

FIGURE 3.17 Verisign, Inc. (VRSN) daily chart, 1999–2000. A flawed late-stage base fails.
Chart courtesy of eSignal, Copyright 2010.

type of formation in January 2000 and bounced off its 50-day moving average on the second low of the double-bottom, which was in fact the very first time the stock pulled back to that key moving average since it broke out and began its price move in late October 1999. This was a textbook secondary buy point, and the stock moved up off the moving average and into new high ground in February 2000. In March the stock began to swing erratically, pulling down over 30 percent in late March and then swinging right back up to its highs—volatility that was out of character for the stock.

Verisign, meanwhile, shown in Figure 3.17, formed an improper double-bottom base where the mid-point of the "W" comprising the double-bottom base was higher than the peak on the left side of the base. In a proper double-bottom the mid-point will be below the peak on the left side, and this is often a flaw, particularly in a base that forms after a significant prior upside price move, that can lead to imminent failure. In Verisign's case, we see that after breaking out from this improper double-bottom base the stock rallied another 25 percent before rolling over and topping for good. In most cases, the big gap-down move off the peak in early March on huge volume was enough to tell you that the move was likely over.

THE THEME OF SUCCESS

In the process of making over 1,000 percent in 1999, some clear themes are evident. The first theme that I believe is most important for investors to understand is the idea that it was not necessarily my thinking that made me so much money. It was, rather frankly, the size of the wave I was riding, and the dot-com bubble bull market of October 1999 to March 2000 was a wave of epic proportion. Just before this massive upside wave appeared, you can see that neither I nor Bill O'Neil, nor perhaps anyone else in the market, had any inkling of what we were about to experience. But when the market turned, despite the fact that we were fairly discouraged and fed up with the market in mid-October 1999, we simply followed our rules and turned with it, buying stocks showing what we believed were driving characteristics that would attract institutional buyers. I didn't make 1,009 percent (that was the exact number) because I was some sort of genius. I simply saw a wave coming and got on with absolutely no idea how long or how big the ride would be. Some simple rules, such as holding a stock for a minimum of eight weeks if it moves up 20 percent within three weeks or less of initially breaking out, provided a simple "collar" that forced me to hold my positions. In a sense, the rule was proven to be quite valid.

Like a surfer who simply jumps on the wave and lets it run its course until it closes out and forces him or her to exit, you simply exercise all your basic rules and techniques to identify, monitor, and then buy a leading stock just as it breaks through the "line of least resistance," where all conditions are lined up like ducks in a neat little row. To a large extent, I think you can chalk up my 1,009 percent performance to being at the right place at the right time: two hot, fast-moving stocks during one of the biggest bubble bull markets in history. Of course, as Bill O'Neil used to tell me, sure there is an element of luck, in that you rely on the magnitude and duration of the bull market to keep your stocks moving higher, but you have to put yourself in those stocks at the right time. In essence, you must work hard to create your own luck!

Making 1,009 percent also did not require that I be diversified in a number of names. I only needed Oracle and Verisign, and in any real bull market this will always be the case. Find one or two big winners, and you will put yourself in the position of making big money in any bull market if you handle them correctly. Oracle and Verisign also did not have picture perfect fundamentals, but understanding their respective roles within the Internet boom was critical in understanding that they would be "big stocks"; in other words, that institutions would have to buy them. This is critical, and it is what Livermore meant when he advised investors to stay in the strongest stocks within the strongest groups.

Another point is that it was necessary to understand that the performance of stocks like Verisign, which was making a mere 2 cents a share in the September quarter of 1999, were being measured and evaluated on the basis of a metric not within the standard "CAN SLIM" fundamental template. In order to capitalize on Verisign, I had to figure out that it wasn't <u>earnings growth</u> that was the driver, but <u>sales growth</u> instead. This was decisive in determining the potential for Verisign. Also, Verisign is a clear example of why P/E ratios are quite simply a "non-determinant" for potential price performance in a stock. P/E ratios don't matter, because the facts prove that they don't.

What I consider to be the most fascinating lesson of my experience as an investor in the dot-com bubble market move that occurred in the last two months of 1999 is that absolutely nobody saw it coming: 1999 proves that a big bull market generally will come when nobody is expecting it, so you must never assume that you can completely ignore the market just because you think it isn't right at any particular point in time. Things can change very quickly in the stock market, and you must absolutely remain attentive and flexible in order to capitalize on what can become opportunities of a lifetime.

The final lesson here is that the basic principles I employed in 1995 and 1999 are easily accessible to any investor who is willing to spend the time and effort to learn them. There is no real magic, since to me successful investing is simply about finding a way to get on board a market-leading "big stock" and then hanging on for as much of the ride as I can. In my view, if I can do it, anyone can. I didn't set out to make 1,009 percent in 1999. I simply put myself in position to capitalize on the biggest bull market of my career at a moment when the ultimate result was unclear and certainly unknowable at the time, but all the conditions were ripe for pushing through the "line of least resistance." It was simply a matter of being there when that line was pierced and then letting the market's trend take care of the rest.

THE SECRET INGREDIENTS

The past two chapters have given you a firsthand view of how big money is made in the market. You may have been surprised to find out that it is not rocket science. The most important ingredients are a decent bull market trend and sound buy and sell rules. There is no need to "out-trade" the market, staying ahead of every wiggle in the general averages. This only puts one in the position of having to be right far too often. It is better to figure out where you are right and then sit tight. So once one has latched onto a big, winning stock, sitting more and thinking less are the two most critical ingredients when it comes to making big money in the market.

Hopefully, you have gained some insight into where one should focus one's attention. Most big, winning stocks, if you use any of the O'Neil tools to screen the market for stocks, will be "in your face" in a bona fide bull market. So it is not as if strong, leading stocks will be hard to find in a bull market. In most cases, it is simply a matter of finding a proper, low-risk entry point, paying close attention to and watching for proper secondary buy and add points as you build and concentrate your position, and then letting the market take care of the rest. Ironically, we find that when we are making big money and our decision making is flowing well as we trade "in the zone," it begins to feel effortless. The key is getting to that point, which is what the rest of this book is about.

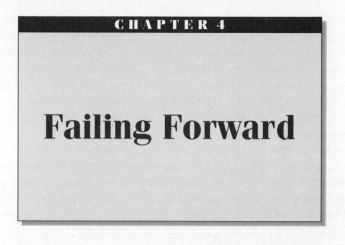

Failing Forward

There have been many times when I, like many other speculators, have not had the patience to await the sure thing. I wanted to have an interest at all times. You may say, "With all your experience, why did you allow yourself to do so?" The answer to that is that I am human and subject to human weakness.
—Jesse Livermore, *How to Trade in Stocks*

As long as the human element is involved in the investment process, then mistakes can be relied upon to litter the landscape of that process. Why do we screw up? Because we're human—a simple answer to a complex problem and perhaps the most difficult aspect of investing to contend with. Failure can result from a single mistake or even a series of mistakes, whether big or small, which often take on a snowballing effect that reaches a final, painful, and climactic conclusion. When failure sets in, and the full extent of the damage inflicted thereby can be assessed, it can be a rather mind-wrenching affair. In the end, however, it can serve as a highly constructive cleansing process. And only by understanding the genesis of our mistakes can we begin to correct them.

In this chapter we examine some of our biggest mistakes, analyzing through them step-by-step as we discuss our thinking and decisions in real time during these periods when we ran into difficulty. More importantly, we show how we gained knowledge by treating our mistakes as useful market feedback, which was then put to profitable use by forcing us to devise solutions and evolve our methods in order to ensure that such mistakes did not occur again. Oftentimes, the mistakes themselves led to the creation of entirely new trading methods or techniques, such as the "pocket pivot," or the broader understanding of concepts, such as what we refer to as the Big Stock Principle. In this way we are able to demonstrate how mistakes are not the bane of traders, but rather the way in which the market lets traders know how and where they need to adjust, correct, and adapt. By accepting our mistakes as part of the market's greater feedback system, we are able to use them to our advantage over the longer-term rather than letting them destroy us.

As a trader and investor you will make mistakes—that is perhaps the only thing we can guarantee about investing. You *may* make money in the markets, you *may* even make your fortune in the markets, and you *might* even find investing rewarding on a number of nonfinancial levels, but in the process you *will* make mistakes. The mistakes may be isolated, or they may pile up as you drift into the realm of a "trader's slump." Such slumps are characterized by periods where you may actually start to believe you have no idea what you are doing. Nothing works, and every trade you put on is like a boomerang that immediately circles back and whacks you on the head, or perhaps some other, more vulnerable part of your anatomy. When this happens it feels very much like what Bill O'Neil used to describe to us as "getting kicked around real good."

We have both experienced such periods, and we believe strongly that what distinguishes great traders from average traders is the ability to re-cover and rebound strongly from a single mistake or a full-blown trader's slump. Trading in the markets requires courage, resilience, and persis-tence, and it is these traits that will serve traders and investors best when-ever they run into those inevitable periods of screwing it all up. We've all done it, whether we are considered "expert" investors or not, and that is because as Livermore observed, we all remain, in the end, quite human. As a trader and investor, insulating yourself from your "human-ness" will likely remain the biggest challenge you will face throughout your trading career or avocation.

THE PSYCHOLOGY OF SUCCESS LIES IN TAMING THE EGO

Ironically, one of the biggest causes of failure can be success itself. This may sound strange, but big initial success in the stock market, as defined by achieving a return well into triple-digit percentages, can easily give one a false sense of investment omniscience and omnipotence. However, it is an extremely destructive illusion rooted in the ego. As a trader, your ego is always your enemy, because as Eckhard Tolle wrote, "The ego is always on guard against any kind of perceived diminishment. . . . It is much more interested in self-preservation than in the truth." Bill O'Neil warned us as we have recorded in our trading diaries that we should "never let the truth become your enemy," and traders who operate within the realm of their egos set themselves up for exactly that.

This inflated sense of all-knowing invincibility was rampant in many investors during the dot-com mania of the late 1990s, and it eventually led to the demise of various colleagues of ours who had made piles of money during the bubble market and had sold out reasonably well near the top. However, some began to believe that it was due entirely to their "brilliance" and that they could make it happen with a wave of their newly found magic investment wand. Thinking that this "Midas touch" of theirs would last forever, many bought "monuments" to their investment genius such as fast cars, second homes, and NetJets memberships. All of this was then reinforced by their own projections of how much they would be worth in 5, 10, 15 years at their current rates of ROI, or "return on investment." Some quit their jobs at William O'Neil + Company, Inc., where we were working, to open up their own shops or go off as independent portfolio managers in 1999 and 2000. Such career moves were made by these traders on the premise that they had completely figured out the markets—even though they had only traded through one brief market cycle, let alone not having had at least 10 years of trading experience in the market.

In a way, big success in the market can become like Mickey Mouse's enchanted broom in the classic animated movie *The Sorcerer's Apprentice*. In this classic Disney allegory Mickey is able to use his rudimentary magical skills to induce a broom to do his work for him, but soon finds that his control of the broom is not as complete as he was led to initially believe, given his success in casting the initial spell over the broom. Ultimately the broom ends up causing a great deal of damage because Mickey doesn't have sufficient knowledge to control it. In the same way, a little success in the stock market can be a dangerous thing. As Bill O'Neil once told one of us, "You start making big money in the market and you think you know something—you don't know anything! It's the market that knows something, not you!" This is a fundamental truth of investing. It's the market that knows something, not you; your job is just to learn how to read and follow the market.

The problem is that once you start making big money in the market, you begin to think you've figured out the market and that it's you and not the market that knows something, and so you start telling the market what to do and where you think it should go, which only serves to take you away from the correct, pure approach of watching the market day-to-day, simply striving to listen to what it is telling you. Ultimately, all you are setting yourself up for is the opportunity to be taught a brutal lesson by the market, which will be more than willing to show you who the boss is. All the intellectualization in the world has never been shown to accurately predict the future of the market. For example, Alan Greenspan's famous "Irrational Exuberance" speech in 1997 was three years short of the actual bursting of the dot-com bubble. Many lost big, and much opportunity cost was borne attempting to call the top of that market based on what one thought should occur, and that the market's rallying tendencies were unjustified and based on "irrational exuberance." The more successful you are as a trader, the greater the tendency over time to try to impose on the market that which you think should occur.

The other problem with making big money in the market is that we live in a society that measures success by material acquisitions. Therefore, becoming a servant of your ego after experiencing a period of great success in the markets is a trap that is quite easy for a trader to fall into given that our modern, materialistic culture encourages such behavior. Anybody who has read *Trader Magazine* gets a front-cover view of the shallow standard of conspicuous consumption and materialism that allegedly drives the trader psyche. Big houses, fast cars, private jets, fine wines, expensive watches, and more are worshiped as signs of success among traders, and are offered up as the ideal of what successful traders should aspire to. We could not disagree more. In our view, material self-gratification should never be one's motive for trading. The best traders generally find that their greatest sense of satisfaction, those moments when they are most at peace, occurs when they are simply trading "in the zone." In this sense, being a successful trader is nothing more than seeking bliss through practicing one's craft well. Ultimately, it is not about the money, although it is true that being a successful trader can make one wealthy, just as being successful in a variety of other vocations can make you wealthy as well. We, however, would urge traders and investors to focus on the joy of practicing their craft and to seek that as their fulfillment. Success and making big money in the market will flow from that ethic. And when you do make big money, as much as possible seek to use your wealth to simplify your life, not to make it more complicated by encumbering yourself with a portfolio of excess materialism. In our view, Henry David Thoreau expressed an ultimate truth when he wrote, "A man is rich in proportion to the number of things he can afford to let alone" (*Walden, or Life in the Woods* [Boston: Ticknor & Fields, 1854]).

So, as you realize your destiny as a successful trader making millions in the market ask yourself whether it is worth using your wealth for the purpose of acquiring so many things that in the end they may end up owning you more than you own them. By seeking to maintain such "O'Neil-style" ethics, you lay the groundwork for successful trading over the long term that will not result in your ultimate demise as you avoid the materialistic ego traps that suck in not just traders, but many other members of our society in any number of walks of life.

Preoccupation with trading and investing as a way to satisfy the needs of the ego is a recipe for disaster. This materialistic ethic stems from a basic lack of understanding of what investing is when distilled down to its essential reality. Like surfers who ride the momentous mass of ocean waves, we must realize that we are not the wave—we only ride the wave, and our skill is in assessing the size and duration of the wave in order to maximize the ride we are able to sustain, and this is the only factor we can control. Ultimately, it is up to the wave to decide just how big and how long a ride we get. The best ocean-wave surfers in the world carry with them a sense of humility based on their experience, which has led to the respect and the deep understanding they have for the power of the ocean and the immense natural forces that drive its movements. In the same way, as traders, we must develop a respect for the power of the markets and the immense natural forces that drive them. The market is simply Wyckoff's "mass mind," and by understanding the message in the market's movements we can maximize our "ride." Like a surfer, misjudging or losing perspective of these forces as we instead emphasize service to the ego can result in a trader being swept away by these same forces and smashed upon the rocks of bad, ego-based investment decisions. As traders we must remain mindful of these forces, and hence develop a strong sense of humility as we operate in the face of such forces.

Bill O'Neil used to tell us that nothing destroys a trader faster than an inflated ego. In observing Bill, we noticed he never let his winnings or his losses affect his judgment, and he never got excited when he was making big money. Even if you called him during a big up day in the markets when you were excited, such as in late 1998 when we owned the big leaders in the market and they were all running like mad to the upside, he was fairly blasé about it all. After expressing your excitement to him about how fast these stocks were moving to the upside and how much money we were making, Bill would, after listening quietly, let out a long, whooshing sigh (the "sigh of exasperation"), and respond with a curt, "Don't talk about your stocks," before abruptly hanging up. It was his own way of saying what Gordon Gekko, the lead character in the movie *Wall Street*, meant when he said, "First rule of investing is never get excited about stocks; clouds the judgment!"

To eliminate the ego you must move beyond your thinking mind to observe how you feel and how your emotions are affecting your physiology. Is your breathing shallow or swift, is your heart beating faster, are your palms sweating, do you feel powerful, do you feel frustration, do you feel elation, do you feel hope, or do you feel a sense of dread? Maintaining awareness of these emotional factors keeps you from becoming wrapped up in them. Eckhard Tolle's books, starting with *Practicing the Power of Now*, deal with this topic in greater deal, which we will also discuss more fully in Chapter 10. He explains that emotional states are simply traps that we allow our thinking mind to fall into. By remaining in the present, and aware of when we are falling into one of these emotional traps, whether a negative emotion like frustration or a positive one like excitement, we simply act and flow in the moment, unencumbered by the ego-mind.

Eliminating the ego also means understanding what your motives for trading and investing are. If you look at trading as solely a means to an end that is primarily materialistic, then you may be more vulnerable to expressions of ego. There is certainly nothing wrong with enjoying the fruits of your labor, but it is necessary to keep it all in perspective. Bill O'Neil would put it in very simple terms, "Now don't start getting carried away with yourself!"

Finally, always maintain a healthy sense of humility and respect for the markets. They operate according to forces that are far larger and far more powerful than we are, and our only task is to try to profitably synchronize our investment decisions to the movements of these immense forces. We ourselves are not the forces, and likewise we do not control them. Like the fishes in the sea, we can only move with them, avoiding the devastation that resistance inevitably brings.

LEARNING FROM OUR MISTAKES

Having both invested in the markets for just about 19 years now, we have logged a sizable blotter of mistakes, some bigger than others. Some mistakes have to do with the macro view of trading while some are more specifically related to trading mechanics. In some cases, mistakes have led to significant new developments in our trading methods. In this section we will examine some of the more significant mistakes from 19 years of investing in the markets and the solutions or lessons that were derived from these experiences.

A Case Study in Overconfidence: Gil Morales

After I made big money in 1995, as I discussed in detail in Chapter 3, I was on top of the world. For the first time in my life I had a significant amount of money to my name, well into six figures, and, to quote Gordon Gekko in the movie *Wall Street*, "At the time it seemed like all the money in the world."

That money alone would have been enough to get carried away with, but another force was working to help inflate my ego. As a broker at PaineWebber, Inc. (now part of UBS Financial Services) my success in the market was also spilling over into my business, which was taking off as well, and as an emerging "big producer" I was given a big, new office with floor-to-ceiling windows on the 30th floor of the Twin Towers in Century City, a city only in name that is essentially a posh cluster of high-rises wedged between Beverly Hills and Santa Monica, California. In many ways Century City serves as a stylish urban setting, away from the grime of downtown Los Angeles some eight miles to the east, that houses the financial, legal, and talent businesses that serve the entertainment-industry wealth that resides in the hills separating West Los Angeles from "the Valley" of San Fernando. It is, as some might say, "a preferred venue."

If there is any single industry where egoistic materialism and self-indulgence are acceptable, even glorified, traits, the retail brokerage business is it. Where else is one likely to witness two brokers getting into a steamy feud over who has a "real" Mercedes-Benz? And, of course, there was what I dubbed the "peacock syndrome," or the tendency for retail brokers to strut around in their well-tailored raiment. Many brokers took serious, perhaps far too serious, pride in their suits, shirts, ties, and shoes. How you folded your handkerchief and placed it in your suit jacket breast pocket, whether you used a single- or double-knot on your necktie, whether your cufflinks were sterling silver, and other pointless fashion details were given special regard. You might often find a small group of three or four brokers in the office admiring each other's tailored suits. Those who did not conform were scorned. I recall one broker, who fancied himself as a "broker to the stars," making fun of my eyeglasses. This struck me as odd, because up until that time, I had taken a rather utilitarian view toward my ophthalmologic needs, and had no idea my eyeglasses would become criteria by which to judge my "fashion-worthiness," and hence worth to society, at least by the standards of retail brokers!

Such was the culture of "consultative" sales in the financial industry. When I was new in the business, one of my sales managers admitted to me that he wanted new "FCs" (financial consultants) to buy a big house and an expensive car, and to get heavily into debt doing so. That way they would be highly motivated to work hard and sell, sell, sell in order to afford their lifestyle. The need for things and more things provided the essential Pavlovian stimulus necessary to inspire brokers to push the "sales process" along. It seemed that this basic premise provided the foundation for the retail broker culture that I was in at the time. The need to express one's worth through mindless materialism forced brokers to sell, and it was management's desire, if not its unstated goal, to have their brokers, their "sales force," out there selling with such material needs in mind.

All of these factors were stewing together in a toxic brew that caused my ego to mutate into a large, bulbous mass. I now fancied myself an "expert" investor of "Livermorian" stature, and I began to believe that I could employ my "hunches" on top of my investment system. The fact that I had made over 500 percent in one stock, C-Cube Microsystems (CUBE), the year before had confirmed my skill, had it not? Reading through O'Neil's book, *How to Make Money in Stocks*, one can find mentions of investors making 100 percent or 200 percent, but I knew of nobody who had ever made over 500 percent in one year, and so I was sure that this made me special. Unfortunately, I neglected to inform the market of my "specialness," as it was getting ready to inflict some painful lessons on my inflated ego.

The Lumisys Lesson In November of 1995 a new company named Lumisys, Inc. (LUMI) came public, and at the time I was very impressed with its business, which consisted of technology used to digitize images for the medical industry. I saw this as revolutionary stuff similar to what C-Cube Microsystems had done with their technology compressed video images for transmission over the Internet and on personal computers. To me, Lumisys represented another company utilizing another type of image-related technology to create innovative new products that changed and made far more efficient the way physicians and medical staff used and accessed medical images such as X-rays. It had to be a winner; I was sure of it.

When Lumisys came public in November of 1995 I was still busy with C-Cube, and so it was easy to remain disciplined and wait for Lumisys to form its first base. This did not occur during April 1996, and by then I had been out of C-Cube for a few months and dabbling here and there with new stock ideas that were not altogether working too well. In 1996 I was relying primarily on Daily Graphs® for my charts, and so was focused mostly on the dailies. Figure 4.1 shows the daily chart of Lumisys in April 1996 when it came flying out of what looked like a five-week base to me at the time, and because I was already in love with the company's products, I didn't need too much persuading to buy what I saw as a perfect massive-volume breakout. However, it did not turn out as perfectly as I thought it would!

In Figure 4.1, the daily chart of Lumisys from April 1996, the trendline breakout looks quite impressive as it occurs on the largest daily volume spike in the entire chart going back to the November IPO date. The breakout also occurs after a shakeout below the 50-day moving average on increasing volume, which I saw as setting up a "shakeout-plus-three" type of buy signal where the stock drops out below the prior lows of the base at around 18 or so and then turns back to the upside. This constitutes the "shakeout," and adding three points to the support low at 18 gives you a buy point at 21, so that when the stock comes through that 21 price level it

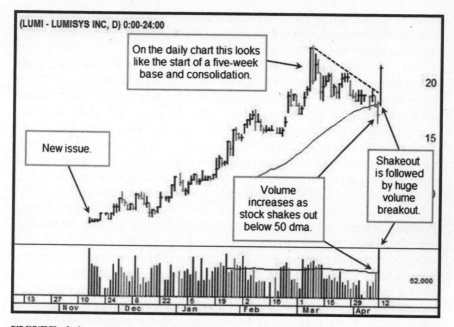

FIGURE 4.1 Lumisys, Inc. (LUMI), daily chart, April 1996.
Chart courtesy of eSignal, Copyright 2010.

is generating a buy signal. In the case of Lumisys, I had a trendline breakout and a "shakeout-plus-three" buy signal. In my mind, this made the breakout even more powerful. Given that I already had a prior bias and that I was already in love with the company's products, I bought this breakout hand over fist in a sheer fit of overconfidence.

One Mistake Breeds More Mistakes　　The first mistake I made here was having a prior bias in that I already believed that the company's products made it a sure win-win situation now that the technicals looked to be falling into place. While you can use your knowledge of a company's business and product line to help develop conviction in a potential winner, such conviction should never be allowed to override your basic system of stock selection and management. Your reasons for buying a stock should first be based on how well it fits the criteria for you to take action on it, based on your particular investment. What you are able to learn about the company should then help you develop the conviction necessary to fully capitalize on a potential big, winning stock. However, such knowledge should never get in the way of operating solely by your investment methodology. It should not work the other way around—don't fall in love with a company's business unless and until your system is telling you to buy the stock for the right reasons first. I was doomed from the start by being in love with Lumisys before I had ever bought a share of the stock. This was a classic case of getting the cart before the horse.

My overconfidence was further encouraged by the fact that I thought that two buy signals—the trendline breakout and the shakeout-plus-three buy setup—somehow gave added power to the stock's big-volume move run for new highs. On this basis I bought the stock aggressively. When I think back on this, my naïveté amazes me, and studying old charts of Lumisys makes that fact even more apparent. Probably the most painful thing about reviewing one's past mistakes is seeing just how much capacity one can have for making incredibly stupid investment decisions.

Figure 4.2, another daily chart of Lumisys breakout shows some other flaws I did not consider in the stock's chart back then. The first was the depth of its base and the fact that the stock came up straight off the bottom of the base without taking any time to digest some very rapid gains as it motored back up through the 50-day moving average and toward new high price ground. The second mistake was getting aggressive; that is, buying a large position, in a stock that traded only 120,000 shares a day on average. The price move that followed the breakout was very playable as a short-term trade, actually, and if one had recognized the flaws in the

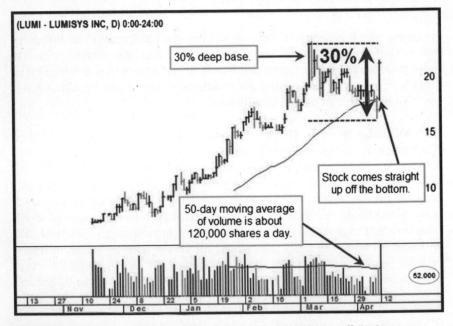

FIGURE 4.2 Lumisys (LUMI), daily chart, 1996—straight up off the bottom. Chart courtesy of eSignal, Copyright 2010.

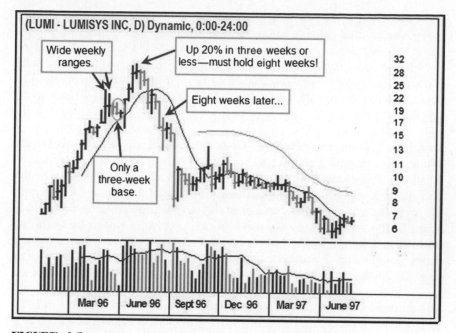

FIGURE 4.3 Lumisys, Inc. (LUMI) weekly chart, 1996–1997.
Chart courtesy of eSignal, Copyright 2010.

breakout one could have sold and taken a profit. Instead I was convinced I
had another C-Cube Microsystems on my hands. And since I was convinced
of this, it was only a matter of holding the stock long enough to realize the
huge upside price move!

The weekly chart of Lumisys (Figure 4.3) also reveals that the five-
week base I thought I saw on the daily chart was only a three-week base.
The first two weeks of the base, as I saw it, were actually up weeks, and
it is only on the first week down that we begin counting weeks in a base.
Also notice that those two weeks had very wide weekly ranges and closed
mid-range. The base itself was not long enough to properly consolidate the
move the stock had made from the time it went public in November 1995 to
April 1996. That move was a threefold move, and it is likely the stock should
have built a longer, more constructive base of at least six weeks in order
to properly digest the prior upside move. On top of it all, even if Lumisys'
base had been five weeks in length, this still would have been too short
for a first-stage base. Generally second-stage base breakouts can have a
base-length of five weeks minimum, but a first-stage breakout should likely
put in more time in order to properly set up a big intermediate-term price
move, particularly if the stock has had a big upside move prior to building
its first base.

Once Lumisys had broken out, it ran up more than 20 percent in only three weeks, thus causing me to invoke the "eight-week rule" whereby a stock that is able to break out and move up that far that quickly must be held for at least eight weeks. As you can see in Figure 4.3, sitting with the stock for eight weeks resulted in getting blown out of the position as it broke down below its original breakout point and headed back to its original IPO price.

Lumisys Leads to Broader Understanding of O'Neil Methods

While Lumisys was a painful lesson, it did help me refine my technique a bit. The first thing I did was stop falling in love with and trying to figure out great company concepts before the stocks themselves showed up on my radar screen. Unless and until the stocks showed up in my weekly scans of the printed Daily Graphs® books, they were not to be bothered with. From then on, I would never buy a stock without consulting a weekly chart to make sure I was buying a stock that has built a proper base of at least six weeks in length. Also, first-stage bases had to be a minimum of six weeks in length. Second-stage bases of shorter five-week durations would be acceptable, but for first-stage bases the stock should be coming out of a longer consolidation, and certainly no less than six weeks in length.

I did not address the problems created for me by the eight-week hold rule since I believed that had I paid attention to the initial factors, such as the improperly short base, I would not have been placed in the situation of invoking the eight-week hold rule to begin with. Based on the difficulty I had in selling the stock because it was so thin, I established a rule of never buying stocks that traded less than 300,000 shares a day. I recall quite clearly when Lumisys was breaking down and how I was frantically trying to sell the stock. For me the situation was exacerbated since I had a number of clients in the stock as well, and I had to get them out first. Every time we entered an order to sell, it took several minutes to get filled since we had to go to outside market makers in Lumisys and bids were scarce. I was so shell-shocked by that experience that I vowed to never buy another thinly-traded stock.

Back in 1996, 300,000 was a reasonable minimum average daily trading volume requirement number, but these days I use a minimum of 350,000 to 500,000 shares in average daily volume when screening for stocks on the long side, and prefer to buy stocks that trade into the millions of shares of stock a day. When I conducted my post-analysis on my Lumisys mistakes I looked at other historical big winners that started out as thinly traded stocks, and I noticed that while they would start out as thinly traded stocks, once they asserted their roles as serious market leaders their average daily trading volume would increase substantially. In general, average daily volume is a sign of the types of investors trafficking in any particular stock.

Stocks with heavy institutional participation tend to be highly liquid and relatively actively traded. Thus the higher the average daily trading volume in a stock, the more likely it has strong institutional participation and sponsorship. As well, I determined that waiting for an IPO's average daily trading volume to "mature" as institutional interest and participation in the stock increased over time was a good way to determine when a stock was approaching "big stock" status, for instance, one that was gaining a strong institutional following and hence could be nearing a strong upside inflection point. This was a key discovery that resulted from my Lumisys experience, and in the end likely made it worth the high "tuition" that I was charged for the education.

To illustrate this concept of average daily trading volume "maturing" as a stock gains leadership status and a larger institutional following, we can observe the weekly chart of Crocs, Inc. (CROX) from 2006 through 2007 (Figure 4.4). Note that the small gray line running through the volume bars, the 10-week moving average of volume, steadily moves higher as institutional investors flock to CROX. In this case, the significantly expanding volume reached a critical mass in April of 2007 when CROX assumed the role of a major market leader in the 2007 bull market and began to move sharply to the upside.

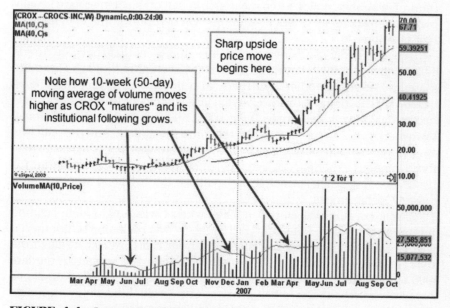

FIGURE 4.4 Crocs, Inc. (CROX), weekly chart, 2006–2007. Chart courtesy of eSignal, Copyright 2010.

The Big Stock Principle Is Born   My experience with Lumisys served as the genesis for what eventually became my Big Stock Principle, a basic underlying principle of O'Neil methodologies that slowly dawned on me over the next couple of years. The essence of the Big Stock Principle is that in any economic and market cycle certain companies appear on the scene that represent the leading edge of what is happening in the economy with respect to the new industries, new economic developments, and other themes that serve as essential drivers for the economy at any given point in time. In turn, because of their status as key companies representing the niches of growth, whether broad or narrow, in any given economic cycle, institutions have no choice but to own these stocks, and once they do they tend to be a staple of institutional portfolios through many market cycles, even when they aren't bona fide leaders. In the 1970s these were stocks like Pic N Save and Tandy Corp., in the 1980s they were stocks like Intel Corp. (INTC) and Microsoft (MSFT), in the 1990s America Online (AOL) and Cisco Systems (CSCO), in the 2000s names like Amazon.com (AMZN), Apple, Inc. (AAPL), Google, Inc. (GOOG), Baidu.com (BIDU), and Research in Motion (RIMM), to name just a few from each cycle out of many, many more. These are the stocks to own in any bull market cycle as they represent the areas to which institutional research will direct money flows, and in the process create huge upside price moves. As well, because of the broad, committed institutional sponsorship in these stocks you have a sort of insurance policy when these stocks sell off since there are usually logical pullback areas where institutions will naturally come in to support their positions.

One of the key characteristics of "big stocks" is that they don't trade 120,000 shares a day on average, they trade several million. Unless there is a cartel of grandmothers out there who instead of buying two shares each of Microsoft and AT&T are buying large blocks of leading stocks, it is institutional money that drives the market, and it is in this river of money flow where you want to set yourself right into the middle. And the only way you can do that is by striving to own the "big stocks" in any market cycle. My horrendous experience in Lumisys led me on the path to discovering for myself this "big stock" principle as I realized thinly-traded stocks cannot possibly be big stocks.

It was not until December of 1998, when I was long a huge position in Charles Schwab & Company (SCHW) as it was rocketing to the upside (Figure 4.5), that I received a quick call from Bill O'Neil, who liked the look of American Online (AOL), another fast-moving winner in the late 1998 bull market. The funny thing about AOL was that during workshops that we also presented at, albeit in a supporting role, Bill would sometimes get moving very fast as he discussed with the audience various leading stocks from many diffrent historical market periods, rapidly pulling up data from his memory, he would refer to AOL as "American" Online, instead of

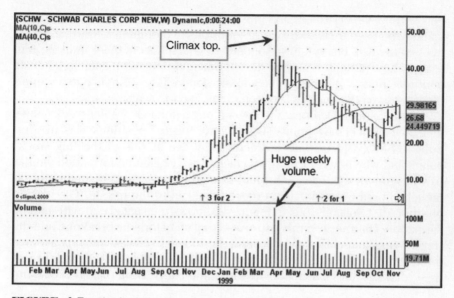

FIGURE 4.5 Charles Schwab & Company (SCHW), weekly chart 1998–1999. Chart courtesy of eSignal, Copyright 2010.

"America" Online, which is the correct name. If you understood how Bill's mind works, which is essentially a vast database of stock market history and information, you realize that this was due to a wire in his brain that was crossing over another wire that was remembering when "American" Airlines was a huge winner back in 1962–1963 when the market started a big rally right in the midst of the Cuban Missile Crisis. I answered the phone, and Bill said one thing: "AOL, now that's a big stock." At that point I had an epiphany, complete with trumpets trumpeting and angels heralding, as the skies opened up and the Big Stock Principle suddenly became clear to me.

I also found that the Big Stock Principle is also at work in short-selling, since the best short-sale targets in a bear market are precisely those stocks that were the big leaders in the immediately preceding bull market phase. Institutions that have loaded up on big leaders will in turn create a wave of selling that continues to wash over the stock in a sustained downtrend during a bear market, and we will have more to say about short-selling when we get to Chapter 8.

Missing the Move in Solar Stocks: Gil Morales

One of the primary pitfalls, at least for me, of managing money in the public realm and with other "partners" in your money management firm is that you will be subject to outside influences from clients and business associates who have their own sets of emotions and opinions. Not that this is necessarily bad, but you have to insulate yourself from these influences in spite of how difficult it may be in real time, particularly if such individuals and influences come from an academic point of view that is outside one's investment methodology's "epistemology," so to speak.

In September–October 2007 I went long a number of solar stock names at exact, perfect buy points. One of my biggest positions was in First Solar (FSLR), which I had correctly identified as one of the "big stock" solars and which was forming a jagged cup-with-handle formation similar to what America Online (AOL) had formed in October 1998, just before it launched on a 67-week, 460 percent price run to the upside. The weekly chart of First Solar (FSLR) in Figure 4.6 shows the jagged cup-with-handle formation. I had noticed this pattern setting up before the breakout, and the three weeks that closed tight around the 10-week (50-day) moving average looked very constructive. I also put together the idea of AOL as a precedent for a "jagged," V-shaped cup-with-handle formation that worked quite

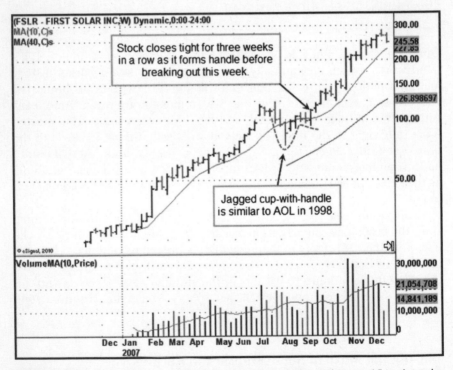

FIGURE 4.6 First Solar, Inc. (FSLR) weekly chart, 2007, a "big stock" in the solar group.
Chart courtesy of eSignal, Copyright 2010.

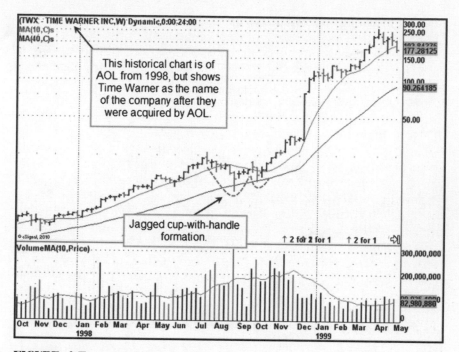

FIGURE 4.7 America Online (AOL), which became Time Warner, Inc. in 2000, weekly chart, 1998.
Chart courtesy of eSignal, Copyright 2010.

well in late 1998 to early 1999. The similarity of FSLR's chart (Figure 4.6) to AOL's from 1998 (Figure 4.7) was very compelling, and the solar group as a whole was also starting to set up technically, with a number of strong patterns in several other potential solar leaders. FSLR also had an interesting, lower-cost technology that did not use the more common polysilicon in its solar cells. In 2007, shortages of polysilicon gave FSLR's non-silicon, thin-film technology an advantage over its polysilicon-dependent competitors.

This was my "big stock" solar stock, and I was playing it big, buying shares along and around the 50-day moving average and the $100 price level before the stock began to break out. On September 21st, volume in FSLR began to pick up early in the trading days, so I began adding to my position, as I intended to get very heavy in the stock on the breakout. You could not ask for a better buy situation, both in FSLR and the group at large, which was breaking out en masse. With such group confirmation, it was clear that a major group move was taking place. As a group, the solar stocks offered a compelling, buyable group opportunity, since the 1999 move in dot-com, Internet-related stocks. Cup-with-handle bases were seen

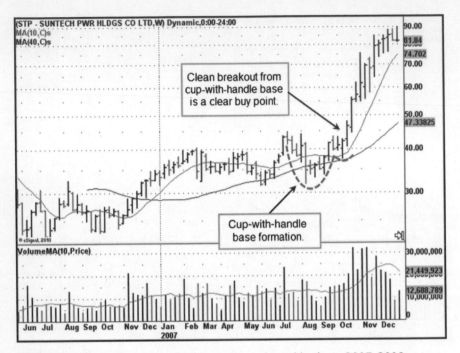

(STP - SUNTECH PWR HLDGS CO LTD,W) Dynamic,0:00-24:00

MA(10,C)s
MA(40,C)s

Clean breakout from
cup-with-handle base
is a clear buy point.

Cup-with-handle
base formation.

VolumeMA(10,Price)

FIGURE 4.8 Suntech Power Holdings Co., Ltd. weekly chart, 2007–2008.
Chart courtesy of eSignal, Copyright 2010.

in stocks like Suntech Power Holdings Co., Ltd. (STP) shown in Figure 4.8, as well as JASO Corp. (JASO), shown in Figure 4.9.

On Friday, October 17, 2007, my business partner wrote me the first of what became a long chain of emails on Friday and continuing into the weekend where he insisted that the market was not acting right, and that I should "lock in" gains of around 10 percent that I had as of Friday's close. To understand how far away this type of thinking is from my style, I should point out that movements, and hence "gains," of 10 percent are actually quite miniscule relative to the normal volatility and movement I experience given my specific investment approach within my overall methodology which dictates that one let one's winners run. One email, which was written with a tone of supercilious authority, in my view, argued against my view that we were in a window of opportunity:

I have gone back to 1985 looking at periods when a NASDAQ rally has occurred on conspicuously light volume including a dearth of major accum[ulation] days. The only NASDAQ advance that even comes close to the present one—when measured by either light volume

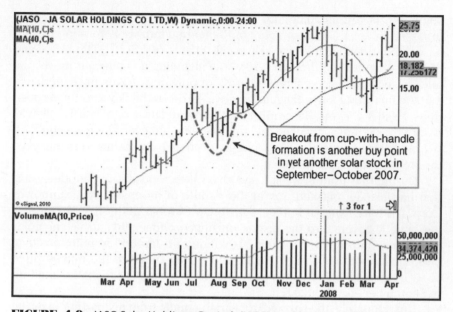

FIGURE 4.9 JASO Solar Holdings Co. Ltd. (JASO) weekly chart, 2007—another perfect cup-with-handle setup in the solar group.
Chart courtesy of eSignal, Copyright 2010.

or major accum[ulation] days—was the July 16, 1996 move, which showed only one major accum[ulation] day in the first eight weeks, but then showed a bunch of them from that point on. As you know, light volume reflects uncertainty among market participants.

My big mistake was in entertaining such drivel. The fact is that I was taught by Bill O'Neil to watch my stocks FIRST and the action of the indexes SECOND. Indexes can weaken, sometimes having intermediate corrections of 7–12 percent with leading stocks holding in tight and building normal, constructive bases. To unload your holdings on the basis of what the indexes are doing is ridiculous given this basic concept. I replied to my partner by citing this exact principle. I received the following response: "At different times, yes, I believe the leaders do provide subtle hints and are more important (e.g., dozens breaking out while the averages languish following a correction). However, the leaders can only go so far amid shoddy demand in the general market."

What makes this exchange so comical is that the immediate week before the weekend when this email exchange took place I had told my trader and Director of Trading Bill Griffith that the move in solars was significant, and that we were in the middle of a perfect window of opportunity to make some decent profits going into year-end. I also felt that the mass, group breakout in solars, with so many of them simultaneously forming perfect base formations such as we see in the charts of FSLR, STP, JASO, and SPWRA (Figures 4.8 through 4.10), was signaling a significant move was under way, and hence a fantastic profit opportunity. Given my experience and the fact that I know the market always tries to buck you off your positions, I told my trader, Bill Griffith, that we would have one "hairy pullback" before these things launched and that we must do everything we could do to hold our positions in solar stocks given some basic parameters that gave the stocks room for a shakeout.

During that trading week I had also taken a position in another solar that had broken out and was in the middle of an upside run, Sunpower Corp. (SPWRA) shown in Figure 4.10. On October 18th SPWRA staged a big outside reversal to the upside on huge volume. Given that the solar group was on fire, I viewed this big-volume turnaround as quite positive, and took a position in SPWRA in one of my funds in the mid-90 price area. In hindsight, I am amazed at just how perfectly the ducks lined up in September–October 2007.

Unfortunately, the barrage of bearish emails from my partner over the weekend of October 17–19, worried about "locking in profits" as well as

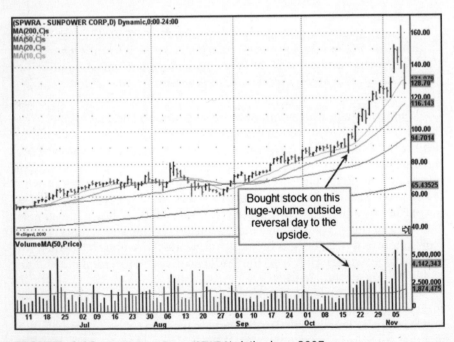

FIGURE 4.10 Sunpower Corp. (SPWRA) daily chart, 2007.
Chart courtesy of eSignal, Copyright 2010.

numerous stories in the media over that particular weekend about the market's resemblance to October of 1987, the infamous Black Monday crash, started to unnerve me and essentially threw me off track.

On Monday, October 22nd, the big shakeout that I had told my trader was coming and through which we must strive to hold our solar stock positions, finally came. Because I had allowed the influences of the bearish media and a bearish business partner within my money management firm to shake me off my predetermined path I veered from my plan. I had already laid out the parameters of how I would handle a nasty market shakeout, which I was fully expecting sometime in October, and I had complete conviction in the solar stocks given the evidence of all the ducks lining up in a row in the group and the window of opportunity that was opening in the market. The lesson here is clear, and I want to make it plain that I do not blame my former partner or the media. I blame myself, because I violated a simple premise of trading, and that is to plan your trade and trade your plan—alone and free of distractions from the emotions and opinions of others! Despite the fact that I knew I was in all the right stocks at the right time, on Monday, October 22nd I dumped my FSLR and other solar stocks, overcome by the fears induced upon me by external influences.

As Figure 4.11 shows, FSLR simply shook out below its 20-day moving average, closed up on the day, and never looked back. I had a huge position in that stock, and I dumped it all that day. I tried to come back into the

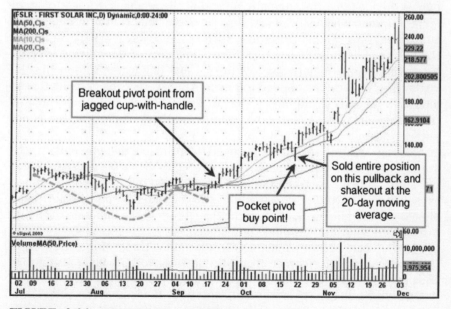

FIGURE 4.11 First Solar, Inc. (FSLR) daily chart, 2007.
Chart courtesy of eSignal, Copyright 2010.

stock later on over the next few days after dumping it, but being so shell-shocked by the initial mistake, I never got my position back. The irony is that on the same day FSLR reversed and closed back in the black and above the 20-day moving average. This is in fact a pocket pivot buy point! I could have simply recognized this and bought all my FSLR back and then some on the very same day I sold it all.

In addition to having the pocket pivot point weapon I didn't have in 2007, today I also use a rule of letting a stock close before selling on any break of the 20-day moving average, as stocks often will reverse intraday to close back above the moving average. If I had this rule then, I would have held FSLR on October 22, 2007. Rather than using a moving average, such as the 20-day or 50-day line, as an "absolute" barrier, I now view moving averages as the median of a "zone" and instead watch how a stock acts "around a moving average." Stocks can frequently venture below a key moving average on a short, intraday basis, or even for a day or two or more, before climbing back above the moving average. It is likely that so many traders are conditioned to sell on breaches of perceived "absolute" support such as right at a moving average line that this naturally carries a stock past a moving average as the momentum of selling, as the stock breaks the line, carries it downward temporarily. This creates price/volume action around the moving average that should be monitored to ensure that the move below the moving average line does not shake one out of one's position. Today, my view of moving average lines and support levels encompasses the idea that they actually represent the medians or mid-points of "zones" around which stocks find support or resistance. In addition, once a stock breaks a key moving average, such as the 20-day moving average for the first time, it must also confirm the "violation" of the moving average by moving below the intraday low of that first day where it breaches the 20-day line. This can be applied to any moving average, by defining this as a clear "violation" if and only if the stock moves below the intraday low of the first day under the moving average, so that one day's action is not enough to confirm such a violation.

The last quarter of 2007 also proved the principle that you must watch your stocks FIRST and the market indexes SECOND, as the NASDAQ chart in Figure 4.12 shows. While the NASDAQ topped out in early November, those very solar stocks whose action I had insisted to my partner that I should be watching instead of getting caught up in the minutiae of the indexes, well, they just continued on higher.

In the end, traders must insist that they trade alone, free from distractions and interference from the outside world, whether such distractions come from business partners, the media, or any other source of external input that can throw you off your path. Remember this rule: Trade your plan, and plan your trade, and do it all with a minimum of outside

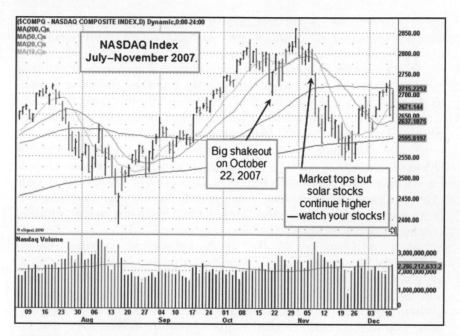

FIGURE 4.12 NASDAQ Composite Index daily chart, July–November 2007. The market tops but solar stocks continue higher, proving that you must watch your stocks first, and the market indexes second.
Chart courtesy of eSignal, Copyright 2010.

influence or input, preferably remaining in the Livermorian ideal of "trader's isolation."

Too Short for Too Long: Gil Morales

My biggest losses have always come on the short side of the market. Since I consider the size of a mistake to be directly correlated to the size of the loss resulting from the mistake, these are then by definition big mistakes. In 2002 I took some serious heat by staying too short too long off the bottom in October of that year. By the second year of the most brutal bear market in 70 years, everyone and everything was negative, and there were plenty of compelling and logical reasons why things were likely to get worse. I remember giving a presentation to a group of institutional investors in a very nice high-rise office building in downtown Los Angeles. During the presentation, we let one eager institutional technician come up and give his view on why the Dow and the S&P 500 had to come down further because they had not yet caught up to the NASDAQ on the downside. There were nods all around the room, and I was one of those nodding heads. After all, the year before, 2001, I had been up over 170 percent, mostly on the short side, and I was still intoxicated by the taste of blood playing the short side of the market.

By the time the bottom in 2002 came around, everyone had become so conditioned to the bear market that nobody could see their way through to the possibility that the market had bottomed. By this time, all of us at William O'Neil + Company, Inc. were so tired of looking for a bottom that we were starting to feel as if we would never see a bottom, and if we did, none of our indicators would help us find it. After a discussion with Bill O'Neil on September 9, 2002, I wrote in my trading diary, "On a super-cycle basis it may be that the market has come into a once-every-20 years, once in every five cycles phenomenon—that's why all the indicators and methods don't work in finding the bottom. This last bull cycle has an extraordinary number of excesses—like a two-headed monster."

As late as September 23, 2002, the market was still suffering from the overhang of gloom and doom, and the following entry from my trading diary gives some idea of how Bill O'Neil perceived the muck of a long, two-and-a-half-year bear market: "Bill feels the administration's emphasis is all on Iraq, where it should be, but he thinks there should be some emphasis as well on the economy. The failed Japanese bond offering is very bad, but also due to the fact that the Japanese have failed to let bad debt fail and allow their system to clean itself out via the 'creative destruction' process that is the hallmark of our system. Weakness in Japan and in Europe is significant, [and] will have an effect on our markets." By the end of September the market was breaking to fresh lows, and at this point I was very short the market going into October 2002. I could feel my saliva glands working overtime as the expectation of tasting blood on the short side again overcame me.

Figure 4.13 shows the NASDAQ Composite Index breaking to new lows in late September into early October. The market was certainly not looking too happy. If you were already as morose about the market as I was, this move to new lows was a sign to get aggressive on the short side. Even Bill O'Neil was looking for more downside, as he called me around October 4th to tell me he was looking at shorting a big-cap tech leader from the 2000 bull market! That's how bad it was looking! Bill told me he believed this particular big-cap tech company has a big problem in that they have bought too many companies. In business you don't want to put yourself in the position of having to manage too much—if you buy fifty companies you then have fifty managements to straighten out. It's just too daunting."

We didn't know it at that time, but we were in for a big surprise. On October 10th, the market bottomed and began to move sharply to the upside, with the NASDAQ Composite Index posting a 4.42 percent move

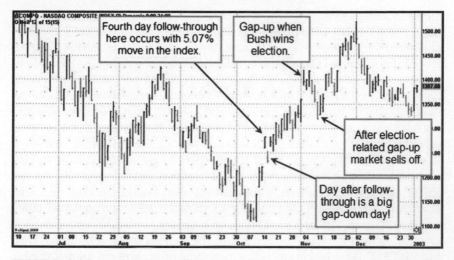

FIGURE 4.13 NASDAQ Composite Index, daily chart, 2002–2003. The bottom of 2000–2002 bear market is finally put in.
Chart courtesy of eSignal, Copyright 2010.

off what would be its final lows in the 2000–2002 bear market. Three days later the NASDAQ put in a fourth-day follow-through, gapping up and rallying a total of 5.06 percent on the day with volume up big. If you were short those first four days off the bottom you felt some serious blast heat as the market launched off the lows. Being heavily short, I was one of those lucky investors standing in the way of this freight train. The follow-through day smacked me good, but the next day the market gapped down, although on lower volume, enticing me to stay short, but the second day after the follow-through gapped back to the upside, and the market began to grind higher over the next 12 days before gapping up again. After that initial gap-up, the market pulled in hard over the next several days, with the NASDAQ pulling down from the high of 1420 that was hit the day after the election to a low five days later at 1319.06.

All of the erratic movements in the indexes kept me trying to short the market, as I could not find any traction on the long side. I still could not see how the market could continue to rally. Then, on November 20th Bill O'Neil called me on my cell phone while I was teeing off at the 11th hole at the country club. Golf outings are far and few between for me, and Bill had never called me on the golf course before, so I knew something was up. He sounded pretty excited as he discussed the Bush Administration's announcement earlier in the day that it would be implementing broad economic stimulus measures, including tax cuts, in their pending economic stimulus plan. At that point Bill told me he thought the firm's institutional advisory group, which I was managing at the time and which was responsible for advising over 500 institutional investor clients of William J. O'Neil + Company, Inc., should "be aggressive on the idea that the market environment is getting more constructive, and that October was likely a permanent bottom." One of the names Bill had identified as a potential, re-emerging type of leader from the prior dot.com bubble market in 1999 was EBAY. As well, he felt that "some new, underplayed names have a good shot at working." I made a note, "Bill likes EBAY," and left it at that. Slowly, however, it dawned on me that, unlike Bill, I was not sensing the flow of the market at that stage. In early October, Bill O'Neil was thinking about shorting stocks, and I was shorting stocks as well. By November, Bill was probably buying EBAY, and I was still shorting the market! I had missed the boat by a long shot. Sure, Bill O'Neil could consider shorting stocks near a market bottom, but the difference is that, unlike me, he recognized that this was incorrect and simply and decisively turned with the market when it counted. Buying EBAY in mid-November 2002 was typical of his ability to smell the big stock when the market began to turn. Watching him do this was a big lesson for me in the wake of my stupidity and stubborn persistence in shorting a

FIGURE 4.14 eBay, Inc. (EBAY), weekly chart, 2002–2003. Bill O'Neil identifies the "big stock" following the market turn in late 2002.
Chart courtesy of eSignal, Copyright 2010.

market that was bottoming and starting a new bull market. I was so blinded by my negativity that I could not see anything positive at the very moment when the market was turning positive.

To confuse matters even more, by December the market was beginning to roll over again as the market's recovery remained uneven, at best. Even Bill O'Neil was feeling a little frustrated, despite owning EBAY, which was still acting well as it continued to track sideways. As my trading diary entry of December 5, 2002, indicates, "Bill says it is difficult to stick with the system. The Dow could pull back to 8200–8400 and the NASDAQ to 1250–1350. The market won't come out of this very well unless the government does something dramatic." The next day a quick call from Bill yielded the following short trading diary entry on December 6, 2002: "The market is just reacting to news—has no rudder. But the real problem remains the post-bubble economy."

At this time gold was beginning a new move to the upside, and Bill O'Neil observed on December 13, 2002: "The move in gold is concerning. It's telling you something!" To me, the market's action in December 2002 got me negative enough to start looking at the short side of the market again. The move in gold was offering another cautionary clue, as I saw it, and on December 20, 2002, I logged in my trading diary the following comment from Bill O'Neil: "Gold responds to fear, but there is some fundamental basis to the recent move in gold. We must get through the next couple of months before we can see where the market is going."

The key point here is that despite the fact that the market's recovery off the October low was uneven and choppy, this was not necessarily indicating that the market was about to go into a bear phase and a new leg to the downside. I learned here that markets are not always black or white. Sometimes they can be gray and uncertain, and the smartest position to take is no position at all—just let the market work itself out. Bill O'Neil understood that while the market was still having a tough go of it, it was more a matter of waiting for the window of opportunity to open wide than taking one side or the other, bull or bear, with respect to the market.

On January 8th, the Bush administration announced a stimulus plan that included accelerated reduction of income tax rates for individuals and the elimination of taxes on dividends for individual investors. On January 23rd, Bill O'Neil conveyed what is an essential stock market truth, and the final lesson of my late 2002 punishment in the markets, which I logged in my trading diary as, "Regardless of how bad things get in the market don't underestimate the power of the government to do something." Accommodating Fed monetary policy combined with a newly elected Bush administration's ability to push through an agenda of tax cuts to stimulate the economy, given the Republican majorities in Congress at the time, meant that the government was going to have its way. By the time the regime of Saddam Hussein collapsed in March 2003, the new bull market was in full swing.

The main theme underlying all of my mistakes that resulted from persistently trying to short a market bottom was that I failed to understand that after a long, brutal bear market, the major market indexes can put in a final, permanent low, but that doesn't mean they have to immediately shift into bull mode. The market is not always black or white, bullish or bearish; and because it was difficult to make upside progress after the October follow-through, that is, was not strongly "bullish," I came to the conclusion that the market must then be "bearish." Jesse Livermore himself said that he preferred to avoid using terms like "bull" or "bear" to describe a market since he believed that prevented him from being objective about what the market was telling him in real time. My need to label the market a "bear" or a "bull" led me to do so deductively, so that if it wasn't definitively bullish, then I "deduced" that it must be bearish. In reality, the market was still in a phase where it was, despite the strong follow-through on October 15 that marked the final low of the great 2000–2002 Bear Market, not in a bull or bear phase, but more accurately in a "recovery" phase. This was a valuable lesson at the time, and helped me avoid getting raked to death on the short side for many years. Then the bear market of 2008–2009 came.

The bear market of 2008–2009 was without question the most unnerving I have ever experienced. Other bear markets were simple affairs for me—I was either in cash or I was selling short. In March of 2008, the end of the first leg down in the 2008–2009 bear market set in with the panic that occurred when Bear Stearns, for all practical purposes, went out of business over the weekend of March 15–16. It likely would have just been another panic low experience for me, but this time something was quite different, because I was now personally involved in the financial crisis. Bear Stearns was the prime broker for both of the private funds I was running at the time, and the funds were domiciled with Bear Stearns. I was staring at the possibility of having my funds lost in a potential Bear Stearns insolvency. Although our Bear Stearns representatives assured us our funds were safe, I didn't assume that I could trust them, as they were only telling us what somebody else higher up was telling them to tell us. The uncertainty of the entire situation over that weekend was quite unsettling. Needless to say, that was not a pleasant weekend for me. Sure, I can handle losing money in the market, but watching money evaporate into thin air because your prime broker went belly up was just too much for me to take. When you find yourself in the grip of an exogenous event that is beyond your control, it is a very uncomfortable feeling. As a trader, I like to think that at least I am in control of my own destiny. In this case, I was in a situation not of my making and quite out of the realm of my control. It was, quite frankly a frightening experience that left me somewhat shell-shocked and with a strange sense of insecurity and foreboding.

The crisis of March 2008 was averted when J.P. Morgan stepped in and bought out Bear Stearns at $10 a share. J.P. Morgan also took over as prime broker of the private funds I was managing at the time, which was ironic since The House of Morgan was considered the safest place to be at the time, and here we were, prime brokered with Bear Stearns, which was going to be saved via a J.P. Morgan acquisition. While we were out of the woods with respect to the possibility of seeing our funds evaporate in a Bear Stearns insolvency, the entire affair left me with a sense of distrust and mistrust, something similar to what people might experience the first time they are in an earthquake. That solid ground you thought you were standing on is now perceived as not being as solid as it used to seem, and so your sense of security is diminished. I suffered from a sort of financial stress-disorder syndrome for several months after that.

As I regained my composure I played the short bear market rally that lasted roughly from March to the beginning of June 2008 successfully. By the end of summer, another leg down in the bear market was brewing, and by September the market began to split wide open. I was again playing the market on the short side, but not as aggressively as I should have. While I did make money on the short side in 2008, finishing up a few percent for the year after posting a deficit in the first three quarters of the year, I felt that I could have been up much more, perhaps 50 percent or more, based on my post-analysis. I was far too timid, and missed what was essentially the "sweet spot" of a severe leg down within an overall bear market that was shaping up to be quite brutal. Again, however, I was letting the opinions of a business partner unduly influence me as he insisted with professorial superciliousness and authority that "nobody can make money on the short side."

I came to realize that making about 10–15 percent on the short side in the last quarter of 2008 represented a very poor showing given the extent and velocity of the downdraft in September–October 2008. I had essentially allowed myself to be influenced by outside forces that led me to become overly cautious and timid in my approach to the short side. Because I had difficulty making money on the short side earlier in the year I allowed others to influence me into believing that my short techniques were deficient and that shorting is simply "too difficult" to execute. What I have learned since then is that the methods detailed in the book I co-wrote with William J. O'Neil, *How to Make Money Selling Stocks Short* are perfectly sound, but the key is to wait for the exact moment when the "line of least resistance" has been broken and the optimal window for short-selling is opening. As you can see in Figure 4.15, the "sweet spot" for short-sellers was essentially a sharply accelerating three-week downside break. If you sat there with

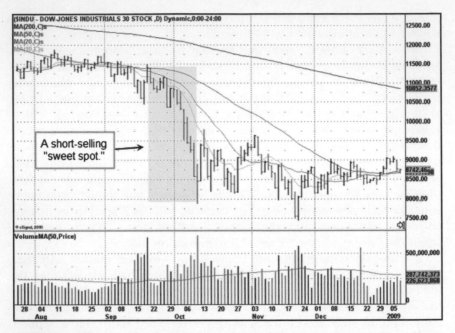

FIGURE 4.15 Dow Jones Industrial Averages daily chart, 2008. The "line of least resistance" is broken for the short-seller, providing a short, "sweet spot" window of opportunity.
Chart courtesy of eSignal, Copyright 2010.

your finger in your ear, you missed the sweet spot. If you caught the sweet spot, that's all you needed, and you could have taken the rest of October through December 2008 off. My colleague Chris Kacher has confirmed that the patterns and methods outlined in *How to Make Money Selling Stocks Short* are deadly accurate when the proper window of opportunity opens, as we will see in Chapter 8, and that this is the key to fully and optimally exploiting a downside break in the market during a bona fide bear market leg down. You must wait for your opportunity! As Livermore said, "There have been many times when I, like many other speculators, have not had the patience to await the sure thing." When it comes to shorting, avoiding danger is best achieved by having the patience to wait for the sure thing. That window in September–October 2008 was that sure thing, and I played it meekly as I had allowed myself to be talked into the idea that "nobody can make money on the short side."

Frustrated by not fully exploiting a massive downside break in September–October 2008, despite being up in a year when the markets were down some 50-odd percent, toward the end of 2008 I became fascinated with the situation in the banking sector, which represented "ground zero" of the bear market. I had already had a visceral experience with the chaos that was engulfing the financial sector with my Bear Stearns experience in March of 2008, and when I began to research the situation it was evident to me that the situation was quite dire. I concluded that the bear market of 2008 would not end until we had seen at least two or three major money center banks go under, such as Citigroup (C), Wells Fargo (WFC), or Bank of America (BAC). At that time I felt that if one could add two-plus-two one could comprehend that the big banks were all insolvent, and it was only a matter of time before the final housecleaning would arrive and that it would be marked by one or more of these money center banks being taken over by the government. At that point the excesses in the system would begin to be allowed to be wrung out of the system, and the market and the economy could go about the process of recovery and rebuilding again.

What I didn't realize was that the excesses were going to be propped up instead, and I severely underestimated the ability of the U.S. government and the Federal Reserve, in concert with central banks and sovereigns across the globe, to orchestrate it so successfully. This was a major mistake, and it was fostered by my belief that by March 2009 the Fed had no traction and that you could "fight the Fed." I had surmised that since preemptive rate cuts throughout 2007 and 2008 combined with $1.8 trillion in bailouts by the end of September 2008 did nothing to prevent the market's sharp break in September–October 2008, the excesses of the financial establishment were going to be washed away in a final break to new lows. In addition, an uncharacteristic reliance on examining the financial statements, the "fundamentals" of the financial stocks reinforced such dire conclusions to the point that I allowed it to override my basic price/volume approach to the markets. This reliance on "fundamentals" coincided with my reading of doom and gloom investment newsletters detailing all that was wrong with the world. My research into the financial crisis took me to all kinds of web sites with their own version of why the crisis would drag down and destroy the global financial system. While their prognostications of Armageddon may yet turn out to be correct, they have little to do with what is going on in the stock market at any particular moment. Unfortunately, given my shell-shocked memories of the Bear Stearns meltdown in March 2008, I was easily persuaded that the worst was yet to come.

Three major factors in my psychology were coming together to create a perfect storm: (1) frustration over not fully exploiting the September–October 2008 short-selling window of opportunity, (2) allowing myself to be influenced by outside sources, and (3) allowing fundamentals and my sense of dread as a result of my experience with Bear Stearns in March 2008 to override my normal reliance on price/volume

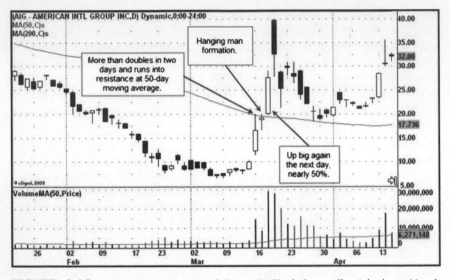

FIGURE 4.16 American International Group (AIG), daily candlestick chart, March 2009.
Chart courtesy of eSignal, Copyright 2010.

action. By March of 2009, newspaper headlines were regularly featuring the word "depression." Given that I have 19 years of experience as a professional investor, this was one time when I could not see the forest for the trees. When everyone is talking "depression" and all looks lost, historically, this is when markets bottom! But I could not see it, and so I kept fighting the market.

Some of the rebounds off their lows in financial stocks such as American International Group (AIG), shown in Figure 4.16, were absolutely insane, or at least I thought so at the time. It flew in the face of the "fundamentals." AIG had collapsed to a low of $6.60 a share by March 9, 2009, and eight trading days later hit $40 a share intraday. As you can see on the chart, on an intraday basis, the stock doubled on one day alone, the fifth day up off the bottom and the second day of a sharp move off the lows that took the stock right up into the 50-day moving average. Notice the long "candle wick" indicating that the stock was hitting some serious resistance at the 50-day line. The next day showed a small "hanging man" type of formation, which is a cautionary sign at the end of a sharp move to the upside, and so I decided AIG could be shorted in size right here. The next day the stock ran to the upside, nearly 50 percent. Given what I knew about the financial state of financial stocks, I considered these moves to be "preposterous," and I was certain that they would immediately reverse course to the downside, despite the fact that there was absolutely no price/volume evidence to

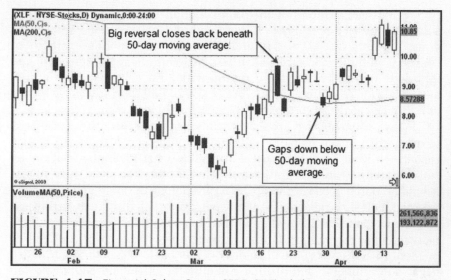

(XLF - NYSE-Stocks,D) Dynamic,0:00-24:00
MA(50,C)s
MA(200,C)s

Big reversal closes back beneath 50-day moving average.

Gaps down below 50-day moving average.

© eSignal 2003

VolumeMA(50,Price)

FIGURE 4.17 Financial Select Sector SPDR (XLF), daily candlestick chart, March 2009.
Chart courtesy of eSignal, Copyright 2010.

indicate that such an occurrence was imminent! As I saw it, the only thing to do was to short the stock again as it got above the 25 price level. Of course from there, the stock gapped up another 10–15 points, finally "kissing" the 40 price level. Shorts in AIG, even persistent shorts that kept shorting and covering as the stock ran up, got hurt badly.

These types of moves off the lows were typical for most of the financials, as the daily chart of the Financial Select Sector SPDR ETF known as the "XLF" in Figure 4.17 shows. For short-sellers like myself who just wouldn't take "no" for an answer, the XLF offered a couple of teases when it broke below its 50-day moving average on heavy volume twice during the latter part of March 2009, gapping down the second time, before launching again to the upside.

They say that wood ticks wait up in the branches of trees, and when an animal passes below the scent of the animal triggers a response in the wood tick whereupon it drops down, presumably onto the subject animal where it then digs in and proceeds with taking a warm meal from its unsuspecting host. If, by chance, the animal passes before the tick drops down and gets to it and the tick instead lands on the ground, perhaps, say on a decent-sized rock, it will attempt to "dig" into the rock until it kills itself, literally grinding itself into the rock. I now refer to this as "tick syndrome" in traders when they persist in digging into a rock; essentially continuing with the same strategy or trade that the market continues to punish. Watch out for "tick syndrome," which I define as a situation that can occur whenever you find yourself stopped out of the same trade twice or more. What I was doing in March of 2009 was entirely opposite to my normal methods of "flowing" with the market; I was in fact "fighting" the market instead, and this alone was a sign that I was on the wrong track. Today, I ask myself a key question from time to time, *Am I flowing with or fighting with the market?* The answer is often useful in getting back on the right track.

In my post-analysis it is clear that the mistakes I made were primarily psychological, and a chain of events and situations served to fuel excessive reliance on what I thought I knew, as well as what I feared, about the instability and potential for further crisis in the global financial system. The events of March 2008 set me off on a psychology of dread and insecurity that had fuelled rising concern on my part regarding the "trustworthiness" of the financial establishment, and this led to my delving into the "fundamentals" of the situation to the point where I was certain it would all be over only when some of the big money center banks began to topple. I also began subscribing to and reading a number of gloom and doom newsletters, which also reinforced my negative views on the market. Also, as a result of missing an opportunity in September 2008 to make big money on the short side by playing what was the true short-selling "sweet spot" too lightly, and given that I "knew" the financials were going down, I was primed to make big money shorting banks, brokers, insurers, commercial REITs, whatever else I was certain was about to collapse as a result of the "final solution" in the 2008–2009 financial crisis.

While all of this doom and gloom made sense from an "intellectual" level, it doesn't mean the market is going to follow any preset path as a result of its "sensibility and logic." Remember this basic principle: The market is going to do what the market is going to do at any point in time, not what you think it should do. Therefore, do not ever allow yourself to get into a state of mind where you begin interpreting the market's action in terms of what you think "should" occur, but rather learn to remain in the present and allow the market to tell you what it is actually doing. Had I adhered to this principle I could have avoided most of my troubles.

As a trader there will be many times when you will be thrown by the market; basically it fools you by throwing you into a situation that is unfamiliar, or cluttered with other exogenous factors. When this happens, you are most susceptible to deviating from your normal rules, and it is precisely such simple, and often minor, deviations that are the cause of most investment mistakes. If you find yourself thrown in this manner, and put into a position where the market is not making any sense to you, then the best course of action is to simply back away and wait for the market to return to a state where you are able to make sense of it. Ask yourself at any time, *Is the market making me want to operate outside of my normal methods?* If so, this may be telling you that it is a good time to back away from the market, a practice Livermore himself admitted he failed at doing many times, which is to insist on "always having an interest" in the market. Not simply backing off to wait for the sure thing to develop can be costly.

One of the big lessons for me after my debacle of March 2009 was that, like Livermore, I did not always have to be in the market, to have "an interest at all times." But this need to always be "doing something" in the market is fed by the fact that since 2005 I have been running money in the public realm for private, high net-worth investors, and this is quite a bit different from managing money in the "cocoon" of William O'Neil + Company, Inc., where I did very well. In the public realm, particularly the hedge fund world, "monthly performance" is ridiculously overemphasized. At O'Neil this was never a factor, and for the most part you were left alone to manage your portion of the internal account in isolation, in keeping with the Livermorian ideal of trading in solitude. Bill O'Neil might saunter into your office once or twice a year, but usually this was for the purpose of going over mistakes, particularly if you were in a trading slump, in the interests of helping you get "out of the ditch." In the public realm, some investors are constantly calling, asking "how're we doing?" over and over again, like Bart and Lisa Simpson in the back of Homer's car incessantly parroting, "Are we there yet? Are we there yet?" With people trying to look over your shoulder constantly and wondering "how we're doing" at every twist and turn in the market this begins to affect your psychology, which is a very fragile thing, particularly for O'Neil–style investing. Professional portfolio managers who are reading this book will likely understand what I am talking about, especially the way that overly skittish investor clients can affect one's psychology. For me, it kept me trading far too long and during periods when I should have been doing nothing, rather than pushing to "do something" in order to meet the unrealistic expectations of investor clients who overly emphasize short-term, monthly performance. Today, I have adopted Ed Seykota's policy of allowing his investors one phone call a year—any more than that and he sends their money back. There is nothing more distracting or damaging to one's fragile psychology than nervous and emotional investor clients—Ed Seykota understands this better than anybody. So rather than entertaining their emotion with soothing comments, he simply amputates the distraction entirely by eliminating the client. I call this, the Seykota Standard, and I now adhere to it.

Another "thematic" lesson that I learned in September–October 2008 and March 2009 was that I was wrong to lose faith in my short-selling investment methodologies in the spring–summer of 2008. Instead, I did not recognize an important principle of short-selling, which is that my short-selling methods work quite well when implemented at the proper stage of a market decline, but lose their effectiveness at certain stages of a bear market. "Tick syndrome" kept me trying to make money in March 2009 on the short side that I felt I "should have made" in September–October 2008. Unfortunately, I foolishly failed to recognize that March 2009 was not September–October 2008 because the market was in a much different stage of the bear market decline, and that it was in fact reaching a full-court-press panic low in March 2009.

There are many academics who will give you hundreds of reasons why you cannot do something, or why something cannot work. If you surround yourself with such individuals, you will never even attempt to accomplish anything for fear of failing. In my view, it is best to limit outside influences when it comes to one's investment thinking, whether that is related to a current market view or perceived opportunity in a particular stock or whether it is related to your methodology. If you choose to converse or consort with other investors, then do so with like-minded investors who will reinforce your investment "epistemology," but for the most part, strive to trade independently at all times.

Jesse Livermore preferred to ensconce himself in the solitude of his special trading office with no opportunity for disturbance. At William O'Neil + Company we used to joke that we should all trade from a room where we would remain "cocooned" from all outside influences, and only our chart books would be allowed to be passed under the door, along with "three squares" (meals) a day. Whenever I had a major cable financial channel on the TV that was mounted on the wall of my office at William O'Neil + Co., Inc. and Bill O'Neil walked in, the first thing he would say is "turn that thing off." Richard Wyckoff wrote: "When you understand stock market science you have no concern about important developments in your morning newspaper." I believe this is the ethic all traders and investors should strive for, and in my view it cannot be emphasized enough. Avoid the sensationalism of the news, of cable financial TV, of the pundits and commentators, because the market will always tell you all you need to know. Many investors concern themselves with "positioning" ahead of major news announcements such as the monthly employment report of the Bureau of Labor Statistics. In my view, there is no need to "position" one's portfolio for a news event as all the market evidence up to that point should already have you positioned on the basis of what the market is actually doing, not what you think it might do based on any number of news event scenarios that have not occurred yet. On its face, this is a silly way to invest, but it is exactly what I was doing in March 2009, and as we have seen it was caused by a confluence of malodorous factors. As traders, we must always remain objective and focused on what the market is telling us in real time, and the best way to do this is to check yourself by constantly stepping outside of your head and questioning the motives of any trade. Justify the trade in your head according to the rules of your methodology and system, not according to scenarios you think might happen or how you are currently feeling, whether that is characterized by fear or elation. Make every trade measure up to the criteria that your investment methodology dictates, and if it does not, nix the trade! By focusing on the criteria of the trade and the market's action, you will also trade with less stress, which is caused by trading in a manner that tries to anticipate rather than flow with the market and individual stocks.

For the record, I should mention that my March debacle in 2009 occurred in only one of the two funds I was managing at the time, and the second, less aggressive fund was left unscathed by the mistakes I made, which were for the most part isolated in the first, far more aggressively managed fund. Both funds were up in 2008, a year when the market was down big, so it was not as if there was any hint of what was to come by year-end 2008 or a pattern of continuous bumbling. During my career I have had several periods where I have drawn down close to 50 percent in aggressively managed portfolios, but such drawdowns have, based on my long-term track record, always been made up over time, sometimes quickly, sometimes not so quickly.

When Base Breakouts Fail During a Bull Market: Birth of the Pocket Pivot: Chris Kacher

The first decade of the new millennium, 2000–2009, has created a whole host of new challenges for traders and investors. While the major market averages in the United States enjoyed steep uptrends and downtrends throughout the 1980s and 1990s, they changed their character after 2003. From January 2004 to mid-2006, the U.S. market tended to move in a lackluster, sideways-to-slightly-upwardly grinding, sloppy market where most textbook, technical breakouts in individual stocks failed. Figure 4.18 shows the grinding nature of this reluctant bull.

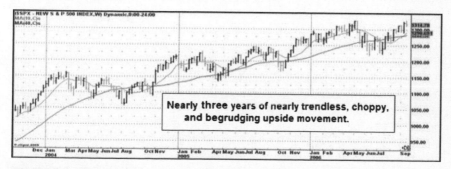

FIGURE 4.18 S&P 500 weekly chart. Nearly three years of difficulty. Chart courtesy of eSignal, Copyright 2010.

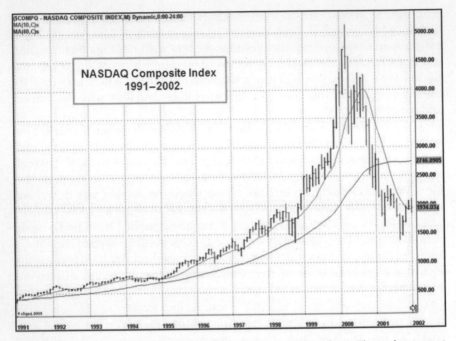

FIGURE 4.19 NASDAQ Composite 1991–2002 monthly chart. Throughout most of the 1990s the market moved in a steady, parabolic uptrend.
Chart courtesy of eSignal, Copyright 2010.

In such an environment it was often difficult to gain an edge, so in mid-2005, I explored other possible trading avenues. My research led me to some useful conclusions, and the pocket pivot point concept was born, which we discuss in greater detail in Chapter 5. That said, even after 14 years of trading success based upon capitalizing on upside moves in the market while sidestepping every significant market downturn since 1992, including the mother of all NASDAQ bear markets from 2000 to 2002 (see Figure 4.19), I began to think on some subconscious level that the markets will always trend, either up or down.

I did not stop to think that the major U.S. market indices could behave in a prolonged, sloppy, reluctant sideways move that would persist for years, so this grinding market action caught me by surprise. That said, certain developing, emerging markets like China and India, as well as commodities in general, were leading, and their bull market was much stronger than the general U.S. market averages. However, outside these specific groups, the environment was considerably challenging. I came to understand that the tone of the markets had changed into something I had not experienced in the 14 years I had traded. It is essential during such challenging periods that traders keep a clear head and not let their emotions control their actions, so they will find the best solution.

My pocket pivot buy point discovery in mid-2005 helped to turn my 2005 performance around so that I was able to turn it into a winning year. Armed with the pocket pivot, in 2006 I was able to achieve triple-digit returns in excess of 100 percent. However, 2007 brought new challenges. Price/volume action in the major market indices misled me through much of 2007, an extremely rare situation. This resulted in a negative return for my market timing model that year, the only other year in 35 years that it had a negative return. During 2007 my timing model produced numerous false signals, as can be seen in Figure 4.20. As it turned out, the fact that the model was generating so many false signals was a big clue that 2007 was indeed a highly unusual year.

While 2007 was the only other year besides 1993 where I logged a negative return for my timing model in its 35-year run, the unusual behavior of the model was helpful in shining a light down these dark and treacherous trading corridors. Numerous distribution days naturally led to sell signals issued by my timing model. However, these sell signals led not to a falling

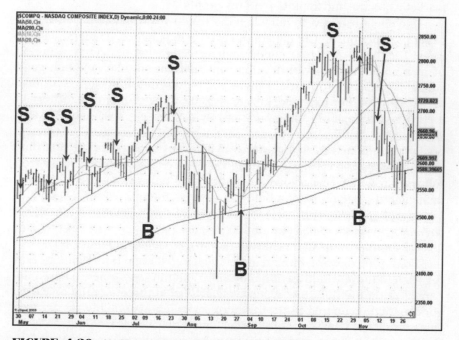

FIGURE 4.20 NASDAQ Composite daily chart May–November 2007. Timing model signals are shown, many of which were false in 2007.
Chart courtesy of eSignal, Copyright 2010.

market but to a market that stubbornly continued to grind higher, and was the first time this had persisted for as long as it did looking back over many decades of price/volume market action. But by capitalizing on the window of opportunity that presented itself in late 2007, and by making full use of pocket pivot points, I was able to reverse my draw downs that had occurred in my own trading account up until August 2007 and finish the year up +30.6 percent despite my timing model being down for the year.

Overtrading: Chris Kacher

Since I always let the stocks have the final say on exactly what degree of market exposure I will take in any environment, I ended up with solid returns for 2007 by buying the fundamentally strongest stocks at proper pivot points and staying heavily invested through September and October of 2007 as the brief window of opportunity was clearly open during those months. Had I invested only during such periods, when the window was clearly open as measured by a buy signal from my timing model together with a confluence of strong, fundamentally sound stocks hitting proper buy points more so than at any other time that year, I would have limited my market exposure and kept more of my profits.

One might ask how to tell when the window is truly open versus only being partially open. The general answer is experience. Traders develop a feel for the market by running their screens each day. Over a period of many months, one will develop sensitivity as to when enough good stocks are starting to hit their pivot points, whether a pocket pivot or a breakout pivot. For example, in August 2006, the general averages turned a corner, and began heading back up. By late August 2006, many stocks with strong fundamentals began to hit my buy screens. Constructive pocket pivot points started showing up all over the place for the first time since October 2005. I began buying the best ones and found myself on full margin within just a few days. The other times when this occurred, launching the beginning of a bull run, were as follows, with the length of window of opportunity in parenthesis: April 2003 (6 months), October 2004 (3 months), October 2005 (2 months), August 2006 (3 months), September 2007 (2 months), and March 2008 (1 month), as shown in Figure 4.21.

From 2005 onward, I found myself well into margin rather quickly during each of these windows of opportunity and thus was able to more fully capitalize on the bull run, which typically lasted three months or less, a short period compared to the 1980s or 1990s, and is one big reason why this decade has been far more challenging. I believe overtrading is one of the toughest challenges for any trader, whether a novice or a deeply experienced professional. It is often far too tempting to let one's prior successes in the market cloud one's judgment. Being trigger happy in the markets

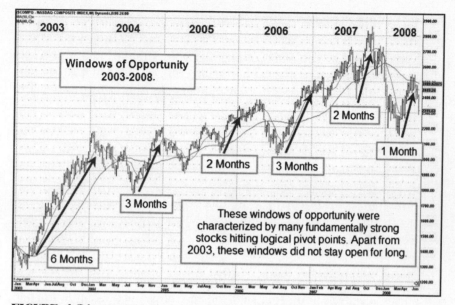

FIGURE 4.21 NASDAQ Composite Index weekly chart, 2003–2008.
Chart courtesy of eSignal, Copyright 2010.

when they are only acting half-right can create losses, especially in the difficult decade of the 2000s.

PROBLEMS, SITUATIONS, AND SOLUTIONS

We have been trading for the past two decades. While any trader knows not to make rookie mistakes such as averaging down, the adventurous ride we have had in the markets has given us a deep perspective on what are often overlooked and unexpected reasons why traders get off track. This ride has not come without "tuition costs," which we might better understand as the price of learning. Such tuition costs have continued to be exacted by the markets since some of our mistakes have occurred even after many years of success in the markets, and should be considered "post-graduate" tuition costs!

What follows is a smorgasbord of our mistakes or mistakes we have observed other experienced traders make. We mention the problem, provide a situational example, and then discuss the solution.

Your Trading Strategy Stops Working

Problem: Your strategy stops working for more than a few months, which tests your patience. You start to question your strategy, and may make changes to it that are detrimental in the long run, or abandon it altogether.

Situation: In 2004 and 2005, base breakouts were not working. The strategy that had always worked in the past, that is, buying the best stocks on base breakouts during bull markets then going to cash during market corrections, was not working as it once had. My business partner, who had many years of experience and was an exceptional trader in his own right, believed base breakouts would no longer work from here on out because the market had fundamentally changed.

Solution: I only briefly believed this because the base breakout strategy is based on human nature, and until human nature changes, markets will generally behave in similar ways. Mark Twain once said, "History never repeats but it often rhymes." So, knowing that, I was not about to abandon my strategy but instead started looking for a way to deal with the markets, which were behaving differently than they had in the 1990s. Consequently, the pocket pivot was born. That said, the base breakout strategy is still perfectly valid but tends to be much more effective during uptrending markets that are in a clear uptrend as opposed to the much more "noisy," sideways markets that typified the market's action in 2004–2007. During this period, however, "pocket pivot" buy points helped build a position in a stock earlier, which in turn gave me more of a cushion in the event the market should have a brief yet normal pullback. Pocket pivots will be discussed in far greater detail in Chapter 6.

Personal Setbacks Can Derail Your Trading

Problem: You suffer a personal setback unrelated to the markets but continue to trade the markets despite your focus being temporarily derailed by the setback.

Situation: A loved one passes away or you get some sort of other dire news.

Solution: Whether it be the death of or breakup with a significant other or other close family member or friend, or one of life's inevitable pitfalls, pratfalls, or personal tragedies, one should take a big step back from trading should such events occur in order to deal with them in a manner that allows one to maintain an even psychology as a trader. In two of the biographies that have been written about Jesse Livermore, *Jesse Livermore Speculator King* by Paul Sarnoff and *The Amazing Life of Jesse Livermore* by Richard Smitten, mention is made of a period when Jesse Livermore had to contend with a death threat against his son, Jesse Jr., as well as the particularly nasty aftershocks of a bad marriage, yet he continued to trade. He ended up giving back the $100 million or so he made going short the market during the early 1930s, equivalent to billions in today's dollars, and became destitute by the late 1930s. Had he maintained his perspective to just not trade while his personal life was in turmoil, he would have kept most of his wealth instead of blowing out his account yet again as shown in Figure 4.22.

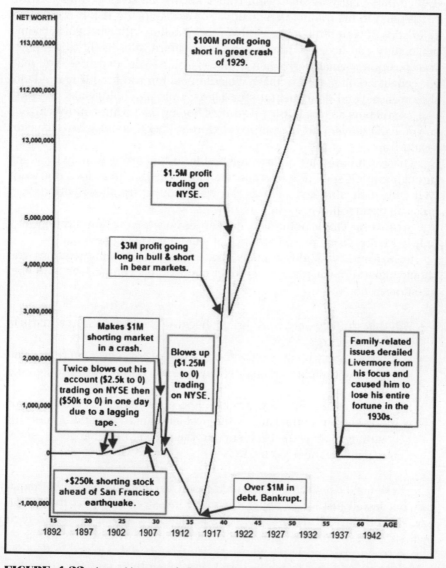

FIGURE 4.22 Jesse Livermore's "equity curve" during his life and trading career. Chart courtesy of eSignal, Copyright 2010.

New Trading Strategies Can Derail Your Trading

Problem: New strategies sound tempting to try because some well-known investor has used the strategy with success. You decide to include this new-found knowledge in your own trading strategy, but you run the risk of it either taking your focus away from your own strategy that has brought you much success, or the new modification is not in harmony with your trading personality. A successful trader knows his strategy must always correspond to his trading personality. For example, the risk/reward characteristics of your strategy must always stay in line with what your trading personality can accept. Otherwise you are more than likely to abandon your position prematurely when it moves against you, or worse, you may get caught holding a particularly volatile position too long if it suddenly slips well beyond your mental stop alerts, thus psychologically trapping you, as you now are put in the position of hoping the position moves higher so you can recover part of your loss before selling it, a dangerous psychological trap.

Those who are particularly vulnerable to this problem may be going through a weak spell due to a specific market period that does not work well with their strategy, such as the way choppy, trendless periods can cross-up trend followers.

Situation: This is potentially dangerous because the new strategy may only work for a brief period or may not suit your trading personality.

Solution: If you add in a new strategy to your existing strategy, you should make sure you place it in proper context. Ask yourself the following questions:

- Will this strategy only work briefly because the change in the markets is just temporary?
- Will this strategy blend well with my existing strategy such that it will still suit my trading personality, psychology, risk/reward profile, and so forth?
- If I incorporate it into my strategy, and my strategy eventually stops working some months later, is the problem due to the addition of this new strategy? Or is the problem that the market has changed in some fundamental manner yet again?

There have been times when changes in the market were only temporary but lasted just long enough for many investors to adjust their strategy. The best investors were able to accommodate this change into their own strategies and then remove this modification when the markets returned to normal. Investors who ran into trouble did not notice that the markets had returned to normal, and thus when their strategy started to underperform as a result of some change they had made to their strategy, they suffered much frustration. Some eventually abandoned their strategy altogether thinking the markets had changed for good. For example, there have been several periods throughout the past 30 years when it has been declared that trend following was dead. Yet the best traders with exemplary 25+ year track records such as Bill Dunn and John Henry, as interviewed in *Trend Following* by Michael Covel, prove that a consistent trend-following approach works brilliantly. These traders are the rare few who continue to trade their strategy even during difficult times when the market is trendless rather than abandoning their strategy and succumbing to the "this time is different" view.

The belief that this time is different has cost traders much money. Using our trend-following example, the many siren calls over the past few decades that trend following is dead has derailed many a trend following and thus can be quite damaging as the markets have always returned to their trending nature. While 2004–2007 were rather lackluster and absent of strong trends, good money could still be made by being invested when the few trending windows of opportunity opened during those challenging years. My timing model, which has averaged just over +33 percent/year since 1974, averaged less than half of that return during 2004–2007 due to the lack of strong trends. That said, money was still made over this period by simply going long or short the QQQQ, an exchange-traded fund that serves as a proxy for the NASDAQ 100 Index. Additional gains could have been made by focusing on the fundamentally and technically strongest stocks when the market was trending, coupled with when the windows of opportunity were clearly open as discussed in the prior section on overtrading.

At any rate, the best trend followers such as Dunn and Henry may lose more than half of their accounts during the most difficult trendless periods as their account audits show drawdowns beyond –50 percent, yet they always more than make up for these losses when the market begins to trend again and thus have always been able to well outperform the general markets in any given market cycle. That said, it is easy to see why most traders would abandon their trend-following strategy. It takes great patience and confidence in one's trading strategy to withstand –50 percent drawdowns in their account without abandoning or changing their strategy.

Of course there are times when certain aspects of the market legitimately change. It is up to the investor to take note of this and make changes accordingly to insure optimal returns. It is good practice to watch the market on at least a weekly basis for such changes. For example, in the late 1990s, the metric of emphasizing a stock's earnings and ignoring stocks that had no earnings changed with the onset of the Internet revolution.

Some successful Internet stocks had no earnings yet had soaring sales. Such stocks often rose hugely over part or all of the bull market in the late 1990s including well-known stocks such as Amazon.com (Ticker: AMZN) and eBay (Ticker: EBAY). Investors who took advantage of this newfound change profited handsomely.

I remember telling Bill O'Neil of my finding. He took serious note. He eventually adjusted his rules to accommodate stocks that had no earnings, but this adjustment did not come immediately. He had been conditioned since the early 1960s to only invest in stocks with strong earnings, as such stocks were the cornerstone of his massive success in the markets. This is where experience can work against even the best investors. To O'Neil's great credit, he eventually adjusted his strategy by allowing his in-house portfolio managers to capitalize on such stocks with no earnings, even though he himself continued to invest only in stocks with earnings.

Market Noise Can Derail Your Trading

Problem: You get caught up in the noise. There is now more financial information available to the average investor than ever before. The thousands of financial web sites on the Internet, financial television channels such as CNBC, and, of course, other forms of news media all serve as potential squawk boxes that can take you away from your focus. Those who are considered experts with big reputations who voice their views can scare one out of their positions. Big headline news events can also be destabilizing.

Situation #1: I remember on January 13, 1999, it was reported that Brazil had devalued its currency overnight. This sparked speculation that South America was going to have a currency crisis that could be compared to the magnitude of the Asian currency crisis of 1997, which knocked U.S. and world markets down considerably. On January 13, 1999, the NASDAQ Composite opened down –115 points, or –5.0 percent as shown in Figure 4.23. I was fully invested at 200 percent using every available dollar I had to ride the uptrend that began in October 1998.

I was a bit shell-shocked to see how much damage my portfolio was about to take shortly before the market opened that morning. My positions consisted of high alpha stocks that thus tended to move two to three times the general market averages, so my portfolio was in for a bit of a downdraft at the open. As tempting as it was to sell my positions right when the market opened, I decided to wait and see if the major averages were going to head lower on big volume after gapping down at the open. This would confirm the gravity of the news. If Brazil's currency devaluation was going to result in a crisis for South America, the market would move lower on big volume after gapping down considerably. I decided I would then sell all positions that also fell below their opening lows. Gil Morales and I frequently

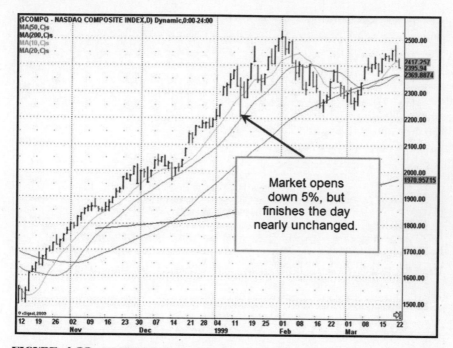

FIGURE 4.23 NASDAQ Composite Index daily chart, October 1998–March 1999. Brazilian currency devaluation sparks deep worries that another currency crisis is at hand. The NASDAQ Composite opens down 5.0 percent but finishes the day nearly unchanged.
Chart courtesy of eSignal, Copyright 2010.

put our heads together before the opening every day when we worked together at William O'Neil + Company, Inc., so I called him to discuss the situation. He quickly replied, "I think . . . we buy!" He was not as heavily invested as I was, so from his perspective it was a potential opportunity to increase his long exposure. Fortunately, the market opened at its low of the day and proceeded to rally. I got scared out of two of my positions, as I was looking for any excuse to reduce my sizeable market exposure whereby I was on full 200 percent margin, but held onto everything else. I ended up staying about 160 percent invested. Instead of being down over −20 percent in one day, my portfolio finished the day down only a couple of percent. It would have finished the day about flat had I not sold anything. Furthermore, I would have finished the day up had I bought stocks such as Cree Inc (CREE) at the open that had gapped down well beyond reason. While I normally would never buy any stock that gapped down, this was a special circumstance of panic getting ahead of reason. I could have bought CREE at its open of 35.4 and sold it had it moved lower, otherwise hold it

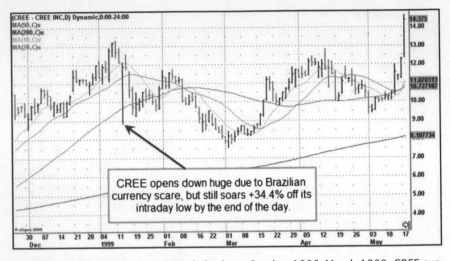

FIGURE 4.24 Cree Inc. (CREE) daily chart, October 1998–March 1999. CREE currency finishes the day up +34.4 percent from where it opened.
Chart courtesy of eSignal, Copyright 2010.

the rest of the day. It finished the day at 47.56, or up +34.4 percent on the day as shown in Figure 4.24. Not bad for a day's work, even in the go-go, dynamic 1990s.

Solution: It is always better to follow the money, not the news. News can scare one out of a winning position (see Figure 4.25). Following the money means paying attention to price/volume action in the stock, which can reveal whether the big, institutional money is flowing into or out of the stock. While you may buy for technical reasons as well as fundamental reasons such as company news, earnings, sales, and return on equity, you should sell solely on the basis of technical reasons and avoid the pitfalls of paying attention to the news. As you can see, it is easy to get knocked off the clean and pure path of effective focus.

Deficient Research Techniques Bring Wrong Conclusions

Problem: The research techniques traders use to refine their strategy are deficient, leading them to the wrong conclusions about how they can improve their existing strategy. They end up modifying their strategy, but when that modification doesn't improve their performance, or worse, hampers their performance, they modify it again as they search for the answer to improved performance, but further modification only makes things worse.

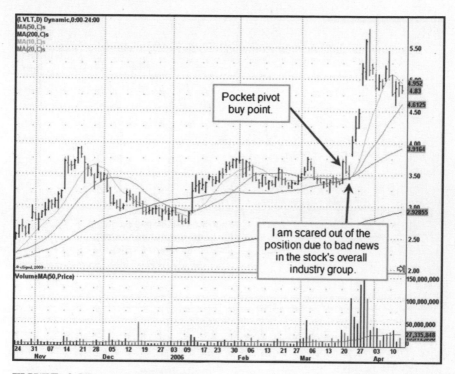

FIGURE 4.25 Level 3 Communications (LVLT) daily chart December 2005–April 2006. LVLT soared the day after I sold it.
Chart courtesy of eSignal, Copyright 2010.

Situation #1: It is a common mistake to assume that just because something holds true over a long period of time, such as 25 years, that it holds true indefinitely. Using a simple example, it was remarked during Thanksgiving of 2009 that the Friday following Thanksgiving is often an up day for the market on light volume, with down days usually being down just slightly, typically between 0 and –0.5 percent. While this does indeed hold true going back 25 years and even 50 years, it was not true in a different era, a period known as the Great Depression. In the 1930s, the Dow Jones Industrial Average was down 5 out of 10 times on the Friday following Thanksgiving: –1.24 percent in 1939, –0.73 percent in 1935, –1.16 percent in 1932, down a big –2.76 percent in 1931, and –1.2 percent in 1930. That said, on the Friday after Thanksgiving in 2009, with 2009 being a truly highly unusual year in the aftermath of the global meltdown of 2008, the Dow lost –1.5 percent.

Solution #1: It is important to take the whole picture into context when sizing up a research discovery. A year such as 2009 was often called

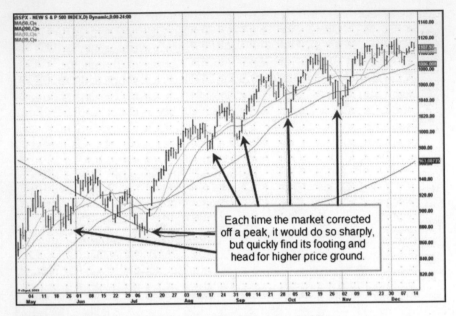

Each time the market corrected off a peak, it would do so sharply, but quickly find its footing and head for higher price ground.

FIGURE 4.26 S&P 500 daily chart, May–December 2009.
Chart courtesy of eSignal, Copyright 2010.

a black swan since it was a time of highly unusual circumstances. The global market meltdown that occurred in 2008 prompted the U.S. Federal Reserve Bank in 2009 to quantitatively ease and print money that would fuel the market higher. This highly irregular situation rendered impotent market indicators that had worked well in the past. Each time it seemed that the market should sharply correct, the market would just dust itself off after a week or two of weakness, then head to higher ground as shown in Figure 4.26.

All discoveries one makes when conducting stock market research must account for possible black swan environments. That said, research is the cornerstone of creating an effective trading strategy. Traders must not rely just on what they read, even if they are convinced the idea is sound, but must also thoroughly test out the idea to prove it has worked in the past and will continue to work into the future. This way, one is not just intellectually but also emotionally secure in knowing the idea is sound. One is then less likely to abandon the idea during brief periods when it stops working by emotionally reacting to its temporary failure. While the Friday following Thanksgiving usually results in a positive day for the general markets, the 1930s were an unusual time just as 2009 was also an unusual year. Putting a research finding into the context of the big picture is essential.

Situation #2: With regard to creating timing models that attempt to time going long, short, or neutral the stock market by way of investing in ETFs that mirror the general market averages such as the S&P 500 or NASDAQ Composite, it is essential that the pieces that define your timing model are properly defined. For example, even if your model is purely systematic in that a clearly defined set of rules apply to your model, you may find that your model is still not a black box in that it still would not be computer programmable. This is perhaps best explained by way of analogy. In the years I worked with William O'Neil, his uncanny ability to interpret the innate quality of a base is nearly unmatched. I equate this to his decades of experience analyzing charts. For example, the difference between a great base, a good base, a marginal base, and all the degrees in between, is contextual, and programming a computer to "see" the subtle differences would be quite the challenge if not impossible. O'Neil's ability to size up "quality" is based on his decades of experience in analyzing millions of charts since 1960.

Thus, erroneous conclusions have been made with respect to the "M" in William O'Neil's CAN SLIM regarding follow-through days, which signal it is time to buy, and distribution day clusters, which signal it is time to sell. For example, some have observed that follow-through days have a low success rate, statistically, and thus are not useful. While follow-through days do indeed have a low success rate, there are ways in which the success rate can be greatly improved by adjusting various parameters such as the threshold level at which the major averages must be up for the day to qualify as a follow-through day. This threshold level should be adjusted based on the average true range over the last "x" number of trading days, depending on how sensitive one wishes the timing model to behave. Average true range is a measure of volatility. A highly sensitive model would react quickly to changes in the general market's average true range. The upside is that it would be quicker to catch such changes. The downside is that it may catch more false signals. A model that has low sensitivity to changes in average true range would react slowly to changes in the average true range. The upside is that it would catch fewer false signals. The downside is that it would be slower to catch changes in average true range thus negatively impacting profitability.

In addition to adjusting the threshold level, clear rules must be made in terms of when the count must be reset. For example, in Figure 4.27, would your rules include October 6, 2009, as a follow-through day?

The NASDAQ Composite had only corrected –5.9 percent from its peak set on September 23. If you defined your rules as having to reset the count whenever the NASDAQ Composite corrects more than –5 percent, then October 6 would not be a follow-through day, assuming you use the rule that follow-through days must occur on the fourth day or later. Of course,

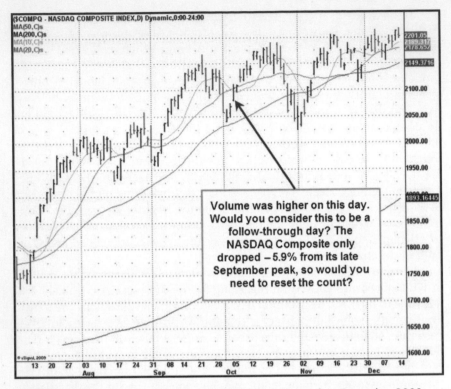

FIGURE 4.27 Dow Jones Industrials daily chart, September–December 2009.
Chart courtesy of eSignal, Copyright 2010.

you could also create a time limit that says the follow-through day must occur no later than "x" number of days after the market begins to rally. Besides what has been discussed, there are other variables that can be accounted for in fine-tuning the predictive value of follow-through days.

Solution #2: It is important to clearly define your parameters when attempting to time the market using a model. Fuzzy definitions will only lead to confusion and misunderstandings. It is also important to consider other variables that can be used to increase the predictive value of the signal.

Situation #2 continued: In terms of distribution days, one could end up making limiting conclusions about distribution-day sell signals. In one case that was published on the Internet, a set of seemingly logical conditions were assigned to distribution days, but upon deeper examination, the conditions were too restrictive. This led to limiting conclusions about distribution days. I use in this example the parameters found at quantifiableedges.blogspot.com/2009/08/distribution-days-quantified.html.

The following hypothetical conditions were:

- The S&P closes above the 200-day moving average since we are looking for a top.
- Sometime within the last 12 days the S&P closed within 1 percent of its 200-day high, which would confirm we are near a top.
- Over the last 12 days there have been at least four distribution days.

Now, let's say we short the S&P on the close of the fourth distribution day using the three conditions above where the fourth distribution day occurs within the last 12 days if it is above the 200-day moving average and has come within 1 percent of its 200-day high in the last 12 days, then we cover the short position 20, 40, or 60 days later.

From this, the conclusion was made that distribution days do not lead to market tops, or falling markets, but that one would actually be better off buying instead of shorting the market.

However, the study has holes. By restricting the S&P 500 to only four distribution days that must close within 1 percent of its 200-day high in the last 12 days then covering the short a fixed amount of time of 20, 40, or 60 days is too restrictive and guilty of overfitting past data. If one were to adjust the number of distribution days to five over a period of "x" number of days, and exclude the rule that the S&P 500 must close within 1 percent of its 200-day high in the last 12 days, the results would be greatly improved. The internal logic of price/volume action in the major market indices held true one hundred years ago and continues to hold true today, outside of a few highly unusual but brief periods such as May–June and October 2007.

A cluster of high-volume down days generally implies that institutions are selling. This often precedes declines in the general market averages. Even in years where there are a high number of false signals where the market moves higher after a sell signal is issued, a proper model should have a failsafe built in to minimize losses during such challenging market periods, such that it can still well outperform the major averages by capitalizing on the times when its signals are correct. It is analogous to letting your winners run and cutting your losses short, a major rule for trend-following success.

Solution #2 continued: The internal logic in any strategy must hold true. One should identify valid concepts first, and then construct a model around those concepts. Traders should not blindly curve-fit their model to data as this could lead to overfitting. Overfitting often occurs when one's model is overly complex, thus it may have too many degrees of freedom relative to the amount of data available. Such a model will have poor predictive ability but will show impressive results in hindsight. Also, don't fall prey to making your model overly complex just to feed your ego.

I remember being so proud of an econometric timing model I created while I was in graduate school in the early 1990s. I showed Bill O'Neil my timing model when I first met him in 1996, and he nodded and smiled politely and said some of my findings may only hold up during certain cycles so always strive for simplicity. Wise words indeed as my timing model, while profitable since 1991, has greatly evolved and simplified since then. As my experience has grown, I have become better at understanding charts and thus able to put distribution days and follow-through days into proper context. In this way I have dropped many of the "training wheels" I used to use. Analogous to this is how I noticed that O'Neil is the quintessential purist when it comes to reading charts. He relies primarily on the price/volume action of daily and weekly charts, the shape of the pattern, the relative strength line, and the 50-day moving average. His decades of contextual experience reading charts allows him to put away almost all other indicators and rely on his vast experience to identify a proper base.

Labels May Simplify But Can Oversimplify

Problem: One finds it easier to fall back on labels such as "cup-with-handle" and "square box" than to put such chart patterns in context with the general market. When I used to give seminars with Bill O'Neil, I would always get questions regarding the shapes of bases. "Does this stock base qualify as a cup-with-handle?" "Is this handle too deep relative to the overall base?" "Why is this not an ascending base? The chart is moving higher in textbook fashion as an ascending base should."

Situation: While such questions are relevant, I found that investors often end up relying too much on the shape of the chart pattern instead of understanding how the stock's base is playing out relative to the general market. This can lead to misinterpretations and missed opportunities. For example, Figure 4.28a shows a chart of Charles Schwab Corporation (SCHW). The base that formed was called a cup-with-handle, yet the cup looks rather defective as it is fairly "V"-shaped whereas a textbook cup-with-handle has a rounded bottom. Further, the handle pulled back a steep –26.7 percent, which was huge relative to the depth of the base of –39.7 percent. However, this cup-with-handle base was buyable since, taken in context of the general market, the base was valid. From August to October 1998, the general market was in the grips of a major bear market as shown in Figure 4.28b. Notice how the general market hit lower lows (Figure 4.28b) between the first bottom on September 1, 1998 and the second bottom on October 8, 1998, yet SCHW's second bottom was much higher than its first bottom. This second bottom would normally be a handle had the market not fallen so far. Further, the "V" bottom would have been rounded had the market not been plummeting.

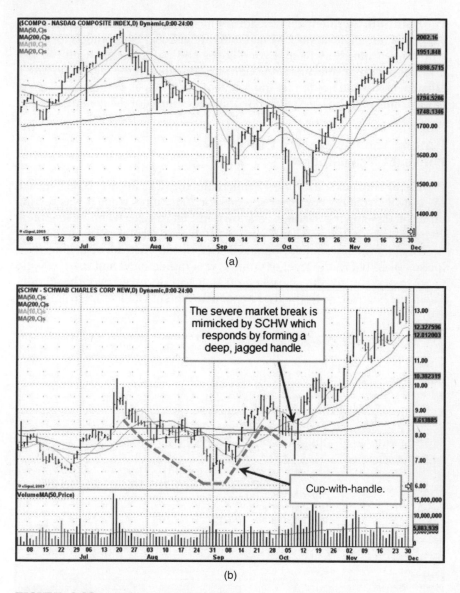

FIGURE 4.28 (a) Charles Schwab (SCHW) versus (b) NASDAQ Composite Index, daily chart, August 1998–December 1998.
Chart courtesy of eSignal, Copyright 2010.

Solution: So you might be asking why use labels if they can be so misleading? The simple answer is that labels are great training wheels for those who are learning how to spot good bases and are generally useful to any investor during normal market conditions. But should the market go into a tailspin, be careful not to rely too much on the "shape" of the overall base. Always interpret the base pattern within the context of the general market.

Waiting Too Long to Sell Due to Unusual Circumstances

Problem: I did not sell Cypress Semiconductor (CY) in early 2008 because I was away from my computer screens for 20 minutes while it was resting on its 50-day moving average, as shown in Figure 4.29. When I came back 20 minutes later, it had fallen 7 percent under my mental sell stop.

Situation: I was quite shocked and upset. Instead of selling it, it looked oversold as the level of volume was rather small and there was no news to account for the sharp sell-off that had occurred over the 20 minutes I had been away. Normally, I never use oversold indicators to guide my

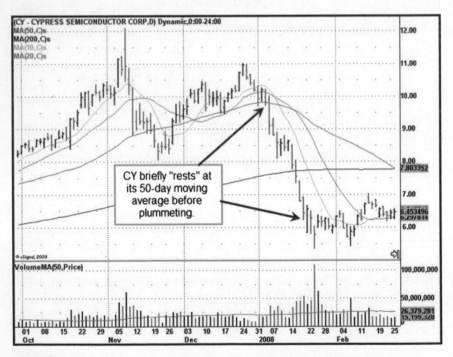

FIGURE 4.29 Cypress Semiconductor (CY), daily chart, January 2008.
Chart courtesy of eSignal, Copyright 2010.

selling since oversold often becomes even more oversold. I just sell the stock if the price of the stock hits my mental sell stop and ask questions later. But in this case, I let my emotions get the best of me. I was upset and felt cheated and figured CY would snap back, so I held it. Near the close, it began to bounce back so I held the position. The next day, it traded higher but only slightly, and then proceeded to sell off another –3.2 percent. I should have sold the stock, but the volume was lower than the day before, so I figured it was truly oversold at these levels, as there was still no news on the stock. The third day, CY sold off another –2.7 percent. Now the stock was –12.4 percent under where I had originally intended to sell it. At this point, it became that much harder to sell. I was psychologically stuck in the position. As has been said, the first sell is the easiest. I had almost always obeyed my mental sell alerts. I was not used to dealing with being stuck in "no man's land." CY proceeded to decline an additional –32.8 percent in the ensuing 10 days, putting it at –41.1 percent from where I had originally intended to sell it. I finally gave in and sold it a few days later on an anemic bounce on January 29, 2008.

Solution: Don't let your emotions cloud your judgment. If events stack up against you and you feel cheated, don't let that derail you from your focus of following your rules. Breaking my sell rule cost me money.

Introducing New Elements into Your Trading

Problem: When I started managing money for Bill O'Neil, I did not have real-time quotes. My quotes were delayed 20 minutes. Over a three-month period, having real-time quotes did me more harm than good. I found that real-time quotes brought me too close to the market action, such that I would get scared out of positions on any sharp intraday reactions in the general market. Having real-time quotes temporarily changed the way I normally traded stocks until I learned to adjust.

Situation: Bill O'Neil once did an informal study of his portfolio managers and found that there was no "edge" gained by having more computer monitors to watch during the trading day. In other words, having more computer monitors to watch did not add to performance and in some cases seemed to cause more harm than good. Sometimes the less information overload you allow to distract you or scare you into making rash moves, the better off you are. One of the best current portfolio managers at William O'Neil + Company, Inc. is a woman who comes into the office later in the morning, a couple of hours after the market has opened, which has an insulating effect and also allows the market time to "settle in" before making any trading decisions. By operating on a longer time frame and not reacting to the opening news and market movement, one may actually block out a lot of the noise that can cause a trader to react in a less than totally objective manner.

Solution: Having too many monitors can be distracting. It can take traders away from their focus and cause them to miss an optimal buy point or sell point. Further, intraday charts can scare one out of a position prematurely. It is better to use daily and weekly charts until one learns to constructively use intraday charts, much as I had to constructively learn to deal with real-time quotes way back in the day.

Opportunities Exist When You Least Expect Them

Problem: The market was in a correction so I was not diligently running my buy screens each day.

Situation: Just because the market is in a correction is no excuse to not run your buy screens each day. I consequently missed out on some excellent opportunities. Some of the best stocks will offer logical pivot and pocket pivot points during weak markets.

Solution: Don't skip running your daily buy screens just because the market may be correcting.

Do Not Overintellectualize

Problem: One enjoys intellectualizing about the market but crosses the line and starts trying to predict where the market will go. I know of no one who has been able to make such predictions with perfect timing. While there are admirable investors such as Jim Rogers who make long-term trend predictions that are often eventually correct, even as Rogers himself admits, his timing can be way off.

Situation: The need to be right will eventually end up costing the investor. This is perhaps why I knew of nearly no scientists at Lawrence Berkeley National Laboratory, the complex adjacent to University of California Berkeley where I obtained my doctorate degree in nuclear chemistry, who were successful investors. They had massive egos as world-class scientists, so they repeatedly made the mistake of trying to tell the market what to do and where it should go.

Overintellectualization is a big trap. Each time one thinks one has mastered the market, one will soon find there is yet so much more to learn. That said, I have read Edwin Lefèvre's book *Reminiscences of a Stock Operator* over 10 times. Each time, I learn new things from reading it. The experiences I have accumulated since I last read the book brings forth new meaning and understanding upon rereading it.

Solution: One must watch the market day-to-day and make investment decisions accordingly. While it may be a seemingly necessary exercise to try to predict where the market will go, one should not let conclusions about the future of the market derail one's focus from the present. Staying in the now means being in tune with the market on a daily basis and will serve to keep one in the focus of quietly listening to what the market is saying. One can then adjust market exposure accordingly.

How to Deal with Trading Slumps

Problem: The market damages your psychology repeatedly through a series of losses, causing a deep slump.

Situation: While slumps can be difficult to overcome, don't become like the aged prize fighter who has lived past his prime, reliving in his own mind former moments of glory, unable to recover his lost youth. More mature market wizards such as Bill O'Neil and Ed Seykota prove that when it comes to investing, age, whether young or old, has little to do with successful investing.

Solution: Chapter 10 will discuss in detail philosophical ways in which you can recover from your slump and repair your damaged psyche.

In the meantime, here are ways to come out of trading slumps:

- Engage your mind in something completely different for a week such as travelling, playing a musical instrument, doing something artistic, or learning a new skill. The new mental stimulation has a way of switching mental gears so your subconscious mind can begin to repair itself.
- Use exercise and a proper diet to jump-start yourself. This will be covered in detail in Chapter 10.
- Keep an active trading diary, which can help your mind reach logical conclusions about why you're in a slump. You can also review your diary to reinforce the lessons you learn.
- Always review your trades to spot weaknesses that are caused by a deficient trading technique, misunderstanding the strategy/improper application of the strategy, or emotional issues that are causing losses.

CONCLUSION

As one can see, many pitfalls await even the most experienced traders. Here are some suggestions on how one can keep evolving as a trader:

- Always keep reading and learning. By 1999, I had read over 200 books on the stock market, having read my first book on investing at age 13. Reading new books even when you think you have learned it all reinforces what you already know and may even give you new ideas on how to optimize your trading strategy. Reread excellent books. Over the years, we have read books such as *Reminiscences of a Stock Operator*, William J. O'Neil's *How to Make Money in Stocks*, and Jack Schwager's two books, *Market Wizards* and *New Market Wizards*, multiple times. Any time a book is read again after one has gained new experiences, the book takes on deeper meaning.

- Feel and embrace the pain of the loss caused by the mistake. Ed Seykota's trading tribe technique, which can be learned at www. tradingtribe.com, is one of the most effective ways to stay on track as a trader. Eckhart Tolle's philosophy of embracing and accepting the pain of loss is equivalent and enormously effective. Both of these techniques will be discussed in Chapter 10.
- Keep an active trading diary that will highlight your mistakes. The act of writing down your mistakes creates a neural trace in your mind that underscores the mistake so you are less likely to repeat it.
- Annotate charts showing your buy and sell points. Carry these charts with you so you drill into your mind proper and improper buy and sell points. Make notes on why you made an error and determine its cause, whether it was simply emotions getting in the way or related to misunderstanding your strategy or misreading clues on a chart.

Jesse Livermore often said that there are far more ways a person can lose money than are imaginable. After experiencing 20+ years' worth of mistakes, we could not agree more. Experience is an amazing teacher if you embrace your failures. Remember that, in reality, there is no failure, only feedback, and that if we learn from our failures, we are actually failing forward.

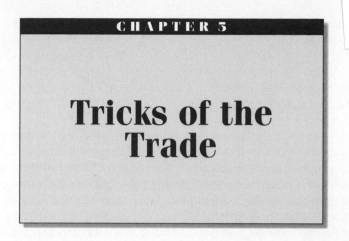

CHAPTER 5

Tricks of the Trade

B
ill O'Neil used to tell us that making big money in the market wasn't about buying the right stocks as much as it was about handling them properly once you've bought them. You can always buy a potential leader as it initially breaks out from a first-stage base at the outset of a big price run, but if you sell it after it goes up 10 percent and it continues up another 190 percent, you didn't handle it properly. This is a critical component of our methodologies, which include a number of specific techniques that can be used in real time to handle positions in strongly performing stocks.

Also as more and more investors and traders use the same tools and have access to all the same real-time news, charts, data, and market indicators, market participants all see the same things happening at the same time, taking on the characteristics of a herd, or at least a market that to some extent watches itself. It is, therefore, understandable that most investors and traders, regardless of their methodology, would like to find some additional tools or tricks, if you will, that can provide them with an edge, both with respect to finding alternative and early buy points relative to standard new-high/base-breakout buy points as well as a coherent system for selling stocks and handling positions in real time, particularly positions in potentially big, winning stocks. If you count yourself among these investors and traders, this chapter will provide some answers and solutions. "Pocket pivot" buy points, gap-up buy points, and selling rules using the 10-day and 50-day moving averages and the Seven Week Rule are more than tricks, although we like to think of them as such. They are, however, very specific rules-based "micro-methods" that should be relatively easy for investors to grasp and implement in their own trading.

DR. K'S LABORATORY: THE POCKET PIVOT ADVANTAGE

In the O'Neil literature you will find many references to new-high "pivot point" buy points, as well as trend line and moving average breakouts, but you will not find any definition of "pocket pivot" buy points. This is because the concept of the "pocket pivot," essentially an early buy point relative to traditional O'Neil techniques, did not exist until it was discovered in Dr. K's Laboratory in 2005 as a result of research studies that were performed for the express purpose of finding a solution to the flattish, compressed, and somewhat sideways moving markets of the mid-2000s (see S&P 500 weekly chart from 2004–2005). Such markets contrast with the more strongly trending market environments seen in the 1980s and 1990s. In simple terms, a "pocket pivot," or "buying in the pocket," is an early base breakout indicator, which is designed to find buyable pivot points within a stock's base shortly before the stock actually breaks out of its chart base or consolidation and emerges into new high price ground.

Having met and talked with a broad range of institutional investors through our affiliation with William J. O'Neil + Company's institutional services department as well as at the workshops we presented at for the company, we gained a distinct and unique appreciation for the fact that institutional investors, such as hedge funds, mutual funds, and pension funds, do not like to buy breakouts to new highs. In fact, they generally prefer to buy stocks off of their lows, and sometimes the lower the better. Of course, if we think about this for just one second we realize that it is the institutions that create the bottoms of chart bases, including the volume/accumulation clues along the lows of a constructive base formation.

The premise of the pocket pivot is simple. If it is the buying of institutions that "carves" out the bottom of a constructive base from which a stock may break out to new highs later on, then we can postulate that the clues of their buying and accumulation in the lower parts of a stock's chart base should be evident, and could offer optimal, low-risk entry points to begin taking a position, particularly if the stock is a proven market leader. Such evidence will show up in the daily chart as well as the weekly chart, but to determine precise "pocket pivot" buy points we make prodigious use of daily charts.

The pocket pivot can give an investor a head start on accumulating a leading stock within a base formation. And in markets where standard breakouts are more often "fake outs" as the example of Dendreon Corp.

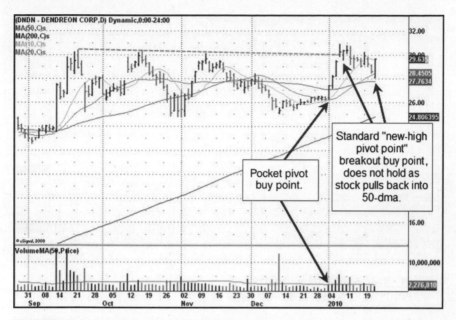

FIGURE 5.1 Dendreon Corp. (DNDN)—a "big stock" bio-tech with a promising new prostate therapy flashes an early buy point.
Chart courtesy of eSignal, Copyright 2010.

(DNDN) in Figure 5.1 shows, the pocket pivot buy point technique can get an investor into a stock at a lower-risk price point and thereby make it more possible for the investor to sit through a pullback if the all-too-obvious new-high breakout buy point fails initially and the stock retrenches, corrects, or sells off.

The pocket pivot was identified after much "lab" research going back through our individual trades since 1991, and then spot back testing through prior decades. Finally, the concept was tested again in real time under fire with actual money, and as an early entry point has proven to be a highly exploitable phenomenon. During the mid-2000s this was especially helpful as many standard new high base breakouts were not working in the shallow and sideways moving markets of 2004–2005. While there were small but sparse windows of opportunity such as one in late 2004 and two very brief windows that opened in mid-to-late 2005, many initial buys at standard, new-high buy points would quickly turn into –7 percent to –8 percent losers within a few days.

When operating with thinner, less-liquid and lower-priced stocks, the pocket pivot can provide a useful buy point that is less obvious to the crowd. When thin stocks break out through obvious resistance levels to

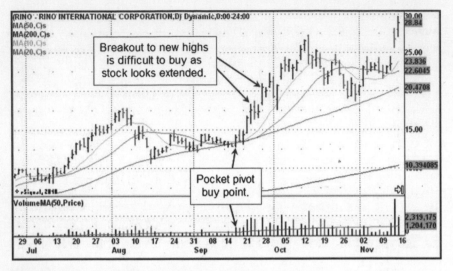

FIGURE 5.2 RINO International (RINO) daily chart, 2009.
Chart courtesy of eSignal, Copyright 2010.

new highs, the crowd tends to see them and hence is more able to run the stocks up, exacerbating the upside price movement. As well, when such thinner stocks begin to sell off, their lack of trading liquidity will exacerbate their downside velocity, which increases the risk inherent in such stocks. In general, stocks that trade less than $30 million in daily dollar volume or less than 750,000 shares a day fall into this category. There are exceptions to this, of course, but as a general guideline these parameters suffice for the purpose of judging a stock's liquidity and associated price volatility and risk.

RINO International (RINO) shown in Figure 5.2 was a relatively thinly traded stock at the time it broke out of a base in late September 2009. Note that the move up through the 15 price area in the latter half of September was fairly sharp, and the stock moved up rather quickly up through the 20 price level before pulling back sharply and finding support at the 10-day moving average. If investors had bought the breakout to new highs, the sharp pullback below the 10-day moving average might have caused them to be shaken out of their position. However, buying on the pocket pivot buy point before the stock rose above the 15 price level would have given investors buying the stock at that point a head start on the stock and put them in a better position to weather any pullback after the stock quickly rallied up through the 17.75 high in the base on the standard new-high pivot point.

Another example of using a less-obvious pocket pivot buy point in a smaller stock is seen in Jazz Pharmaceuticals (JAZZ), a thin, low-priced stock with a strong fundamental picture given its strong pipeline of new and existing products at the time. The move up through the 50-day moving average on December 9, 2009, occurred on a material increase in volume after the stock had been exhibiting very tight price action as it drifted into the 7.00 price area on extremely light volume. The fact that the pocket pivot occurs right after this extreme volume dry-up is highly constructive, and while the stock does not launch to the upside it does build a tight, sideways consolidation with virtually no selling volume in the formation.

Once a thin stock like JAZZ begins to move higher, its price moves, one way or the other, can be exacerbated by its small size and lack of trading liquidity; hence buying a solid, reliable pocket pivot point as the stock acts very "quietly" provides a strong entry point as one tries to build a position in the stock. Watching for pocket pivot action in smaller, thinner stocks with potentially strong fundamental outlooks can be rewarding, as the examples of RINO and JAZZ illustrate.

CHARACTERISTICS OF POCKET PIVOTS

A pocket pivot point generally occurs within the stock's chart base, before the standard new-high breakout buy point appears. Pocket pivots can also appear as continuation buy points as stocks move higher after launching out of a chart base or consolidation. Price/volume action and base formation leading up to a pocket pivot point are of paramount importance in identifying a proper pocket pivot buy point. Pocket pivots are also signs of strength within the base of a leading stock and as such have some predictive value with respect to the potential of a stock to continue higher. A stock will often break out of its base within a few days or sooner of a proper pocket pivot point, assuming the general markets are also acting bullish or are in a bull trend.

When looking for pocket pivot points, limit your universe of potential candidates to fundamentally strong stocks with constructive basing action leading up to the pocket pivot point. This would include characteristics such as tight price closes within the weekly chart, as well as high-volume spikes with supporting or upside action on the weekly range, or other evidence of accumulation within the base. We would avoid wide-and-loose bases since the premise of accumulation that the pocket pivot concept is based upon is not generally evident on the charts of stocks forming wide-and-loose bases. Pocket pivots within such faulty patterns are therefore more prone to failure. In addition, it is necessary to compare the overall base formation to the action of the major market averages formations such as the NASDAQ Composite and S&P 500 Indexes, to see if the stock's base formation is constructive relative to the overall averages. For example, a pocket pivot that occurs within the base of a stock that is acting and holding up much better than the market averages would carry more weight than one that occurs in a stock that is acting much more erratically or negatively than the general market and leading stocks as a whole.

DEFINITION OF A POCKET PIVOT BUY POINT

Pocket pivot points in fundamentally strong stocks are preferable, and in particular one should constantly monitor the "big stock" leaders in any bull cycle for potential pocket pivot points. The Internet stocks in 1999, Apple and Google in 2004, and solar stocks in 2007 would have been areas to focus on for monitoring pocket pivots during those particular bull market years and cycles.

The idea behind a pocket pivot is that one is buying the stock "in the pocket," as a less-obvious but valid and reliable buy point within the stock's base. While many different buy points in a stock's chart can meet the definition of a pocket pivot, some can be improper, as we will see later in some of the examples.

Similar to what you would want to see in a proper base formation, a stock should be showing constructive price/volume action preceding the pocket pivot. Just prior to the pocket pivot, as the stock is moving within its overall base structure, tighter price formations, that is, less volatility should be evident in the stock's price/volume action as viewed on its chart. The stock should have been "respecting" or "obeying" the 50-day moving average during the price run that occurred prior to the time the stock began building its current base. This indicates that the stock's character is such that it can be expected to continue to do so. Therefore you can use the 50-day moving average in such a case as a sell guide if the stock begins to violate its prior "character," for instance, its habit of "obeying" or "respecting" the 50-day moving average. If the stock's character is such that it tended to "obey" or "respect" its 10-day moving average on its prior price run before building its current base, then you might expect to use the 10-day moving average as your guide for selling the stock. The stock's price/volume action will ultimately determine whether you should use the 10-day or 50-day moving average as your guide for selling the stock.

Except in very rare cases, such as in the aftermath of the crash of late 2008, pocket pivots should only be bought when they occur above the 50-day moving average. Ideally, the stock's price/volume action should become "quiet" over the previous several days, which contrasts with the much

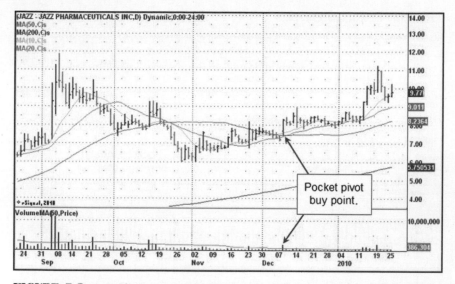

FIGURE 5.3 Jazz Pharmaceuticals (JAZZ) daily chart, 2009–2010. Very quiet side-ways action with volume drying up followed by upside volume spikes, especially on the pocket pivot day.
Chart courtesy of eSignal, Copyright 2010.

larger and stronger volume move that comes on the pocket pivot itself. On the pocket pivot you want to see up-volume equal to or greater than the largest down-volume day over the prior 10 days. We call this the proper "volume signature." If the volume has a habit of being choppy, in other words varying greatly from day to day, then you increase this to 11–15 days. Visually, this means that there should not be a lot of big, "spiking" down-volume bars in the chart over the prior 10 days as well as the stock's over-all base formation. Ideally, volume should be relatively consistent over the prior 10 days, preferably drying up, and then should "burst" higher on the day of the pocket pivot, as is evident, for example in Jazz Pharmaceuticals (JAZZ) in Figure 5.3.

POCKET PIVOTS AND STANDARD BREAKOUT BUY POINTS

Sometimes a pocket pivot will coincide with a standard new-high base breakout buy point, a classic O'Neil "pivot point." If the pocket pivot co-incides with a base breakout, then volume does *not* have to be at least as great as the down-volume day over the previous 10 days, but should be

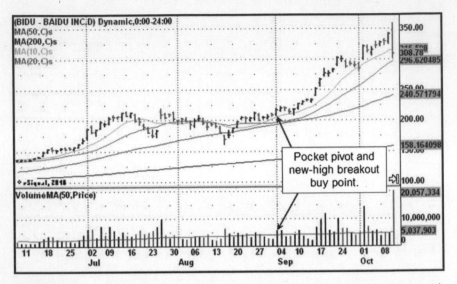

FIGURE 5.4 Baidu, Inc. (BIDU) daily chart, September 2007. A pocket pivot with volume increase of 39 percent but still the highest volume in the prior 10 days, which sets up a buyable breakout that lacks the 50 percent volume increase preferred for a standard new-high breakout.
Chart courtesy of eSignal, Copyright 2010.

acceptable breakout volume. In the example of Baidu, Inc. (BIDU) in Figure 5.4, we can see that the volume on the new-high breakout of September 4, 2007, which is also a pocket pivot point by definition, was the highest over the prior 10 days, but would not have to be if the volume on the breakout is of sufficient magnitude required for any standard new-high, pivot point type of breakout buy point. In this case, the volume on the breakout was 39 percent above average, when you would normally want to see volume come in at 50 percent above average or more. However, given the "pocket pivot" rule where volume on the pocket pivot only needs to be the highest compared to any down-volume day over the prior 10 days, this breakout was actually buyable as a "pocket pivot," even though a 39 percent volume increase is not necessarily preferable on a standard pivot point breakout. BIDU's base on this breakout was "V-shaped" and somewhat volatile due to the general market sell-off at the time, but the stock did hold its 50-day moving average after dipping below it for two days in mid-August. The stock then set up again above the 50-day, 20-day, and 10-day moving averages before staging the pocket pivot on September 4th, 2007.

We see in the BIDU example how a standard breakout pivot point that does not meet the 50 percent volume increase preferable for such a classic

O'Neil-style buy point can still be acceptable if it meets the pocket pivot volume rule whereby the upside volume on the day of the pocket pivot should exceed any downside volume in the pattern over the prior 10 days. The converse of this example is where the new-high breakout has a volume increase of over 50 percent, meeting the requirement for such standard breakout pivot points, but the volume is less than the highest down-volume day in the prior 10 days, which does not meet the requirement for a pocket pivot buy point. With BIDU, the pocket pivot volume requirement was met, but the 50 percent standard breakout pivot point volume requirement was not, making BIDU buyable only as a pocket pivot buy point.

First Solar (FSLR), shown in Figure 5.5, is a good "flip-side" example of the BIDU situation. In FSLR's case, the stock formed a cup-with-handle formation and then staged a proper breakout through the top of the handle on September 21, 2007, with volume 52 percent above average, meeting the volume requirement for a standard breakout pivot point from the handle. However, note that the volume on September 21st was lower than the big downside volume spike we see on the chart that occurred seven days before the volume spike on the pocket pivot and breakout buy point day on September 21st. In this case, FSLR was buyable as a standard handle breakout pivot point, but not as a pocket pivot, since volume was not higher than the downside volume spike of seven days prior.

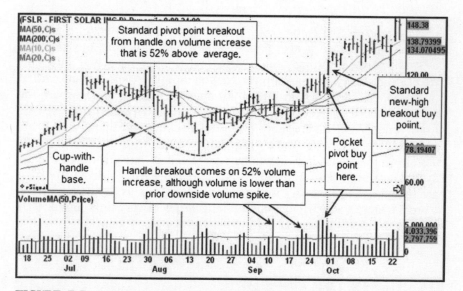

FIGURE 5.5 First Solar (FSLR) daily chart, September 2007. Not enough volume on the handle breakout for a valid pocket pivot, but 52 percent increase over average is sufficient for a standard handle breakout pivot point.
Chart courtesy of eSignal, Copyright 2010.

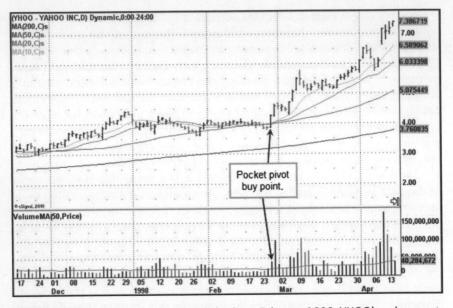

FIGURE 5.6 Yahoo!, Inc. (YHOO) daily chart, February 1998. YHOO's volume pattern qualifies it as both a pocket pivot and standard base breakout pivot point buy. Chart courtesy of eSignal, Copyright 2010.

Note that on September 28th FSLR flashed a valid pocket pivot buy point one day before it also flashed a new-high breakout buy point as the stock pushed through the 123.21 high in the base and into new high price ground. The pocket pivot got you into the stock one day earlier.

Yahoo!, Inc. (YHOO) in Figure 5.6 illustrates an example where the breakout is both a pocket pivot and a standard O'Neil base breakout type of buy point. After a very quiet period of backing and filling as it drifts just below its 50-day moving average and volume dries up, YHOO bursts back above the 50-day line on volume that is higher than any down-volume day in the prior 10 days. But this is also a breakout from a seven-week flat base that was showing very tight weekly closes, just as the daily chart in Figure 5.6 shows a nearly one-month-long series of very tight and orderly action in the daily closes just before the pocket pivot occurs.

BUYING "IN THE POCKET"

Whether buying pocket pivots in the base or within an uptrend, pocket pivots should ideally occur after consolidation of some sort. Naturally, the length of consolidation of buying within a base will be longer than the length of buying within an uptrend, also known as continuation pocket pivots. That said, some of the strongest price performers may only rest long enough to hit their 10-day moving average briefly before bouncing higher on volume, which, if conditions we have discussed in this chapter are met, would qualify as a proper pocket pivot buy point. This presents the investor with a multitude of possible buy points to get on board top-performing stocks and enables investors to initiate a position in a leader even if they missed the initial base breakout.

To better understand the entire concept of "buying in the pocket," we will review a short Pocket Pivot Model Book of pocket pivots that occur within a stock's base and which often give investors an early entry point in a fundamentally sound, leading stock building a proper base during a bullish market backdrop. We will then discuss buying pocket pivots in an uptrend, or continuation pocket pivot points, in a subsequent section of this chapter.

In March of 2007, Nvidia Corp. (NVDA) was rounding out and coming up off the second low of a potential base formed in the first quarter of 2007. This base was roughly 30 percent deep, and along the lows the stock was picking up some big volume support, as we see in Figure 5.7. The big volume spikes are positive signs off the lows of the potential base, and

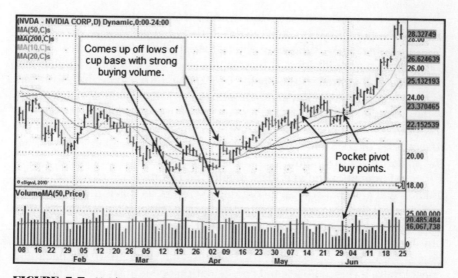

FIGURE 5.7 Nvidia Corp. (NVDA) daily chart, first quarter 2007. Two large upside volume spikes in the pattern constitute prior constructive action occurring in the pattern before the pocket pivots occur.
Chart courtesy of eSignal, Copyright 2010.

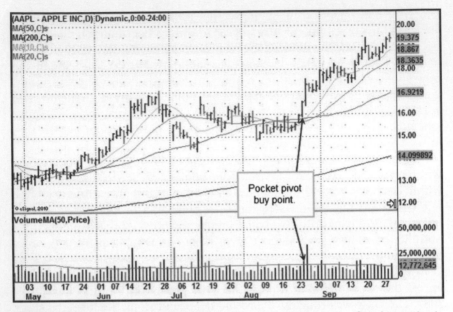

FIGURE 5.8 Apple, Inc. (AAPL) daily chart, August 2004. The first buy point in AAPL's sharp 2004–2005 price run was the August 25 pocket pivot.
Chart courtesy of eSignal, Copyright 2010.

they provide a constructive backdrop and context to the pocket pivots that occur later on in the formation on May 11th and May 31st.

Apple, Inc.'s (AAPL) pocket pivot on August 25, 2004 (Figure 5.8), was the earliest buy point for AAPL after the NASDAQ Composite Index had bottomed and turned to the upside on August 13th. Coinciding with this market bottom and follow-through on August 18th, which signaled a new general market rally phase, AAPL's August 25th pocket pivot was the first buy point in what became a very strong price advance that lasted into the first quarter of 2005 and during which the stock nearly tripled in price from the pocket pivot buy point.

Fundamentally sound stocks staging big upside price moves on heavy volume will always show up on our daily screens, as this is always a meaningful initial flag that a more sustained upside price move is brewing. But because of their extended condition after the run-up they are often not buyable without taking on greater risk. Following any strong price run-up over several days, however, a stock will inevitably begin to pull back and consolidate. If this pullback and consolidation occur in an orderly and constructive fashion, it is useful to watch carefully for potential pocket pivots to form as the stock finishes up its short consolidation following the sharp price run-up and sets up again. Verisign, Inc. (VRSN) in late 1998 provides a very good example in Figure 5.9.

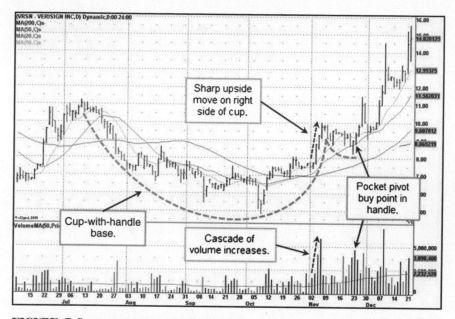

FIGURE 5.9 Verisign, Inc. (VRSN) daily chart, 1998. A pocket pivot buy point occurs within the handle of a cup-with-handle base formation.
Chart courtesy of eSignal, Copyright 2010.

In early November 1998 Verisign, Inc. (VRSN) had a sudden, sharp, three-day upside price burst as it pushed up the right side of a potential cup formation with a cascade of volume increases. As VRSN pulled back and formed a handle to fill out what was shaping up to be a cup-with-handle base formation, it drifted downward within the handle and then briefly dipped below the 20-day moving average on an intraday basis before closing above the 20-day moving average. The next day, on November 24, 1998, VRSN pushed up off of its 20-day moving average on volume that was higher than any down-volume days over the prior 10 days, a pocket pivot buy point. Two days later the stock cleared the high of the handle in the cup-with-handle formation for a standard new-high base breakout buy point. VRSN then pulled back sharply for two days, but held the 20-day moving average, right around the pocket pivot buy point of five days earlier. Buying the pocket pivot would have made it easier to sit through the sharp pullback after the new-high base breakout.

Another interesting example is Riverbed Technology, Inc. (RVBD) in May of 2007 (Figure 5.10). On April 25, 2007, RVBD had a big one-day gap-up move that sent the stock flying up off the lows of a 4½-month base formation and through its 50-day moving average. Obviously, this move could be considered a pocket pivot buy point, but it became extended very quickly and so may not have been so easy to buy in real time. In any case,

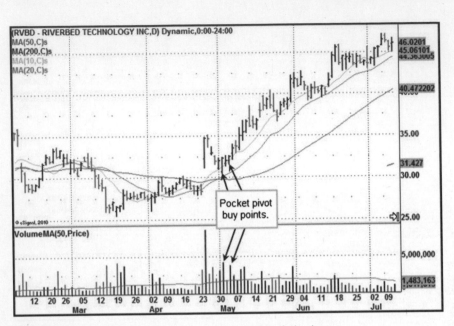

FIGURE 5.10 Riverbed Technology, Inc. (RVBD) daily chart.
Chart courtesy of eSignal, Copyright 2010.

the huge-volume gap-up move through the 50-day moving average was an initial flag of strength in the stock, and the ensuing pullback and consolidation of that sharp, one-day price move were relatively orderly as the stock drifted lower, holding the 10-day moving average on a closing basis. Right off the 10-day moving average there were two upside days on May 2 and May 4, 2007, where the volume was higher than any downside-volume days over the prior 10 days in the pattern, hence each qualified as a pocket pivot buy point. Notice also that as the stock pulled down into the 10-day moving average, volume dried up on each of the days just before each of the two pocket pivot points, an additional sign of constructive action.

Sometimes pocket pivots occur in a base formation just before a stock is about to announce earnings, implying an information leak somewhere as volume picks up during the regular trading day and the stock stages a pocket pivot type move. As an example, we can look at Intuitive Surgical, Inc. (ISRG) on October 25, 2005, the day that the company announced earnings after-hours (Figure 5.11). Despite the intuitive uncertainty of the earnings announcement, the stock's price/volume action was telling another story as ISRG poked its head up above its 50-day moving average on strong, above-average volume. By monitoring the big stock leaders and checking their price/volume action going into an earnings announcement, it is possible to use pocket pivots as a sign that taking a position in the

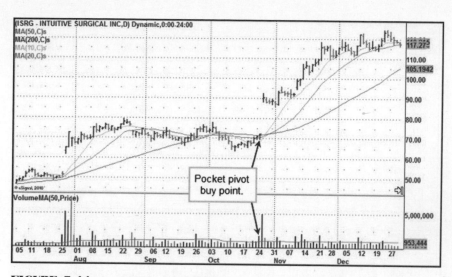

FIGURE 5.11 Intuitive Surgical (ISRG) daily chart, October 2005.
Chart courtesy of eSignal, Copyright 2010.

stock just before the earnings announcement is less risky than might otherwise be perceived. If the stock is showing pocket pivot action, including strong volume at the close of the day when the company announces earnings, then a position can be taken near the close of the normal trading session once it is clear that volume will exceed the highest down-volume in the pattern over the prior 10 days. Pocket pivot buy points going into earnings announcements are playable, in our view, and position sizing can be scaled to one's risk tolerance, and whether one is adding to an existing position or initiating one.

Pocket pivots are often relatively quiet buy points within a stock's base formation. Amazon.com (AMZN) in the latter half of 1998 was working on a rather choppy base formation as it bounced along its 200-day moving average (Figure 5.12). By the time it was starting to work its way back higher up the right side of the base, selling volume was subsiding quite significantly, setting up a pocket pivot buy point on October 29th as the stock came up off the 10-day moving average on volume that was greater than any down-volume day in the pattern over the prior 10 days. Within three weeks the stock was breaking out of the 4½-month base formation and into new high price ground.

Buying "quiet" pocket pivots can at times require some patience, but being able to sit with a partial position taken on a pocket pivot buy signal as long as the stock continues to track sideways tightly and constructively within its base formation can have its rewards. Once an initial position is

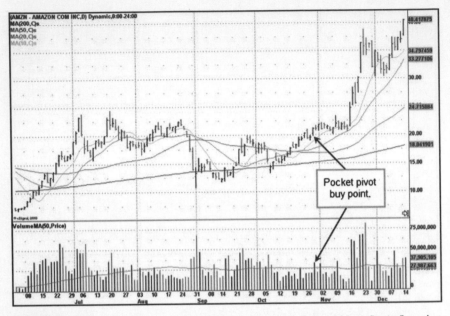

FIGURE 5.12 Amazon.com (AMZN) daily chart, October 1998. A "quiet" pocket pivot buy point as the stock works its way up the right side of a base.
Chart courtesy of eSignal, Copyright 2010.

taken on a pocket pivot buy point that is well "in the pocket," it can be doubled up on if a second pocket pivot a little higher in the pattern shows up, or if the stock stages a standard base breakout. We saw one example of this in the Jazz Pharmaceuticals (JAZZ) example in Figure 5.3 near the beginning of this chapter, and Infospace, Inc. (INSP) in Figure 5.13 is a similar type of situation.

INSP sets up a constructive "context" for its pocket pivot buy point by first staging a shakeout through the lows of the base it has formed from mid-July into the end of October 1998. Note how the stock undercuts a prior low within its base structure on September 24th as volume picks up sharply at 123 percent above average. This appears as a breach of support and hence is interpreted as a bearish development for the stock. However, this is too obvious, so the crowd is faked out here as the very next day INSP gaps to the upside and moves back up into the base structure on heavier volume than the previous day's gap-down decline and breach of "support" at the lows of the base. This is a very constructive "shakeout," which is simply part of the process of bringing in strong hands and cleaning out weak hands that every stock goes through as it forms what may later become a basing formation for an eventual successful upside price move. INSP then drifts down slightly over the next several days as volume dries up

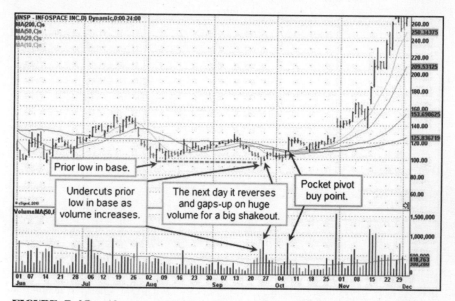

FIGURE 5.13 Infospace (INSP) daily chart, 1998. A constructive "shakeout" in the base creates a meaningful, positive context for the ensuing pocket pivot buy point. Chart courtesy of eSignal, Copyright 2010.

precipitously, setting up a very favorable context for the ensuing October 7th pocket pivot buy point. INSP holds above all of its moving averages following the pocket pivot as it moves tightly sideways and eventually resolves in a gap-up base breakout at the end of November 1998. Following that standard base breakout in late November, INSP did a little backing and filling, and several pocket pivots occurred in the pattern at that point, but we will leave those to the reader to identify.

Blue Coat Systems (BCSI) flashed a pocket pivot buy point in its base on May 15, 2007 (Figure 5.14). This was followed by a breakout to new highs that came right back in to test the pocket pivot point a couple of times before the stock began moving higher again. Buying the pocket pivot here gives the investors a slightly lower entry point that may make it easier to hold through any of the initial pullbacks to the 10-day moving average that ensued in the stock over the next seven days following the pocket pivot.

Before Charles Schwab Corp. (SCHW) cleared to new highs in late 1998, it produced a very clear, high-volume pocket pivot buy point as it began pushing out of a jagged handle within an overall cup-with-handle base formation in October of 1998. What makes this particular pocket pivot compelling is that it was also a handle breakout that occurred on the exact same day as the market follow-through on October 15, 1998, that ended the short, sharp three-month bear market of that year and signaled a new

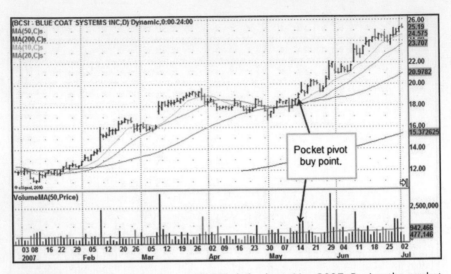

FIGURE 5.14   Blue Coat Systems (BCSI) daily chart, May 2007. Buying the pocket pivot on May 15th made it easier to sit through the "uncertain" breakout action that ensued.
Chart courtesy of eSignal, Copyright 2010.

rally phase for the market. SCHW was a big leader in the market rally that began off the October 1998 lows, along with America Online (AOL). A lot of money was eventually made in these stocks when we were managing money for Bill O'Neil back then, but despite this SCHW did not go galloping right out of the gate following that October 15th pocket pivot buy point. It noodled about the 10-day moving average for another two weeks before staging a new-high breakout and starting its sharp ascent to the upside. See Figure 5.15.

Pocket pivot points can sometimes add clarity to the price/volume action in the chart patterns of stocks that are not quite perfect. For example, Sunpower Corp. (SPWRA) built one base in late February to March of 2007 from which it broke out as the general market was coming out of a correction and following-through back to the upside, initiating a new general market rally phase. SPWRA's chart formation was a little erratic (Figure 5.16), but the pocket pivot point of March 27th provided a clear, early buy signal that came only a few days after the March 21st market follow-through. SPWRA rallied approximately 38 percent higher before pausing to build another base, this time a cup formation from which it then proceeded to break out without ever pausing to build a handle, which may have thrown investors trying to buy the stock as they waited for the handle to form. However, all of this could have been avoided by using pocket pivot buy points instead. June 5th was the first pocket pivot buy point, but the

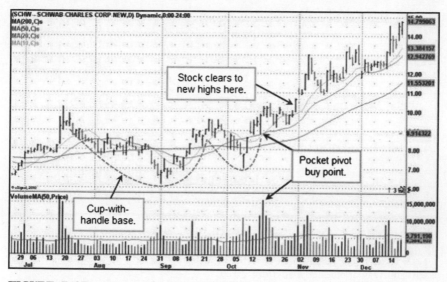

FIGURE 5.15 Charles Schwab Corp. (SCHW) daily chart, October 1998.
Chart courtesy of eSignal, Copyright 2010.

stock immediately pulled back, which could have stopped out investors
using a tight stop on the pocket pivot buy. However, one week later, on
June 14th, SPWRA flashed another pocket pivot buy signal on which the
stock could have easily been bought back in time to catch the ensuing
price move.

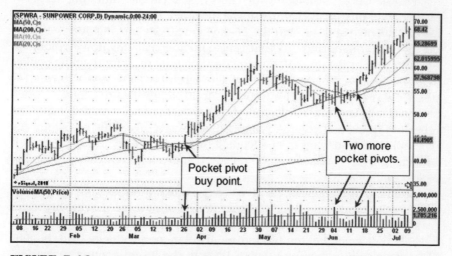

FIGURE 5.16 Sunpower Corp. (SPWRA) daily chart, 2007. Plenty of pocket pivot
buy points providing excellent entry points on the stock.
Chart courtesy of eSignal, Copyright 2010.

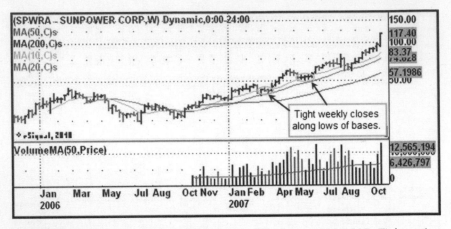

FIGURE 5.17 Sunpower Corp. (SPWRA) weekly chart, 2006–2007. Tight action along the lows in two separate bases seen on the daily chart is also confirmed by the weekly chart.
Chart courtesy of eSignal, Copyright 2010.

The price/volume action along the lows in both of SPRWA's bases was fairly tight, and in the second cup-base was extremely tight. This was also confirmed by the weekly chart (Figure 5.17), which showed a series of four tight weekly closes right along the lows of the base coinciding with the tight sideways action shown in Figure 5.16 from late May to early June 2007, as well as three tight weekly closes at the end of March 2007.

Potash Corp. Saskatchewan (POT) is a classic "bursting" type of pocket pivot buy point that occurs as the stock bounces up off the 50-day moving average and through the 10-day and 20-day moving averages on a big spike in volume and one that is also greater than any down-volume in the pattern over the prior 10 days, per our volume rules for defining pocket pivot buy points. This pocket pivot on March 30, 2007 (see Figure 5.18) was a low-risk entry point for a roughly fourfold upside price move. Notice how POT was tracking tightly sideways throughout most of March 2007 as it quieted down and volume remained below average. This is exactly the type of action you want to see leading into a pocket pivot buy point as it sets the proper "context" for the pocket pivot to have a higher probability of success.

Stocks that start out their lives as sizzling hot initial public offerings often begin trading and within a short period of time are moving higher as they break out of chart patterns that on first glance do not appear to be buyable. For example, the big moves in solar-energy stocks back in 2007 also resulted in a huge number of IPOs in the group coming to market. These were often hot-IPOs right out of the gate, and among these hot IPOs was LDK Solar Co., Ltd. (LDK), shown on a weekly chart in Figure 5.19.

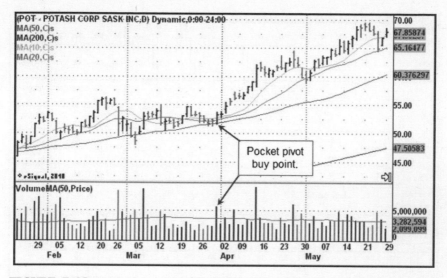

FIGURE 5.18 Potash Corp. Saskatchewan (POT) daily chart, 2007. The pocket pivot buy point occurs as the stock "bursts" up through three moving averages. Chart courtesy of eSignal, Copyright 2010.

Right after coming public LDK formed a short, four-week, V-shaped cup formation from which it then broke out of on no discernible volume increase, since the stock had very little history on which to base average daily trading volume. If investors were looking for a "sound" base off of which to buy LDK after it came public, it was not cooperating as it simply

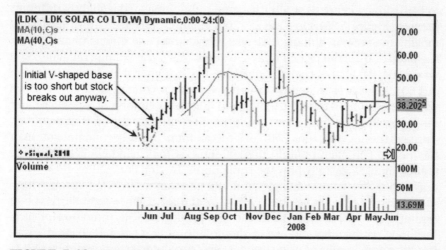

FIGURE 5.19 LDK Solar Co., Ltd. (LDK) weekly chart, 2007. A short, V-shaped base does not look buyable on the weekly chart. Chart courtesy of eSignal, Copyright 2010.

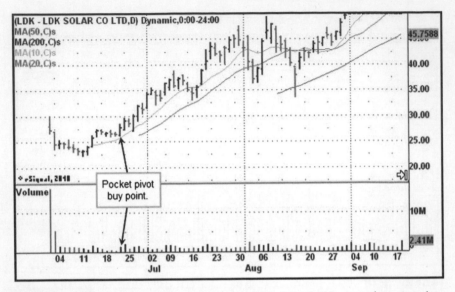

FIGURE 5.20 LDK Solar Co. (LDK) daily chart, June 2007. A pocket pivot buy point presents itself in what otherwise looks like an unbuyable V-shaped base on the weekly chart (Figure 5.19).
Chart courtesy of eSignal, Copyright 2010.

took off to the upside after briefly pulling back from its offering price of $27-a-share.

Setting the weekly chart aside, however, and focusing on the action in LDK's daily chart right after it came public revealed a slightly different picture (Figure 5.20). On June 22, 2007, LDK bounced up off of its 10-day moving average on volume that was higher than any down-volume day in the pattern over the prior 10 days. Interestingly, the volume on June 22nd was 1,204,400 shares traded, only 100 shares higher than June 8th, which at 1,204,300 shares traded was the highest down-volume day in the pattern within the prior 10 days. Strictly speaking, the definition of a pocket pivot buy point held on June 22nd, but if one hesitated to buy on that day, then the next trading day, June 25th, offered an immediate, second pocket pivot buy point. The main point in this example is that using pocket pivot buy points changes entirely how we think about buying compelling IPOs. Generally, the O'Neil methodology would dictate that we wait for a proper base of at least six to eight weeks to form, or at least a "high, tight flag" type of formation. In the case of LDK, the stock built a rather nondescript little V-shaped pattern that did not fit the definition of a "proper" base. Viewed from the perspective of using pocket pivots to determine proper buy points within patterns, LDK was entirely buyable as early as June 22, 2007.

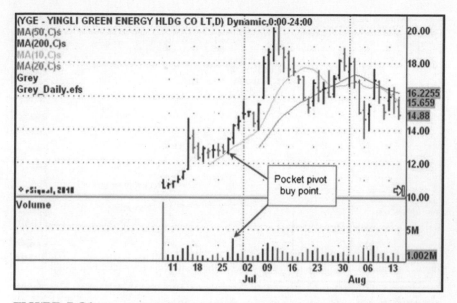

FIGURE 5.21 Yingli Green Energy (YGE) daily chart, June 2007. A pocket pivot buy point on June 27, 2007, provides a ready entry point 13 days after the IPO date and before the stock has built any kind of "proper" chart base formation. Chart courtesy of eSignal, Copyright 2010.

It is not necessary to look at a weekly chart of Yingli Green Energy (YGE) to determine that the short flag formation it formed on the daily chart (Figure 5.21) was of insufficient length to be considered a "proper" high, tight flag formation since it only had one week down in the flag. However, in evaluating IPOs pocket pivots offer an entirely different approach to buying such hot IPO stocks—an approach that is not as dependent on the idea of the stock having to build a proper base formation first. On June 27, 2007, YGE moved up off its 10-day moving average on volume that was the highest in the pattern since the IPO date 13 trading days earlier, hence meeting the technical definition of a pocket pivot buy point.

BOTTOM-FISHING WITH POCKET PIVOTS

Some pocket pivots can occur as stocks that have corrected and declined a significant amount finally "hammer out" a bottom after several weeks or months of base-building along the lows of the decline. The severe market break that began in September 2008 took a lot of former "big stock" leaders

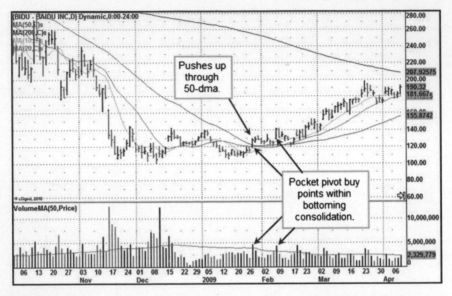

FIGURE 5.22 Baidu, Inc. (BIDU) daily chart, 2009 market bottom. Two pocket pivot buy points mark the start of a "bottom-fishers rally" in the stock.
Chart courtesy of eSignal, Copyright 2010.

from the immediately preceding bull phase down sharply. Some of these stocks eventually declined over 70 percent or more from their bull market price peaks, at which point they began to stabilize and probe for potential bottoms. After several weeks or months the stock will have finally started to "round out" a potential bottom. It is at this point that investors should be alert to potential pocket pivots as they will often show up in a stock that is potentially coming up off its lows and ready to stage some sort of material rally off the bottom.

Baidu, Inc. (BIDU) was one such former leader that declined 73.8 percent off of its bull market price peak and by late November 2008 was trying to probe for a bottom (Figure 5.22). This process went on for the next two months before the stock was finally able to regain its 50-day moving average on a pocket pivot buy point on January 28, 2009, well before the market itself had bottomed. Note that once BIDU had climbed back above the 50-day moving average on the pocket pivot it never broke back to the downside as it "obeyed" the 50-day moving average.

Another big stock leader that declined precipitously in the severe market break of late 2008 was medical robotics pioneer Intuitive Surgical (ISRG), which had declined 84.86 percent off of its bull market price peak at its ultimate low. After peaking out at 359.59 in December of 2007, ISRG finally began trying to find a bottom as it dipped below the 90 price level

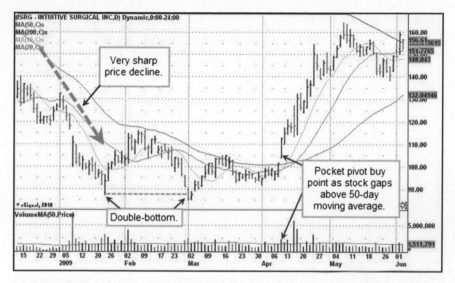

FIGURE 5.23 Intuitive Surgical (ISRG) daily chart, 2009. A pocket pivot point marks the turning point—a "line of least resistance" is clearly broken.
Chart courtesy of eSignal, Copyright 2010.

twice in late January and then early March 2009 to form a double-bottom bottoming formation, not to be confused with a "double-bottom" chart base formation, which is formed as part of a stock's overall uptrend during a price advance.

Once the double-bottom had been put in at the lows ISRG advanced up to its 50-day moving average (Figure 5.23), before backing down again and moving tightly sideways through the end of March and into early April 2009. The general market had already followed through on March 18, 2009, signaling a new general market rally phase, and ISRG gave a pocket pivot buy point signal on April 9th at 103.75. This led to a very sharp price advance over the next four weeks that took the stock over 60 percent higher. By the end of 2009, ISRG had surpassed the $300 price level. If one had been lucky enough to enter the stock on the pocket pivot buy point day, April 9th, the ensuing upside move provided enough cushion to potentially allow one to sit through a longer upside price move.

Using pocket pivot buy points can be applied similarly to stocks in deep bases, such as Baidu, Inc. (BIDU) in April of 2007 (Figure 5.24). BIDU was in the midst of trying to find a bottom following a decline of 30.8 percent off of its January 2007 price peak of 134.10, and as it was dipping down below and tracking along the 95 price level there was a noticeable decline in selling volume. This is visible in Figure 5.23 throughout the

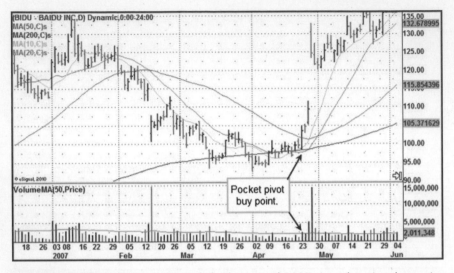

FIGURE 5.24 Baidu, Inc. (BIDU) daily chart, April 2007. A pocket pivot buy point three days before a huge gap-up in the stock turns out to be a very profitable buy signal.
Chart courtesy of eSignal, Copyright 2010.

first three weeks of April, roughly, before the stock "burst" up through its 50-day moving average on the necessary volume increase for a pocket pivot buy point on April 24th. Three days later BIDU was gapping up toward new price highs as it launched on a price run of over 100 percent in only 11 weeks from the pocket pivot buy point. We often see pocket pivot buy points show up in a stock's chart pattern a few days, sometimes even only one day, before a major price gap-up, providing a material and potentially hugely profitable clue that enables us to buy the stock and be in position to benefit from the gap-up.

Research in Motion (RIMM) in mid-August of 2007 provides a fantastic example of a "deep in the pocket" pocket pivot buy point two days up off of the absolute low of a deep double-bottom type of formation that is only four weeks in duration, insufficient for a "proper" double-bottom base formation (Figure 5.25). On August 15th RIMM began to roll over, closing below its 50-day moving average. Volume was not particularly heavy given the break through the 50-day line, coming in at only 9 percent above average for the day. The next day volume picked up sharply, and RIMM reversed back to the upside, but remained below its 50-day moving average. On August 17th, RIMM gapped back above its 50-day moving average, and with very strong volume coming into the stock right off the market opening it was immediately buyable as a pocket pivot buy point.

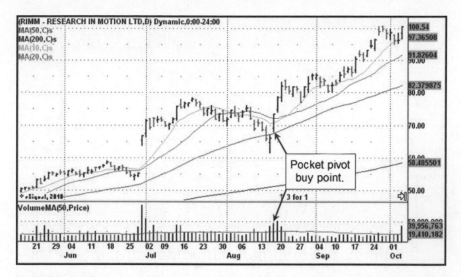

FIGURE 5.25 Research in Motion (RIMM) daily chart, August 2007. As it starts to roll over, RIMM experiences a sudden reversal of fortune as a pocket pivot buy point shows up two days off the bottom.
Chart courtesy of eSignal, Copyright 2010.

Pocket pivots have proven to be useful in "bottom-fishing" as they provide more reliable reference points for buying stocks as they attempt to rally off the lows of a severe, prior price decline or a very deep base formation of 30 percent or more.

CONTINUATION POCKET PIVOTS: USING THE 10-DAY MOVING AVERAGE

Once stocks have broken out of a base and are in an uptrend, heading higher in price, finding low-risk points at which to add to one's position in a strongly-acting stock is not always so easy. Waiting for a pullback to a prior standard base breakout pivot point or the 50-day/10-week moving averages is always possible, but having the ability to confidently pinpoint actionable buy points using pocket pivots within an uptrend is a highly useful, additional arrow in our quiver. In general, we focus on the 10-day moving average as our buy guide when determining "continuation" pocket pivot buy points within a stock's uptrend. As always, we maintain a volume requirement that the pocket pivot off the 10-day moving average come on volume that is greater than any down-volume day in the pattern over the prior 10 days.

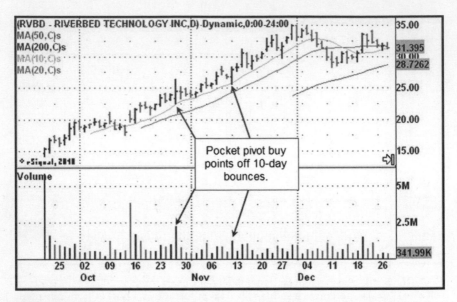

FIGURE 5.26 Riverbed Technology, Inc. (RVBD) daily chart, October–November 2006. Pocket pivots forming along the 10-day moving average are buyable. Chart courtesy of eSignal, Copyright 2010.

Riverbed Technology (RVBD) offers a good example of a stock "obeying" or "respecting" its 10-day moving average as it trends higher (Figure 5.26). Two pocket pivot buy points occur in the uptrend as it bounces up off the 10-day moving average on October 27 and November 13, 2006. Notice that once RVBD stops "respecting" the 10-day moving average and closes below the line it can be considered as a short-term sell signal, something we will cover a little later on in this chapter.

Apple, Inc. (AAPL) first emerged as a big leading stock in the latter half of 2004 as it was riding the iPod wave, initially breaking out of a cup-with-handle base in March of 2004, just as the NASDAQ Composite was already three months into a correction. As the market continued to correct into the summer of 2004, AAPL formed two more bases, breaking out on August 25th, just five days after the NASDAQ Composite Index staged a fourth-day follow-through on August 18th, signaling the start of a new potential rally phase for the general market. As AAPL made upside progress following the August 25th breakout to new highs, it more or less obeyed the 10-day moving average, as Figure 5.27 shows. A few days before earnings were to be announced on October 13th, the stock dipped below the 10-day moving average and bounced off of its 20-day moving average. As it was coming up off the 20-day moving average, on the day that earnings were to be

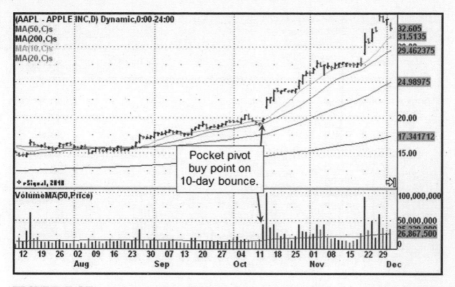

FIGURE 5.27 Apple, Inc. (AA PL) daily chart, October 2004.
Chart courtesy of eSignal, Copyright 2010.

announced, AAPL flashed a pocket pivot buy point as it came up through the 10-day moving average on volume that exceeded any down-volume days in the pattern over the prior 10 days. After the close AAPL handily beat analysts' estimates, gapping up the next morning as it was off to the races. We played AAPL very heavily in 2004, buying on the day of the gap-up. Back then we did not have knowledge of pocket pivot buy points, and looking back on these stocks with benefit of hindsight and the pocket pivot, we see many opportunities that could have been taken advantage of in stocks like AAPL.

After gapping up on the October 13, 2004, earnings announcement, AAPL continued moving higher (Figure 5.28), finding support along the way at the 10-day moving average. On October 27th AAPL staged a move up off the 10-day moving average with the proper volume action required for a pocket pivot buy point. The only potential problem with this particular pocket pivot was that its move started just above the 10-day moving average, rather than at the moving average, or just below it. In this case the pocket pivot could be considered to be somewhat extended, something we will get into in more detail a little bit later. However, because of the very tight price action that preceded it, one could invoke some discretion and buy it anyway. Normally, because the pocket pivot began at a point somewhat above the 10-day moving average it might be considered extended. Interpreting pocket pivots, however, requires analyzing them within the

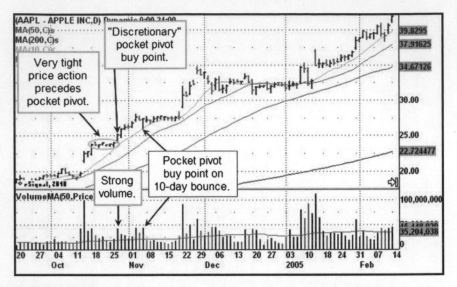

FIGURE 5.28 Apple, Inc. (AAPL) daily chart, November 2004. AAPL bounces up through the 10-day moving average for a pocket pivot buy point.
Chart courtesy of eSignal, Copyright 2010.

"context" of the price/volume action within the uptrend or base in which they form. In this case, the "context" of very tight price action before the pocket pivot made it buyable, even though it had the slight flaw of starting its move above the 10-day line. Seven days later, AAPL had a small, intraday shakeout down to the 10-day moving average, bouncing right off the line and closing up for the day on volume that was greater than any down-volume day in the pattern over the prior 10 days.

First Solar (FSLR) provides an example of three different variations on a pocket pivot buy point that form around the 10-day moving average (Figure 5.29). The first pocket pivot, which forms on February 13, 2007, starts right at the 10-day moving average and moves up off the line with the required volume signature. The second pocket pivot in the pattern on May 4, 2007, occurs after the stock moves below the 10-day and 20-day moving averages and bounces off the 50-day moving average back up through the 10-day moving average on heavy volume, qualifying it as a pocket pivot buy point as well as a buy point on the move to new highs after bouncing off the 50-day moving average with big upside volume support. Finally, a third pocket pivot occurs on June 12, 2007, when FSLR moves below the 10-day moving average, bounces off the 20-day moving average, roughly, and ends up closing up on the day just above the 10-day moving average on volume that is the highest volume in the pattern over the prior 10 days.

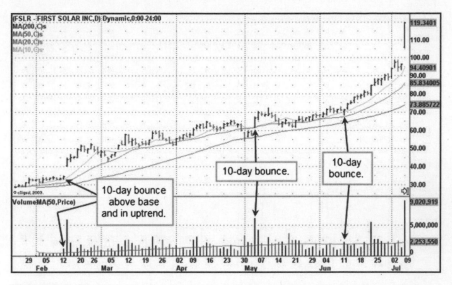

FIGURE 5.29 First Solar, Inc. (FSLR) daily chart, 2007. Three different types of "10-day bounce" pocket pivot buy points occur in the stock during the first half of 2007.
Chart courtesy of eSignal, Copyright 2010.

In general, proper pocket pivots that form on 10-day bounces do so from a position right at or just below the 10-day moving average as the stock is travelling in an uptrend after breaking out from a proper chart base of six to eight weeks or more. Paying close attention to the "context" of the pocket pivot by looking for constructive action in the pattern, such as very tight, sideways movement, leading up to the pocket pivot also helps one to determine when the rules can be bent just a little bit as a "discretionary" pocket pivot buy point is exercised as we saw in Figure 5.28.

IMPROPER OR "DO NOT BUY" POCKET PIVOT POINTS

Just as there are "proper" pocket pivot buy points, there are also "improper" pocket pivot buy points. There are probably as many reasons or criteria to not buy a pocket pivot point as there are reasons or criteria to not buy a standard base breakout. Here we cover some of the basic flaws that we have observed in pocket pivot points that fail. Given that the pocket pivot point is a relatively new discovery, we anticipate that this discussion

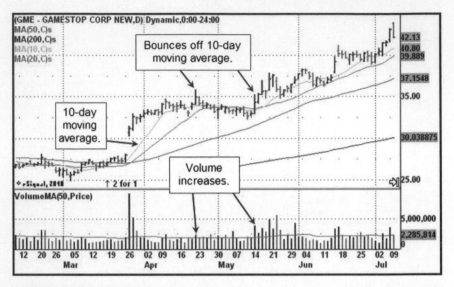

FIGURE 5.30 GameStop Corp. (GME) daily chart, April–May 2007. Two pocket pivots in the pattern, but only one is "proper."
Chart courtesy of eSignal, Copyright 2010.

will prove to be incomplete, as over time many more such flaws will likely be catalogued as our research into the topic continues.

Something to watch out for are pocket pivots that occur when a stock takes a quick dip to the downside and then makes a straight "V" back up to new highs, such as what we see in GameStop Corp. (GME), shown in Figure 5.30. Notice how the pocket pivot on April 23, 2007, moves straight up to new highs after gapping down to a point just above the 20-day moving average two days earlier. This is a little "straight-down-and-straight-up" V-shaped type of move that is suspect, particularly after the stock has already been trending higher over several weeks as GME was doing following its big gap-up breakout in late March. Generally the stock will need more time to consolidate its gains. With this in mind, note how the second pocket pivot point in the pattern on May 15th was more constructive as it moved up through the 10-day and 20-day moving averages after the stock was drifting downward on relatively "quiet" volume.

It is important to determine whether a pocket pivot point may be too "extended" from its 10-day or 50-day moving average when it begins its move on the pocket pivot point day. Sometimes this can occur after the stock has been "wedging" upward, in other words moving higher within its pattern on successively lighter volume. Normally you want to see a stock drift downward on volume that is declining and drying up. When it

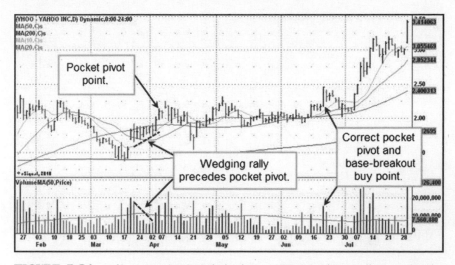

FIGURE 5.31 Yahoo!, Inc. (YHOO) daily chart, 1997. A wedging rally provides the wrong context for a flawed pocket pivot in April, while tight price action sets up a favorable context for a successful pocket pivot buy point.
Chart courtesy of eSignal, Copyright 2010.

drifts upward instead, this is called "wedging action," and it is not constructive. Pocket pivots occur after wedging in a stock, such as we see in Yahoo! (YHOO), shown in Figure 5.31. Notice how YHOO wedged upward just before flashing a pocket pivot buy point on April 7, 1997, and this pocket pivot soon failed as the stock broke to the downside. YHOO needed more time to set up, and through the end of May into mid-June the stock moved very tightly sideways as the price/volume action provided a much more constructive "context" for the correct pocket pivot buy point which occurred in June and did set up again, becoming very "tight" within its chart pattern through the end of May and into the first three weeks of June. Again, we see that "context" is important. The wedging action in late March and early April provided an improper context for the April 7th pocket pivot buy point, while the tight, sideways price action in late May and early June provided a constructive and proper context for the correct pocket pivot point that occurred on June 20th.

The same situation holds for GameStop Corp. (GME) in Figure 5.32. From late January into most of February 2007 GME wedges up in its base formation before bursting up through the 50-day moving average with the requisite pocket pivot volume signature. However, as with the YHOO example in Figure 5.31, this wedging rally preceding the pocket pivot creates a weak context for the pocket pivot, and it fails immediately when the stock violates the 50-day moving average. After the stock puts in more time

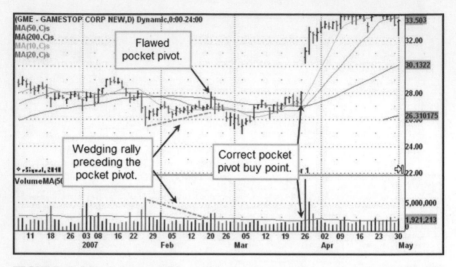

FIGURE 5.32 GameStop Corp., (GME) daily chart, 2007. Like YHOO, GME discovers that context is everything when it comes to pocket pivot buy points.
Chart courtesy of eSignal, Copyright 2010.

building its base, undercutting the lows of the base in early March 2007, and then working its way back above the 50-day moving average toward the end of March, it flashes a correct pocket pivot buy point on March 26, 2007. This is clearly a pocket pivot as the volume, while just about average, is still higher than any down-volume day in the pattern over the prior 10 days as the stock moves right up off the 50-day moving average and back up through the 10-day moving average, a 10-day and a 50-day bounce type of pocket pivot buy point.

Pocket pivot points that begin their move from a point that is above the 10-day moving average can in most cases be considered as "extended" and hence risky to buy. Let's look at GameStop Corp. (GME) again (Figure 5.33), this time following up on the example we saw in Figure 5.30. Recall that the pocket pivot buy point on May 15, 2007, was a proper one, but note on Figure 5.31 that another pocket pivot point occurs four days later on May 21st, which begins from a point that is well extended from the 10-day moving average. This fails three days later. On July 9th we see another, similar pocket pivot point that starts from a point that is extended from the 10-day moving average, and is therefore flawed. It too fails in short order.

A little earlier in this chapter we looked at the "10-day bounce" pocket pivot points that worked in First Solar's (FSLR) chart during 2007, but there were also some flawed pocket pivots in the 2007 chart that did not work (Figure 5.34). Pocket pivots that occurred on March 22nd and April 16th both started from points well extended up from the 10-day moving average, which immediately flags them as "do not buy pocket pivot points."

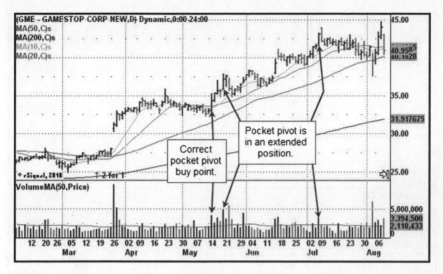

FIGURE 5.33 Gamestop Corp. (GME) daily chart, 2007. Two flawed pocket pivots that begin from points extended above the 10-day moving average.
Chart courtesy of eSignal, Copyright 2010.

Keep in mind that when we talk about the pocket pivots "starting from points extended from the 10-day moving average" what we mean is that the extreme low point of the daily price range on the day of the pocket pivot point on the chart should be at a point right at the 10-day moving average or just below it. If that point is noticeably above the 10-day moving

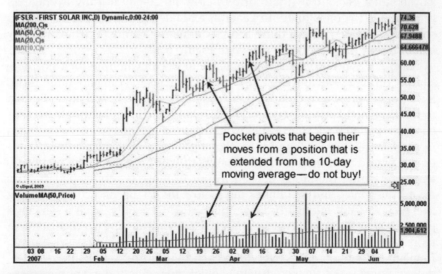

FIGURE 5.34 First Solar (FSLR) daily chart, 2007.
Chart courtesy of eSignal, Copyright 2010.

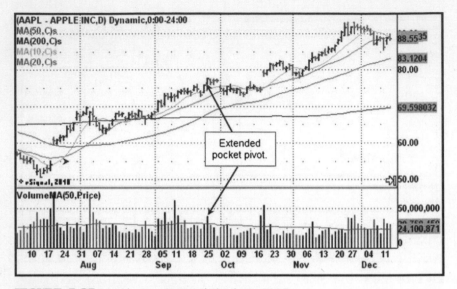

FIGURE 5.35 Apple, Inc. (AAPL) daily chart, 2006.
Chart courtesy of eSignal, Copyright 2010.

average, then the pocket pivot is considered to be "extended," and hence is very risky to buy into.

Similarly, we see a visibly extended pocket pivot point occur on Apple, Inc.'s (AAPL) chart in September of 2006 (Figure 5.35) that fails as the stock backs down and drifts below its 20-day moving average as it continues to consolidate. In general, extended pocket pivot buy points should be avoided unless there is an extenuating context such as we saw in a different AAPL example shown in Figure 5.35.

Another type of flawed formation can occur when a stock corrects sharply off of a peak and then just as quickly tries to come up, often forming a pocket pivot as it comes up the right side of a V-shaped up-and-down move. Riverbed Technology, Inc. (RVBD) in Figure 5.36 illustrates this concept as it pulled back sharply below its 10-day and 20-day moving averages in early December 2006 and then shot right back above both moving averages in one fell swoop to flash a pocket pivot buy point. The real problem here is that the stock needed to put in more time consolidating its prior price gains, and a pullback just below the 10-day and 20-day moving averages was not enough to accomplish this. Generally, such a V-shaped pullback should come down and touch the 50-day moving average, a much more reliable area of support for such a sharp pullback off a price peak. Remember that context is everything, and this sort of "break-and-recover" type of move is not the constructive, quiet type of action we prefer to see preceding a pocket pivot buy point.

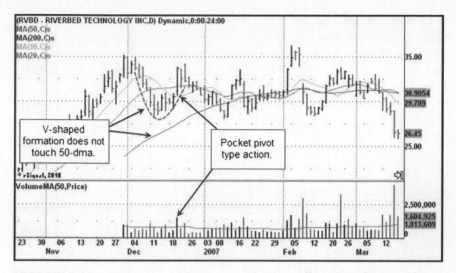

FIGURE 5.36 Riverbed Technology, Inc. (RVBD) daily chart, 2006–2007. A V-shaped pullback does not touch the 50-day moving average, providing a weak context for the ensuing pocket pivot point to succeed.
Chart courtesy of eSignal, Copyright 2010.

While it may seem intuitive, it is worth mentioning that one should never buy pocket pivot points that are occurring within an overall downtrend, as opposed to a constructively downward sloping base formation. Baidu, Inc. (BIDU) was in a severe downtrend during the sharp bear market break in the latter months of 2008, but it still managed to flash a couple of sharp, upside pocket pivot point type moves on the way down (Figure 5.37). Each of these failed immediately, and illustrate why pocket pivot points in a downtrend should simply be ignored. Even if a downtrend in a stock eventually turns out to be the left side of a cup-type base formation as it bottoms and then starts turning back to the upside, one should still generally seek to buy pocket pivots that occur on the right side of a such a cup, ideally in the top half of the base or at least at or above the 50-day moving average, and generally not in the lower one-third of the base.

USING MOVING AVERAGES AS SELL GUIDES

Stocks that have shown a tendency to "obey" or "respect" the 10-day moving average for at least seven weeks in an uptrend should often be sold once the stock violates the 10-day line. If they don't show such a tendency,

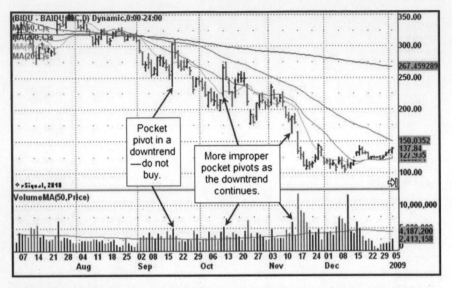

FIGURE 5.37 Baidu, Inc. (BIDU) daily chart, 2008. Pocket pivot points within an overall downtrend should be ignored.
Chart courtesy of eSignal, Copyright 2010.

then it is better to use the 50-day moving average as your guide for selling. This is what we call the Seven-Week Rule, and it can help prevent you from selling a stock prematurely if it is simply not its nature to hold the 10-day moving average and it tends to do so often. Our studies of pocket pivots indicate that a pocket pivot buy point which results in an uptrend that is shown to obey the 10-day moving average for at least seven weeks following the initial pocket pivot should be sold upon its first violation of the 10-day line. A "violation" is defined as a close below the 10-day moving average followed by a move on the next day below the intraday low of the first day. The example of Apple, Inc. (AAPL) in Figure 5.38 shows a stock that obeys the 10-day moving average all the way up until early December 2006 when it finally closes below the 10-day moving average, the day with the arrow pointing to it, and then the very next day moves below the low of that day. The inherent logic is that if a stock has been holding above its 10-day moving average for several weeks or more it likely has been trending. Our studies show that after such moves back below the 10-day moving average, stocks will tend to rest for a while, allowing the nimble investor the opportunity to take a profit and then lie back as the stock rests, consolidates, and potentially sets up for another move to the upside. The strongest stocks may not rest for very long, so it is important to be flexible and ready

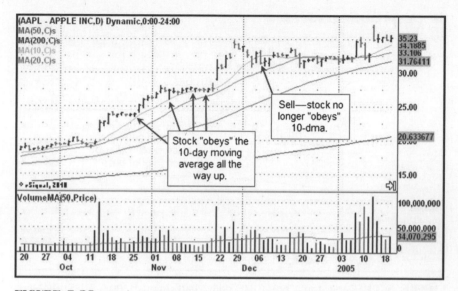

FIGURE 5.38 Apple, Inc. (AAPL) daily chart, 2004. AAPL obeys the 10-day moving average until early December, when it finally closes below the 10-day moving average.
Chart courtesy of eSignal, Copyright 2010.

to jump on any new pocket pivot points that may appear in the pattern going forward.

DR. K'S LABORATORY: BUYING GAP-UPS IN LEADING STOCKS

There is nothing more alluring for a trader than a stock that is gapping up hugely on tremendous volume. Despite this, we tend to view gap-ups as being extended and hence do not have the confidence to buy them, even though they may very well be signaling that the stock having the gap-up is potentially a very powerful, big, winning stock. Sometimes big gap-up moves can occur as simple new-high base breakouts, and if the gap-up move is within 5 percent of the high in the base at any point, it is buyable on that basis alone. We see this in GameStop Corp. (GME) in Figure 5.39, which gaps up on August 23, 2007. Notice that GME had tried to break out earlier at the beginning of August but failed, pulling back and testing the lows of its base. This gives the base a sloppy look, but when it finally does break out of this base on a huge-volume gap-up move, the strong gap-up action entirely exonerates any questionable price/volume

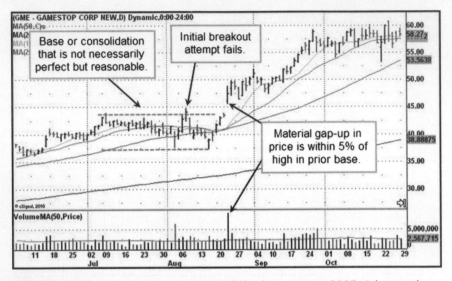

FIGURE 5.39 GameStop, Corp. (GME) daily chart, August 2007. A huge-volume gap-up base breakout to new highs.
Chart courtesy of eSignal, Copyright 2010.

action within the base. This is one basic rule of gap-up breakouts—they negate or "exonerate" any negative or weak action in the base, such as the erratic, failed breakout of GME in Figure 5.39. That said, gap-ups should not be bought back if the stock is in a clear downtrend. GME in this example is, however, a simple gap-up situation that is easily determined as buyable since it is also a clean new-high base-breakout.

Apple, Inc. (AAPL) in Figure 5.40 is another gap-up move that is also a new-high base breakout, and hence is buyable on this basis. Gap-ups that are also base breakouts are the most powerful base breakouts, and hence should almost always be bought when they occur in fundamentally strong stocks. Relative to other types of gap-up moves that are more extended, buying gap-up breakouts is simple stuff. Gap-up breakouts that are immediately extended more than 5 percent to 10 percent and gap-up moves that occur within an uptrend are far more tricky to buy, but it can be done using some rules we've come up with based on our studies of gap-up moves.

The first rule of buying gap-ups is that it should only be done in quality, leading stocks with strong fundamentals. Buying big gap-ups in speculative $2 bio-tech or Canadian uranium mining stocks is not what we are talking about here. Gap-up moves in "junk," that is to say stocks that do not represent fundamentally strong leadership or at least potential leadership should be avoided as gap-up buy candidates. Stick to stocks that trade at least $5 million a day in average daily dollar volume, and preferably much higher.

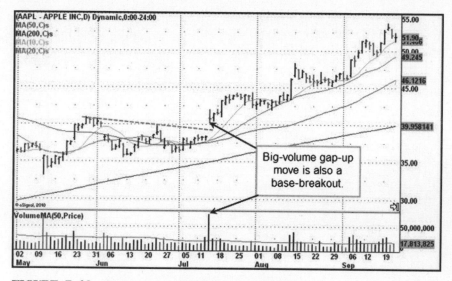

FIGURE 5.40 Apple, Inc. (AAPL) daily chart, July 2005.
Chart courtesy of eSignal, Copyright 2010.

A gap-up in a pattern should be fairly obvious, in that one should be able to eyeball on a stock's daily chart all the major gap-ups that are on the chart. We define a "major gap-up" as follows: (1) The stock gaps up at least 0.75 times its average true range (ATR) over the previous 40 trading days, though there are cases where the weeks leading up to the gap-up are volatile, such that 0.75 times its ATR is insufficient; thus if the gap does not look clear within the context of the chart pattern, it is best avoided; (2) its volume on the gap-up day should be at least 1.5 times, or 150 percent of, the 50-day moving average of daily trading volume. Average true range measures the volatility of a stock, which can be calculated each day by using the greatest of the following: (1) the current high less the current low, (2) the absolute value of the current high less the previous close, or (3) the absolute value of the current low less the previous close. By keeping a running tally of this for the most recent 40 days and maintaining a moving average of that tally each day, one can determine the average true range (ATR) over the preceding 40 trading days. In general this means that the more volatile a stock is, the greater its gap-up must be in order for it to be considered a valid "major gap-up."

Sometimes, when dealing with new issues that have very little trading history, having a 40-day ATR or a 50-day moving average of volume is not possible. In such a situation, as we see in the example of Riverbed Technology, Inc. (RVBD) shown in Figure 5.41, one can eyeball the ATR

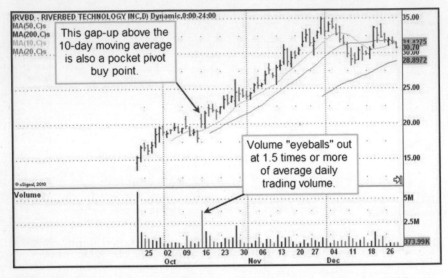

FIGURE 5.41 Riverbed Technology, Inc. (RVBD) daily chart, October 2006. Chart courtesy of eSignal, Copyright 2010.

and determine whether volume increase is sufficient to be approximately 1.5 times or more of 50-day moving average of daily volume.

Despite the fact that they can look somewhat "scary" to buy, most massive gap-ups in quality leaders that meet the conditions of a "major gap-up" can be bought, with the proviso that they hold the intraday low of the gap-up day's trading range. In Figure 5.42, Amazon.com (AMZN) gaps up on massive volume on October 23, 2009, and never trades below the intraday low of that day's trading range. Also note the tremendous power of the gap-up as expressed by the huge buying volume that comes into the stock at that point. Notice how the stock closes near the high of the day. Gap-ups can be bought at the beginning of the trading day, since the strongest names will often continue higher that same day after they gap-up, such as in the case of AMZN. Buying a gap-up at the end of the day that closes at its high is okay, but you have to allow for that much more downside based on our gap-up sell rules, which we will discuss later in this chapter. Alternatively, one could buy half of one's intended position at the open, and half at the close. The real trick with handling major gap-ups is where to sell if the stock starts to fail in the days after the gap-up. The basic rule is that the stock should hold the intraday low of the gap-up day, but once the stock is up and running higher from the gap-up day, where and under what conditions do you sell? Depending on the quality of the stock, and its behavior around the 10-day and 50-day moving averages as it trends higher, this can vary.

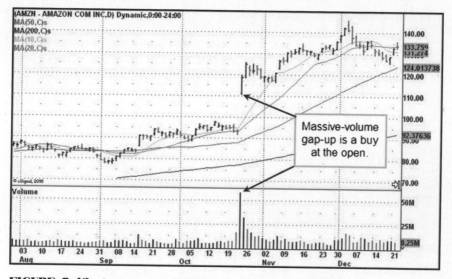

FIGURE 5.42 Amazon.com (AMZN) daily chart, October 2009. Chart courtesy of eSignal, Copyright 2010.

The two general sell rules for handling major gap-ups once a position is taken on the gap-up day, preferably near the lows of the intraday trading range, are as follows.

Rule #1

Sell if the stock violates its 10-day moving average, for instance, closes under the 10-day line and then trades below the low of that day. Exceptions occur if (1) the stock violates the 10-day moving average in intervals of less than seven weeks in duration as a matter of course in its price history prior to the gap-up day; (2) the stock is in one of the following industry groups: semiconductors, retailers, or commodities, including oils and precious metal; or (3) the stock has a market capitalization greater than $5 billion. For these three exceptions, it is better to use a 50-day moving average violation, defined the same way we would with a 10-day moving average violation, as your sell signal. Otherwise the Seven-Week Rule holds for stocks that show a tendency to hold above their 10-day moving average for intervals of seven weeks or more within their price patterns prior to the gap-up. If a stock adheres to the Seven-Week Rule then it is prima facie a stock that tends to hold the 10-day moving average; therefore, once it breaks this moving average, it should be sold because it is now changing character by failing to hold the 10-day line. Conversely, stocks that violate

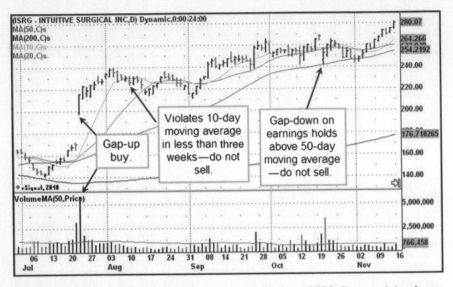

FIGURE 5.43 Intuitive Surgical, Inc. (ISRG) daily chart, 2009. Because it is a large-cap leader and does not adhere to the Seven-Week Rule, ISRG should only be sold on a 50-day moving average violation, not a 10-day violation.
Chart courtesy of eSignal, Copyright 2010.

their 10-day moving average all the time do not adhere to the Seven-Week Rule; hence we use the 50-day moving average violation as the sell signal for such stocks. For stocks that meet the Seven-Week Rule, then a violation of the 10-day moving average can be used as the point at which to sell at least half the position. An ensuing violation of the 50-day moving average can be used to sell any remaining balance.

In the example of Intuitive Surgical (ISRG) from 2009 (Figure 5.43), ISRG violates its 10-day moving average within three weeks of the gap-up day on August 11th, and so does not meet the Seven-Week Rule. ISRG is also a quality, large-cap leader with a market cap well in excess of $5 billion. Therefore, we must use the 50-day moving average violation as our sell signal. This turns out to be the correct strategy, as even a sharp gap down on October 21, 2009, the day after the company announced earnings, was not enough to force the stock below the 50-day moving average as it held support there, retested it once more, and then turned back up to new highs.

Figure 5.44 shows how well Baidu, Inc. (BIDU) held its 10-day moving average following the gap-up day of March 4, 2009. BIDU did not violate its 10-day line for three months after the gap-up, far longer than the minimum of seven weeks required for the stock to meet the Seven-Week Rule. Based on the rule, once BIDU violated the 10-day moving average one should have

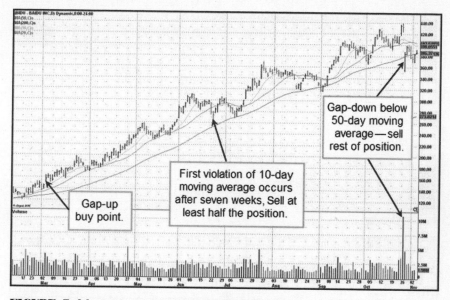

FIGURE 5.44 Baidu, Inc. (BIDU) daily chart, 2009.
Chart courtesy of eSignal, Copyright 2010.

sold at least half of any position taken on the gap-up, selling the rest once the stock had gapped down below the 50-day moving average on October 27th. There is always the option of simply selling the entire position on the first violation of the 10-day moving average, which is what we would be more inclined to do, since this allows us to lie back and wait for lower-risk re-entry points to show up, such as a possible pocket pivot buy point. A bird in the hand is always worth two in the bush, and as Bernard Baruch said, "I made my money by selling too soon."

Rule #2

In the days following the gap-up, sell if the stock trades below the intraday low of the gap-up day. One can allow the stock to close first before deciding whether to sell on an intraday move below the gap-up day's intraday low. Stocks with higher volatility can be given a little more room than those with lower volatility. Also watch for pullbacks just under the intraday low of the gap-up day that are close to and hence might find support at the 10-day, 50-day, or 200-day moving averages.

In the example of Riverbed Technology, Inc. (RVBD) in Figure 5.45, note how the pullback after the gap-up dips below the intraday low of the gap-up day, but closes up on the day, finding intraday support off both the

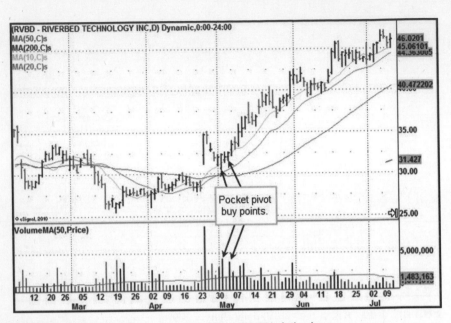

FIGURE 5.45 Riverbed Technology, Inc. (RVBD) daily chart.
Chart courtesy of eSignal, Copyright 2010.

10-day and 20-day moving averages. This particular day is also a pocket pivot buy point since the stock comes back up through the 10-day moving average on volume that is greater than the largest down-volume day in the pattern over the prior 10 days—a "10-day bounce" pocket pivot. It is always important once you are shaken out of a position by adhering to your stop-loss points that you continue to monitor the stock you have just sold for the right reasons in case it turns around and flashes some sort of buy signal such as a pocket pivot buy point. In RVBD's case, if you sold the stock intraday as it was moving below the intraday low of the gap-up day, you could have turned around and bought it right back on the basis of the pocket pivot buy point. In this manner we are ready to use all the tools at our disposal, including the pocket pivot point, to help us in handling a gap-up buy situation.

Unlike RVBD, Apple, Inc. (AAPL) in Figure 5.46 breaks below the low of its gap-up day on October 20, 2009, triggering a sell signal. Note that AAPL also simultaneously violates its 10-day moving average only six days after the gap-up day, sealing its fate as a failed gap-up move. AAPL does eventually back and fill for several weeks before moving to new highs again, but once the gap-up day fails there is no point in continuing to play out the position; it should simply be closed out at a relatively small loss without further argument.

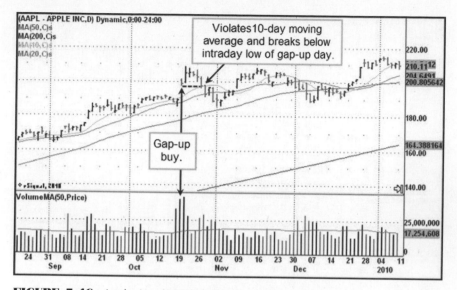

FIGURE 5.46 Apple, Inc. (AAPL) daily chart, October 2009.
Chart courtesy of eSignal, Copyright 2010.

SELLING TECHNIQUES USING THE 10-DAY AND 50-DAY MOVING AVERAGES

Alert readers may have noticed that the sell rules for pocket pivot points are the exact same rules that are used for gap-ups. This is because these sell rules are all based on the Seven-Week Rule that we use for determining whether to use the 10-day or 50-day moving average as our guide for selling a stock, and this can be applied to any stock at any stage of its price trend. While the 20-day is used to some degree as well, we tend to focus more on the 10-day and 50-day moving averages as our primary guides for selling stocks and/or cutting back positions.

It doesn't hurt to repeat the Seven-Week Rule, which is that any stock that shows a tendency to hold above its 10-week moving average for intervals of at least seven weeks should always be sold when it violates the 10-day moving average. Conversely, stocks that do not show this tendency should be sold when they violate their 50-day moving average.

Sohu.com (SOHU) held its 10-day moving average for just about 2½ months in 2003 (Figure 5.47) as it nearly tripled in price from late March 2003 to mid-June before finally violating its 10-day moving average, at which point it should have been sold based on the Seven-Week Rule. Since SOHU held its 10-day moving average for more than seven weeks after it

also see pg 176

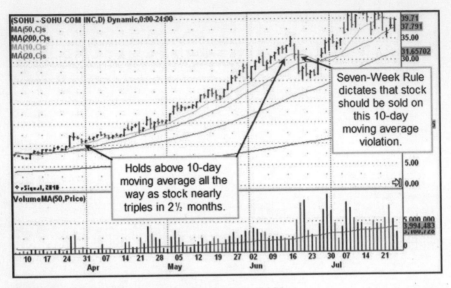

FIGURE 5.47 Sohu.com (SOHU) daily chart, 2003.
Chart courtesy of eSignal, Copyright 2010.

broke out in March of 2003, the 10-day moving average was your selling guide on that upside move. Once the stock broke the 10-day moving average, you would have sold it on this basis. You can then lie back and wait for another buy point, either a standard base breakout or a pocket pivot point, to show up.

Crocs, Inc. (CROX) gapped up very sharply in early May of 2007 (Figure 5.48) and launched higher. After the gap-up day, which was buyable based on our gap-up buying rules discussed in the previous section, CROX held its 10-day moving average for more than seven weeks, invoking the Seven-Week Rule whereby the 10-day line would be used as your guide for selling the stock. It was not until late June of 2007 that CROX finally violated its 10-day moving average. Remember that we use the term "violated" to specify the precise technical action we are looking for, which is that after the first day the price closed below the 10-day moving average, the stock must move below the intraday low of that first day to meet the definition of a moving average "violation." The second day down through the 10-day moving average in Figure 5.48, which also breaks down through the 20-day moving average, was the confirming violation of the 10-day line.

Mosaic Co. (MOS) in Figure 5.49 would also use the 10-day moving average as a selling guide following its breakout in late August 2007, since it did not violate the 10-day line for at least seven weeks following the

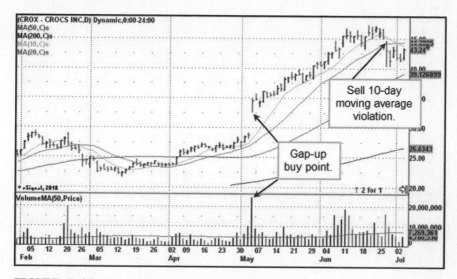

FIGURE 5.48 Crocs, Inc. (CROX) daily chart, 2007.
Chart courtesy of eSignal, Copyright 2010.

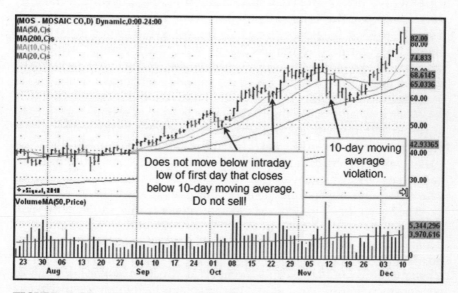

FIGURE 5.49 Mosaic Co. (MOS) daily chart, 2007.
Chart courtesy of eSignal, Copyright 2010.

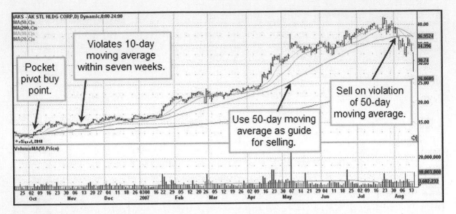

FIGURE 5.50   AK Steel Holding Corp. (AKS) daily chart 2006–2007.
Chart courtesy of eSignal, Copyright 2010.

breakout. Note that while MOS did actually have two days where it did close below the 10-day moving average, it did not meet the definition of a moving average "violation" because the stock never moved below the intraday lows of those first-day closes below the 10-day moving average, as the chart shows. This is important to keep in mind since you will never sell a stock for which the Seven Week Rule is invoked on the first day it closes below the 10-day moving average. You must first see the stock move below the intraday low of that first-day close under the 10-day line. This is one of the primary "tricks" to using the 10-day moving average as a selling guide per the Seven Week Rule.

When a stock violates the 10-day moving average within seven weeks of its buy point, whether a base breakout or a pocket pivot point, as AK Steel Holding Corp. (AKS) did in October 2006 (Figure 5.50), then the 50-day moving average is to be used as your selling guide. Once it finally violated its 50-day moving average in August 2007, it would have been sold with a 150 percent gain from the initial buy point in early October 2006.

The Seven Week Rule is a very simple concept that works quite well. In general, the way to handle a stock that does not violate the 10-day moving average for at least seven weeks from the buy point, whether a base breakout pivot point or a pocket pivot point, then a violation of the 10-day moving average can be used as the point at which to sell at least half of your position, if not all of it. If half the position is held following the 10-day moving average violation, then a violation of the 50-day moving average can be used to sell the other half. If a stock violates the 10-day moving average within seven weeks of the buy point, then a violation of the 50-day moving average signals to sell the stock. One minor difference about how the 50-day moving average as our selling guide is that if the volume is appreciably greater on the first day the stock penetrates the 50-day moving average, then it can simply be sold at that point. However, if the volume is not appreciably greater, then wait for the stock to meet the strict definition of a "violation" of the 50-day by moving below the intraday low of the first-day close below the 50-day moving average before selling it.

PUTTING IT ALL TOGETHER

As we were careful to point out at the beginning of this chapter, pocket pivot buy points, gap-up buy points, use of the 10-day and 50-day moving averages as sell guides, and the Seven Week Rule are not viewed as separate "tricks," but rather as a holistic group of interrelated techniques that we have found very useful in practice. All of these components come together as concrete means of dealing with positions in big, leading stocks that have outstanding profit potential if handled properly. To illustrate this, let's go through three "trading simulations," for lack of a better term with three subject stocks from the market rally that began in March 2009:

1. Apple, Inc. (AAPL)
2. Cerner Corp. (CERN)
3. Green Mountain Coffee Growers (GMCR)

For readers interested in similar real-time analysis of individual stocks, see the Follow the Stock section on our website: www.virtueofselfishinvesting.com.

Apple, Inc. (AAPL) 2009

Apple, Inc. (AAPL) flashed a pocket pivot buy point on April 16, 2009 (Figure 5.51), nearly a month after the general market logged a follow-through day, signaling a new general market rally phase. On the pocket pivot day volume was the highest in the prior seven days, and was also higher than any down-volume day in the prior 16 days, thus meeting the 10-day minimum required for a proper pocket pivot "volume signature." AAPL began its move on the pocket pivot day reasonably close to the 10-day moving average, which qualified as a buyable pocket pivot. A second pocket pivot on May 26th came right off the 10-day moving average, at which point one could buy enough shares to fill out a "full" position. Notice that AAPL does in fact violate its 10-day moving average relatively quickly after each of the

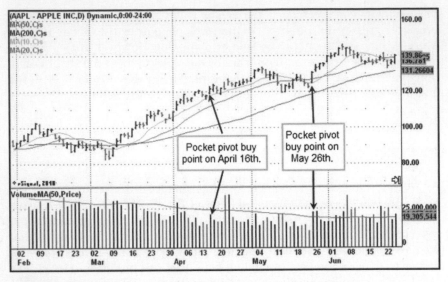

FIGURE 5.51 Apple, Inc. (AAPL) daily chart, first half of 2009.
Chart courtesy of eSignal, Copyright 2010.

two pocket pivot buy points. This dictates that we use the 50-day moving average as a selling guide for now.

As AAPL continued higher it presented another pair of pocket pivot buy points on October 2nd and October 19th, 2009 (Figure 5.52). Volume on the October 19th pocket pivot was clearly the highest in the prior 10 days, while the volume on October 2nd qualified because it was higher than any down-volume day in the prior 3½ weeks. The day after the October 19th pocket pivot on the gap-up was buyable, but would have stopped you out of your position on the move below the intraday low of the gap-up day. On December 7th, AAPL violates the 50-day moving average, and since applying the Seven Week Rule dictates that the 50-day line will be used as a selling guide, the stock is sold. During the 2009 market rally, AAPL was a "big stock" leader that was supported every time it pulled back to its 50-day moving average, which after a while became something of an "insurance policy" as institutional investors came in to support one of their most favored growth holdings, no doubt.

Cerner Corp. (CERN) 2009

Cerner Corp. (CERN) was a quiet leader in the 2009 market rally and had a habit of staging new-high base breakouts on less-than-convincing volume. Promises of material, increased government spending on information

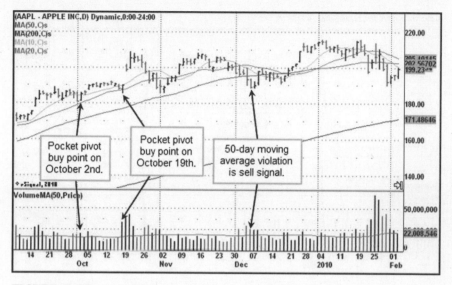

FIGURE 5.52 Apple, Inc. (AAPL) daily chart, second half of 2009. Chart courtesy of eSignal, Copyright 2010.

technology, or "IT," for the medical industry were a driving theme for CERN's price move, and there were enough pocket pivot buy points that could have been utilized to take a position in the stock.

The first pocket pivot point presented itself on April 24, 2009 (Figure 5.53), and a 10-day moving average violation occurred within seven weeks of that buy point on June 3rd. Applying the Seven Week Rule indicates that we will use the 50-day moving average as a guide for selling the stock. Also, at around $6 billion in market capitalization, CERN was a large-cap stock, which also argues for using the 50-day moving average as our selling guide. On July 7th CERN actually penetrates the 50-day moving average, but volume is only 22 percent above average daily volume, so we would then wait to see if the stock moves below the intraday low of this first-day penetration of the 50-day line in order to define it as a "violation," and hence a sell signal. Since this did not happen, we do not sell the stock, allowing it to climb back above the 50-day moving average and soon to present another pocket pivot buy point on July 23, 2009. Even though volume is only average, it is the highest volume in 11 days, qualifying as pocket pivot volume, and occurs after four orderly, low-volume down days. As well, prior strength was seen in the pattern with the huge up-volume day on July 16th, six trading days before the pocket pivot buy point.

On September 1, 2009, CERN violates its 50-day moving average, which the Seven Week Rule indicates would be our guide for selling

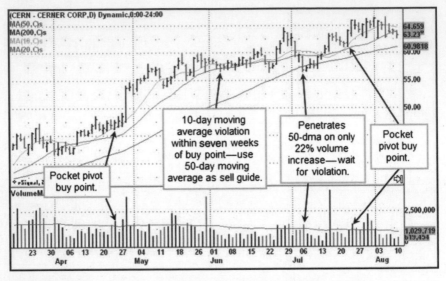

FIGURE 5.53 Cerner Corp. (CERN) daily chart, April–August 2009.
Chart courtesy of eSignal, Copyright 2010.

the stock. However, this is an example where an exception can be made, because while the stock is below the 50-day moving average it is also at an area of support defined by prior lows in the pattern on July 23rd and August 19th, along which a dotted line has been drawn in Figure 5.54

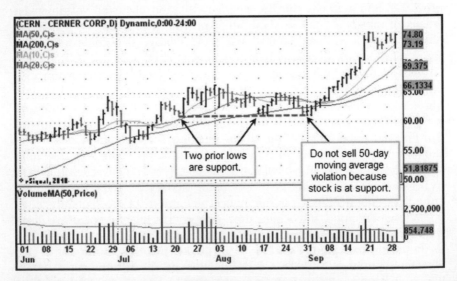

FIGURE 5.54 Cerner Corp. (CERN) daily chart, June–September 2009.
Chart courtesy of eSignal, Copyright 2010.

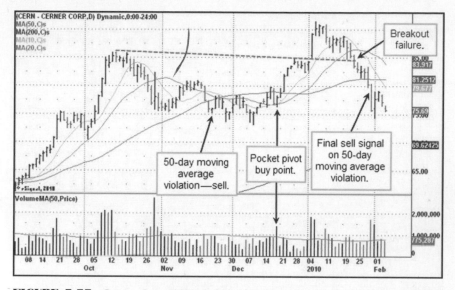

FIGURE 5.55 Cerner Corp. (CERN) daily chart, October 2009–February 2010. Chart courtesy of eSignal, Copyright 2010.

CERN finally did violate its 50-day moving average with a valid sell signal at that point on November 11th. The stock backed and filled a bit more under the 50-day moving average before presenting a pocket pivot on December 18th (Figure 5.55). As we discussed previously in the section on pocket pivots, pocket pivots under the 50-day moving average are risky to buy, and this particular pocket pivot is in fact below the 50-day line. However, it did work for a period of time as the stock broke out to new highs on January 5, 2010, but this breakout failed soon thereafter, and the stock violated the 50-day moving average on January 29, 2010. In this case, however, it would have been prudent to begin cutting back and selling CERN off as it broke down through its new-high base breakout pivot point at around the 85 price level. Note, a minor pocket pivot emerged on January 4, 2010, but the same sell rules would apply as CERN's breakout soon failed.

Green Mountain Coffee Roasters (GMCR) 2009

After one of the worst market corrections in stock market history, Green Mountain Coffee Roasters (GMCR) showed signs of life from November 2008 through February 2009. Even though the major averages broke below their lows set in November 2008, GMCR held its ground and resisted the general market downtrend in February. On March 12, 2009, the Dr. K market direction model issued a buy signal as the market had a bona fide

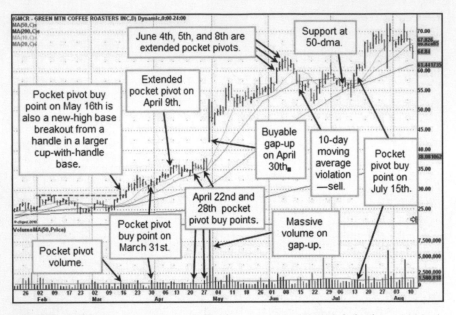

FIGURE 5.56 Green Mountain Coffee Growers, Inc. (GMCR) daily chart, 2009. Chart courtesy of eSignal, Copyright 2010.

follow-through day. The nice thing about the systematic portion of the market direction model, which will be discussed in the next chapter, is that it does not care how bad things look on a fundamental basis because it focuses purely on the price/volume action of the major market indices. On March 16th, just two trading days after the follow-through day, GMCR flashed a pocket pivot buy point that was also a new-high base breakout, but with volume only 12 percent above-average it was insufficient for a standard O'Neil–style base-breakout pivot buy point (Figure 5.56). However, because the volume on that day was higher than any down-volume day in the pattern over the prior 10 days, it met the proper "volume signature" required for a pocket pivot buy point. By closing mid-bar, however, it was somewhat weak, but nevertheless fulfilled the pocket pivot criteria, so a small position in GMCR could have been bought on that day.

On March 31, 2009, GMCR presented another pocket pivot buy point. Note how the low of the day rests right on top of the 10-day moving average, and finishes the day up on appreciably higher volume. Additionally, the trading days leading up to this pocket pivot point were below-average volume days, a sign of healthy consolidation. Note that April 9th is not a pocket pivot buy point because it is slightly extended. This should be visually clear, but an additional clue is that the low of its trading range is above the 10-day moving average. April 22nd, on the other hand, qualifies as a high-quality pocket pivot buy point because of the strong, high volume and also because the days leading up to this pocket pivot are orderly, having very tight price closes over the prior four days leading up to the pocket pivot on the 22nd, hence the "context" of this pocket pivot is very constructive. Another pocket pivot buy point on April 28th qualifies for the same reason.

By the time GMCR had its gap-up buy point on April 30, investors probably had accrued a fairly substantial position in the stock if they had been buying at the pocket pivot points. Depending on one's position sizing risk tolerance levels, one could add to their position here. If investors owned no GMCR, they could initiate their position here. As with most all gap-ups that meet our requirements, it is best to buy at the open of the trading day. Stocks often will move higher from their gap-up point for the rest of the trading day. Our requirements for buying at the open are that the market has been behaving bullishly, that is, the market direction model is not on sell, the stock meets our minimum liquidity requirements, the stock has not been in a downtrend, and the stock is fundamentally strong.

Continuing along, we note that June 4th is not a pocket pivot point because it is slightly extended with the low of its daily price range visibly above its 10-day moving average (Figure 5.56). The same reasoning would apply to June 5th and June 8th even though volume is high on all three days. On June 16th, GMCR violates its 10-day moving average for the first time in more than seven weeks, so at least half the position can be sold here. On July 8th, GMCR touches its 50-day moving average and could be bought here for those who prefer to buy on weakness around the 50-day moving average. Buying on strength versus buying on weakness within an uptrend is a matter of trading personality. July 15th shows a pocket pivot because it just barely meets the volume requirements, and even though the low of its trading range is above its 10-day moving average, it is not extended when taken in context of the overall chart pattern as the stock is just breaking out of a base. So part or all of the GMCR sold on June 16th could be bought back here. While the price paid on July 15th is slightly higher than the price sold on June 16th, capital used for GMCR was not at risk in GMCR as it traded mostly sideways during this period.

Moving to Figure 5.57, we see that on July 20 GMCR could be bought again on the basis that it had hit its 50-day moving average and was now moving to new highs on high volume. This is a standard new-high breakout following a bounce off the 50-day moving average. The stock then flashes another pocket pivot buy point on July 30th as the stock undercuts its 10-day moving average and then finishes with a strong close on huge volume. The wide trading range for that day is due to the bulls wrestling with the bears over its earnings report, and by the end of the day the bulls had

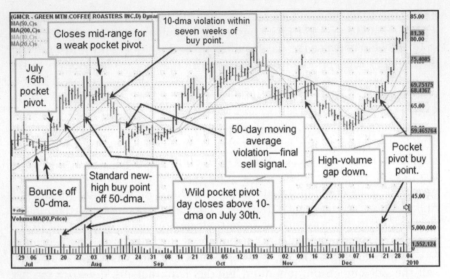

FIGURE 5.57 Green Mountain Coffee Growers, Inc. (GMCR) daily chart, 2009. Chart courtesy of eSignal, Copyright 2010.

won. Then a few days later a weak pocket pivot that closed mid-range as it stalled a bit occurred on August 7th. GMCR is finally sold on August 18 as it violates its 50-day moving average.

Important Note: The 10-day moving average violation on August 11 is not a sell signal because while GMCR obeyed the 10-day moving average for at least seven weeks prior to its 10-day violation in June and thus was sold upon violation of its 10-day moving average, the count is reset once the stock reverses trend either by basing for at least three weeks or at least touching its 50-day moving average once. GMCR violates its 10-day moving average in its fifth week after resuming its uptrend the week of July 13; thus the 50-day moving average would be used as the sell guide.

Late in the year, GMCR tried to break out to new highs again in late September but failed on that breakout attempt. Interestingly, the stock built an entirely new base and flashed a pocket pivot buy point on December 18, 2009, and continued to move higher into January 2010.

Note that had an investor initiated her first buy in GMCR on July 15th and then continued to buy on July 20th and July 30th, then she should pay heed to the maximum 7–8 percent sell loss rule. Had one bought equal dollar positions at the close on each of these days, one would have had an average cost of 65.45. One might not want to wait for a violation of the 50-day moving average at 58.13 since this is an 11.2 percent loss from their average cost. On the other hand, a stock like GMCR is relatively more volatile so that, armed with this knowledge, one might institute a 10 percent stop-loss for such a stock. In practice, however, you want to limit your losses to as little as possible.

CONCLUSION

By fully utilizing the concepts of pocket pivot buy points, gap-up buy points, and the Seven Week Rule with respect to the use of the 10-day and 50-day moving averages as sell guides, all in combination with orthodox O'Neil buying rules such as standard new-high/base-breakout pivot points, we can gain an edge in our position entry points relative to where the "crowd" might be compelled to come in and buy a stock. As well, these techniques provide critical assistance in how we handle a big, winning stock during its uptrend, both adding to and cutting back our positions along the way as the stock flashes buy points and moving average violations that help us handle risk and maximize our profit exploitation of such a stock. This chapter has provided a good deal of the "meat" with respect to how we maneuver the twists and turns of the market as we handle a potentially hugely profitable position in a big leader, and concretely answers the classic question every investor is faced with when they first buy a potentially big, leading stock: "Now what?"

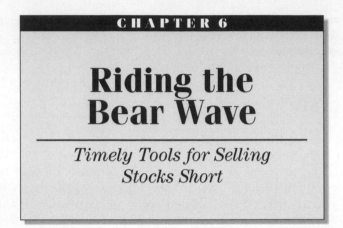

CHAPTER 6

Riding the Bear Wave

Timely Tools for Selling Stocks Short

I n essence, our short-selling philosophy is the mirror image of our up-side, bull market philosophy where we seek to capitalize on the huge upside price moves in the "big stock" leaders of any bull market cycle. For us, short-selling is simply playing the second half of what we can think of as a stock's "life cycle." Young, entrepreneurial companies start their life cycles off with a bang as strong fundamentals, new products and services, and dynamic new industry conditions help them to gain a strong institutional following as mutual funds, pension funds, hedge funds, and other large, institutional investors take positions in the stock. Systematic and sustained institutional accumulation of a leading stock drives the stock price inexorably higher, resulting in your classic O'Neil–style "big, winning stock." As the company matures and conditions change, such as the emergence of newer, more efficient, competing technologies, processes, or concepts, the flow of institutional money into the stock will inevitably slow. In some cases, the company merely becomes a slow-moving, underperforming "has-been." In other cases, and those that typify the kind we are most interested in, that institutional money flow can reverse very sharply as the institutional investors that piled into an innovative, entrepreneurial young company on the upside quickly begin to pile out. When institutions begin exiting their sizable positions in such a manner, a former leading stock can come under severe, sustained distribution that sends the stock plummeting ever lower, and completes the stock's "life cycle."

More than five years have passed since *How to Make Money Selling Stocks Short* was published. This chapter can be considered (at least for

Gil's part) the first update to that work, though the book very much remains an excellent primer on O'Neil–style short-selling methods. While this chapter can stand on its own, we recommend that *How to Make Money Selling Stocks Short* be read as an introduction to this chapter. While that book focuses primarily on the use of weekly charts to illustrate short-selling techniques, the point where the rubber meets the road is, in fact and in the reality of real time, on the daily charts. Exactly how and where one sells a stock short is critical in being able to capitalize on a prime short-sale opportunity, and this chapter expands on the precise timing of short-sales using daily charts. In addition, we will discuss some new ideas in short-sale chart formations and set-ups, which add to our arsenal of topping formations that provide the necessary structure to our short-selling methods. Previously, our universe of viable, short-sale set-ups consisted of the standard head & shoulders (H&S) type of formation and its derivative, the late-stage-failed-base (LSFB).

THE GOLDEN RULES OF SHORT-SELLING

There are six basic principles and rules that govern our short-selling activities and provide the philosophical foundation upon which our O'Neil–style approach to short-selling is built. We refer to these as the six Golden Rules of Short-Selling and they refer primarily to what sorts of stocks we seek to short with respect to leadership status and liquidity, when we seek to short them, how we handle stop-loss points on short positions, and how we establish profit-taking rules.

Obviously, when the "big stock" leadership in any bull market begins to top and roll over, this has macro-implications for the general market and usually signals the onset of a bear market. By definition, the leadership that led the market on the upside will often lead it to the downside as money flows out of the stock market during a bear market. Therefore, we want to focus on short-selling in those few names that were big, winning stocks and that had huge price moves in the immediately preceding bull market. In a bear market, what has gone up the fastest often has the best chance of coming down the fastest. So we can establish our first two Golden Rules of Short-Selling:

1. Sell short only when the market is in a clear bear market trend, and as early in the bear market cycle as possible. If you are shorting late in a bear market, after the market has been trending lower over many

months, you may very well be late to the party. Short-selling very late in a bear market can be catastrophic, so beware of this. In particular, if the market has come down significantly off its peak and everyone around you is talking about selling the market short then be especially attuned to the contrarian implications of such a bearish preponderance.

2. Focus on those "big stock" leaders that had huge upside price moves in the immediately preceding bull market phase and that are showing significant topping signs. This means you will likely only be dealing with a relatively small universe of proper short-selling candidates.

   As we will see later in this chapter, major topping formations, such as a head & shoulders top, can take 8–12 weeks or more after their absolute tops to develop. Some can take longer, and in some exceptional cases can take only a scant few weeks before a stock literally appears to blow out of the sky. The critical point in most short-selling cases is that bullish sentiment in a former, big winning leader is often very persistent in the stock. From a psychological perspective this makes perfect sense, since human nature is pretty much what it is and has always been. Investors who missed the big "rocket stock" and never bought it as they watched it go higher will see it start to break down off its peak for the first time and want in on the missed opportunity. Brokerage analysts may come out and recommend the fallen leader as a "strong buy" because it is seen as "cheap" after the sharp price break off the peak. In this manner, "residual" bullish sentiment in a former leader will persist in bringing money into the stock and bouncing it back up within its pattern. It takes time to wring out all of the bullish sentiment in a stock, which is why most short-sale candidates take 8–12 weeks or more to set up properly before they break to the downside. In most cases, larger-cap stocks with a broad institutional following will take longer to break down, while relatively smaller stocks can tend to break down much more quickly, usually within 12 weeks of their price peaks.

3. Seek to short former, big leading stocks 8–12 weeks after their peak price following a major upside price run.

   In most cases, "big stock" leaders will be fairly liquid traders with average daily trading volume well in excess of 1–2 million shares. In general, we prefer a minimum of 2 million shares in average daily trading volume for our short-sale candidates. Stocks that trade a few hundred thousand shares a day should generally be avoided, unless an investor intends to deal in much smaller position sizes relative to one's account equity. We also impose an absolute maximum position size for stocks trading less than 1 million shares a day at less than or equal to 0.5 percent of the average daily trading volume. Therefore, for a stock that trades 300,000 shares a day, an appropriate maximum absolute position size of 1,500 shares or relative position size of 5 percent of one's account equity, whichever is less, is recommended for less than the most seasoned short-sellers. Stocks that trade only a few hundred thousand shares a day are quite thin and hence subject to very rapid price run-ups, which can cause a great deal of damage, even if your position size is relatively small. Therefore, Golden Rule of Short-Selling rule #4 is:

4. Only sell short stocks that trade a minimum of 1–2 million shares a day, and preferably more. In general, avoid thinly-traded stocks as short-sale candidates, as risk can correlate inversely to a stock's trading liquidity.

    Stop-losses on short positions should range around 3–5 percent. If you are down 3 percent on a position and the stock is trading above-average volume as it rallies from your short-sale point, it is best to implement the 3 percent threshold for your stop-loss with the idea that the stock can always be re-shorted if the rally suddenly fizzles out. Also, if a stock you are short generates a pocket pivot type of upside buy signal, you can often just cover the stock right there. Otherwise, if the stock is rallying weakly, a 5 percent stop can be used, sometimes 1–3 percent more if so desired. Stops on short positions are still dependent on one's position size, personal psychology, and risk tolerance. One way to handle stops is to use a "reverse-layering" technique by "peeling off" portions of the position as a short position rallies against you, say ⅓ of the position when it is 3 percent above your short-sale price, another ⅓ when it is 5 percent above, and the last ⅓ once the stock has rallied 7 percent past your short-sale price point. Other "permutations" of this strategy might be ½ the position at 3 percent and the other ½ at 5 percent, or ½ at 5 percent and ½ at 7 percent. As you gain experience in short-selling, you might find a particular permutation of stop-loss policies that works best for you, but whatever the case it is extremely important to always have a clear exit plan and point for any short position that is taken. Standing in the way of a sharp rally through indecision or hesitation, what we refer to as "freezing up," can be very dangerous. Hence, Golden Rule #5 states:

5. Set stop-losses at an average of 3–5 percent, using the tighter 3 percent stop if the stock begins to rally against you on strong, above-average volume. A "layering" technique can also be used by "peeling off" and covering portions of the position as the stock rallies against you a series of specified percentage thresholds, such as covering ⅓ at 3 percent, another ⅓ at 5 percent, and the final ⅓ at 7 percent, or any other permutations. Stops are dependent upon personal psychological

preference and risk tolerance, so short-sellers should try to determine what works best for them in real-time.

Because stocks will often have sharp upside rallies within their macro-downtrends, it is wise to set reasonable profit objectives for any downside move you expect a stock to make once you have taken a short position in the stock. In most environments profit targets should be 20–30 percent. If you find that short positions are breaking closer to 15–20 percent before rallying and wiping out your profits, then you can adjust this, or again use a "layering" technique where you cover ½ the position when it is showing a 15–20 percent profit and the remainder when it is showing a 20–30 percent profit.

Alternatively, the 20-day moving average can sometimes be used as a guide for a trailing upside stop on any short position that is showing a decent profit. Once a stock has broken down from a proper short-sale set-up and topping formation and has been in a downtrend for at least a few days to a few weeks, the 20-day is often a useful reference point for a legitimate upside turn and rally in a stock, and hence offers what can be a nearby trailing stop. In Figure 6.1 we see First Solar, Inc. (FSLR) as it broke down from a large, wide, loose, and improper late-stage cup-with-handle type of formation. Note the loose and very long handle with very few tight weekly price closes. This is the macro-formation from which FSLR topped in late 2008.

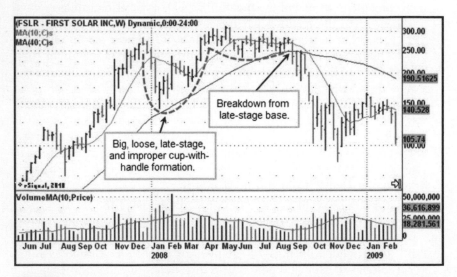

FIGURE 6.1   First Solar, Inc. (FSLR) weekly chart, 2007–2008. FSLR tops out in a big, late-stage-failed-base short-sale set-up.
Chart courtesy of eSignal, Copyright 2010.

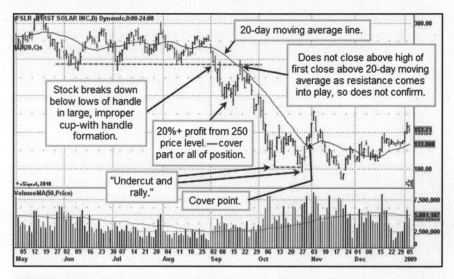

FIGURE 6.2 First Solar, Inc. (FSLR) daily chart, 2008. The 20-day moving average provides a useful guide for a trailing stop as the stock breaks down and rapidly trends lower.
Chart courtesy of eSignal, Copyright 2010.

In Figure 6.2 we can see FSLR's breakdown in detail on its daily chart. The stock breaks support along the lows of the handle at around the 250 price area, which corresponds to the weekly chart in Figure 6.1 which is the macro-view. After FSLR breaks decisively through this support zone in the lows of the handle, it stages one rally back up toward resistance and the 250 price area. Because (1) the stock did not move above the intraday high of the first day that it closed above the 20-day moving average and (2) the move up into the 20-day also corresponded to solid resistance at the 250 price area and the lows of the handle, this would not be considered a cover point, necessarily. However, notice that the move from 250 down to 200 represented a 20 percent profit, roughly, so part or all of the position could have been covered there, nicely illustrating the implementation of the 20–30 percent profit objective rule. The stock could have then been re-shorted on the move back up to the 20-day moving and the lows of the handle, which represented stiff potential resistance at the 250 price area.

Note that as FSLR came down to the 100 price level it bounced once and then re-tested that 100 low by coming down to a point just below it, setting up an "undercut and rally" situation, which also provided a potential profit-taking/short-covering point. Watching for lows that are retested and undercut can be useful in determining when to cover part or all of a short position, as it is very common for stocks to fake out shorts by undercutting a prior low, whether near-term (within the last week or two) or intermediate-term (several weeks to a few months), which is seen as a "breach of support" that is simply too obvious to work. Hence stocks will have a tendency to "undercut and rally" as they trend lower. Watching for such undercuts can help determine when a short position should be covered in part or in total. From this we derive Golden Rule #6:

6. Once a short position is showing a profit, set a downside profit target objective of 20–30 percent or use a "layering" technique, covering ½ the position once a 15–20 percent profit is showing, and the other ½ at a 20–30 percent profit. Alternatively, once a short position is showing a good profit one can use the 20-day moving average as a guide for a trailing stop. If the nearest moving average above the stock's current price is the 50-day or 200-day moving average then they can be used in place of the 20-day moving average line. Watch also for undercuts of prior lows as potential rally points at which all or part of the position can be covered.

SHORT SALE SET-UPS

The key to successful short-selling lies in waiting for the proper window of opportunity to open. This requires waiting and watching as potential short-sale formations that begin to form complete their chart patterns. There are three primary short-selling set-ups that we use, the head & shoulders top, the late-stage-failed-base, and the punchbowl of death double-top. Each has its own unique characteristics, but sometimes patterns can overlap and can be therefore be interpreted as a "hybrid" of two or even all three of these formations, as we will see later in this chapter. Ultimately, the exact shape and label we assign to a particular topping formation is less important than the actual price/volume action within the pattern that indicates the stock is very likely under systematic and sustained distribution.

One feature that each of these topping formations and short-selling set-ups have in common is a sharp downside price break and breakdown on massive volume, which occurs right off the peak of a sharp upside price run of several months or more. Heavy volume selling off the top after a sustained uptrend usually signals the first wave of distribution in a former market leader, and it is at this point that such a stock should be placed on one's short-selling watch list as it potentially continues to form some sort of valid topping formation. Screening for stocks with heavy-volume price breaks on a daily and weekly basis is the most effective way to catch potential short-sale targets as they initially come under distribution. Keep in mind that in not all cases will a price break down off the peak in a former leader result in the stock building an overall topping formation. Leading stocks can and often do simply correct and build new chart bases from which they begin new price advances. It is possible to build elaborate screens that identify head & shoulders formations, but this is not necessary. Keeping a watch list of "broken" leaders that have had big-volume sell-offs off the peaks of big price runs in the immediately prior bull market phase is sufficient.

The Head & Shoulders Formation

The basic "mechanics" of a head & shoulders topping formation are best illustrated with the picture-perfect, textbook example of Crocs, Inc. (CROX) in 2007–2008 (Figure 6.3), one of the few true "poster children" of the head & shoulders topping formation. The prerequisite for any short-sale set-up

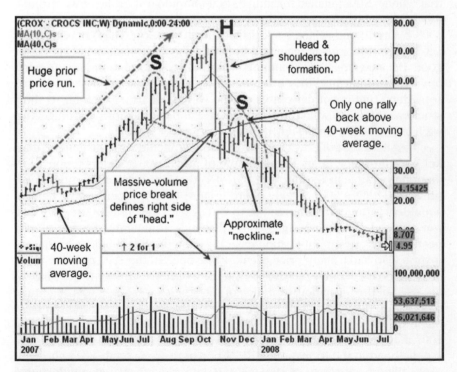

FIGURE 6.3 Crocs, Inc. (CROX), weekly chart, 2000–2008—the modern "poster-child" example of the head & shoulders top formation.
Chart courtesy of eSignal, Copyright 2010.

and topping formation is a substantial prior price run, such as CROX's 13-month upside romp through late 2006 and most of 2007. In October of 2007 CROX was slammed off its absolute price peak on massive selling volume, as Figure 6.3 shows. The stock then bounced to form a single right shoulder that briefly rallied above the 40-week (200-day) moving average before breaking down again. Note that the right shoulder forms below the left shoulder in the head & shoulders formation, which is the optimal configuration as it indicates severe weakness in the stock. As well, the left shoulder can represent a stiff area of resistance if the right shoulder forms below it in the pattern.

Once the head & shoulders formation has "filled out" it is possible to draw a "neckline" along the lows of the left shoulder, head, and right shoulder. In CROX's case, the neckline slopes downward, and hence is a "descending neckline." This is also an optimal configuration, as a downsloping or descending neckline is much weaker than a neckline that is flat or upward-sloping (ascending). Initial downside breaches of the neckline can often result in "fakeouts" as the stock turns and rallies briefly. Note that when CROX finished forming its right shoulder it broke down through its neckline, but after spending three weeks below the neckline in January 2008 it turned and rallied back up into its 10-week (50-day) moving average before rolling over again and breaking down through the neckline for good. Because breaches of support within topping formations are often too obvious, and because they often occur as gap-downs on the daily charts, something that is not detectable on the weekly charts, we prefer to short stocks as they rally weakly into logical resistance or a moving average line, such as the 50-day or 200-day moving averages (Figure 6.4).

To get an idea of how these formations coincide with the general market, let's first look at another example of a head & shoulders topping formation, this time in Garmin, Ltd. (GRMN) that occurred at the exact same time. In GRMN's 2007 weekly chart (Figure 6.5), we can see the head & shoulders formation set up similar to CROX with the initial big upside price run, the end of which is signaled by the huge volume price break off the peak. GRMN was an interesting case because the left shoulder in the formation also had a sharp price break-off its peak in the 120 price area peak on very heavy volume, so that by the time GRMN broke off the peak of the head in the formation, evidence of the stock's weakness was beginning to stack up decisively. This distribution in the left shoulder and the head made GRMN a prime short-sale target as the market began to top in late 2007. Following the second price break off the peak, which finished forming the head in the formation, GRMN began to work on its right shoulder as it rallied back above its 10-week (50-day) moving average on declining volume. This is the point at which we want to watch the stock's rally for signs that it is running out of gas as it rallies on declining volume.

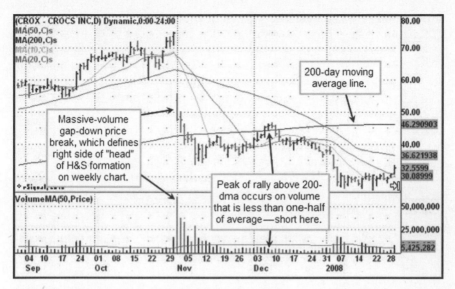

FIGURE 6.4 Crocs, Inc. (CROX) daily chart, 2007.
Chart courtesy of eSignal, Copyright 2010.

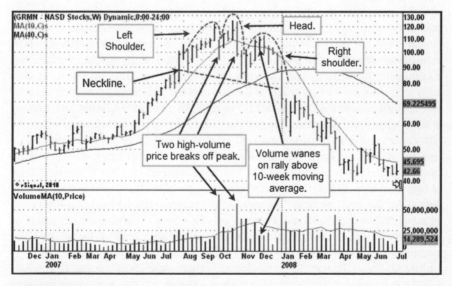

FIGURE 6.5 Garmin, Inc. (GRMN) weekly chart, 2007–2008. GRMN sets up in a head & shoulders topping formation.
Chart courtesy of eSignal, Copyright 2010.

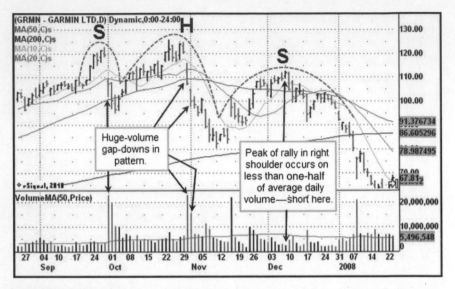

FIGURE 6.6   Garmin, Inc. (GRMN) daily chart, 2007–2008. Very low volume as the peak of the right shoulder is the optimal short-sale point.
Chart courtesy of eSignal, Copyright 2010.

By examining the daily chart of GRMN (Figure 6.6) we can see the rally in mid-November 2007 that took the stock back above the 50-day (10-week on the weekly chart) moving average in early December. As GRMN reached what would become the peak of the right shoulder, daily trading volume declined precipitously as can be seen on the chart. Volume on the peak day was less than half of average daily volume for the stock, a strong sign of declining demand for the stock on the rally. In most cases, when volume on a rally within a right shoulder gets to –35 to –40 percent below average or lower, around one-third to one-half of average daily volume or less if you eyeball it on the chart. We call this a "volume dry-up" day, which can be shortened to the acronym "VDU," but we prefer to call it a "VooDoo" day. When it occurs, the odds of the stock giving way to the downside as it runs out of gas begin to increase, particularly if selling volume begins to increase sharply following the weak-volume up days in a rally/bounce. In most of the best examples, a very light-volume up day right around the peak of the right shoulder will mark the end of the rally as the stock will roll over to complete the right shoulder. Notice also that once GRMN starts to decline off the peak of the right shoulder it drops below its 50-day moving average but still manages to rally a couple of times back up into the moving average on light volume before rolling over altogether and plunging through the neckline of the head & shoulders, as I've delineated on the weekly chart of GRMN in Figure 6.6.

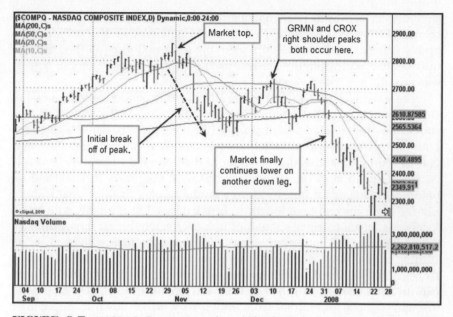

FIGURE 6.7 NASDAQ Composite Index, daily chart, 2007. The market top coincided with tops in big, leading stocks CROX and GRMN.
Chart courtesy of eSignal, Copyright 2010.

The timing of short sales also coincides with the action of the general market. It is important to understand that the head & shoulders formations of both CROX and GRMN did not form in a vacuum; they topped and formed their short-sale set-up formations as the market itself was building its top. Figure 6.7 shows the NASDAQ Composite Index in late 2007 as it built its overall top before plunging lower in early 2008. By comparing Figure 6.7 with the daily charts of CROX (Figure 6.4) and GRMN (Figure 6.6) you can see that both stocks initially peaked out right at the exact same time as the NASDAQ Composite Index. Once the NASDAQ Composite had broken down off its late October 2007 price peak, this initial decline was followed by nearly two months of backing and filling, which also coincided with CROX and GRMN building the right shoulders within their overall head & shoulders topping formations.

How topping patterns form is largely a function of the general market and usually peaks in the right shoulder of a head & shoulders topping formation, coinciding with peaks in general market rallies that occur after an initial break off the peak, just as CROX and GRMN built their patterns in a manner that is very much in synchrony with the NASDAQ Composite, e.g., the general market. Short-sale target stocks that may be building right shoulders in an overall, potential head & shoulders topping formation must be watched within the context of the general market as the two are inexorably linked. CROX and GRMN were big leaders during the bull market rally of 2007, and when the general market topped in late October 2007 it was no surprise that these stocks topped as well.

The examples of CROX and GRMN illustrate quite well the head & shoulders template that encompasses all the critical characteristics one should look for when identifying a head & shoulders top. While these were both examples of head & shoulders formations with one right shoulder, you will run into stocks that form more than one right shoulder, but this is often a function of the general market as it continues to back and fill before breaking down further as well as the stock's "institutional status." Big-cap favorites can take longer to break down, but normally as a stock forms two or more right shoulders it will typically break down through the neckline in the pattern at some point that coincides with the market starting a new down leg in an overall bear market. For example, while stocks like CROX and GRMN topped with the market in late 2007, larger-cap favorites like Apple, Inc. (AAPL) and Baidu, Inc. (BIDU) continued to build topping formations from which they broke down in September 2009, nearly a year after the October 2007 market top, as the market began a second major down leg in the 2007–2009 bear market (Figure 6.7). After the initial break off the peak in late 2007, we can see the backing-and-filling phase in the last two months of 2007 before the first real down leg of the bear market took CROX and GRMN with it. Another phase of backing-and-filling through most of 2008 finally ended with a second major down leg that began in September 2008. This was the point where another wave of leaders began to break down from their topping formations, which is typical of most bear markets (Figure 6.8). Leading stocks will begin to come apart and break down on each successive down leg during a bear market.

This is a very important concept to keep in mind as we discuss the other topping formations and set-ups that we look for in our short-sale operations later in this chapter. The market offers optimal windows of opportunity with each major down leg within an overall bear market, and it is critical that investors remain patient and vigilant in order to come in on the short side just as the market is starting another down leg and the optimal window of opportunity is opening.

Monsanto Co. (MON) in 2008–2009 (Figure 6.9) is an interesting head & shoulders example that formed in the midst of the bear market following the top in October 2007. Note that MON did not top with the market in October 2007, but instead continued higher as it nearly doubled in price by the summer of 2008 during what was actually a bear market rally within the overall 2007–2009 bear market environment.

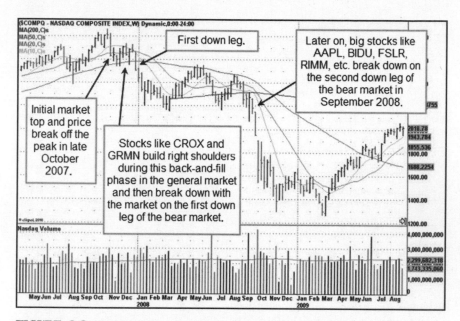

FIGURE 6.8 NASDAQ Composite Index weekly chart, 2007–2009. Leading stocks top in "waves" that coincide with each new down leg in an overall bear market. Chart courtesy of eSignal, Copyright 2010.

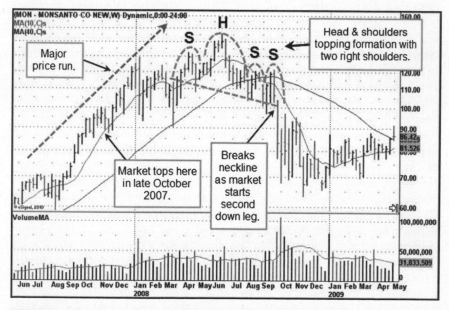

FIGURE 6.9 Monsanto Co. (MON) weekly chart, 2007–2009. Chart courtesy of eSignal, Copyright 2010.

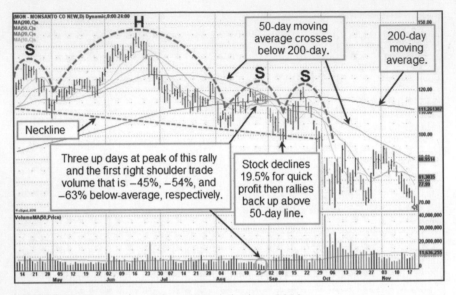

FIGURE 6.10 Monsanto Co. (MON) daily chart, 2008.
Chart courtesy of eSignal, Copyright 2010.

Eventually, however, MON began to form a head & shoulders topping formation after peaking in June 2008. Although it is not labeled on the chart in Figure 6.9 you can see the high-volume price break off the peak in June that defines the right side of the "head" in the formation, after which MON forms two right shoulders, roughly, and then finally breaks down through its neckline at the exact same time that the market begins its second major down leg in the bear market. In MON's daily chart (Figure 6.10) we can see that right around the peak of the first right shoulder the stock showed three up days where volume was –45 percent, –54 percent, and –63 percent below average daily trading volume, indicating that demand for the stock was potentially drying up. The stock then breaks down through its 50-day moving average down 19.5 percent to the neckline of the head & shoulders formation. As we discussed previously in this chapter, the first break through the neckline is usually a fakeout as it sucks in shorts and natural sellers before undercutting the neckline and then turning and rallying. In this case, MON rallied back up to a point just above its 50-day moving average to form the second right shoulder in the pattern.

Note that as the second right shoulder began to form MON's 50-day moving average had crossed below its 200-day moving average (corresponding to the 10-week moving average crossing below the 40-week on the weekly chart), a bearish "black cross." If an investor had successfully shorted MON off the peak of the first right shoulder as upside volume was drying up, the first break down to the moving average would have yielded a quick profit, and the ensuing rally could have been monitored for a potential failure point. Typically, stocks forming right shoulders will rally to a point just above the 50-day or 200-day moving averages, at which point a reversal back below the specific moving average, whether the 50-day or 200-day, can be shorted. After forming the peak of the second right shoulder MON breaks down to its neckline again, hovers around for a couple of days before splitting wide open to the downside.

Relatively smaller stocks like the CROX and GRMN examples will tend to break down faster, often only forming one single right shoulder in the head & shoulders formation, while very large-cap leader "favorites" like a MON can form two to three or more. Ultimately, however, the final break down will occur at the same time as a new down leg in a continuing bear market, so it is imperative to conduct short-sales in synchrony with the beginning of a new market down leg.

Late-Stage-Failed-Base (LSFB) Set-Ups

The second primary short-sale set-up and topping formation is the late-stage failed-base (LSFB), a corollary to the head & shoulders top that is usually seen more frequently than the head & shoulders formation, but which can also be seen as part of a head & shoulders formation, as we shall see a little bit later in this chapter. The LSFB, as we call it, forms when a stock breaks down from a late-stage base, which can happen after a failed breakout attempt or with the stock simply falling out of bed from a late-stage base formation. As always the pattern will have a big upside price run preceding it. After a long price run, each successive base that a leading stock forms on the way up becomes more and more obvious. When a stock finally builds a very late-stage base, usually the third or later base formed on the way up and after the initial breakout that began the price move several months earlier, it becomes very obvious to the crowd, which is then set up to be fooled.

When the LSFB gives way to the downside it can often do so very rapidly, but just as often can break down through a major moving average, such as the 20-day or 50-day line, first and then back-and-fill several times as it rallies back up into the moving average before splitting wide open. In the most ideal example, Sunpower Corp. (SPWRA) in 2007 (Figure 6.11) was a late-stage, V-shaped cup-with-handle formation that failed very rapidly. SPWRA's weekly chart shows that the breakout attempt from this cup-with-handle formation occurred on light weekly volume as the stock stalled out and reversed to close at the very low end of the weekly trading range. Two weeks later, the stock pierced the 10-week (50-day) moving

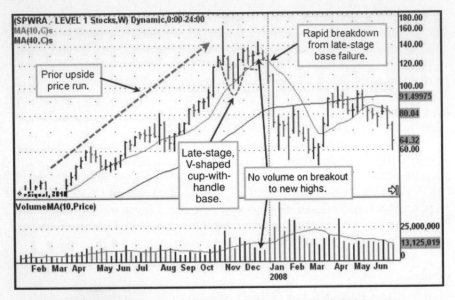

FIGURE 6.11 Sunpower Corp. (SPWRA) weekly chart, 2007–2008.
Chart courtesy of eSignal, Copyright 2010.

average and plummeted to the downside in rapid order, losing over 50 percent of its value in just about three weeks.

As always, the daily chart (Figure 6.12) gives a much better picture of how the breakout failure occurs, and we can see that the initial V-shaped cup-with-handle base formed after the stock had put in a climactic type of price run into the peak on the left side of the cup. After the cup forms a handle, the breakout day comes on just average volume, making it suspect, and the ensuing days roll over as volume actually dries up.

For seven days the stock drifts down toward its 50-day moving average before bursting through the moving average on very heavy volume and moving sharply lower. In this case shorting the immediate breach of the 50-day moving average would have been the proper entry point. The stock plummets rather quickly from that point, pausing for three days in a short, inverted bear flag, what we also like to think of as "walking the plank." The third day in the "plank" or inverted bear flag, volume dries up to a very low –36 percent below-average, a VooDoo day. Using a stop at the prior day's high, it would be possible to add to a short position in the stock at this point. SPWRA did not waste any time making a beeline right through its 200-day moving average to the downside where it finally stabilized for several weeks underneath the 200-day line. SPWRA would have given a very quick 25–30 percent profit, which is where our profit rules might come into

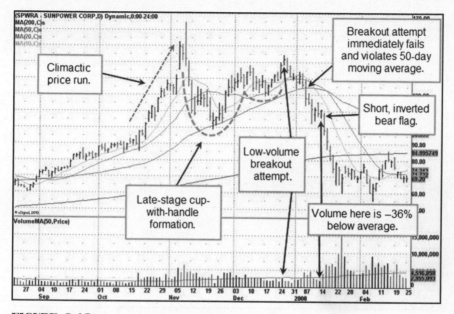

FIGURE 6.12   Sunpower Corp. (SPWRA) daily chart, 2007–2008.
Chart courtesy of eSignal, Copyright 2010.

play and cause us to cover our short on this basis, which would obviously be premature given the extent of the additional downside that actually ended up occurring. The key here is to assess the velocity of the break-down, so that if it is extremely weak to the downside as it collapses on heavy volume, one can use the 10-day moving average as an upside stop. Notice how SPWRA's 10-day moving average trails just above it on the way down once the stock breaks the 50-day moving average.

"Big stock" fertilizer play Potash Corp. Saskatchewan (POT) is an in-teresting example of a late-stage-failed-base that eventually morphs into a head & shoulders formation (Figure 6.13). Focusing on the LSFB, how-ever, gets you into the stock on the short side a lot sooner. After breaking out from a late-stage five-week base in June 2008, POT drifts higher on de-clining volume before pulling back to its 10-week (50-day) moving average, which it tests for the next three weeks before finally failing and breaking down toward the 40-week (200-day) moving average. A final rally up into the 40-week line occurs just as the 10-week line crosses below the 40-week line, a bearish "black cross," before the stock splits wide open, literally blowing apart in four weeks.

While the weekly chart of POT makes it look rather easy, the daily chart (Figure 6.14) paints a slightly different picture as it demonstrates

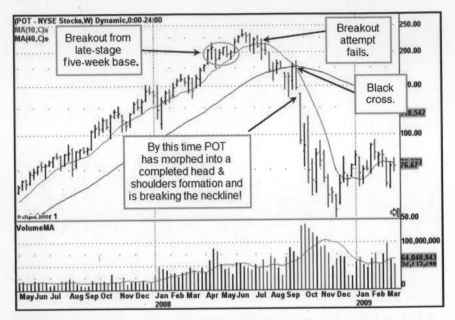

FIGURE 6.13 Potash Corp. Saskatchewan (POT) weekly chart, 2008. Chart courtesy of eSignal, Copyright 2010.

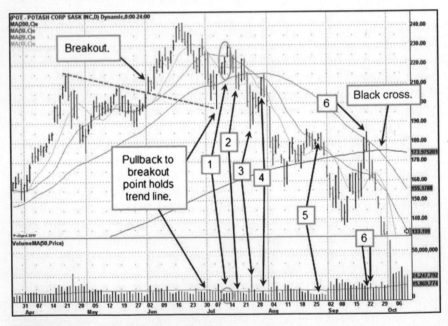

FIGURE 6.14 Potash Corp. Saskatchewan (POT) daily chart, 2008. Chart courtesy of eSignal, Copyright 2010.

how persistence is necessary in successful short-selling, as well as waiting for the exact right moment to short the stock. POT's initial breakout from the five-week late-stage base was actually a short trendline breakout that occurred on reasonably strong volume. The stock actually looked very strong as it pushed higher on several higher-volume up days, but eventually this all gave way as the stock descended back down toward the trendline breakout and the 50-day moving average, corresponding to the 10-week moving average on the weekly chart (Figure 6.13). In Figure 6.14 we can follow the numbers as we track the stock's steady but somewhat stubborn breakdown. (1) A very low bounce occurs off the 50-day moving average and rallies to a point just above the 20-day moving average. A retest of the 50-day moving average briefly looks successful at (2) for one brief day before the stock breaks down again. At this point it appears that some support at (3) is coming from the five-week base from which POT had previously broken out as the stock seems to rally right out of "thin air" and back up into the 50-day moving average at (4) on below-average volume. Note that the next day the stock actually touched the 50-day moving average on intraday basis, and that volume was very light, showing that the stock ran out of upside fuel at that point. POT broke down hard from there before finding support at the 200-day moving average where it rallied up into and around the 20-day moving average, which we would use as a reference for a trailing upside stop. Note that POT was unable to clear the 20-day line on any volume at (5), which is a VooDoo day with volume coming in at –44 percent below average on the day. The stock then broke down again through the 200-day moving average before rallying once more into the 50-day moving average in a violent rally that accompanied a similar violent rally in the general market.

If we take a chart of the S&P 500 Index and label it 1 through 6 as we have in Figure 6.14, we come up with Figure 6.15, which gives a good idea of how POT's breakdown was correlating to the general market action. In fact, POT was breaking out of its five-week late-stage base about two weeks after the actual top in the S&P 500. As the market continued to move lower throughout most of June 2008, POT's price action reflected this as its breakout began to fail and the stock flailed around its 50-day moving average, as we saw in Figure 6.14. You can also see how the little twists and turns in POT from points 1 through 4 correlate to some degree with the twists and turns of the general market. The movement from points 5 to 6 most certainly was a function of the general market, and the jagged break and final two-day "jack-up" rally into point 6 in POT's daily chart clearly mimics that seen in the S&P 500 chart. The window of opportunity becomes opens wide at point 6.

We cannot stress the importance of monitoring the general market when stalking your short-sale targets in individual stocks. In most cases,

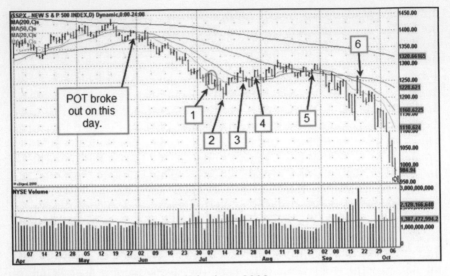

FIGURE 6.15 S&P 500 Index daily chart, 2008.
Chart courtesy of eSignal, Copyright 2010.

stocks' topping patterns can be seen to move in synchrony, at least to some degree, with the general market.

As was mentioned earlier, short-sale set-ups and topping patterns can overlap, and in more than a few cases we observe a combination of topping patterns that occur as pieces of the overall topping process. Research in Motion (RIMM) in 2008 is an excellent example of at least two topping formations overlapping. To illustrate this we begin with the RIMM daily chart (Figure 6.16) which shows two distinct patterns up around the top between early May and late August 2008.

The first breakout occurs right at the very peak of RIMM's long-term upside price move in mid-June from a four-to-five-week base formation. The breakout quickly rolls over into the end of June and breaks to the downside. It was likely not possible to enter a short on the gap-down breakout failure given that the stock was already extended to the downside and well through the 50-day moving average. However, when it comes to short-selling, opportunity can often knock more than once, even twice, within a stock's overall topping phase. As we see in Figure 6.16 RIMM recovers to some extent to form a short, cup-with-handle formation with a handle that is moving straight across rather than drifting slightly lower as is preferred in a proper cup-with-handle formation (See O'Neil's *How to Make Money in Stocks*, 4th edition). Notice that as the stock finishes the handle it wedges up just a bit, logging a VooDoo volume signature as trade declines –36 percent and –37 percent below average on these two days, respectively.

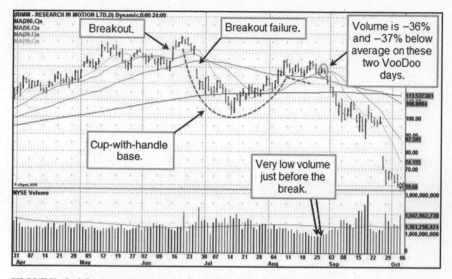

FIGURE 6.16 Research in Motion (RIMM) daily chart 2008.
Chart courtesy of eSignal, Copyright 2010.

This breakdown in late August coincides with the market's breakdown at the same time, as we can reference back to in Figure 6.15. The weakness in the late-stage cup-with-handle formation is accented by the heavy-volume gap-down in late June that marks the right side of the cup in the formation. The rally coming back up into the handle on the right side of the cup shows a general pattern of declining volume as the stock progresses into the end of the handle and flashes two VooDoo days right at the end, just before it begins to break down sharply. This is where the stock can be shorted.

What is most interesting about RIMM, however, is its hybrid combination of two LSFB's teaming up to form an overall head & shoulders topping formation with a "pinhead" that consists of the breakout from the five-week late-stage base up to the stock's ultimate peak in June, and then the one-week decline that marks the breakout's official failure. The handle in the ensuing cup-with-handle formation forms the right shoulder of the head & shoulders formation, which eventually pierces the neckline and plummets to the downside, as we see in Figure 6.17.

RIMM points out the importance of focusing on weak price/volume action within the pattern, looking out for potential VooDoo volume signatures within wedging little rallies or consolidations rather than obsessing over the precise "shape" and "label" you want to give the pattern. Short-sale set-ups all have some basic characteristics that can be summed up as

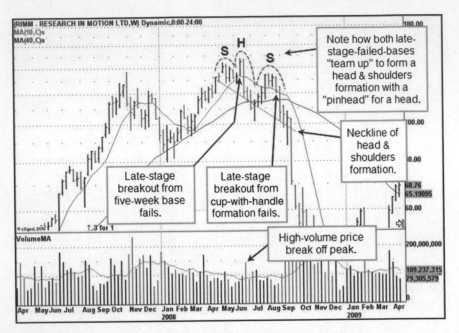

FIGURE 6.17   Research in Motion (RIMM) weekly chart, 2008.
Chart courtesy of eSignal, Copyright 2010.

follows: (1) a big, prior price run-up of several weeks to several months; (2) a high-volume break off the peak that takes the stock below a critical moving average, such as the 50-day or 200-day moving averages; and (3) a series of weak rallies back up into the moving averages where we seek to find optimal short-sale points based on the VooDoo day concept.

Punchbowl of Death (POD) Set-Ups

Late-stage-bases that fail and set-up as LSFBs can often occur from cup-with-handle formations that are wide and loose. When these cups begin to get more than 50 percent deep in what is essentially a rapid price break down from a peak price that follows a prior huge price run-up, they become something more than mere "cups." What they become, quite frankly, are "punchbowls," hence the short-sale set-up and topping formation we refer to as the Punchbowl of Death or POD formation.

The basic concept behind the POD formation is a rapid price run-up in a "hot" leading stock followed by an equally rapid price decline of more than 50 percent. When the stock declines so sharply, investors who missed the first run to the upside see the stock as extremely "cheap," driving the

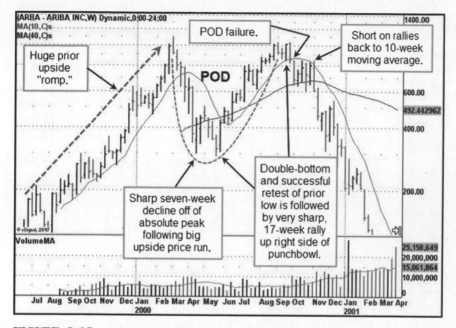

FIGURE 6.18 Ariba Corp. (ARBA) weekly chart, 2001.
Chart courtesy of eSignal, Copyright 2010.

stock up rapidly back up to its prior highs, giving the impression of a giant double-top, "cup," or as we refer to it, "punchbowl." The problem with a second priced run-up to the right side of the punchbowl is that it is simply too rapid to be sustained, and so it breaks down very quickly from that point. As in the example of Ariba, Corp. (ARBA) in Figure 6.18, a high-volume failure of the peak of the punchbowl's right side marks the beginning of the final decline.

ARBA demonstrates this as the POD failure occurs with the stock breaking the 10-week (50-day) moving average on very heavy volume. Several rallies back up into the 10-week line occur before one last rally precedes a final break through the 40-week (200-day) moving average, after which the stock plummets precipitously. In most cases a POD should be of a short time duration, anywhere from 28 to 40 weeks or more, but often the shorter the better. ARBA has a 26–28 week long POD formation in the example shown, but in longer POD formations, such as we will see in Charles Schwab Corp. (SCHW), the formation can be a year in duration but should also have a very sharp run up the right side of the punchbowl. It is the rapid run-up to old highs in a former, beaten-down leader that is the critical characteristic in any POD that determines whether the formation

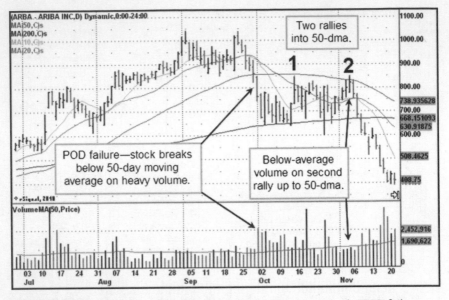

FIGURE 6.19 Ariba Corp. (ARBA) daily chart, 2001. Shorting the POD failure. Chart courtesy of eSignal, Copyright 2010.

is sustainable and hence prone to failure. Long, rambling punch bowl-like formations with gradual slopes up the right side of the formation are not what we are looking for in a POD.

As the daily chart of ARBA shows (Figure 6.19) the mechanics of shorting a POD failure are very familiar since they do not differ very much from what we've seen in our previous discussions of the head & shoulders and LSFB set-ups. Essentially, a breakdown from the peak of the right side of the POD occurs on heavy volume as the stock breaks through the 50-day moving average until it finds support at the 200-day moving average and rallies back up into the 50-day moving average at point 1. Another test of the 200-day is followed by another rally at point 2 right into the 50-day moving average, and this rally occurs on a number of below-average volume days. Both points 1 and 2 would serve as logical short-sale entry points, and profit-taking rules would likely have you covering around the 200-day moving average and then shorting the second rally into the 50-day moving average at point 2 on the chart. In this example the rallies pushed right into the 50-day moving average and were halted in their tracks at the line. In other cases, as with head & shoulders and LSFB short-sale set-ups, the stocks often will rally to points just above the 50-day moving average after the initial breakout failure off the right side of the POD.

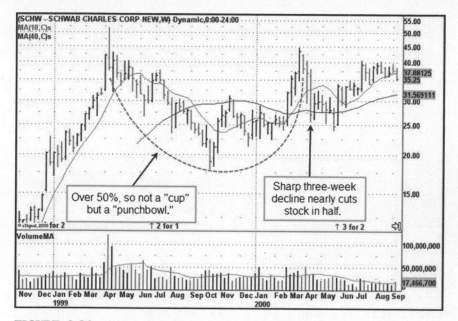

FIGURE 6.20 Charles Schwab Corp. (SCHW) weekly chart, 1999–2000. Chart courtesy of eSignal, Copyright 2010.

Charles Schwab Corp. (SCHW) in 1999–2000 is an example of a longer-term POD that is nearly a year in duration (Figure 6.20). In this case the stock displays a necessary characteristic for such a long-duration POD formation to be valid as a short-sale set-up, and that is the very rapid, four-week price run-up on the right side of the one-year-long punchbowl. This rally closes in new high price ground on a weekly basis before immediately gapping down the next week and beginning a rapid descent that takes the stock down about 40 percent. Had SCHW instead rambled higher, slowly climbing up the right side of the punchbowl, it would likely not have had a sharp break off the peak. The rapid run up the right side does not allow for any consolidations that would weed out weak hands and bring in strong hands as the stock builds a base, moves up, builds another base, and moves up in a slow-moving ascent. By running up so sharply, the stock creates a lot of weak hands who are now seeing a big profit in the stock they bought lower in the POD and are likely to sell, as well as catching some overhead supply from the left side of the formation from investors who bought near the peak in March 1999. For these reasons, as well as the action of the general market which topped in March 2000, SCHW's POD failure worked very well on the short side.

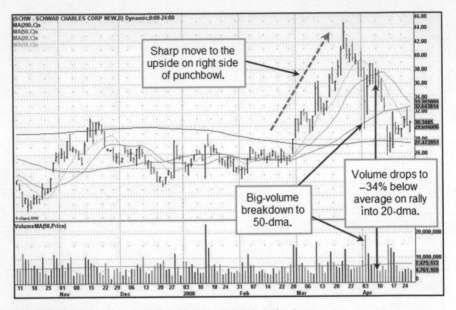

FIGURE 6.21   Charles Schwab Corp. (SCHW) daily chart.
Chart courtesy of eSignal, Copyright 2010.

The daily chart of SCHW (Figure 6.21) shows the rapid ascent up the right side of the POD and the subsequent breakdown back through the 20-day moving average on the down side. This results in a very sharp break down to the 50-day moving average, at which point the stock bounces violently back up into just above the 20-day moving average. The stock backs down below the 20-day moving average and the third day up around the 20-day moving average flashes a volume dry-up (VDU) or VooDoo volume signature as trade drops to –34 percent below average. This is the point at which to short the stock. Later on, once the stock drops below the 50-day moving average, rallies up into the 50-day line to become shortable as we see on the very far right of the daily chart in Figure 6.21. Another example observed at the same time and which played out very similarly to SCHW, but which we do not show here, was America Online (AOL) in 1998–2000. We leave it to the reader to investigate AOL (at one time TWX following the merger with Time-Warner Co.) on their own.

During the 2007 general market rally otherwise "dull" shipping stocks, that is, the stocks of companies that put "stuff" on big boats and move them around the globe so consumers around the world can get their "stuff," became all the rage as the group launched on a massive upside price run. The leader of the pack at that time was Dryships, Inc. (DRYS) which had a tremendously steep upside price run through most of the year

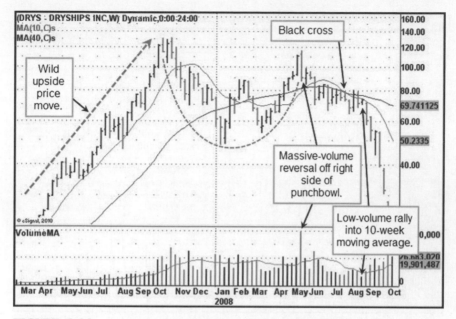

FIGURE 6.22 Dryships, Inc. (DRYS) weekly chart, 2007–2008. Chart courtesy of eSignal, Copyright 2010.

(Figure 6.22). When the general market topped in October 2007, the shippers, as one of the big "darling" groups in the bull rally, topped with it. DRYS, and its shipping brethren all collapsed, plummeting over 50 percent from their bull market price peaks, as we see in DRYS' weekly chart. In January 2008, however, the stock found a bottom, retested it once on the weekly chart, and then took off on a steep eight-week run up the right side of the POD. Interestingly enough, DRYS has a sharp, climactic type of run at the end of the rally up to the peak on the right side of the POD, which is potential topping action that should be watched for as a stock comes up the right side of a POD. This can provide a clue that is useful in developing conviction to short the stock once you see the first high-volume reversal at the peak on the right side.

When viewed on a weekly chart, DRYS short-sale set-up looks almost exactly like a POD that was formed by Reading Railroad in 1907. Copyright issues prevent me from showing that chart here, but it is fascinating to see the exact same pattern work the exact same way, even though they occurred 100 years apart. But then, as O'Neil and his predecessor like to say, the stock market is simply human nature on parade, and as long as human psychology remains the same we can expect that the same chart patterns and set-ups, whether on the long side or the short side, will continue to reappear both now and into the indefinite future.

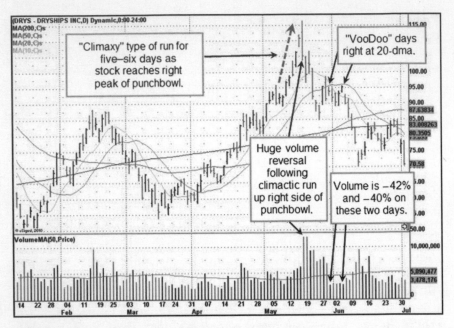

FIGURE 6.23 Dryships, Inc. (DRYS) daily chart, 2008.
Chart courtesy of eSignal, Copyright 2010.

After running rapidly up the right side of the POD, DRYS quickly flames out as it reverses on very heavy volume, breaks down below its 10-week (50-day) and 40-week (200-day) moving averages, and then proceeds to bump up into both of those moving averages for the next 11 weeks before blowing apart completely as the general market broke down in September 2008 (refer to Figure 6.15)

You can see in Figure 6.23 that DRYS looks very similar to ARBA and SCHW on the daily chart, reversing sharply on huge volume right off the peak of the right side of the POD, crashing down through first the 20-day moving average before rallying up into the 20-day line twice with volume drying up sharply on two VooDoo days right at the line, as the daily chart shows. The second rally up to the 20-day moving average reversed as volume that was –40 percent below average indicated a severe lack of demand for the stock at that point, and so it gapped down the next day as volume picked up meaningfully. Once the stock breaks down through the 50-day and 200-day moving averages, those moving averages become reference points for short-sale points as the stock rallies twice up into its 200-day moving average before rolling over again in early July 2008. One of the things working against the POD at the peaks are the mad rushes to the upside that characterize both the left and right peaks of the POD formation. The first one on the left side results from a normal, but sharp bull market–related rally in the stock, usually a stock that is considered one of the hot leaders of any particularly bull market phase. The second rush up the right side of the POD occurs so quickly, without ever taking time to shake out weak hands and bring more strong hands into the stock, so that the wild run becomes unsustainable. DRYS' run up the right side of the POD gets so out-of-control that it culminates in a climactic-type of five-to-six-day run to the peak before the stock reverses back to the downside. The stock is often shortable on the first high-volume reversal off the peak on the daily chart, but once it breaks, the 20-day moving average rallies back up into the 20-day line and can be used to short into as they come up on weak volume, certainly like the VooDoo volume signature days seen at the 20-day in the DRYS example.

Another instructive Punchbowl of Death short-sale set-up can be found in Apple, Inc. (AAPL) during late 2007 into September 2008, which actually began forming its POD top with a late-stage-failed-base (LSFB) short-sale set-up in late 2007, as we see in the weekly chart (Figure 6.24). During the period in which AAPL formed its POD top, other "big stocks" of the bull market that ended in late 2007 like Baidu, Inc. (BIDU) and First Solar (FSLR) formed POD tops of their own, roughly in synchrony with AAPL. We leave it to readers to investigate those on their own and instead focus

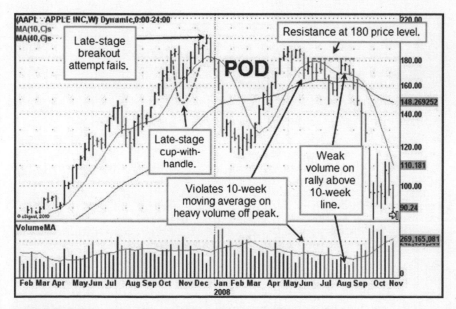

FIGURE 6.24 Apple, Inc. (AAPL) weekly chart, 2007–2008.
Chart courtesy of eSignal, Copyright 2010.

on AAPL. Following the late-stage failure in late 2007–early 2008, AAPL's stock price was cut nearly in half in six short, brutal weeks. It then bottomed after 12 weeks and turned to the upside, scampering back toward the 200 price level in a mere eight weeks. This made the entire POD a short 20 weeks in duration. AAPL was a "big stock" favorite in the immediately prior bull market, and so it spent a lot of time bouncing between its 50-day moving average and resistance at the 180 price level on the upside, and the 200-day moving average on the downside, before finally giving way and splitting wide open in conjunction with the market break in September 2008.

We will split the view of AAPL's price/volume action during 2007–2008 on the weekly chart (Figure 6.24) into two daily charts for a more detailed look at how AAPL broke down on both the left and right sides of the punchbowl. Figure 6.25 shows the breakdown from the late-stage cup-with-handle formation AAPL formed in late 2007, moving higher even after the general market had topped in late October 2007 before it finally topped in late December. Note that once AAPL broke down through both the 20-day and 50-day moving averages, it only spent another six days backing and filling as it wedged up into its 50-day moving average on weak volume. The rallies into the 50-day line were the optimal short-sale points, and put you in position to benefit from the ensuing, sharp break to the downside

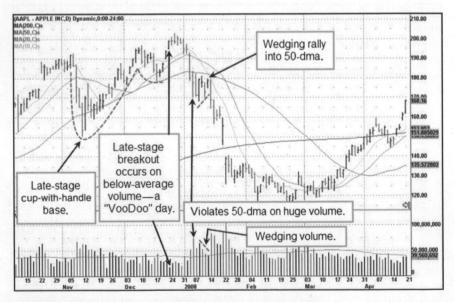

FIGURE 6.25   Apple, Inc. (AAPL) daily chart, 2007–2008.
Chart courtesy of eSignal, Copyright 2010.

that extended into February of 2008. It is interesting to note that the break-out day for AAPL came on VooDoo volume that was –56 percent, less than half, of average daily trading volume for the stock. This was a clear sign of a lack of demand for AAPL as it cleared to new highs and failed to hold the highly-publicized 200 price level.

AAPL's move into the 200 price level was reminiscent of Jesse Livermore's comments regarding his play in Anaconda Copper back in 1907, when he said, "It was an old trading theory of mine that when a stock crosses 100 or 200 or 300 for the first time the price does not stop there but goes a good deal higher, so that if you buy it as soon as it crosses the line it is almost certain to show you a profit." When Anaconda Copper cleared the 300 price level for the first time in 1907, Livermore observed the action in the stock, "I figured that when it crossed 300 it ought to keep on going and probably touch 340 in a jiffy." Anaconda, however did not act as it should, and Livermore noted that "Anaconda opened at 298 and went up to 302¾ but pretty soon it began to fade away. I made up my mind that if Anaconda went back to 301 it was a fake movement. On a legitimate advance the price should have gone to 310 without stopping. If instead it reacted it meant that precedents had failed me and I was wrong; and the only thing to do when a man is wrong is to be right by ceasing to be wrong" (Edwin Lefevre, *Reminiscences of a Stock Operator Illustrated* [Hoboken: John Wiley & Sons, 2004], 101). A modern-day example of Anaconda Copper, AAPL could not clear the 200 price level in late December 2007, and that action was further confirmation of its bearish, topping action, and the stock began to break down rapidly.

Once AAPL had broken down into the February 2008 lows, it began to turn in March and rallied back up in an eight-week rush into the right peak of the POD formation (Figure 6.26). Note that as AAPL came up to the peak, upside volume was below average, while two above-average selling spikes hit the stock on the way up. The stock made a little double-top right around the 190 price area, with weak –36 percent below-average volume on the second top.

Once AAPL began to fail off the right side of the POD, it took several weeks before it completely broke to the downside at the same time that the general market broke in September 2008. The last-gasp rally that AAPL logged when it pushed up into logical resistance at the 180 price level was the optimal spot to begin shorting the stock. Note also that there is a little, wedging (e.g., up on the day with very light volume) day with volume –45 percent below average, a VooDoo volume signature. Shortly thereafter the stock begins to roll over and busts through all of its moving averages in a matter of days as the general market began a very sharp down leg in September. It is important to note that short-sale reference points occurred throughout the backing-and-filling phase that began in late June and

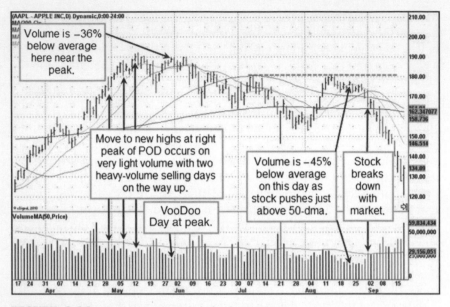

FIGURE 6.26 Apple, Inc. (AAPL) daily chart, 2008.
Chart courtesy of eSignal, Copyright 2010.

continued until the stock split wide open in September. In most cases, light-volume moves up into or just above a key moving average or a logical area of support, such as the 180 price level in AAPL's daily chart, were the best spots to short shares of AAPL in 2008.

Some of the most rapidly-rewarding POD formations to play can be those that occur in very "hot" IPOs such as the solar stocks in 2007–2008. Hot IPO merchandise can often start "flying off the shelves" when a particular theme catches the investing community's eye, such as the Internet stocks in 1999–2000 or the solar stocks in 2007–2008. Often, hot IPO stocks that go straight up have a nasty habit of coming straight down, particularly if they are coming in on the tail end of all the excitement over a particular theme, such as Trina Solar (TSL) was in 2007 (Figure 6.27). TSL had a great move from its initial IPO date in late 2006, but after that it had several failed breakout attempts from what were essentially IPO POD type formations in that they had the straight up and then straight down, followed by straight up again, look that typifies these unsustainable, speculative rocket moves in such stocks.

TSL's weekly chart in Figure 6.27 actually shows two shortable POD formations, a "double-POD" rarity. These are both very short patterns of about 8 weeks and 12 weeks, respectively, and both PODs have a right peak that is characterized by a high-volume reversal week on the chart.

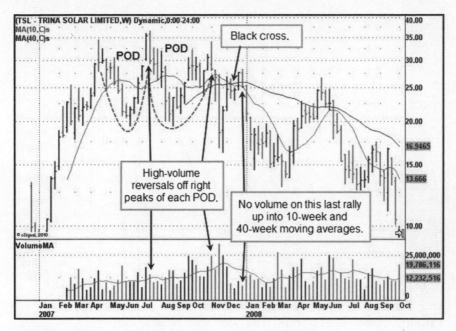

FIGURE 6.27   Trina Solar Ltd. (TSL) weekly chart, 2007.
Chart courtesy of eSignal, Copyright 2010.

If we break this down into two separate daily charts for each POD formation (Figures 6.28 and 6.29), we see that the mechanics are roughly the same as we've seen in the prior POD examples of ARBA, SCHW, and AAPL that we've discussed previously. The first POD that TSL formed is shown in Figure 6.28, and again we see the high-volume reversal right off the right peak of the POD, marking the end of the stock's upside rush. This is then followed by a series of jerks back up into the 32 price level that start to define a clear area of resistance. On the third and fourth rallies up into and around the area defined by the 20-day moving average and the 32 price level resistance, volume begins to lag, and the stock becomes shortable at this point. The breakdown is very rapid from that point.

The breakdown off the right side of the POD that TSL formed in Figure 6.28 led to another wild, upside rally, but in this case the stock pauses to form a handle through most of October 2008 (Figure 6.29). When it tries to break out, the high-volume reversal off the peak of the right side of the POD rears its head yet again in this example and clocks the stock, knocking it straight down through its 20-day, 50-day, and 200-day moving averages in a matter of three days. The stock then rallies weakly back up into the 50-day moving average before breaking down and gapping lower. You

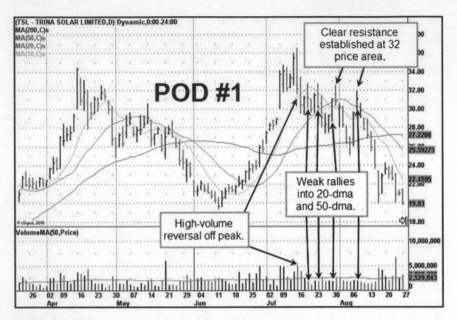

FIGURE 6.28 Trina Solar Ltd. (TSL) daily chart, 2008.
Chart courtesy of eSignal, Copyright 2010.

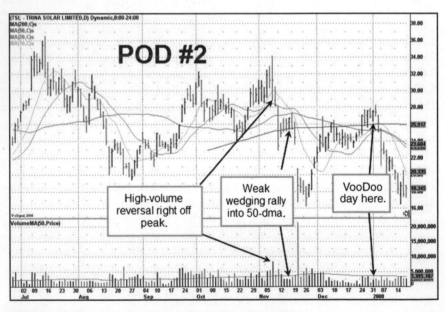

FIGURE 6.29 Trina Solar Ltd. (TSL) daily chart, 2008.
Chart courtesy of eSignal, Copyright 2010.

can here see why taking profits when a short-sale position becomes extended to the downside is critical in handling these types of plays. After the sharp gap-down in mid-November TSL, it then rallies back up into the 50-day and 200-day moving averages before it finally flashes a low-volume VooDoo day at the peak of a rally into the end of December 2007 and then rolls over altogether.

Other examples of IPO PODs during the solar stock craze of late 2007 are Yingli Green Energy (YGE) and LDK Solar Ltd. (LDK), which readers can study on their own.

The Punchbowl of Death short-sale set-up and topping formation can be a very rewarding one, particular if a short-seller is able to identify the "rush" up the right side of the POD and wait for the first high-volume reversal day to short the stock off the right peak. Some very quick, sharp profits can be gained thereby, as the examples we've discussed have demonstrated, but once the stock has broken down off the right side there are numerous areas and points where the stock can be shorted again as one "campaigns" it on the short side.

SHORTING ROCKET STOCKS

A high-probability short-selling method we've discovered, which is unrelated to the normal types of short-sale situations we look for in the head & shoulders, late-stage-failed-based, and Punchbowl of Death short-sale set-ups is what we call Exploding Rocket Stocks. Rocket stocks are defined as "hot" stocks that move at least 4.5 times from their high-volume launch point, which usually occurs on a breakout from some sort of consolidation on volume that is greater than twice the normal average daily volume. The 4.5-fold move generally occurs in four weeks or less as these stocks launch like "nuclear" rocket stocks. But after launch, nuclear rockets eventually blow apart, and history has shown that these rocket stocks do the same, usually within a few weeks after their launch. Thus, ample profit opportunities abound by going short at the right time, and the time value can be enormous. Rocket stocks are shorted after their high volume climax run as they break below any day's intraday low, which generally is the first sign that the climax top is at its end. While this is a risky, more volatile technique, the reward is that the odds are fantastic. 95.7 percent of all rocket stocks short-sale set-ups from 1991–2008 were profitable, and 84.2 percent of all rocket stocks short-sale set-ups fell at least 50 percent off their absolute price peak on the "rocket ride." Knowing this, it can be advantageous to pyramid your short position as the stock continues to fall to potentially –50 percent from its peak.

The risk is that the 4.3 percent of stocks that don't work will hit their sell stops, which we place at the absolute high of the pattern. Thus, you will know your exact risk in percentage before placing the trade, and there it is imperative that you size your positions accordingly. Your stop might be quite a distance from where you initially shorted the stock, so that 15.8 percent of the time, expect to have to hold a position that could go against you by more than 17 percent before becoming profitable. But the upside is that this means that 84.2 percent of the time your position will go against you by less than 17 percent before you reap a substantial profit. While these percentages can be tough to sit through, knowing that 95.7 percent of these patterns are profitable, with 84.2 percent of them being substantially profitable should greatly help your confidence.

It is safest to cover your position once the stock has fallen 50 percent from its peak since most stocks fall at least 50 percent from their peak before staging a potentially large rebound. For potentially higher profits, you can cover half your position and wait to see how the stock behaves before covering the other half.

Also, for stocks that move up at least 6.5-fold from their launch point price, 65 of 66 rocket stocks that we studied fell at least 50 percent from their peak. If we include the examples from the climax top in March 2000, the tally increases to 73 of 77 rocket stocks that fell at least 50 percent from their peak.

Note, for 2009, the black swan year, most of all the junk-off-the-bottom stocks that went up in price at least 4.5 times did so over a period of more than four weeks, so these would not qualify as rocket stock short-sale candidates. Remember that we are looking for "nuclear rocket-powered" thrust; thus stocks that qualify are those that streak higher in price at least 4.5 times in usually four weeks or less. Such behavior is rare; thus there are typically only a couple of such stocks that behave this way in any given year. But when you do spot such a stock, your risk/reward is extremely favorable. That said, obtaining a proper borrow from your broker in these stocks, which tend to be thinner, smaller names, is not always easy, and we have found that we are only able to borrow such stocks for short-selling for half the stocks that show up as rocket stock short-sale candidates. When the set-up is right, and the stock's shares can be borrowed for shorting, we have found that such situations can almost be like "free money."

Let's look at an example of a rocket stock set-up in Interdigital, Inc. (IDCC) during 1999–2000 (Figure 6.30). In highly unusual situations, after a stock has moved up at least 4.5 times its launch price in four weeks or less, a stock might settle down, tighten up, and move sideways in a constructive manner, which is what we are initially looking for in a proper "launch point" for the stock. Note that if a stock trades sideways for more than two weeks, such as IDCC did from late November 1999 to early December, then

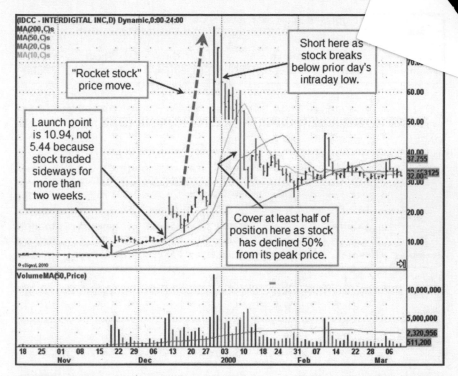

FIGURE 6.30 Interdigital, Inc. (IDCC) daily chart, 1999–2000. A "rocket stock" short-sale set-up.
Chart courtesy of eSignal, Copyright 2010.

its launch point price is reset. Thus, after this November–December consolidation of more than two weeks duration, IDCC's launch point is reset to 10.94, from 5.44, the high of the prior consolidation that the stock hit about ⅔ of the way through November 1999.

Once the stock tops, the first day down off the peak is your reference day, using the low of that day's trading range as your trigger for the short sale. In the IDCC example, this would have been triggered on the second day following the peak, when it dropped below the intraday low of the first day off the peak.

Keep in mind that with these rocket stock set-ups we are looking for massive thrust, and this thrust can occur with low-priced stocks, so while the price of the stock may be well under what we would ever consider buying, history shows that such stocks offer excellent short-sale set-ups, and such stocks will attract massive levels of volume from their launch point, so that getting the stock borrow in order to legally initiate your short position is possible.

TABLE 6.1 Examples of Short-Sale Set-Ups Observed Between 1998 and 2004

Examples	Launch Point Date	Launch Point	Peak	Gain (x-times)	Short Short Date	Short Point
IDCC	12/10/1999	10.94	82	7.5	01/03/2000	62.9
OXGN	05/20/2003	2.3	19.4	8.4	06/11/2003	11.25
SIEB	02/01/1999	12.31	70.63	5.7	02/05/1999	42.69
MACE	04/05/2004	2.11	14.8	7.0	04/14/2004	9.61
IDSA	02/06/2004	2.38	23.75	10.0	03/03/2004	19.7
UBID	12/18/1998	36.94	189	5.1	12/24/1998	147.9

Examples	Failure Cover Point	Max % Against*	Actual % Goes Against**	Falls >50 % from Peak?	Reward at 50 % from Peak	Trading Days to 50 % Reward Point
IDCC	82.1	30.52%	25.60%	y	34.8%	7
OXGN	19.5	73.33%	14.60%	y	13.8%	7
SIEB	70.73	65.68%	0.00%	y	17.3%	<1
MACE	14.9	55.05%	0.00%	y	23.0%	<1
IDSA	23.85	21.07%	9%	y	39.7%	54
UBID	189.1	27.86%	8.40%	y	36.1%	12

*This would be the maximum percent your initial short entry would move against you, which is the high of the pattern.
**This is the actual percent your initial short entry moved against you, which is far less than the maximum. Thus in practice, the risk in these short-sale set-ups is manageable, especially when considering that such patterns have a high probability of breaking down to 50 percent of their peak price.

Table 6.1 shows the statistics for six rocket stock short-sale set-ups observed between 1998 and 2004, including the IDCC example discussed previously. Even though big gains can be made in a short time, and the odds are greatly in your favor, keep in mind that the amount of room you may need to give such a short-sale set-up might be more than you are normally used to giving, so position size accordingly so that you don't get shaken out of your position prematurely.

CONCLUSION

As we've seen in the numerous examples in this chapter, short-selling can provide a source of quick profits in a bear market. However, playing the short side of a bear market is inherently more risky than playing the long side of a bull market because bear markets tend to have sharper upside "jerks" within their overall downtrends, which can run in short-sellers who come in late on a stock's decline. Timing your short-sales properly, waiting for that proper window of opportunity to develop in conjunction with a breakdown in the general market, is even more important than when buying stocks on the long side of a bull market. Investors who have little experience short-selling should start out with only small capital commitments relative to their overall portfolio value, say 5–10 percent maximum. As one gains great experience one can decide whether one is comfortable taking larger positions. Stay smart from the start!

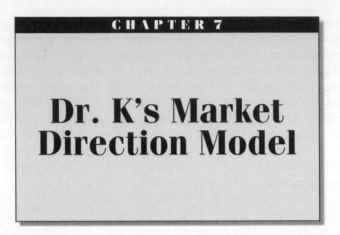

CHAPTER 7

Dr. K's Market Direction Model

I t may seem decidedly *un*-O'Neil to consider using a market direction model, essentially a systematic program for generating valid buy and sell signals for the general market indices. While a market direction model may seem like a "timing model," we do not ascribe that term to it, since it does not adequately describe our approach in using such a model. A market direction model, in contrast to a timing model, should be used as a critical tool in understanding when you are in a bull market, favorable to taking long positions, or in a bear market, favorable to taking short positions. In this chapter we will discuss the refinements that we have incorporated along with basic O'Neil concepts of upside market follow-throughs and downside market distribution days to produce what we consider to be the refined framework of a market direction model, and hopefully clear up some of the confusion surrounding the precise price/volume action that characterizes potential turns and reversals in the direction of the general market direction. Readers who have further questions should contact Dr. Chris Kacher at chris@mokainvestors.com, or can refer to the web site: www.virtueofselfishinvesting.com.

TIMING THE MARKET

A timing system must start by containing internal logic that makes sense; then the system can be built around this internal logic. This is where many years of market experience are necessary. This avoids the black box situation of overfitting data where data is fit to predict the past but has little to no predictive value on the future. Unfortunately, so many timing systems available on the Internet for a subscription fee lack internal logic but manage to boast high theoretical returns because they have overfitted their past data. Such systems are great at predicting the past but fail when tested under real-time market conditions. This is perhaps why such skepticism abounds when the words "timing model" or "timing the market" are mentioned. But just because most timing systems do not work, does not mean all timing systems do not work. We highly recommend Robert Koppel's book *Bulls, Bears, and Millionaires* (Dearborn Financial Publishing, 1997), where the author and Mike Dever discuss the perils of model design and overfitting data.

I have been timing the markets real-time, under fire since 1991, the first successful year where I strongly outperformed the major U.S. market averages. My model is a statistical formalization of price/volume action of the NASDAQ Composite and S&P 500. I developed a set of rules that guides this model and has guided my trading over the years. It is largely responsible for my long-standing track record, as verified by the big four auditor KPMG and for the degree of my exposure to the market on the long or short side. My model keeps me on the right side of the markets as it excels at catching intermediate term trends near their starting points. It has never missed a major drop in the market, including the sudden precipitous drop in October 1997, and has always gotten me on board near the beginning of major bull markets including the challenging year of 2009 when it signaled a major buy on March 12, 2009. That said, sideways, choppy markets are the model's weakness, and drawdowns are almost always the result of such erratic market behavior. Fortunately, such periods are rare. Incidentally, my model was inspired by the "M" in William O'Neil's CAN SLIM. The fourth edition of his book classic *How to Make Money in Stocks* (McGraw-Hill Companies, 2009) that discusses CAN SLIM in detail is now available, and I highly recommend it, even if one has read earlier editions. CAN SLIM screens for stocks that have the characteristics winning stocks tend to share before big price moves, and the "M" is the market timing portion of CAN SLIM.

There has been much confusion over the years about what constitutes a proper distribution day and a proper follow-through day. In the years we worked as portfolio managers for Bill O'Neil, we noticed a degree of confusion even within our group of top-performing portfolio managers that were trading Bill's investment capital. When Bill and I gave investment seminars, we would frequently get asked to give further clarification on distribution days and follow-through days from those who read about the two concepts in *How to Make Money in Stocks*.

Part of the confusion comes from the many possible permutations concerning price/volume action including the shape of the price bar, where it closes in relation to the prior day, the day on which the follow-through day occurs, and how much the NASDAQ Composite or S&P 500 has to fall to initiate a follow-through day count, among other possible issues. The other part of the confusion may come from not having exact rules. For example, some may assert that a day like August 28, 2009, is not a distribution day because the market indices did not fall at least –0.2% on the day. This creates confusion since it does not take into account the *shape* of the price bar, because in fact that day had a long upside tail. If you have a long tail on higher volume, and the NASDAQ Composite closes about even, this is a distribution day since the index tried to move higher earlier in the day but eventually closed at the low end of the range. The shape of this day, therefore, would define it as a distribution day—the intraday rally attempt was met by selling. Requiring the index to fall at least –0.2% before calling a distribution day without taking into careful consideration the shape of the price bar and close seems illogical.

Another part of the confusion comes from high-frequency trading algorithms which can increase volume on the downside during corrections and pullbacks leading to false sell signals. Filtering out this type of trading volume results in fewer false sell signals. While this can somewhat improve results, it is important to note that sell signals in timing systems including one that filters out such high frequency trading volume were largely unprofitable on the short side in 2009 mainly because the overall trend of the market was up. Likewise, buy signals in timing systems were largely unprofitable in 2008 on the long side because the overall trend of the market was down. That said, a good timing system will profit well on true signals while losing little on false signals. Thus even during challenging periods, a timing system's true signals should more than make up for the small losses from false signals. And over the entire cycle, typically three to five years, an excellent timing system should clearly outperform the major market averages.

Distribution Days

A distribution day can be thought of as a trading day where there is more selling pressure than buying pressure on that given day as evidenced by increased volume combined with negative price action, either a down day or a day where the index shows signs of reversal and/or churning. If enough distribution days, usually five, occur within a short time frame of typically 20 trading days or less, then a sell signal is generated. Volume must be higher than the prior day's volume to qualify for a distribution day, but the closing price does not necessarily have to be lower than the prior day's closing price. For example, if the stock has a long upside tail, closing less than 0.1 percent higher on the day and in the lower 25 percent of its daily

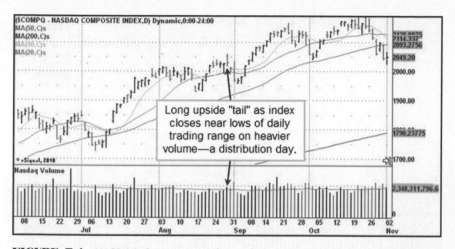

Long upside "tail" as index closes near lows of daily trading range on heavier volume—a distribution day.

FIGURE 7.1 NASDAQ Composite Index. A long upper tail closing near the lows of the day on higher volume is a distribution day.
Chart courtesy of eSignal, Copyright 2010.

trading range on higher volume, then that would be a distribution day. An example of this type of distribution day is shown in Figure 7.1.

Also, if a stock makes little price progress on substantially higher volume on any given day, this can also indicate distribution in the form of churning, a situation where more selling than buying is occurring, but the selling is masked by the fact that the day's closing price closed slightly higher than the closing price the day prior. That said, make sure the big volume is not due to options expiration or index rebalancing, such as occurred on September 18, 2009 (Figure 7.2). Had this been a day where volume was not skewed by the monthly options expiry or periodic index rebalancing, then we would certainly view it as a distribution day. However, because volume may have been skewed by an options expiry on this particular date, it has to be viewed with some skepticism since the market did finish up on the day. If the market had closed down, with a long daily range showing material volatility on the day, then the potentially skewed volume would have to be taken for what it is, a down day on heavier volume, hence a distribution day. In the case of churning with a very narrow daily price range, as in Figure 7.2, this is less clear; thus we are less inclined to see it as a negative day in and of itself. Of course, confirming or disconfirming action over the next few days can help clarify the action on an options expiration day, such as our example in Figure 7.2.

You could also have a situation where the day is lower on higher volume than the prior trading day yet it is not a distribution day because it closes in the top half of its daily trading range for the day and also

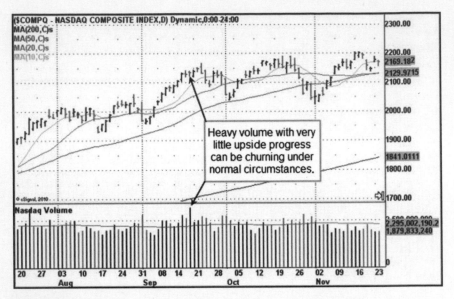

FIGURE 7.2 NASDAQ Composite Index daily chart, March 8, 2008.
Chart courtesy of eSignal, Copyright 2010.

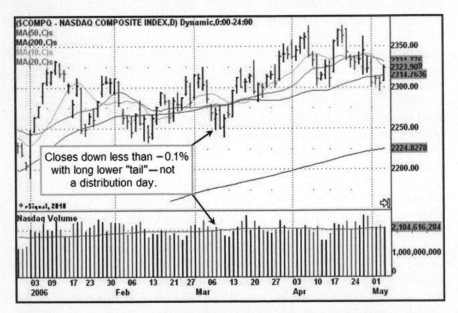

FIGURE 7.3 NASDAQ Composite Index daily chart, March 8, 2006. The index closes down less than –0.1 percent (–0.04 percent in this case) with long lower "tail"—not a distribution day.
Chart courtesy of eSignal, Copyright 2010.

closes down less than –0.1 percent, as Figure 7.3 illustrates. On March 8 the NASDAQ Composite closed down on heavier volume, but because it closed down –0.04 percent and because it closed well in the upper half of its daily trading range, it was not a distribution day. In some cases, this action can actually be viewed as constructive. At the very least, this type of distribution day where the stock has a wide daily range and closes in the uppermost part of the daily range is not in fact a distribution day. We would also view a day where the daily trading range was very narrow, or tight, and the index closed down less than –0.1 percent as not being a distribution day. We find the –0.1 percent downside minimum requirement for a distribution day to be more reliable than using –0.2 percent. Bear in mind that we are not trying to be controversial here; that is simply what the statistical work shows.

One important point in our discussion of distribution days is that we only use the NASDAQ Composite Index to count distribution days. This is because over the past several years we have noticed an increasing number of false sell signals from the S&P 500, which, while often having smaller gains in uptrends or smaller losses in downtrends than the NASDAQ Composite, still carries more noise within its pattern, and thus more risk by way of generating more false signals. For the same reason, and also due to the narrowness of the index, I do not use the Dow Jones Industrial Average, which is an index of only 30 big-cap stocks, which more often than not do not adequately represent the leadership in any bull market.

Follow-Through Days

A follow-through day is a buy signal that usually occurs after the fourth day of a rally attempt. O'Neil used to define a follow-through day as a move of more than 1 percent (the threshold level) on one of the major market indexes on higher volume than the prior day on the fourth through seventh days of a rally attempt off the bottom. This rally attempt by definition occurs after the NASDAQ Composite or S&P 500 has suffered a correction. The rally count begins on the first day the index closes higher after making new lows, but can also begin on the day the index actually closes at a new low but the close is mid-range or higher on the day, indicating potential supporting action off the lows. For example, the mid-range close on massive volume on October 8, 1998 (Figure 7.4), which might otherwise be considered a big distribution day since the index did in fact close down more than –0.1 percent on heavier volume, should actually be considered the first day of a rally attempt and hence the first day in the "rally count." When the index closes mid-range with very heavy volume, it should almost always be viewed as accumulation, not distribution.

In very rare instances, a follow-through day can occur on the third day of the rally attempt but all three days must be up on increasing volume

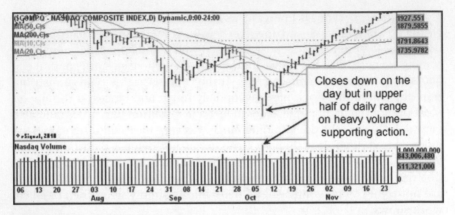

FIGURE 7.4 NASDAQ Composite Index daily chart, October 8, 1998. The index closes in the upper half of its daily trading range on heavy volume, indicating heavy supporting action that qualifies it as the first day of a rally attempt.
Chart courtesy of eSignal, Copyright 2010.

such as January 15–17, 1991, on the NASDAQ Composite, or the prior three weeks must be relatively tight such as the weeks leading up to the follow-through day on January 5, 1987.

Threshold Levels

The threshold level represents the minimum percentage gain that either the NASDAQ Composite or S&P 500 must be up, often on the fourth through seventh days of a rally attempt off the lows (though this is not an absolute requirement) to qualify as a follow-through day. These levels seldom change as the NASDAQ Composite and S&P 500, but at various times O'Neil has adjusted this to 2 percent or 1.7 percent based on his perceived volatility in the indexes. When the indexes have demonstrated over a period of many weeks that their volatility has changed, then O'Neil has more or less eyeballed the required threshold level to adjust for increased or decreased volatility. Adjusting threshold levels for index volatility is correct, in our view, and statistical studies of market volatility and follow-through days over history indicate that the optimal threshold level remained at 1 percent for both indices from 1974 to 1998, then increased to 1.7 percent from January 1998 to December 2002 due to the evident increase in volatility in the months leading up to January 1998. This volatility stayed at a high level over this period, until 2003, when the threshold level was readjusted again to 1.4 percent.

It is important to note that the threshold level is not always the same for both indices, either. In January 2004, it was 1.1 percent for the S&P

500, as this index was showing clear signs of reduced volatility while the NASDAQ Composite's threshold level remained at 1.4 percent. In 2008, when the market's volatility increased again sharply, the threshold level was increased again to 2.1 percent for the NASDAQ Composite Index and 2 percent for the S&P 500 Index. Currently, as of this writing in early 2010, the required percentage increase for the NASDAQ Composite and S&P 500 Indexes to qualify as a follow-through day, their threshold levels, is at 1.5 percent for both indices. Therefore, currently, and keep in mind that this will be adjusted if and as market volatility changes in the future, our definition of a follow-through indicates that the NASDAQ Composite or S&P 500 indexes must be up at least 1.5 percent on increased volume from the prior day, often on the fourth through seventh days of a rally attempt off the bottom.

Fail-Safes

Should the model issue a false signal, fail-safes have been built into the model to minimize drawdowns. This would explain why the maximum drawdown over the model's entire 35-plus year run is just –15.7 percent, yet the model's average annual return between July 1974 and December 2009 is +33.1 percent.

Systematic versus Discretionary

The model's back-tested returns from July 1974 to December 2009 were +33.1 percent annually with a maximum drawdown of –15.7 percent. These theoretical returns were achieved by going 100 percent the NASDAQ Composite Index on a buy signal, going 100 percent short the NASDAQ Composite on a sell signal, or going to 100 percent cash on a cash signal. The signals are purely systematic, so there is no position sizing or override. The NASDAQ 100 Index (QQQQ) ETF makes an excellent proxy for the NASDAQ Composite, but note that the QQQQ did not exist prior to 1999, thus for consistency, we continue to use the NASDAQ Composite as the benchmark for calculating the model's performance based on its systematic signals.

The discretionary portion of the model allows for discretionary override should there be ample evidence to override the systematic signal. There is also discretion with respect to which ETF instrument is used. With 2-times and 3-times leveraged ETFs available for trading these days, leverage can be implemented or adjusted based on the use of such ETFs. This discretion is based on the strength of the signal, so that, theoretically, a very strong buy signal might cause us to buy a 3-times leveraged index ETF, such as the SPXU, for example.

CHART EXAMPLES

What follows are some actual buy and sell signals generated by the model along with our commentary. We have included the most challenging years of our trading careers, namely 2008–2009, so you can see how the model functions when fully challenged by difficult market conditions. We have also included the difficult period known as the Crash of 1929–1930 to show how the model functions in an entirely different era using the same systematic rules. These charts should help give you a clearer understanding of the various types of follow-through days (FTD) and distribution days (DD) that can occur. Readers who have further questions should contact Dr. Chris Kacher at chris@mokainvestors.com, or can refer to the web site address www.virtueofselfishinvesting.com.

A few notes about the charts:

- Black tick marks correspond to distribution days (unless the black tick has an explanation saying it is not a DD). "B" corresponds to a buy signal, "S" corresponds to a sell signal, and "N" corresponds to a neutralization of the immediate prior signal, whether buy or sell.
- Buy signals are neutralized during the trading day once the NASDAQ Composite trades below the lower of the following: (1) the low of the buy signal day or (2) in the case of a gap-up, the closing price the day before the gap-up buy signal day. Of course, if a sell signal occurs, the buy signal is neutralized. If the NASDAQ Composite has hit new intraday highs for at least five trading days since the buy signal, then reverses, the buy signal is neutralized once the close of the day on which the buy signal occurred is exceeded on the downside.
- Sell signals are neutralized during the trading day once the high of the sell signal standby day is exceeded on the upside, or if a buy signal occurs before then.
- Once a number of distribution days are reached within a brief period, usually five in a rolling 20-day period, the model goes to "sell signal standby." Once the low of the sell signal standby day is exceeded to the downside, the model issues a sell signal.
- After a buy signal, there may be distribution days that had accumulated before the buy signal day. Thus, a new sell signal standby could be issued if the next distribution day occurred within the 20-day rolling time-frame period. To reduce the number of false sell signals, the model cannot go to sell signal standby on the first distribution day after the buy signal is issued unless that distribution day went below the low of the day on which the buy signal occurred.

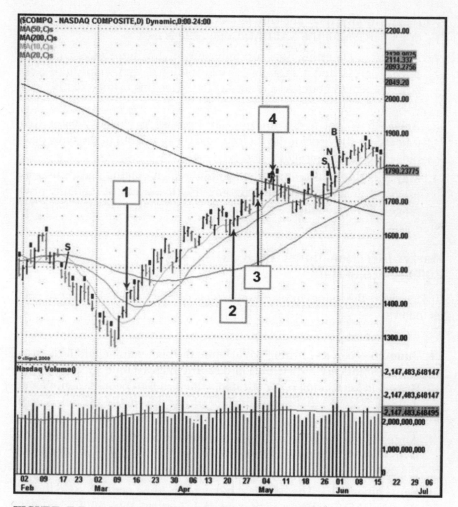

FIGURE 7.5 NASDAQ Composite Index daily chart 2009.
Chart courtesy of eSignal, Copyright 2010.

Market Direction Model Analysis
2009—First Half

We can follow the model's interpretation of the market action in Figure 7.5, the first half of 2009, as follows:

1. **March 12** = third day of rally attempt for NASDAQ Composite, which in this case and as in most cases is too soon. However, this is the fifth day in a rally attempt for the S&P 500 and thus counts as a

follow-through day. The threshold level of 2 percent for the S&P 500 or 2.1 percent for the NASDAQ Composite is met.

2. **April 22** = Churning days are unusually high-volume days with little price progress, and thus qualify as distribution days. Volume here is not large enough to count as a churning day, thus this is not a distribution day.

3. **April 30** = Not a distribution day because it closed greater than 0.1 percent above prior day's close, and the upper tail of the daily price range is not long enough.

4. **May 6** = Not a churning day despite the high volume and little price progress, thus not a distribution day. The lower tail of the daily price range was long enough.

Market Direction Model Analysis 2009—Second Half

In Figure 7.6, the model interpreted signals during the second half of 2009 as follows:

1. **June 26** = Not a churning day despite the high volume and little price progress thus not a distribution day. The high volume was due to the Russell indices being reconstituted, which caused people to move into and out of stocks that were added or dropped from the various Russell indices, thus artificially boosting and skewing the overall volume.

2. **August 28** = Distribution day because the index closes down less than 0.1 percent above the prior day's close and in the lower 25 percent of the daily trading range, giving it a long "upper tail."

3. **September 16** = The S&P 500 Index is up +1.53 percent even though the NASDAQ Composite is only up +1.45 percent, thus the +1.5 percent threshold level requirement is met on at least one of these two indices.

4. **September 18** = Churning days are unusually high volume days with little price progress, and thus qualify as distribution days. Churning days also tend to have wider intraday price ranges. This was thus not a churning day and therefore not a distribution day. Volume was artificially high due to options expiration.

5. **October 6** = The rally attempt count was not reset because the NASDAQ Composite Index corrected less than 6 percent, thus is still in its original rally attempt and qualifies as a follow-through day. This is an example of an unusual situation where the follow-through day occurs well past the 7th day of the rally attempt.

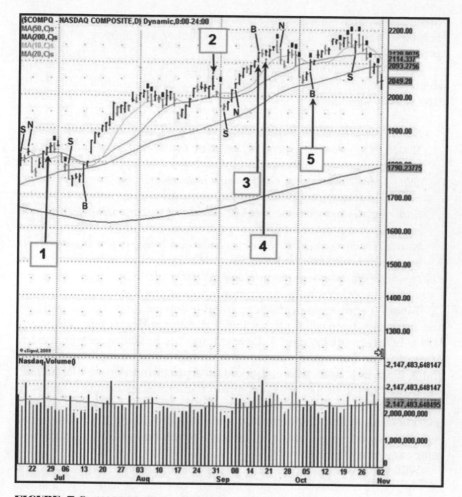

FIGURE 7.6 NASDAQ Composite Index daily chart, 2009.
Chart courtesy of eSignal, Copyright 2010.

2009 Commentary

The year 2009 was what William O'Neil himself called the most challenging year of his career, a career that spans over half a century! It was a year led by junk-off-the-bottom (JOB) stocks, while the more quality names often floundered. Many technical indicators that had worked for many years stopped working in 2009 since 2009 was the year of the Fed "funny money" market manipulations as the Federal Reserve, in concert with central banks around the globe, injected huge amounts of liquidity into the financial system while holding interest rates near zero. Every time a correction seemed imminent in 2009, the market would stabilize and turn back up to new highs, as it ground its way higher in a choppy, whipsawed uptrend.

Even the Decision Moose market timing site run by William Dirlam, which has a sound track record, wrote the following in their January 15, 2010, weekly summary:

> *Looking back, 2009 was the worst year I can remember for the Moose (+1 percent), especially relative to the S&P (+26 percent). Of the last four non-cash switches post-2008 crash, two (T-bonds and gold) were losers. One (EPP) was a winner, and the latest (ILF) is flat to slightly underwater. It shows how government intervention can distort normal market activity by truncating trends and causing price spikes (bonds) and collapses (gold). It also shows how extremely volatile price action can render an intermediate term trend-following mechanism virtually useless in the short term. (www.decisionmoose.com/uploads/2010.01.15.pdf).*

Table 7.1 shows top-performing trend-following funds whose portfolio managers have been celebrated in Jack Schwager's *Market Wizards* books, Michael Covel's book *Trend Following*, and the highly successful Turtles investors. The Turtles were spawned from market wizards Richard Dennis and William Eckhardt, who embarked on a program to prove that individuals who had the proper psychological characteristics could be taught to trade profitably. In the process, many of the individuals they trained went on to become highly respected and successful traders in their own right. As you can see from the table, many had a tough time in 2009 despite their prior exemplary track records.

William O'Neil used to tell us that new bull markets always are around the corner. The window of opportunity will open once again. One just has to have patience and not take one's eye off the ball. That said, our Market Direction Test Fund, which we began with actual money on June 1, 2009, finished the year up nearly 30 percent after fees, and is up 53.8 percent after fees as of May 31, 2010. Despite the many false signals generated in 2009, the Dr. K Market Direction model made significantly more profit in correct signals than losses it took in false signals. This is due to a fail-safe that is built into the model, as I discussed earlier.

The first highly profitable signal for the market direction model in 2009 was in gold. Gold had a perfect set-up, breaking out on September 2, 2009, (Figure 7.7), a breakout equivalent to earlier pocket pivot and standard base breakouts in gold seen in September of 2007, just before the yellow metal went on a sharp upside price run.

TABLE 7.1 Trend Following Wizards 2009 Performance

Fund Name	Assets Under Management	2009 Performance (percent)
Abraham Trading	N/A	−5.56%
Aspect Capital	$473 million	−9.11%
Chesapeake Capital	N/A	+0.41%
Clarke Capital	$1.046 million	−29.78%
Drury Capital	$18 million	+9.05%
Dunn Capital	$151 million	−0.58%
Eckhardt Trading	$220 million	−4.80%
EMC Capital	$445 million	−14.29%
Hawksbill Capital	$212 million	−15.32%
Hyman Beck & Co.	$51 million	+3.96%
JWH & Co.	$462 million	−17.28%
Man AHL Diversified	$18 million	−16.40%
Millburn Ridgefield	$1.414 million	−8.66%
M Rabar Market Res.	$1.137 million	+6.93%
Saxon Investment	$222 million	+10.37%
Superfund	$11 million	−24.46%
Transtrend	N/A	−11.28%
Winton Capital	$4.768 million	−4.63%

Source: Jez Liberty, www.automated-trading-system.com/.

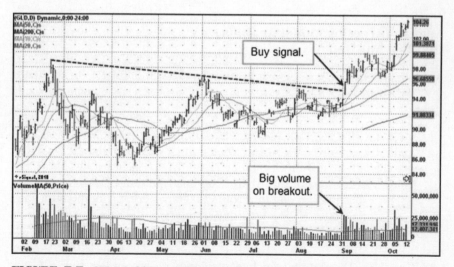

FIGURE 7.7 SPDR Gold Trust ETF (GLD) daily chart, 2009. Gold breaks out in early September 2009, issuing a clear buy signal before trending sharply higher. Chart courtesy of eSignal, Copyright 2010.

Using the discretionary portion of the model, whereby we use the strength and context of the buy signal to determine which ETF vehicle to use, leveraged positions were taken in gold and gold-related instruments such as the Market Vectors Gold Miners Index ETF (GDX) and the GLD. The model also did well in July on the long side in the NASDAQ Composite and S&P 500 indices when it took positions in the 2-times leveraged NASDAQ 100 Index ETF (QLD) and the 3-times leveraged S&P 500 Index ETF (UPRO). Thus, during the June 1, 2009, to December 31, 2009, period, the model did very well the few times it was right, which more than offset the far more frequent times it was wrong. However, each false signal resulted in relatively tiny losses when it was stopped out, thus the Market Direction Model fund was able to finish June 1, 2009, to December 31, 2009, up nearly +30% after fees.

Note that in the FAQ section, which follows later in this chapter, there is a discussion of the hypothetical performance the model might have had in 2009 by going 100 percent long or 100 percent short the 3-times leveraged Direxion Technology Bull ETF (TYH) purely on buy, sell, or neutral signals issued by the systematic model. During the test period from the March 12, 2009, follow-through day to August 24 2009, the date the calculations were made, a return of +90 percent could have been made, while keeping in mind one would have had to sit through a drawdown of −18.4 percent (Figure 7.12).

Market Direction Model Analysis
2008—First Half

The first half of 2008 is shown in Figure 7.8. The numbers in the figure correspond as follows:

1. **January 2** = Buy signal is neutralized intraday as the NASDAQ Composite Index moves below the closing price of December 20, 2007, before the gap-up day on December 21, 2007 (see "A few notes about the charts" at the start of this Chart Examples section). Because today is the fifth distribution day in a rolling 20-day period, the model issues a sell signal standby. The next day, January 3, the model issues a sell signal as the NASDAQ Composite moves below the low of the standby sell signal day.

2. **May 14** = Distribution day because index closes up less than 0.1 percent over the prior day's close and in the lower 25 percent of the daily price range.

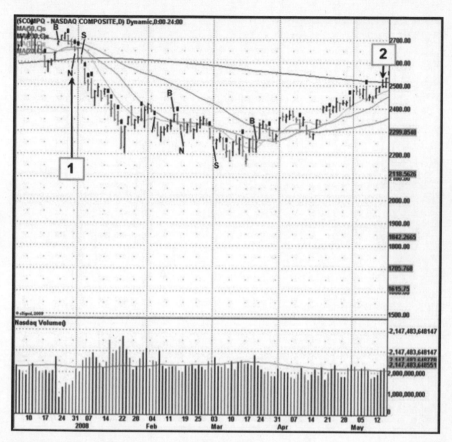

FIGURE 7.8 NASDAQ Composite Index daily chart 2008.
Chart courtesy of eSignal, Copyright 2010.

Market Direction Model Analysis
2008—Second Half

Figure 7.9 shows the NASDAQ during the second half of 2009, with the model interpreting the action as follows:

1. **May 16** = Distribution day because closes down –0.19 percent, more than –0.1 percent.

2. **June 12** = Not a distribution day for two reasons: (1) closed in top three-quarters of day's trading range and (2) was up more than 0.1 percent. Nevertheless, the prior day's sell signal standby went to sell signal today since its intraday low had been broken.

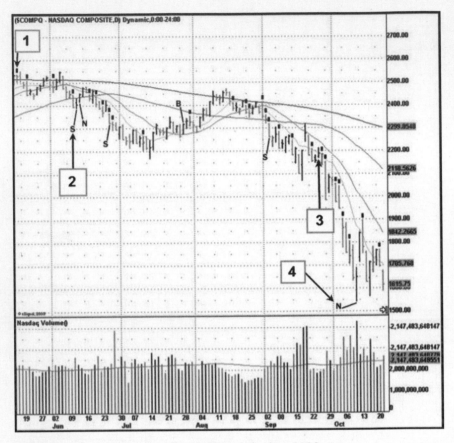

FIGURE 7.9 NASDAQ Composite Index daily chart 2008
Chart courtesy of eSignal, Copyright 2010.

3. **September 25** = Not a follow-through day because neither the
   NASDAQ Composite nor the S&P 500 meets the threshold level of 1.5.

4. **October 10** = Sell signal is neutralized on this exceptional day of
   record volume that closed in the top ½ of the day's trading range.

Market Direction Model Analysis 1929–1930

Figure 7.10 shows the Dow Jones Industrials in 1929–1930 with the model's
interpretation of the action as follows:

1. **September 25, 1929** = Not a distribution day because the daily price
   range has a long lower tail and the index closes down less than –0.1 percent on the day.

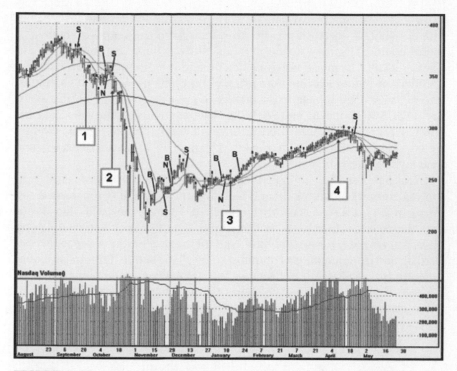

FIGURE 7.10 Dow Jones Industrial Average Index daily chart 1929–1930. Chart courtesy of eSignal, Copyright 2010.

2. **October 15, 1929** = The model goes to "sell signal standby" even though it is the first distribution day after the buy signal. This is because the index went below the intraday low of the buy signal day (see "A few notes about the charts" at the start of this Chart Examples section).

3. **January 16, 1930** = The model does not go to sell signal standby because it is the first distribution day after the buy signal (see "A few notes about the charts" at the start of this Chart Examples section).

4. **April 11, 1930** = This is churning on high volume and is therefore a distribution day.

STEALING THE MODEL'S SECRETS

Even if some were able to reverse-engineer the model and utilize it on a wide-scale basis, it should not affect the predictive nature of the model.

Even if a large number of people were to buy or sell on the basis of the model's signals, there should be no effect given the massive number of highly liquid ETFs in existence, and this model is but a tiny grain of sand in a sea of ideas. The model is not a black box, thus a programmer would have a difficult if not impossible time programming the model into a computer. The rules used are subject to the quality of prior price/volume formation of the NASDAQ Composite and S&P 500. Thus, even though the rules are hard and fast for the systematic model, they still depend on this quality characteristic. Being able to size up "quality" is based on 20+ years of experience in analyzing charts in detail since 1989.

This nature of "quality" is perhaps best explained by way of analogy. In the years I worked with William O'Neil, his uncanny ability to interpret the innate quality of a base is nearly unmatched. I equate this to his decades of experience analyzing charts. For example, the difference between a great base, a good base, a marginal base, and all the degrees in between, is contextual, and programming a computer to "see" the subtle differences would be quite the challenge if not impossible. Of course, a computer could be programmed to isolate specific charts that fit general characteristics, then those charts could be sifted through in more detail by human effort. But then, properly built stock screens already do much of that work.

TIMING MODEL FAQ

Over time, I have found the most instructive way to teach is by the Socratic method, namely, by vigorous question and answer format. Here are the most common questions I have received over the years with respect to my Dr K Market Direction Model (Dr K MDM). Should you have additional questions, please email me directly at chris@mokainvestors.com or go to www.virtueofselfishinvesting.com as the existing Q&A file will be updated regularly.

Should I expect returns similar to those achieved by the model?

Keep in mind the model's returns are theoretical prior to June 1, 2009 and that high returns come with drawdowns that you may find are outside your comfort zone. Thus, choose 1-times, 2-times, and 3-times ETFs, depending on your risk tolerance. The Market Direction Model™ is up +53.8 percent from June 1, 2009–May 31, 2010 (one year's returns) in a test fund using actual money, with exposure to the market less than half the time. In a separate account that is not using actual money, I wanted to see how my system held up against a volatile instrument such as the 3× technology ETF TYH, going 100 percent long on buy, 100 percent short on sell, and 100 percent cash on a neutral signal. Such instruments did not exist until the last year, so this gives big opportunity for profit that did not exist before. From June 1, 2009–May 14, 2010, it is up +183.9 percent, and as of May 31, 2010, it is up +215.1 percent. Of course, due to the highly aggressive nature of this account, drawdowns as high as −18.5 percent were not unusual but that is the price to pay to get to +215.1 percent. Note, had you been using a 1-times ETF, your gains would be roughly $\frac{1}{3}$ of those shown, but so would your drawdowns. Thus the worst drawdown recorded by the model is −15.7 percent in 1999 based on the NASDAQ Composite which is, by definition, a 1-times vehicle. Also note, the long term returns of +33.1 percent from July 1974–January 2010 are based on the NASDAQ Composite; a 1-times vehicle. If one were to have invested in ETFs such as TYH that were roughly 3-times the movement of the NASDAQ Composite had they existed then, returns would be roughly 3-times the amount but, more important, so would be the drawdowns.

Figure 7.11 should give you an idea of how the model works. It capitalizes on trends when the signal is profitable as denoted by the [Big Gains]

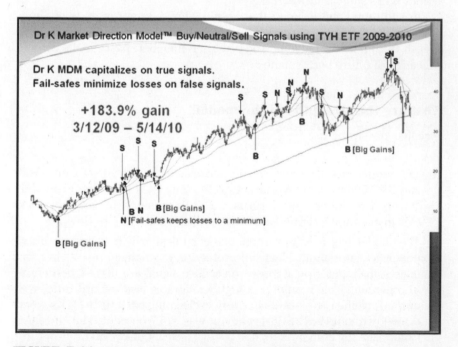

FIGURE 7.11 Direxion Daily Technology Bull ETF (TYH) daily chart, 2009.

moniker, then a fail-safe mechanism kicks in to limit losses if the signal is false.

For nearly two decades, the model has been a big driving force to our trading success as it keeps us on the right side of the market. The model's returns of +33.1 percent/yr for the systematic portion date back to July 1974. The last few years have been highly challenging due to sideways, choppy, often trendless markets. That said, the model was still able to outperform with a +17.3 percent/yr return going back to January 2005, beating the major indices and the top timing sites, and actual returns were greatly enhanced by buying top quality stocks in top industry groups on buy signals, especially during mid/late 2006 and late 2007. Furthermore, a +51.9 percent (17.3 percent x 3) return could be achieved since the birth of 3-times ETFs such as TYH/TYP that make good proxies for 3-times the NASDAQ Composite. In other words, such instruments tend to return 3-times what the NASDAQ Composite would return. That said, a +90.2 percent return could have been achieved from TYH/TYP since the March 12, 2009 follow through buy signal through August 24, 2009, the date the study was done (see FAQ below). Keep in mind you would have had to withstand an −18.4 percent drawdown on the way to +90.2 percent. For those with lower risk appetites, there are also the 2-times ETFs such as QLD/QID and 1-times ETFs such as QQQQ/PSQ.

In addition, keep in mind that results above do not include commissions, taxes, dividends earned, or money market interested earned while in cash from a neutral signal. And always remember, past results are not indicative of future performance.

What are the strengths of the model?

I see five key strengths:

1. The model has substantially outperformed the NASDAQ Composite and S&P 500 over every market cycle going back 35 years. From July 1974 to December 2009, returns are 33.1 percent/year. The model excels in catching intermediate term trends, whether up or down.

2. The model has a self-protection mechanism which keeps its drawdowns to a minimum. This self-protection mechanism results in more false signals but typical losses on a false signal are just −1 percent to −1.5 percent. This results in a highly favorable risk/reward ratio, well outperforming the markets in every cycle going back to 1974. Its worst drawdown in its entire 35+ year run was −15.7 percent. The NASDAQ Composite, by comparison, had a −78.4 percent drawdown.

3. The model buys the fundamentally strongest stocks at pocket pivot points and breakout pivot points when the model signals a buy. The web site www.virtueofselfishinvesting.com provides stock suggestions so you can make potentially larger gains since we all want to achieve that brass ring 100 percent return in a year's time if the market allows.

4. The model buys inverse ETFs (or shorting ETFs) when the model signals a sell.

5. The model uses $2\times$ and $3\times$ ETFs to boost returns especially in this challenging environment.

What are the weaknesses of the model?

I see two key weaknesses.

First, trendless volatile markets are the most difficult. This would include periods such as:

1. **May 4, 2009–July 10, 2009:** Four false signals in a row.

2. **February 1999–August 1999:** Five false signals in a row, a profitable signal, then another five false signals in a row. This resulted in the model's largest drawdown of –15.7 percent in its 35+ year run. As you can see in the performance figure above, the drawdown during this period is still small relative to the overall performance of the model. The NASDAQ Composite, by comparison, had –78.4 percent as its worst drawdown.

Interestingly, I achieved my highest return for 1999 in both my personal account of +451 percent and my O'Neil firm account of +566.1 percent because I went long the right stocks on buy signals. As an aside, my returns in my personal account were significantly higher than +451 percent because I did not invest money earmarked to pay for taxes that year, but kept it in my trading account. Thus, at a total tax rate of +50.5 percent (federal, state, etc), my starting capital base that year as well as for 1997, 1998, and 2000 was significantly less. However, there was no way using normal accounting standards that KPMG, who did the verification, could account for this. My higher return that Kevin Marder cites in his book *The Best: Conversations with Top Traders* (M. Gordon Pub. Group, 2000) accounts for this.

Increased volatility seen in 2009 has shown false signals to lose typically between 1.5 to 2.5 percent instead of the normal 1 to 1.5 percent.

Case in point: Actual results from March 12, 2009, to August 24, 2009, the date this study was done, which experienced two uptrends and a period of trendless volatility where the system had four false signals in a row

(100 percent long on buy signal, 100 percent short on sell, 100 percent cash on neutral).

	NASDAQ Composite	$1 Becomes	TYH (3x ETF)	$1 Becomes
3/12 Buy	1426	1.21	45.3	1.63
5/28 Short	1728.9	1.18	73.8	1.5
5/29 Neutral	1768.2	1.18	79.9	1.5
6/1 Buy	1828.6	1.16	88.1	1.46
6/17 Short	1795.5	1.14	85.3	1.39
6/19 Neutral	1831.1	1.14	89.4	1.39
7/7 Short	1770.1	1.13	81.3	1.33
7/13 Buy	1793.2	1.27	85	1.90
8/24	2018.0 (close)	**+27%**	121.4	**+90%**

Figure 7.12 shows this graphically.

As you can see, using TYH yielded a +90.2 percent return from March 12, 2009, to August 24, 2009, which is stellar; however, you had to endure four false signals which totaled to a –18.4 percent drawdown, on the way to being up +90.2 percent. Had you traded a 1× ETF instead such as QQQQ, which is a good proxy for the NASDAQ Composite, you would have made a +27 percent return, but with just a –6.6 percent drawdown. You must decide your own personal risk tolerance. Keep in mind the model has outperformed every market cycle back to 1974 as well as January 1929–December

FIGURE 7.12 Direxion Daily Technology Bull ETF (TYH) daily chart, 2009. Chart courtesy of eSignal, Copyright 2010.

1932, and has had only two down years, 1993 and 2007, in its 35+ year run. It has averaged +33.1 percent annually July 1974 to December 2009.

The second key weakness is that, on very rare occasions, the model may still issue a sell signal even though top quality stocks are breaking out of sound bases. This occurred in March 1996 when stocks such as Iomega (IOM) broke out. I started buying such stocks, overriding the sell signal from my model. Fortunately, such times are extremely rare. Ultimately, when it comes to stock selection, let the stocks tell you what to do. If enough good names are breaking out of sound bases, start buying. If the names you hold are hitting your sell alerts, sell without question.

How can I use this site to boost my returns since we are living in such challenging times?

Returns can be boosted by going long or short 2-times or 3-times leveraged ETFs that serve as good proxies for the NASDAQ Composite. Since many ETFs highly correlate with each other, there are many to choose from, including EWZ (Brazil), FXI (China), and India MSCI ETF, which is traded on the Singapore exchange and www.virtueofselfishinvesting.com provides suggestions on which ETFs are likely to outperform. However, if you wish to stay as close as possible to the NASDAQ Composite, the best ETFs would be the 2-times leveraged bull and bear NASDAQ 100 Index ETFs, the QLD and the QID and the 3-times leveraged Direxion Tech Bull and Bear ETFs, the TYH and the TYP.

You can also do what I've done since 1991, the first year I was able to handily beat the U.S. market averages. Buy top-quality stocks in top industry groups when my model signals a buy. It has been shown that in 2009 the market behaved abnormally. The best-performing stocks were low-grade "junk-off-the-bottom" (JOB) stocks while higher-quality CAN SLIM type stocks completely underperformed. However, buying the highest-grade stocks at pocket pivot points and normal breakouts such as Shanda Interactive Games (SNDA), NetEase.com (NTES), Baidu, Inc. (BIDU), Green Mountain Coffee Roasters, Inc. (GMCR), and STEC, Inc. (STEC) in March, April, and May 2009 would have produced solid returns. Don't create bad habits of buying junk just because the market is temporarily askew.

How has the Dr. K Market Direction Model done against some of the best timing sites in the Internet?

We calculated the performance of two of the best-performing timing sites that have been on the Internet for at least five years.

The top performing sites as tracked by TimerTrac show 23 sites that have track records at least five years or longer. I omitted sites with shorter lifetimes since there have been a few that have been around since mid-2008, made massive gains on the short side, but the inherent logic of their system is suspect such that these models may underperform the markets once the highly unusual black swan period of 2008–2009 ends. Following are the total returns (not annualized) over the prior five years as of June 2009.

Rank	Strategy Name	Gain/Loss %	Trades in Time Frame
1	PsiTrade	128.04%	445
2	Market Systems II-DD	105.81%	634
3	Premium Trust NDX Trader	53.75%	153
4	Premium Trust SPX Trader	42.41%	135
5	KT QQQ-a	41.71%	504
6	Premium Trust RUT Trader	35.10%	109
7	TimingCube	15.93%	23
8	Bonner Mutual Fund Signal	13.60%	0
9	Performance Signal Short Term	13.22%	107
10	Vinny Index VM Allocation	4.01%	61
11	FundSpectrum	2.20%	15
12	Q5TrackerLT	−4.80%	21
13	Highlight QQQQ (Pre−Close)	−10.86%	59
14	Q5TrackerST	−13.06%	84
15	Highlight QQQQ (After Close)	−14.27%	59
16	Highlight SPDRs (Pre-Close)	−14.72%	62
17	Highlight DOW (Pre-Close)	−18.33%	56
18	Highlight SPDRs (After Close)	−22.22%	62
19	Highlight DOW (After Close)	−25.77%	55
20	Vinny S&P Index	−26.95%	35
21	Stockbarometer.com QQQ Trader	−31.79%	124
22	KT Mid Term	−33.78%	91
23	Q5TrackerIT	−43.20%	34

Upon closer investigation, it seems many sites with five year or longer track records could not beat the markets, which should not come as a surprise, and the top two performers shown in the next table had stellar returns in 2008, which catapulted them to the top of the list and skewed their annualized returns to what you see in the next table. However, prior to 2008, their returns were less than impressive. Based on their annualized performance records, following are the results of the top two timing sites versus the Dr K Market Direction Model (Dr K MDM).

May 2000 to July 2009	PsiTrade	17.04%/yr	PsiTrade inception: May 2000	**Dr K MDM Systematic +20.8%/yr**	**$100,000 becomes $565,650**
April 2003 to July 2009	Market Systems II-DD	10.4%/yr	Market Systems II-DD inception: April 2003	**Dr K MDM Systematic +20.7%/yr**	**$100,000 becomes $324,090**

In addition, the maximum drawdowns in the Dr. K Market Direction Model were lower, so the model beat the top two timing sites tracked by TimerTrac on both an absolute return basis and on a risk/reward basis. Keep in mind that these two sites have logged signals real-time with Timer-Trac whereas the model's signals are theoretical but are largely responsible for my long-term audited track record as an investor in individual stocks for two decades. That said, the model's theoretical returns are based on my having bought 100 percent NASDAQ Composite (QQQQ is a good proxy) on a buy signal, shorting 100 percent NASDAQ Composite (PSQ is a good proxy) on a sell signal, and moving to 100 percent cash on a neutral signal.

After examining TimerTrac, I then focused on three sites I believe have sound long-term track records: Timing Cube, Decision Moose, and Investor's Business Daily (IBD) Big Picture/market commentary. IBD is an excellent resource I still use to this day. I focused on roughly the last 4½ years (January 2005 through July 2009) which represent the most challenging period to timing models. These years were fraught with much sideways, trendless action as well as numerous false price/volume signals in 2007.

Mike Scott, a former engineer who is now a full-time individual investor and a notable market research and data wizard, showed me his spreadsheet of IBD's market calls all the way back to 1994. The Big Picture column began in 2003, but he painstakingly went through old issues of IBD to ascertain changes in market direction given by the paper. Next, I show IBD's returns going back to 1994 as well as over the prior 4½ years when the Big Picture column was running.

Here are the results of top-performing sites for the most difficult period—the prior four and a half years (this comparison was made in August 2009).

Period	Site	Return	Configuration	Comparison	Dr K $ Growth
Jan 2005–July 2009	Timing Cube	11.5%/yr	100% long/short model gave best results (100% NASDAQ Composite 100 long, short, or cash).	Dr K MDM Systematic +17.3%/yr*	$100,000 becomes $207,680
Jan 2005–July 2009	Decision Moose	13.4%/yr	100% long only (100% various Exchange Traded Funds (ETFs) such as EPP, EWJ, ILF, bonds, GLD).	Dr K MDM Systematic +17.3%/yr*	$100,000 becomes $207,680
Jan 2005–July 2009	IBD Big Picture	8.4%/yr	100% long NASDAQ Composite when "market in rally," 100% short NASDAQ Composite when "market in correction," 100% cash when "market under pressure."*	Dr K MDM Systematic +17.3%/yr*	$100,000 becomes $207,680
Dec 1994–July 2009	IBD Big Picture	14.8%/yr	100% long NASDAQ Composite when "market in rally," 100% short NASDAQ Composite when "market in correction," 100% cash when "market under pressure."*	Dr K MDM Systematic +31.1%/yr	$100,000 becomes $5,183,788
July 1974–July 2009	Long-term Historical Return of Dr K MDM Systematic	+33.4%/yr*	100% long NASDAQ Composite on buy signal, 100% short NASDAQ Composite on sell signal, 100% cash on neutral signal.**	Dr K MDM Systematic +33.4%/yr*	$100,000 becomes massive = this is how William O'Neil made his money***

*Going to cash yielded better returns for IBD than not going to cash when "market under pressure." Using these same parameters, Dr. K MDM's +33.1%/yr return since July 1974 is massively larger than its return of +17.3%/yr since January 2005 especially over such a long time frame. The large difference is due to the action of the major U.S. indices over the prior few years. Consequently, the prior few years have been extremely challenging for timing systems. These years were fraught with much sideways, trendless action as well as numerous false price/volume signals in 2007.

**I also spot-tested my model of the late 1920s and early 1930s using the Dow Jones Industrial Average to make sure my systematic rules would work in completely different eras. My belief is that charts are human nature on parade and day-to-day price/volume action form the chart patterns we see, and since human nature has not changed, these patterns repeat with statistical significance.

***O'Neil has been compounding his wealth since 1958. The key is to stick with a system that works over many market cycles, even during the challenging times where it may seem the system no longer works. The very few trend followers with 25+ year track records were managing billions (John Henry, Bill Dunn, etc.) because they stuck with their system even when the market was in a challenging, choppy, trendless phase.

Reasons why the systematic portion of my model outperformed IBD's big picture market calls:

- It is important to keep in mind IBD is not putting out their market calls as a timing model for ETFs. Readers use IBD's signals typically as follows: to buy the right stocks on a buy signal, to possibly tighten sell stops on a "market under pressure" or equivalent signal, and to keep stops tight and not buy any new stocks on a sell signal. IBD's Big Picture daily column should be read each day, and I believe IBD is the finest financial newspaper in the world. The Dr. K MDM results are based on having bought 100 percent NASDAQ Composite (QQQQ is a good proxy) on a buy signal, shorting 100 percent NASDAQ Composite (PSQ is a good proxy) on a sell signal, and moving to 100 percent cash on a neutral signal. Of course, results can be further improved by individual stock selection on buy signals.
- My model has a self-protection mechanism that limits losses regardless of price/volume action.
- The systematic portion of my model has no discretionary intervention. I learned over the several years I worked with William O'Neil that the market can fool even the best. I figured if someone with Bill O'Neil's market experience could get whipsawed in his market calls during challenging periods, perhaps it is better to stick with the set of systematic rules that have statistically proven themselves based on actual price/volume action of the major indices. Bill always said opinions don't matter, just the facts, and price/volume is as factual as it gets. That said, my model does have a discretionary component that I added in mid-2009. My intuition says the discretionary component can further boost the returns of the model, which is wholly systematic. But opinions do not matter, including my own. Time will tell whether my discretionary intervention can enhance my model's systematic returns. Even though I have great confidence in my abilities, I cannot assume I am immune to what caused whipsaws in O'Neil's own market calls during challenging periods.

Sidebar: Here is where Bill O'Neil is one of the best, if not the best: He jumps on the stocks with huge potential near the beginning of a new trend, then pyramids his winning positions. This makes all the difference in performance and accounts for the years in which he has achieved triple digit returns.

- The model has no gray area of what constitutes a distribution day or a follow-through day. The timing method that he discusses in his book caused some confusion among many followers of his methods. Some have asked, What if the day finishes higher by a small amount but has a shooting star tail? How do you define a distribution day caused by churning? How many distribution days over what time period are necessary to signal a sell? What is the percent threshold required for a follow-through day? Is it still a follow-through day if the volume is well under average but is still higher than the previous day? and so on.

Why has the Dr. K Market Direction Model done so much better over the long 35-year time frame from 1974 to 2009 compared to the past few years?

The past few years have been extremely challenging for timing systems. These years were fraught with much sideways, trendless action as well as numerous false price/volume signals in 2007. That said, there are ways to boost your return in these challenging times. Returns can be boosted by going long or short 2-times or 3-times ETFs that serve as good proxies for the NASDAQ Composite. Since many ETFs highly correlate, there are many to choose from. However, if you wish to stay as close as possible to the NASDAQ Composite, the best ETFs would be the 2-times QID/QLD and the 3-times TYH/TYP. See the discussion on the returns the model would have achieved using the TYH during 2009 in the FAQ "What are weaknesses of the model" of this chapter.

Some market timing web sites show huge returns. What should I watch out for?

When you check the seemingly impressive returns on a timing site, here are very important questions you should ask:

- How has the site performed on an annualized basis since January 2005?
  Most all sites fall short here. The past few years have been most challenging to timing sites. Some sites that show high returns overall are due to making abnormally huge returns in 2008 while making only mediocre returns in 2005–2007. Such inconsistent returns are likely to cause an ulcer!
- How many switches are made?
  Some sites switch 75–100+ times/year. This drives up commission costs.
- Has the site switched its strategy midstream?
  Read the fine print. Some sites report high annualized returns, then show that the strategy was optimized midstream. In other words, they modified their strategy midstream but their reported returns are

skewed to reflect the best possible results. They may also skew their results by reporting returns as if the whole run were live, when in reality, it was only live since the modification to their strategy was made.

- The total return is massive.

Ignore total return. It is meaningless. Total returns are often massive and therefore easily boggle the mind. For example, the model's +33.1% annual return since July 1974 would give a total return of 2,560,467%. Stated another way, $1 would have become $25,605. With enough time, the power of compounding is powerful indeed. Our book *How We Made Over 18,000% in the Stock Market in 7 Years* was titled that way because that huge percentage is intriguing to the potential reader, but this massive percent should be broken down into annualized returns, which make more sense: 18,000 percent averages out to +110.5 percent annually over these seven years. As an aside, my annual returns were actually higher than +110.5 percent because I did not invest money earmarked to pay for taxes each year when I was trading the markets, but kept it in my trading account, thus, at a total tax rate of +50.5 percent (federal, state, etc.) back in 1997–2000, my starting capital base each year was significantly less. However, using normal accounting standards there was no way that the accounting firm of KPMG that performed the verification could account for this. My return of 70,000 percent as cited by Kevin Marder in the book he co-authored with Marc Dupee, *Conversations with Top Traders* accounts for this.

- Does the web site show theoretical signals going back many years but its live signals are less than a year old?

This situation would apply to the timing model that appears on www.virtueofselfishinvesting.com. This is the first time that the model's timing signals have been made available to the public. Do your due diligence. Check to see if the creator of the model has any prior performance track record or otherwise that demonstrates a high level of competence. Googling the name of the person who created the model can be an effective way to find information to get a clearer picture.

In addition, keep in mind that some sites may boast high theoretical returns over a long period. It is essential to know if they possibly overfit the data to create those high returns. As discussed earlier in this chapter, overfitting occurs when excessive attention is paid to past data while failing to account for the system's predictive value going forward. This is a common trap that affects many timing systems, which is why so many fall short. The system may yield impressive results over a historical 20-year period because the parameters were fit to maximize profits over that period. But going forward, the returns will fall short because the system was overfit.

What is discretionary intervention, and how does it apply to this model?

While the primary force behind my model will be systematic since it has proven out over the years as a guide to my trading, I will on some occasions issue a sidebar discretionary signal to alert the www.virtueofselfish investing.com member. Again, while my intuition says such discretionary intervention should improve the systematic results, I hold to my original thought: I figured if someone with O'Neil's extensive market experience could get whipsawed during challenging, trendless markets, perhaps it is better to stick with the set of systematic rules that have statistically proven themselves based on actual price/volume action of the major indices. O'Neil always said opinions do not matter, just the facts, and price/volume is as factual as it gets.

Examples of discretionary intervention include:

- Enough leading stocks breaking out of sound basing patterns, such as we saw in March 1996 when stocks such as Iomega (IOM) were breaking out to new highs.
- A huge confluence of reliable secondary indicators showing either strength or weakness in the markets, which runs counter to the current direction of the model.
- Highly unusual one-time news events that are forward-looking that could override the systematic model.

Should I use the systematic or discretionary portion of the model in my own trading?

The systematic portion has the 35+ year historical advantage. The discretionary portion has the advantage of position sizing and the occasional override. In practice, position size depends on the strength of the signal. I will give an example here that was a loser to illustrate the challenges of working with the model. It would be easy to give any of the many examples that were profitable, but I've always believed that more learning comes from challenging situations. Thus on the weak November 9, 2009, buy signal, I only bought a 50 percent position in QQQQ. As distribution days continued to mount, my model found itself on a standby sell signal. Once the sell signal was triggered on November 19, 2009, I immediately switched to a 30 percent position in FAZ which is the 3-times leveraged Direxion Financial Bear ETF. I switched into FAZ because the financials had lagged the major indices for months and a 30 percent position in the FAZ is effectively a 90 percent short position in the XLF, the SPDR Financial ETF. I then bought an additional 30 percent position in FAZ once the NASDAQ

Composite index broke below the lows of November 19, 2009. Once new lows were made again on November 27th, I bought a 30 percent position in TYP, the 3-times leveraged inverse ETF called the Direxion Tech Bear that is also a good inverse proxy for the NASDAQ Composite Index—it will rise when the NASDAQ falls. I decided to diversify into TYP even though I was most bearish on the financials given the fundamental backdrop of the United States economy at the time, but I did not want to be too heavy in any one triple-leveraged ETF. Having this 90 percent position in triple-leveraged inverse ETFs put me at an effective 270 percent short exposure and an average cost below where I had bought the three positions; thus I had reasonable cushion.

In practice, investors can decide whether to work off the discretionary portion using leveraged ETFs or the plain-Jane systematic portion where the model simply goes 100 percent long or short the QQQQs if it is not in cash. Also note that after November 27, 2009, the market turned back up yet again as so-called quantitative easing by the Federal Reserve continued to help the markets move higher, a recurring theme since March 2009. After November 27th, the model's self–protection mechanism kicked in, which reversed profits but protected capital, so that losses were contained to less than –3 percent.

What if I am only able to act on signals at the open of the following trading day?

For signals that are issued either intraday, some users will only be able to act on the signal at the open the next day. In practice, this should balance out since on some days, the market may have moved lower, giving such users slightly better entry points than users who bought intraday, and other days, the market may have moved higher, giving such users slightly worse entry points than users who bought intraday.

How can I know that your rules that guide your model will continue to work?

The rules the Dr K Market Direction Model™ follow are not our rules, nor Wall Street's rules, but the market's rules. They represent statistically significant results culled from the major market averages going back more than 20 market cycles (back to the 1920s) as well as studies done on how the behavior of leading stocks and secondary indicators affect the market.

We are in a highly unusual market environment, and with the advent of high frequency trading and the like, a few question whether price/volume action and trend following are still applicable. My answer is a resounding yes. As mentioned earlier in this chapter, the Market Direction Model™ is up +53.8 percent from June 1, 2009–May 31, 2010 in a test fund using actual money, with exposure to the market less than half the time. In a separate account that is not using actual money, I wanted to see how my system held up against a volatile instrument such as the 3x technology ETF TYH, going 100 percent long on buy, 100 percent short on sell, and 100 percent cash on a neutral signal. From June 1, 2009–May 14, 2010, it is up +183.9 percent, and as of May 31, 2010, it is up +215.1 percent.

The bottom line is that trends still occur even in these highly unusual times. Just ask Michael Covel who wrote the excellent book *Trend Following* which contains in-depth interviews with successful long-time trend followers John Henry, Bill Dunn, and Ed Seykota. And yes, while such noted trend followers have been encountering difficulty since 2009, they are no stranger to steep drawdowns, and in their 25+ year careers, have always more than recovered, thus maintaining the integrity of their long term track records. In their careers, there have been periods where trend following and price/volume action was declared dead but what makes them unique is they continue to apply their systems through thick and thin, knowing the markets will always trend again.

The key in creating any model is to be completely objective and listen to what the market is telling you as you study the data. The ego and the need to be right have no place in the world of model-building. Once you have decided to use a model to guide your trading, thoroughly understand its weaknesses so you don't end up abandoning it. As prior examples of this, too many trend followers had declared trend following dead at junctures when the market stopped trending, such as 2004–2006, 1993–1994, and 1976–1977. As 200 years of market history has shown, trends will occur often enough to keep the likes of William O'Neil, Ed Seykota, John Henry, and Bill Dunn gainfully employed.

Is the systematic portion of your market direction model a black box in that it is computer programmable?

This is only partially true. Some of the rules I have built are not black box but subject to the quality of prior price/volume formation of the NASDAQ and S&P 500. Thus, even though the rules are hard and fast for the systematic model, they still depend on this quality characteristic. Being able to size up 'quality' is based on my many years of experience in analyzing millions of charts since 1989.

This is perhaps best explained by way of analogy. In the years I worked with William O'Neil, his uncanny ability to interpret the innate quality of a base is nearly unmatched. I equate this to his decades of experience analyzing charts. For example, the difference between a great base, a good base, a marginal base, and all the degrees in between, is contextual, and programming a computer to 'see' the subtle differences would be quite the challenge if not impossible.

CONCLUSION

The rules the market direction model follow are not my rules, nor Wall Street's rules, but the market's rules. They represent statistically significant results culled from the major market averages going back more than 20 market cycles as well as studies done on how the behavior of leading stocks and secondary indicators affect the market.

The key in creating any model is to be completely objective and listen to what the market is telling you as you study the data. The ego and the need to be right have no place in the world of model building. Once you have either built a model or use a model to guide your trading, thoroughly understand its weaknesses so you don't end up abandoning it. Too many trend followers, as one example, had declared trend following dead at junctures when the market stopped trending, such as 2004–2006, 1993–1994, and 1976–1977. As 200 years of market history has shown, trends will occur often enough to keep the likes of William O'Neil, Ed Seykota, John Henry, and Bill Dunn gainfully employed.

CHAPTER 8

Our Bill of Commandments

W hen we talk about the Ten Commandments of Bill O'Neil, it is important to understand that we do not mean commandments that were issued directly by him, like Moses coming down from the mount with two stone tablets etched by the hand of God. For us, these "commandments" are more subjective, in that what we are referring to is a compilation of some of our favorite but less obvious rules and principles for life and the markets that Bill O'Neil conveyed to us on a daily basis, outside of what is found in his books and seminars. Our trading diaries are filled with scores of essential lessons that we have found can apply to life as easily as they apply to the stock market. Anyone who has spent over 50 years in an industry that sits at the hub of global enterprise, as Bill O'Neil has, will have certainly learned a few things about dealing with people, dealing in business, and dealing with all the moving parts of life in general. For the purpose of passing such information on to the reader, we find it simplest to distill these down to some basic ideas, concepts, rules, and principles that we can simply label the Ten Commandments of Bill O'Neil.

MISCONCEPTIONS

As well, there are many misconceptions and myths about O'Neil and his organization that we find preposterous, particularly those that are promulgated for the sole purpose of bringing the man and his methods down. A lot of it is born of envy, but most of it is just plain and deliberate ignorance of who and what O'Neil is. For example, in the midst of the grimness of the 2000–2002 dot-com bubble-bursting bear market, a professional portfolio manager was asked on financial cable TV when he thought the brutal bear market would finally come to an end. His response was immediate and contemptuous, "This bear market will be over when that momentum investor's newspaper, *Investor's Business Daily*, goes out of business!"

In most cases ignorance is bliss, but in this case ignorance was little more than ignorance, as such a statement reflects a profound misunderstanding of Bill O'Neil and the O'Neil organization, which includes not only *Investor's Business Daily*, but also the institutional investment advisory and research firm of William J. O'Neil + Company, Inc., a nationally recognized and ranked publications firm called O'Neil Data Systems that prints much more than just chart books, and several other, smaller and not-so-smaller sister companies.

If you were a portfolio manager at William O'Neil + Company, Inc., as we were at that time, you knew that the last thing that would ever happen during the bear market of 2000–2002 would be IBD going belly up. The O'Neil organization consists of many different businesses, some of which, like the nationally top-ranked printing firm of O'Neil Data Systems, were strong cash cows, and so if any of the other organizations had a lean year, there were plenty of well-run enterprises elsewhere in the organization to pick up the slack. We can also tell you that the internal portfolio management group, which was essentially responsible for managing the organization's capital, also did very well. Bill O'Neil himself attests to this by writing in his book, *The Successful Investor*, that "Our internal money management group operating from our Data Analysis holding company produced a 1356 percent net return in the five-year period ending June 2003." It is clear that unless you can beat Bill O'Neil in the market, you cannot beat him in business, and where others may be forced to fold up their operations when profitability goes on vacation, O'Neil has the wherewithal and mix of complementary businesses to outlast the difficulties of down economic and market cycles as well as the financial challenges of taking on start-up ventures such as IBD was at one time.

When we hear someone use the term "momentum investor" to describe Bill O'Neil, the investment firm of William J. O'Neil + Company, Inc., or *Investor's Business Daily* it is always meant in a pejorative sense, almost as a convenient shorthand for dismissing, discounting, and diminishing O'Neil and his methods. By using this pejorative sense, O'Neil's detractors imply that he advocates the mindless buying of high-octane stocks as they streak ever higher. In our view, nothing could be further from the truth, and we offer the following example as proof, one of the countless numbers of examples going back more than 25 market cycles, nearly 100 years.

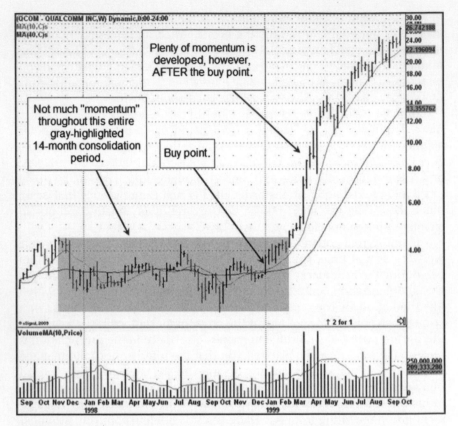

FIGURE 8.1   Qualcomm, Inc. (QCOM), weekly chart, 1998–1999.
Chart courtesy of eSignal, Copyright 2010.

In 1999 one of the biggest winning stocks of that market cycle was Qualcomm, Inc. (QCOM), shown in Figure 8.1. After a 14-month period of sideways consolidation as highlighted in Figure 8.1, QCOM broke out of a cup-with-handle formation and launched on a tremendous price run. At the time of purchase, QCOM is not exhibiting any real "momentum" per se as it is only just starting to emerge from a long-term consolidation. At this point the company is also showing huge earnings and sales growth, strong profitability, compelling products, and materially significant institutional sponsorship. When all the ducks are lined up, both fundamentally and technically, the stock is purchased. While there are prescribed add points on the way up, there is certainly no mindless "momentum investing" going on, as if how fast the stock is going up is the only criteria for purchasing the stock in the first place. If momentum investing means buying strong fundamental stocks with a large institutional following as they emerge from a proper consolidation or sideways range and then capitalizing on the ensuing huge upside price move, then so be it. Otherwise, as Bill O'Neil would say, the portfolio manager who referred to IBD as "that momentum investor's newspaper" is all wet.

SURVIVING BY KEEPING EGO IN CHECK

With over 50 years of experience, O'Neil is, by sheer definition, a senior survivor of the professional investment business, and in the process he has seen many other professional investors and investment firms come and go. Most of the failures he has witnessed in the investment industry were caused by excessive ego and the dangerous psychological effect that sudden wealth can have on people who have a tendency to simply get carried away with money and themselves. Money is certainly capable of becoming the root of all evil, as it can lead an individual down unsustainable paths of self-indulgence. Because of this, the taste of significant and material success in the markets, as we discussed in Chapter 3, can absolutely be fatal.

With more than 50 years in the business, O'Neil has more than a few stories to tell regarding the lessons of investment excess and folly. We recall several of these stories, such as the one about a broker he knew at Hayden Stone, a smart kid out of Yale who had bought a lot of big-growth stocks in the 1960s like Brunswick and American Photocopy and had made a lot of money, but when they started coming down, he began to proclaim his infallible approach as a newly declared "long-term investor." To put it simply, he rode all these hot stocks all the way up, and he rode them all the way down, and in the process put himself out of business. Another fellow Bill knew as a broker was a guy who borrowed $150,000 (a lot of money in the early 1960s) to leverage himself up into Solotron, a big high-tech glamor stock in the 1960s. The stock hit 275 and topped. He held it all the way down from 275 to 8, losing his job, losing his wife, and having a stroke after going bankrupt. These are lessons about what happens to those blinded by initial success with a stock or in the market in general.

In June of 1999, Bill pointed out the photo of Steve Case, CEO of dot.com wunderkind stock America Online (AOL), which was making the rounds in the financial print media. The photo showed Case coming out of a government building after giving his testimony with respect to antitrust actions the U.S. government was pursuing against Microsoft, Inc. (MSFT). Case had a big, smug smile on his face. Nobody understand human nature as well as Bill O'Neil, in particular when it came to the managements of certain companies who can get carried away as a result of their heady success. O'Neil recognized the tell-tale signs of overconfidence which can lead some top corporate managers to become overextended and full of themselves. O'Neil correctly predicted that AOL's best days were likely behind it, and after making another retest of its highs in late 1999, AOL declined from a high of 267.76 in December of 1999 to 24.31 at the bear market lows in 2002, saving itself from the ignominy of the affair by buying out and changing its name to Time Warner, Inc. in 2000, a move that turned out to be ill-considered but not uncommon for a management that had taken on a false sense of omniscience and omnipotence.

Bill O'Neil's approach to the business has evolved from his perception that in order to survive in this business, and even in life itself, one must maintain perspective and not get carried away with one's success and the trappings of wealth. He understands the pattern of psychology and behavior that ensues after one makes a lot of money in the markets. Once traders find they cannot duplicate this magic wealth creation feat immediately and at will, since it takes a nicely trending market to make such huge gains and thus requires the market's cooperation, they resort to riskier trades, a conversion to "long-term investing" or leveraging schemes to maintain the growth of their wealth and expanding pattern of conspicuous consumption.

In this manner, the organization reflects this ethic. The O'Neil campus where Data Analysis, Inc., *Investor's Business Daily*, William O'Neil + Company, Inc, O'Neil Securities, Inc., and the other O'Neil sister companies are located is rather modest and Spartan. We used to joke that the big status symbol for one's office at O'Neil was not getting new carpet, but getting new duct tape to repair the rips in your old office carpet! All joking aside, you will not find a Google-like "habitat" where extravagant and self-indulgent perks are an intrinsic part of the environment. You come to work for Bill O'Neil to learn how to make money in the markets, and lots of it, not to get a daily massage or have your laundry done. This frugal behavior is borne from O'Neil's Depression Baby sensibilities as well as an underlying wisdom and long-term understanding of how otherwise rational and successful investors become prey to the various ego and vanity-related psychological pitfalls of the investment business. And it is not as if O'Neil doesn't advise making one's stock market profits real by occasionally rewarding oneself with a new car (just don't make it a Ferrari!) or some other recognition and reinforcement of a successful stock market investing expedition. But balance and modesty are always called for, and the lessons that O'Neil teaches in this regard are lessons that all investors and traders should heed. In many ways, the United States could learn a lesson here as well, since the financial crisis of 2009 was a symptom of the country getting carried away with the unsustainable concept of "liberty and free money for all."

THE FIRST COMMANDMENT

The First Commandment among the many rules and principles applicable to life in general and stock market investing in specific that we heard many times from Bill was "Never get carried away with yourself." The basic idea is that one should remain impervious to the illusions and trappings of wealth, as they often lead one to become "carried away" to the point where excess of one sort or another ultimately leads to one's demise. This is critical.

Despite avoiding failure and demise as a result of his experience in understanding the root causes of such common investor afflictions, there have been many who take a certain smug sense of satisfaction in trying to predict Bill O'Neil's demise, albeit with little luck. The comments of the portfolio manager cited at the beginning of this chapter who predicted that the brutal 2000–2002 bear market would end when and only when *Investor's Business Daily* had gone out of business, turned out to be quite wishful in their ignorance and inaccuracy, but are in fact not too uncommon. When you are successful you can often become the target of another negative human emotion: envy.

One example of this type of envy occurred when we had heard a rumor that O'Neil had taken a "hit" in semiconductor "hot stock" Cymer, Inc. (CYMI). Supposedly the big break in the stock (Figure 8.2) had caused big losses for O'Neil and this was seen as potentially deleterious. If any of this was true, you would have known it by talking to Bill, who never loses focus no matter what the market throws at him. As it turned out, whatever losses that may or may not have been sustained in CYMI didn't seem to have any effect on O'Neil, since even if it was a big "hit," it was probably nothing greater than he had ever seen before and come back from in his long career. To this day, we still don't know whether this was true or just another rumor put out by those who had a sad desire to see O'Neil fail, but what we do know for sure is that two years later O'Neil and his stable of internal portfolio managers, of which we are proud to have been a part of at the time, were putting up quadruple-digit percentage gains in the market.

THE SECOND COMMANDMENT

The ability to come back from periods of difficulty with courage and persistence is embodied in O'Neil's Second Commandment: "Never operate from a position of fear." If you are fearful in the markets, either as a result of taking a recent loss or some other mistake, or even as a result of being nervous about the level of risk you are taking, then you are putting yourself in the position of making an unclear and hence incorrect decision. Either adjust your position to eliminate the fear, or come to the realization that if you

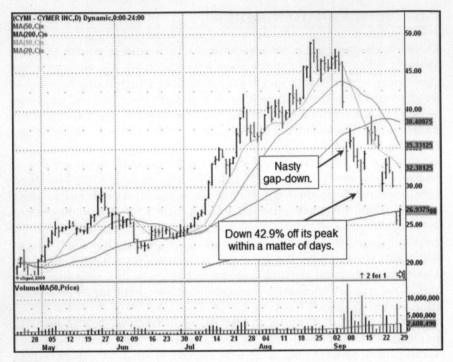

FIGURE 8.2 Cymer, Inc. (CYMI), daily chart, 1997. O'Neil takes a licking, but keeps on ticking!
Chart courtesy of eSignal, Copyright 2010.

are chronically fearful in the markets, then you have no business investing in them.

This principle of always operating from a position of strength was also manifested in O'Neil's approach to business. As a firm, we were probably unique in that since we were so intimately tied to the stock market, we used it as a forecasting tool for our own business. When the market topped, and a potential bear market began, we knew that the market was beginning to discount an economic slowdown. When this would occur, O'Neil would often order a 10 percent cut in each firm department's expenses, allowing the firm to get out ahead of a business downturn and actively place itself in a position of strength, prepared to deal with the oncoming economic train wreck. Operating from a position of strength also means having no debt, and so the firm did not rely on any debt in its operations. Cash flow was king, and with the regular and successful ventures into the stock market by the internal portfolio management team, the firm stayed well ahead of the game. Operating from a position of strength, therefore, also necessitates that if one is in a position of weakness, then that position must be corrected immediately so that the principle is adhered to.

THE THIRD COMMANDMENT

O'Neil deals with detractors and critics by turning their negativity into a positive. When it came to naysayers and backbiters, O'Neil simply invoked what we have labeled O'Neil's Third Commandment, and that is that "You learn more from your enemies than you do from your friends." In typical O'Neil fashion, a negative is turned into a positive, and criticism from third parties is seen as little more than a potential learning experience. In fact, this rule embodies a certain level of truth in that it is your enemies who scour you and your activities, looking for any little flaw they can blow out of proportion to serve their ends, which is to bring you down. In the process, however, they can help to reveal areas where you may have a weakness or flaw; a "deficiency" as O'Neil loved to say. Meanwhile, you can always depend on your friends to only see the best in you, which for those seeking self-improvement is not very useful. As a critic, O'Neil loved to play the role of the benevolent detractor, ignoring your successes and instead focusing on picking apart and revealing your mistakes. As is standard in the proprietary money management business, we were each paid a percentage of the gross profits on the account we managed for O'Neil, so that if you were managing, say $2 million and ran it up to $30 million, you would get a percentage of the gross profits of $28 million. In 1999, managing money for Bill O'Neil was the place to be when it came to compensation, and after a huge 1999 we might have expected Bill to come in with the big bonus checks and spray us with his adulation and admiration for doing such a fantastic job in 1999. No such luck! Instead, he immediately began going over his notes and reviewing all our bad trades and dumb mistakes. His conclusion: "If you had done everything exactly right, you could have been up 1,000 percent!"

THE FOURTH COMMANDMENT

In this way, we became acquainted with O'Neil's Fourth Commandment: "Never stop learning and improving, and the only way to do this is by constantly analyzing your mistakes and correcting them." As we all know, everyone constantly talks about their successes in the stock market, but few focus on their mistakes. O'Neil makes a point of focusing on his mistakes.

THE FIFTH COMMANDMENT

To this end, O'Neil invokes the Fifth Commandment: "Never talk about your stocks." The tendency to get excited and tell everyone how well you are doing in the markets is one that O'Neil abhors. By sticking to a simple policy of never talking about your stocks, you eliminate the ego-feeding urge to trumpet your success. Try implementing this rule, and see how it changes your perspective on how you handle your stocks.

THE SIXTH COMMANDMENT

The Fifth Commandment may in fact help you stick to the Sixth Commandment: "Don't get giddy at the top," because that is usually the time to be selling.

If Bill O'Neil were given a choice of being able to use only one type of chart interval, he would pick weekly charts. At least this is what he once told us, and there is good reason for this. First of all, O'Neil shuns reacting to news and other noise, including unusual intraday price swings. Intraday charts to O'Neil are virtually useless. At one time, he felt that having real-time quotes were a distraction, since operating on a 20-minute delayed basis did not seem to be a burden to his applied temporal frame of reference. O'Neil is on the hunt for "big stocks" that are heavily trafficked in by institutional investors, whose deployments of cash constantly move into big, winning stocks that are at the cutting edge of any economic growth cycle. Institutional investors buy and sell their stock positions over a period of many weeks, sometimes even months, so their activities are not likely to be picked up by an intraday chart, and in most cases probably not by a daily chart either. For this reason, weekly charts are the preferred "visual tool of choice."

THE SEVENTH COMMANDMENT

Thus the Seventh Commandment is, "Use weekly charts first, and daily charts second. Ignore intraday charts." Weekly charts eliminate a lot of the noise inherent in short-term fluctuations while providing meaningful clues with respect to potential accumulation by institutional investors.

THE EIGHTH COMMANDMENT

The use of weekly charts as one's primary method of discerning accumulation in a particular stock is also in keeping with what we call the Big Stock Principle, which distills the O'Neil methods down to their essential, driving element which is Commandment #8: Find a big stock and then find a way to own it in size.

THE NINTH COMMANDMENT

Probably one of the most important rules that O'Neil taught us, and one which we have not always found it easy to abide by is the Ninth Commandment, "Be careful who you get into bed with." This has nothing to do with one's love life, although in an age of communicable diseases it still stands as practical advice in this regard, but rather who you deal with in life's more mundane business affairs. O'Neil believes strongly that trust and integrity between two people are the most important variables in life and in business, and it is not often that one finds this in their relationships and dealings with other individuals. In the investment business in particular this is a critical teaching, simply because the investment area is full of Bernie Madoff–like characters who will steal you blind, as well as those of a less insidious, but just as insincere, phony, and conniving class of individual that can be found in any business. When you do find people with whom you share deep integrity and trust, they become colleagues worth keeping in one's life—friends toward whom one will gravitate throughout life as anchors of trust in a world where finding trust and integrity can be a challenge. O'Neil used to say that life and business will throw plenty of enemies and detractors at you, so choose your friends, partners, and associates carefully and wisely!

THE TENTH COMMANDMENT

One of O'Neil's overwhelming traits is his intense dedication and passion for the markets, something that led us to postulate the Tenth and Final Commandment, "Always maintain insane focus." Maintaining "insane focus" doesn't mean becoming a workaholic, since this implies that one is simply a mindless slave to one's job. What it means is finding one's passions in life so that the "work" that we do as we express these passions of ours is never really work. Not everyone is lucky enough to work at what they love, but to O'Neil it was something to strive for in life, and maintaining insane focus is another way of saying that people should always seek and pursue their passions in life, one way or the other. It is what makes life worth living, and by relentlessly pursuing our passions we attain the state of insane focus that in turn drives high levels of success. In O'Neil's view sitting around drinking beer, watching TV, and playing video games never struck him as a worthwhile, much less interesting, activity. As O'Neil used to say, "Don't just 'dabble,' dive in!"

To understand this, it helps to understand that O'Neil never saw any reason to take a vacation. Vacations are for people who hate their jobs, and O'Neil would tell us that if we could afford to leave the office for a three-week vacation, then we were proving we weren't very important to the operation. In 1999, we knew that the last time O'Neil had taken a vacation was in 1982, taking the family on a trip into the Oregon wilderness where they stayed in a log cabin with no phone, no television, and no other way to contact the outside world. As his son Scott and his wife related at the time when they each told us the story, Bill O'Neil brought up chart books and for most of the time in the "wilderness" he had his nose buried in these same chart books. After just a few days, O'Neil became quite bored and ended up leaving early to get back to his passion, the market, and the rest of "civilization." O'Neil's "insane focus" meant that he could never find solace in any wilderness setting simply because this was not his passion. For some, such as the great wilderness photographer Ansel Adams, camping for weeks at a time in Yosemite Valley in the Sierra-Nevada mountain range of eastern California is part of their passion in life, and in this regard Ansel Adams displayed his own version of "insane focus." Certainly, trading in the market was no more a part of his "insane focus" in life than camping in the wilderness was part of Bill O'Neil's "insane focus." And that is the whole point to O'Neil Commandment #10.

CONCLUSION

Overriding all of these rules, rules that go beyond many of the rules most investors are familiar with through his books and other writings, is a basic concept of always striving to operate with purity and simplicity. O'Neil doesn't get bogged down with tracking a multitude of indicators, relying instead on pure price/volume behavior as an old tape reader to discern where the big money is flowing in any market environment. Through his own experience and study, O'Neil understands that some indicators have a limited lifespan, and that 15 years was only a slice of the big picture. O'Neil keeps his system pure and simple. He doesn't get bogged down in minutiae. The indicators he does use have proven themselves over many market cycles. They were just as useful back in the 1920s, an entirely different era, as they are today, because they are based on human nature, which has remained constant. O'Neil primarily relies on the elements of price/volume behavior of the leading stocks and major indices on weekly and then daily charts, the shape of the patterns the stocks and indices trace out, relative strength, the relative strength line confirming new highs, institutional sponsorship, the accumulation/distribution rating, group rank, and the 50-day moving average. If you want to witness simplicity in action, work with Bill O'Neil, and you will soon realize that all your market indicators, gadgets, and gizmos are not necessary to the process of making big money in the market.

Since we both left the nest of O'Neil several years ago, the essential truths behind these commandments have become obvious to us as we have dealt with the world "outside of O'Neil." In any case, they are useful guideposts by which you can govern certain aspects of your conduct, attitude, and behavior, and hopefully help you stay focused, stay on track, and as Bill O'Neil used to advise us, "keep your nose clean." Of course, all of these commandments were conveyed to us while we were managing money for Bill O'Neil, during a time when we were working in the trenches with the man, an unforgettable learning experience we cover in detail in the next chapter.

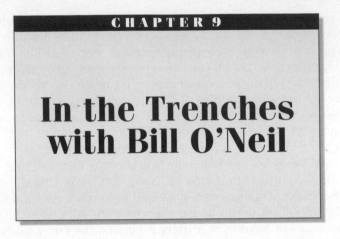

CHAPTER 9

In the Trenches
with Bill O'Neil

The period of 1998 to 2005, particularly the dot-com bubble and crash, were exhilarating periods to be working at William O'Neil + Company, Inc. managing money for the firm alongside Bill O'Neil and other very knowledgeable and talented traders at the firm, such as 1994 U.S. Investing Champion Lee Freestone, Al Savoyan, Ross Haber, Charles Harris, and Mike Webster, to name a few. They say that timing is everything, and we both were very lucky to be managing money at William O'Neil + Company, Inc. during the latter half of the 1990s, a decade that featured a parabolic move in the market (Figure 9.1). Working closely with Bill O'Neil during this fascinating market period, as well as the ensuing 2000–2002 bear market and the new "recovery bull" that began in 2003 provided one-of-a-kind lessons as we took careful notes of our real-time market discussions with him on a daily basis. What follows is an abridged edition of our combined trading diaries during our tenures at the firm, each of which could constitute an entire book in its own right.

1997–1998

Late 1997 was a difficult time to make any money in the market, and by early 1998 the market was pushing into new high ground following the sharp market break and correction that culminated in a 554.26-point sell-off in the Dow Jones Industrials, the largest point drop in its history at the time, on October 27, 1997. In late February, Bill O'Neil observed that

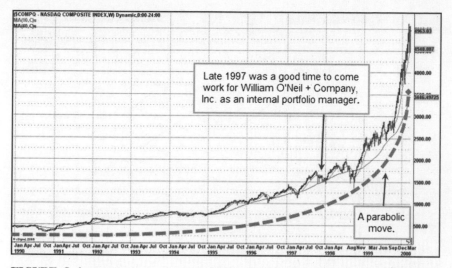

FIGURE 9.1 NASDAQ Composite weekly chart, 1990–2000. The 1990s was a Parabolic Decade.
Chart courtesy of eSignal, Copyright 2010.

leadership in the rally to new highs was being shared by growth stocks and larger-cap, consistent earnings-generating, established companies. As he would advise at the time, "This is a two-pronged market today—stick to companies with earnings consistency—this is what institutions are likely to buy." Larger-cap stocks of established companies with steady, reliable earnings growth of 10–15 percent and a long-term record of profitability, while not attractive as classic high-growth CAN SLIM type stocks, do have periods where they come into favor by institutions, and in this sense O'Neil was relying on his understanding of what we have come to call The Big Stock Principle, as he concluded what institutions were likely to buy in the market environment of 1998. In his observations, O'Neil emphasized that the simplest, most reliable way to identify leading groups in any market cycle is to pay close attention to the new high list and note which groups are consistently making the list. There is no need to create industry group "velocity" charts, no special color-coding of industry group movements, and no reliance on so-called top-down analysis.

Industry Group Comparison Invalid

One group moving well in early 1998 was the Computer–Software/Services group, adding some confirmation to the strong action in personal computer

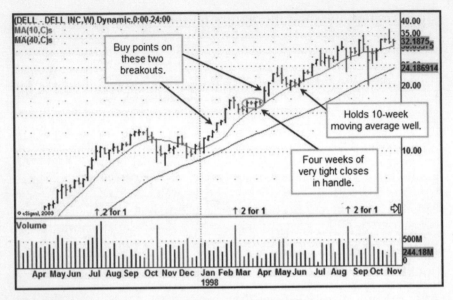

FIGURE 9.2 Dell, Inc. (DELL), weekly chart, 1997–1998.
Chart courtesy of eSignal, Copyright 2010.

maker Dell, Inc. (DELL), which by April of 1998 had staged two buyable breakouts following the market low in late 1997, as Figure 9.2 shows.

DELL's upside trend was a relentless continuation of a price move that began in 1995 and continued right into the market top in March of 2000. The personal computer group was a strong one in 1995, and the Computer–Software/Services group, including stocks like Computer Business Solutions (CBSL), Compuware (CPWR), and Computer Sciences (CSC), was a follow-on type of play to the move in PC stocks like DELL. A large installed base of personal computers, particularly in the business world, meant that companies providing technical and other services for personal computers (PCs) would find fertile ground for growth. Many analysts at that time viewed the move in PC stocks in the 1990s as being like the move in television stocks like Motorola (MOT) during the 1950s and 1960s, for example, and so felt that this comparison and historical precedent, as they saw it, meant that PC stocks had more or less run their course. O'Neil vehemently disagreed with this assessment as he felt televisions were purely for entertainment, whereas PCs were more of a "knowledge" tool for creating efficiency in the workplaces and organizing our personal lives. For this reason, he felt that any comparison to the move in television stocks in the 1950s and 1960s with the move in PC stocks in the 1990s as overly simplistic, as it was not an apples to apples comparison and hence was not valid.

In the first half of 1998, the weekly chart of DELL was confirming O'Neil's view, and offered clear proof that price/volume action tells you everything you need to know, hence the opinions of analysts who tried to intellectualize about the potential price moves of PC stocks by comparing them to the television stocks of the 1950s and 1960s were entirely useless. When we were looking at the DELL chart in April of 1998, it was showing very tight price/volume action as it moved straight sideways, closing tight for four weeks in a row before launching higher as we see in Figure 9.2. Notice also that the four weeks circled in Figure 9.2 showed two weeks up and two weeks down, with trading volume higher on the two weeks that were up and which had found support off the 10-week moving average, while volume declined on the two weeks down in that tight little consolidation. O'Neil commented at the time that this sort of pattern could just be bought right in the handle given how tight it was closing and the associated support off the 10-week, or 50-day moving average.

An Incredible Nose for Market Action

As the market moved into April of 1998, it had been steadily moving higher in a very tight, coherent trend that began in February and continued throughout March. O'Neil considered this very constructive. As he pointed out, "Tightness in the indexes while in an uptrend is constructive." Figure 9.3 shows this tight trend in the Dow Jones Industrials Index. What

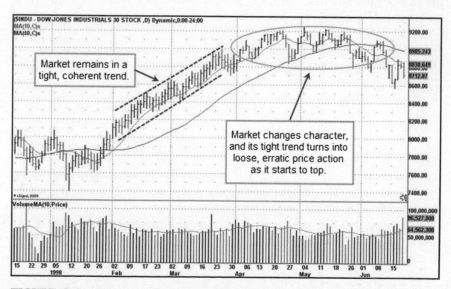

FIGURE 9.3   Dow Jones Industrials daily chart, 1998. A tight trend in February and March is highly constructive, until it begins to change character.
Chart courtesy of eSignal, Copyright 2010.

is significant here is that once this characteristic changes, in other words, the tight, coherent trend begins to morph into a volatile, choppy, and decidedly less "trending" state, it gives a strong clue that something is amiss. Indeed, the market began to wobble in the summer of 1998, and while the major market indexes were all able to make a marginal higher high by mid-July 1998, this breakout to new highs was a bull trap, and the market quickly began to fail to the downside as the continued shockwaves from the Asian Contagion of 1997 that caused the big October 27, 2007, break in the market began to hit the headlines.

O'Neil could smell something, which told him something was very wrong. On May 28th he called to point out, "Banks and brokers were hit hard today and did not rally. The financial crisis could be spreading. There is validity to the Asian crisis—it's not just 'some' news but A LOT of news." Problems in the Philippines and Indonesia, among other places on and around the Asian continent were creating palpitations in the market, and it is interesting to note that the break in brokers and banks on May 28th, occurred as the "tight, coherent trend" of February through March (Figure 9.3), changed character and the market began to wobble around its highs. Merrill Lynch (MER), shown in Figure 9.4, gapped down hard on May 28th, but this did not lead to any further serious price breaks in the stock as it turned around and broke out again in early July. However, it gave off a certain odor, certainly one that O'Neil did not like. When MER and other financials like Lehman Brothers (LEH) and Morgan Stanley (MS) tried to break out into new high price ground in early July 1998, they all failed and began to break down severely in a classic bull trap. Note the descent

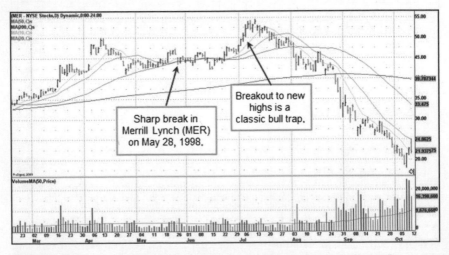

FIGURE 9.4 Merrill Lynch (MER) daily chart, 1998. A classic "bull trap."
Chart courtesy of eSignal, Copyright 2010.

of MER's chart as it began to break below its 200-day moving average in late August. Investors who witnessed the severe breaks in financials in March of 2008 might notice the similarity to the 1998 break in financials.

By mid-August, O'Neil noted the 12-year cycle followed by big downside market breaks in recent history, such as in 1962, 1974, and 1987. As the market began to roll over in August, O'Neil saw another big market break coming on the heels of this 12-year cycle. He projected that "Right now the market looks like it will need to undercut the low at 7500. We can project downside risk to 7000–7500. Mutual funds are loaded up with stock and they can't do anything about it, so they will start to have their performance questioned, creating fears that they won't be able to come back. Notice that the NYSE short interest ratio currently shows zero shorting on the way down—this is ominous."

As a "tape-reader" from the old school, Bill O'Neil has an incredible nose for the market, and his sixth sense derived from years of experience and careful observation gives him an uncanny ability to sniff out a change of character in the market. As the tape began to act in a way that he considered ominous, he surmised that its character was signaling a drop of significant magnitude.

O'Neil always looks at market declines and their potential magnitudes within the context of the longer-term chart. As the market began to break in late August of 1998 a logical end point for the decline was, as he saw it, a likely undercut of the lows of early 1998, as Figure 9.5 illustrates. The

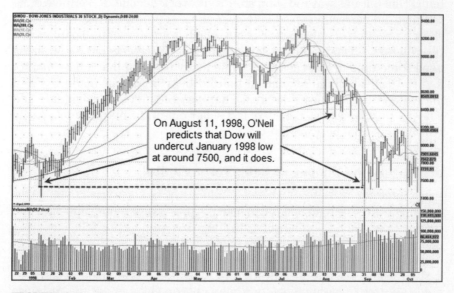

FIGURE 9.5 Dow Jones Industrials daily chart, 1998. O'Neil correctly projects the extent of the market's correction in late 1998.
Chart courtesy of eSignal, Copyright 2010.

intraday low of the lowest close in January of 1998 was around 7500, hence O'Neil quickly concludes that this is the first likely area for the market decline to stabilize and attempt to bottom. Price undercuts of large support areas often fake out the crowd, which sees such breaches of support as an area to sell stock aggressively or even to go short. And as we all know, when the crowd leans one way the market will usually lean the other way.

As the indexes sat on top of their 200-day moving averages, O'Neil observed, "Support at the 200-day is too obvious so it will probably break it." At this stage, he emphasized that while we would watch our stocks first and the indexes second, nevertheless, "It is very important to stick to your sell rules." Always being one to interject some optimism and positivity into the conversation, he quickly added, "It's also important to have a rule that will keep you in a stock once you buy it. For example, if you buy a stock on a breakout, then you must stay with it for six weeks or until it hits the 8 percent stop loss point." While this comment had nothing to do with what was going on in the market at that time, it is interesting to note that this quote from O'Neil in our trading diaries shows that as the eternal optimist he always has one eye on the bull side of the market, and is just as worried about selling a stock too soon before one has given it a chance to work as he is about following sell rules in a market decline!

O'Neil was dead-on in his projection of a market undercut and bottom at around the 7500 price level on the Dow, as Figure 9.6 shows. Five days off the first low in early September the market staged a follow-through day, but O'Neil felt this was too soon after a six-week decline. Nevertheless, he felt that the correction was likely over as he set forth his assessment, "A short correction of only six weeks but which is greater than 20 percent is a bear market. It is possible the adjustment has been made and we probably need some time to back and fill." While many believed that a bear market had to "last" a certain amount of time to be a valid bear market, O'Neil understood that a downside break that was of sufficient magnitude and velocity to scare and shake every last seller out of the market could easily constitute a valid bear market.

Sizing Up the Collapse of Long-Term Capital

By October the collapse of a hedge fund known as Long-Term Capital was causing a stir. The fund had relied heavily on leverage in implementing the strategies of its Ph.D.-brandishing, Nobel-prize-winning portfolio managers and so had borrowed heavily from banks and brokers of all stripes, and its collapse in turn led to fears of a domino effect whereby the global financial system would begin to melt down. But when the Fed stepped in and lowered rates by 25 basis points, or $\frac{1}{4}$ percent, on October 14th in response to the Long-Term Capital Crisis, the market was immediately off to the

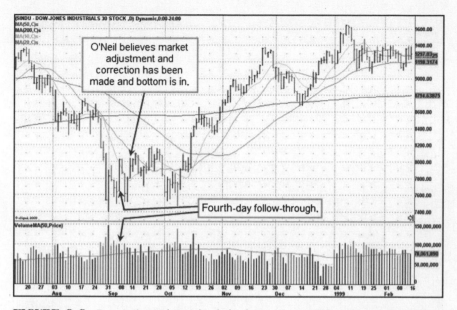

FIGURE 9.6 Dow Jones Industrials, daily chart, 1998–1999. A 20 percent decline in six weeks is a bear market by any other name.
Chart courtesy of eSignal, Copyright 2010.

races. Interestingly, most market participants remained shell-shocked by the frightening events and simply could not believe that the market could turn out of this so quickly. As well, most market strategists made the fatal error of considering a six-week, 20 percent correction in the market as "insufficient" for a bear market, and hence were calling for additional downside once the market finished consolidating this latest downside leg in what they saw as a continuing bear market.

Despite the fact that the crowd was skeptical, O'Neil reverted to his "Livermorian" core as he noted, "Basic economic conditions right now are not as bad as other bear periods," making the case that underlying conditions were sufficiently positive to support a rally attempt by the market.

A Controversial Stock Recommendation

Sometimes O'Neil would "make a statement" to the institutional clients of William O'Neil + Company, Inc. by making a controversial selection to put on the firm's institutional buy list, known at the time as the O'Neil Select List, but which most followers of O'Neil know as the New Stock Market Ideas or NSMI service containing recommendations on both the buy and avoid side of the market to institutional clients willing to pay $65,000 and

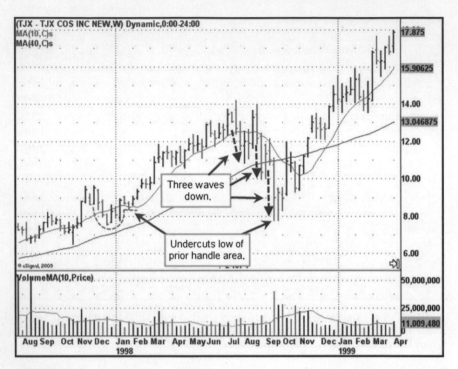

FIGURE 9.7 TJX Companies (TJX), weekly chart, 1998. O'Neil introduces the three waves down bottom-fishing technique.
Chart courtesy of eSignal, Copyright 2010.

up for such a service. You had to admire his boldness in seeking to demonstrate his confidence in underlying conditions by selecting a retail stock, TJX Companies (TJX), as a buy recommendation for the O'Neil Select List. However, this selection came as a bit of a shocker, since TJX was just coming up off its recent bear market lows, as we see in Figure 9.7, and we can only surmise that O'Neil intended it this way for the express purpose of making a statement about his market view at the time in what we used to call "classic Bill mode." O'Neil understood that the U.S. economy is primarily a consumer economy, and this was observed empirically in that most historical big winners in the market over history had a consumer orientation.

Further background to this recommendation comes in the form of comments O'Neil made to us in February 1998. As we noted in our trading diary: "Consumer (read: retail) stocks should be emphasized at this time. Over the last 4–5 years the tech sector has been the glamour group, which has performed well, while the big retailers like Wal-Mart and Home Depot sat it out. Now Bill sees them beginning to re-take a leadership position due to the general economy and the impact of baby-boomer spending. Bill sees a big move in these stocks from here which could have the same magnitude as the move they had in the early 90s. Also, brokers can be considered part of the retail boom: Schwab, Merrill Lynch, Morgan Stanley, etc. are all becoming more consumer-oriented and financial services is taking on a broader appeal as more highly-educated baby boomers begin to emphasize their own financial futures. This makes them more like consumer stocks. Finally, the Internet stocks can be considered retail stocks as well, and this further confirms the coming retail boom."

When O'Neil put TJX on the institutional buy list it caused quite a stir as some wondered whether he had fallen off his rocker. But as he explained, "It looks like bottom-fishing but there is an important concept here. First, TJX is a leader in discount retailing. It corrected 50 percent with three waves down. After the third wave down the need to sell is too obvious, and it also undercut the low on the handle formed in January 1998 which is a logical bottoming point. It is typical in a bear market for a good stock to drop deep into its prior base."

As Figure 9.7 shows, O'Neil was far from being "off his rocker," and TJX continued higher, nearly doubling from where he had recommended it. This recommendation became notable not only because it worked, but because it demonstrated to our institutional clients that we had techniques for buying stocks off their bottoms, as institutions overwhelmingly love to buy things when they are down. After all, who do you think creates all that "support along the lows" in the base formations of leading stocks?

Institutional Clients Provide Insight into Sponsorship Dynamics

During difficult or unsettling times in the market, it was common for O'Neil to meet with some of our largest institutional clients. Among these was Boston-based Fidelity Management & Research, O'Neil's first institutional client in the business. O'Neil loved to tell the story of how, as a 26-year-old broker at Hayden Stone in the early 1960s he first called Jerry Tsai, manager of the flagship Fidelity Fund back then, and started giving him stock ideas that worked out very well. Tsai gave the upstart O'Neil a 5,000 share order, which at the time was a huge "ticket" to write, as it meant some nice commissions would be earned. O'Neil knew that the account was being handled by a senior partner at Hayden Stone, and so he went in to his sales manager with the order. The manager saw no reason to turn down what was good business for the firm and told O'Neil to go ahead and send it into the wire room for execution, and that they would work out the conflict with the senior partner later. As it turned out, Jerry Tsai insisted that O'Neil be put on the account and earn the commissions, which was fair considering that the order resulted from O'Neil's ideas, and not those of the senior partner.

We remember during an IBD workshop in 1995, long before we worked at the organization, Bill O'Neil got up in front of the audience and held his palms horizontally, facing and parallel to each other, separate by about 2 feet of vertical space. He then said, "Fidelity gets a stack of research this big from us every week." O'Neil is well-regarded by his biggest institutional clients, and going in to see a manager of some $100 billion fund somewhere was a routine affair. Generally, O'Neil would go in and present a fund manager of such stature 8–10 of his biggest stocks and best ideas in the market at any given time. In this manner, O'Neil also has gained an intimate understanding of the workings of the minds of institutional portfolio managers given the array of challenges and objectives that they face. Coming back from one such meeting in October of 1998 where he had just met with the manager of a fund with 12-figures in assets under management, O'Neil pointed out that a fund this size could take three to six months to sell a 3 percent position. He also pointed out that as a big index like Microsoft (MSFT) goes up it often becomes a bigger percentage of the S&P 500, so any money manager who benchmarks his performance against the S&P 500 is forced to keep up by becoming more heavily weighted in the stock, and so is compelled to buy more. This in turn drives the stock higher in a spiraling effect.

Disagreeing with Wall Street

By December 1998 O'Neil was quite bullish. On December 2nd a report came out from a major market strategist asserting at the time that since new highs had not been confirmed by breadth, and only six of 30 Dow stocks were at new highs, the market was simply going to have a "good rally" without longevity. This strategist cited the fact that the broad market was lagging the Dow, and that European markets did not confirm the moves in U.S. markets, adding that he would not be surprised if the market retested its October lows. O'Neil quickly pointed out that our methodology does not rely on breadth confirming new highs, and that Europe, beset with lagging "semi-socialist economies," was not relevant. As well, O'Neil considered the Dow irrelevant since it was not leading at the time anyway (Figures 9.8 and 9.9). O'Neil was more focused on giving credit to the Fed rate cuts which lay the fundamental foundation for our firm's case.

Wall Street's obsession with the "Dow" and with "breadth confirming" was always something that O'Neil could not understand. And his voice would sometimes take on a vociferous tone as he would bark his views over the phone with decisive precision. O'Neil insisted that it is the leading index that is always telling you what is going on in the market, and at

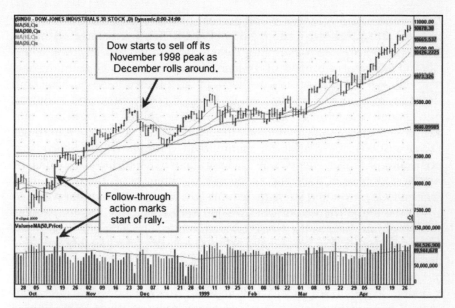

FIGURE 9.8 The Dow is lagging.
Chart courtesy of eSignal, Copyright 2010.

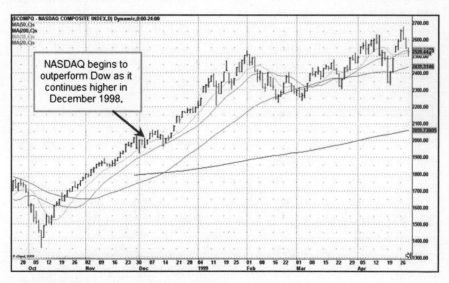

FIGURE 9.9 The NASDAQ is leading.
Chart courtesy of eSignal, Copyright 2010.

the time the NASDAQ was in the process of overtaking the Dow, as Figures 9.8 and 9.9 show. While we do not show an advance/decline line on these charts, breadth was in fact coming up strongly off its lows; hence the improvement of breadth at the margin was significant. Concerning oneself with what the Dow was doing, what 30 "old economy" stocks were doing in an otherwise vibrant era of Internet connections and shrinking cell phones, was utter nonsense to O'Neil, who felt at the time that market analysts were underestimating the depth of the economy. As always, O'Neil looked to the market for confirmation of his views, and he saw that something stronger was clearly going on under the surface as evidenced by the steepness of the trend as the market came up off the bottom with tremendous power and strength. In hindsight, we know what that was, and it was the initial tremors of what would later become the dot-com bubble market of late 1999 as the NASDAQ shifted into high gear and rapidly left behind its larger-cap, "old economy" brethren, the S&P 500 and the Dow Jones Industrial Index.

In October–December of 1998 a number of "deep" chart patterns were working very well, which was a bit unusual. However, it was necessary to make this adjustment and allow for more volatility in chart base patterns due to the market's rapid and steep correction of 20 percent in only six weeks. Also, there were examples of historical market environments where such patterns showed similar "jagged" behavior, particularly in their handles, such as Peoplesoft (PSFT) in 1994, shown in Figure 9.10, which has since been acquired by Oracle Corp. (ORCL). PSFT formed a long "macrobase" consisting of two failed breakouts from improper "sub-bases" within the overall structure. The third base was relatively more constructive than the prior two failed "sub-bases" and had a deep handle, which looked

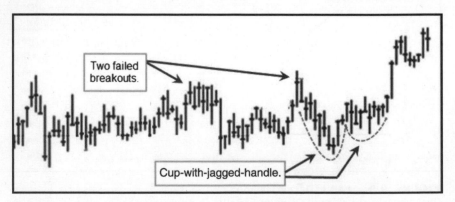

FIGURE 9.10 Peoplesoft (PSFT), weekly chart, 1994. An old scan shows the jagged handle in Peoplesoft's cup-with-handle base, the third base in this overall "macro-base" formation.
Chart courtesy of eSignal, Copyright 2010.

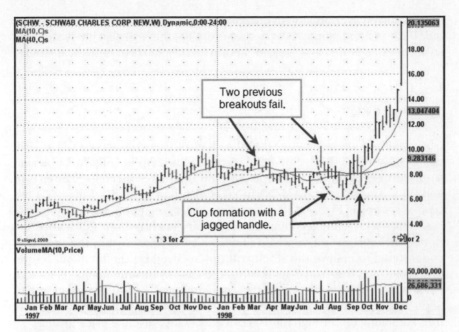

FIGURE 9.11 Charles Schwab Corp. (SCHW), a "jagged" cup-with-handle formation works on the third breakout try, confirming the Rule of Three.
Chart courtesy of eSignal, Copyright 2010.

wrong. But the breakout from this base ended up working as Peoplesoft had a huge move from that initial, correct buy point. In 1998 we saw similar "jagged" patterns in stocks like America Online (AOL), Charles Schwab Corp. (SCHW), shown in Figure 9.11, and even Sun Microsystems (SUNW in 1998, today JAVA). At first O'Neil wasn't sure what to make of these patterns, but enough of them were working by December 1998 to confirm that the exaggerated price ranges in their chart bases were indeed a function of the market's correction of 20 percent in only six weeks.

Peoplesoft is also instructive in that it illustrates the Rule of Three whereby a stock will form a large "macro-base" structure as it tries to break out of three successive "sub-bases" within the overall structure but fails on the first two, only to succeed on the third try. O'Neil believed that the Rule of Three was valid because the first two breakouts that failed conditioned the crowd to expect the third breakout to fail, but as the market always seeks to fool most investors most of the time, it ends up working. We saw this sort of formation occur with Charles Schwab Corp. (SCHW) in October of 1998 with the third breakout from a cup-with-handle "sub-base" working as the stock launches higher. The jagged "V-shaped" handle is due to the steep correction in the general market. It is important to understand that one should not get overly focused on the precise shape of a base since it must be taken in context with the pattern that the general market is tracing out. If the general market is extremely volatile, this will also likely show up as more exaggerated and "jagged" action on the charts of individual stocks.

1999–2000

Observant readers will notice that the chart of Qualcomm (QCOM) in 1999 which is shown at the beginning of the previous chapter (Figure 8.1) is also similar to the examples of Peoplesoft and Charles Schwab in Figures 9.10 and 9.11. Amazon.com (AMZN) in 2009 also had a similar Rule of Three type of set-up, as Figure 9.12 shows. Two prior breakouts within a "macro-base" that is actually trending upwards very slightly both fail before the third breakout from a cup-with-handle base works. Again, the crowd is conditioned to believe the stock will not succeed on the breakout by the third time, and the crowd, as is often the case at turning points, is fooled. Once AMZN cleared the top of the cup-with-handle base it formed in late September 2009 it never violated its 10-week (50-day) moving average before launching up through the 100 price level into all-time price ground.

In any case, the precedent of Peoplesoft in 1994 was helpful in discerning these jagged bases, and stocks like America Online (AOL) and Charles Schwab (SCHW) were rocketing higher. On March 16, 1999, we put out a

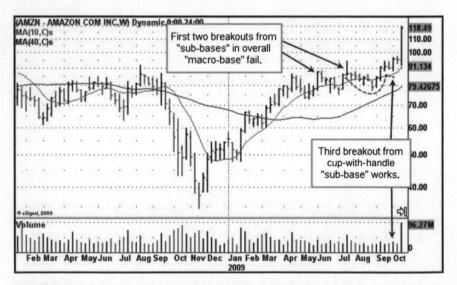

FIGURE 9.12 Amazon.com (AMZN) weekly chart, 2009. The Rule of Three is at work again in AMZN's September 2009 breakout.
Chart courtesy of eSignal, Copyright 2010.

price target on Schwab based on some similar historical examples as well as some simple price target analysis based on earnings growth, forward earnings estimates and any potential P/E expansions in Schwab. At the time Schwab was trading at a split-adjusted $90 a share, and O'Neil was looking for a $140 price target on the upside. Most of the institutional sales force was incredulous, thinking that Schwab had "come too far too fast." Again, the misperception of overwhelming upside strength as a reason to be negative on a stock because it is just "too high" is seen at work here. In about four month's time, Schwab had gone from a split-adjusted $28 a share to nearly $90, and it wasn't finished yet. O'Neil was using an historical precedent in establishing his price target for Schwab. He had noticed that Quotron Systems, a hot stock back in 1979, had come out of a similar base as Schwab's, and the magnitude of its move indicated that Schwab could go to 140. As it turned out, Schwab eventually topped out at 155, a little higher than O'Neil's 140 price target.

The Use of Historical Precedence

Using historical precedence when trying to figure out possible price targets for stocks he owned was one technique O'Neil employed when trying to figure out just how far a big, winning stock that he owned could go. O'Neil believes that the chart patterns are essentially maps of psychology, and that chart patterns will remain useful as long as human psychology remains the same. For this reason, he felt that if a stock he owned today exhibited very similar chart characteristics to a big, winning stock from the past, then using the stock from the past as a "historical precedent" in order to guide his handling of a stock in the present was valid. In the case of Schwab and its similarities to Quotron Systems of 1979, it turned out to be quite valid.

O'Neil understood that it is the big institutional investors that run the market, and since big fund managers all think the same, then the chart patterns of the stocks they traffic in generally will show their psychology at work. O'Neil looked for institutional support, and in his observations he found that stocks which have upside price runs and then consolidate, forming a base structure of one sort or another, usually need five weeks of pulling back in order to digest their gains as some institutional investors finish accumulating their positions and others sell part of their positions after the stock has run up because it has either become "overvalued" within their framework of how they look at stocks and also because they will trim a position that goes up too far, too fast and hence becomes a larger-than-normal percentage of their portfolio. For example, if fund manager A can only have 2 percent maximum position sizes in his fund, and he buys 2 percent of stock XYZ which then doubles, becoming more like 4 percent of the portfolio, he may have to cut that position back to 2 percent if it becomes too heavy of a weighting in his portfolio. As this process occurs, and the stock consolidates, other institutions who like the stock will accumulate on pullbacks. One interesting rule that O'Neil had was that after a stock has consolidated and built a base of at least five weeks, then usually the stock can be bought on pullbacks that are near to or undercut the prior low of the base in the sixth week or later. In many cases after a stock has based for at least five weeks the 50-day, or 10-week, moving average has a chance to catch up to the stock, at which point it serves as critical support.

By the end of April 1999, O'Neil was beginning to have his doubts about the market, which was in a choppy uptrend and running into some trouble as the Dow was trying to clear the 11,000 level. Distribution in the form of higher-volume down days as the Dow approached the 11,000 mark looked suspicious to O'Neil, particularly when he combined this with the action in leading stocks. As we quote him in our trading diaries, "One of the problems is that most, if not nearly all of the big leaders have undergone serious distribution and liquidation. Even the retailers, which are considered a steady, stable sector, are getting hit." Pointing out the current weekly chart of Home Depot (HD) shown in Figure 9.13, O'Neil gave a quick assessment of what was wrong with the stock. "It broke out at 20 in early 1998 and ran up to the 50 area, then built a big, loose base in the summer/fall of 1998, broke out again in October, then had a smaller run up to 60, and then built

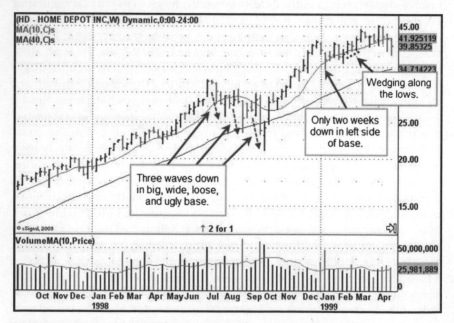

FIGURE 9.13 Home Depot (HD) weekly chart, 1998–1999.
Chart courtesy of eSignal, Copyright 2010.

a base around 55–60. There are only two down weeks in that base on the left side which is characteristic of an improper base. You need to see four to five down weeks on the left side which allows the psychology to set up correctly by shaking out ALL the weak holders before it moves up. The three weeks before it broke out were all wedging up slightly."

Authors' Note: O'Neil is a natural teacher with a natural feel for developing talent in this manner, and these short "market school" sessions where he would call us to talk about a real-time example in the market that illustrated a lot of the concepts he teaches in his books and workshops were always a privilege and a treat given that we were receiving "one-on-one" real-time instruction from one of the stock market's greatest mentors.

This concept is very important in order to understand a proper base formation. O'Neil was concerned that breakouts from improper bases were failing, as in the case of Home Depot, and this was a bad sign for the market. Note the Three Waves Down type of structure similar to the example of TJX Companies (TJX) in Figure 9.7. The critical point here is that the base Home Depot formed in early 1999 only came down two weeks before it started drifting back upward again. As it tried to break out in late February, it was not pulling back but was instead wedging along the lows for three weeks as it drifted higher on light trading volume. Normally, a stock should pull back a little as volume dries up before launching out of a base. Because Home Depot's base was faulty, by late April 1999 it was starting to roll over.

1999—A Challenging Year!?!

Throughout much of 1999 the market's trend was a slow, choppy, and grinding upside affair that would break out to new highs and then pull back in again, which it did several times in succession. All the while there were reasons to become bearish, and reasons to become bullish. Throughout all the "chop and slop" there were some stocks that continued to go about the business of breaking out of sound bases, moving up, building another base, breaking out, and moving up again. Most of these were stocks that were simply stair-stepping their way higher as they slowly built up for the parabolic move that was coming at the end of 1999, but which nobody saw coming in late spring.

On May 20 O'Neil called to discuss two of these new leaders, Broadcom (BRCM) and Qlogic (QLGC), and to go over how to set price targets for Broadcom. O'Neil frequently discusses how to use price-to-earnings ratios and their associated expansions during a stock's uptrend to come up with price targets, but there are actually three different methods that can be used. We've already seen how O'Neil used the example of Quotron Systems in 1979 as a historical precedent to set an upside price target for Charles Schwab Corp. (SCHW), which had a similar chart pattern. This is the

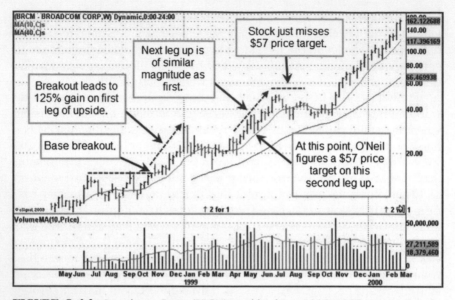

FIGURE 9.14 Broadcom Corp. (BRCM) weekly chart, 1998–1999. Measuring the first up leg in BRCM's chart pattern to estimate the extent of subsequent upside price moves.
Chart courtesy of eSignal, Copyright 2010.

second type of method he employs to determine price targets, and there is a third, even simpler method, which O'Neil describes as follows as we observe the chart of Broadcom in Figure 9.14 (note that the chart is not split-adjusted, so prices mentioned in the following diary entry are three times the prices shown in the charts, which we put in parentheses): "If you have a big position in Broadcom and have pyramided properly, now you have to figure out where the stock could go to. This is the more difficult half of capitalizing on a big winner—buying the stock is easy. The process can go one of two ways. First, look at the prior base which was formed from July through September 1998. The stock broke out at 40 (13.33) and ran up to 90 (30), a 125 percent run. The stock's most recent breakout is now at 77 (25.67) coming out of the base formed between January and April 1999. Figuring it could make a similar move as the move from 40 (13.33) to 90 (30) would take the stock somewhere to 173 (57.66). Also note the number of weeks of the move from 40 (13.33) to 90 (30) was 11 weeks. So you would figure the next move from 77 (25.67) should go about the same duration. If you hit your price target of 57.60 within five weeks, you would not sell as this indicates a lot of power, and a big leader will not run up and poop out after five or seven weeks. Your durations should be comparable. This also assumes that BRCM is in fact a big, institutional leader and not a thin, wild thing that could go up five weeks and blow up. Some thin, wild things can do exactly that—but a big institutional, heavy-trading leader will not."

O'Neil also reiterated the use of a similar historical precedent to generate price targets. At O'Neil we had "model books" of all the big, leading stocks that were huge winners in prior historical cycles going all the way back to the 1880s, and these were very helpful in finding historical precedents that could be used in assessing stocks we were handling in real time. O'Neil describes this process as follows, "A third way to gauge the potential move is to look for a similar leader in the model books. If BRCM has gone up 33 percent in the first five weeks since breaking out at 77 (25.67) look for another big leader in the model books that also moved up 33 percent in the first five weeks. Don't pick a second-tier leader—look for a big leader that is similar in its base structure and how it acts right out of the chute. Maybe there are some similar industry characteristics but this is not necessarily a key thing."

By June 6th O'Neil was starting to look for a bear market to develop, as he believed the market was topping. He ran through the process he believed was unfolding: "Note that the market topped in late April when Schwab and AOL topped. At that point the Dow started running up due to buying in cyclicals. The market will top in a couple of ways: First, distribution occurring on the Dow sucks in shorts who are then run in and the market moves to new highs and then rolls over, making a final top. The second is as you get distribution in the big leaders one other index keeps going up which fakes everyone out. This divergence camouflages the real top in the market." Despite the bearish evidence in the market, the indexes soon stabilized in mid-June before turning and making a run for new highs, as Figure 9.15 shows.

In Chapter 1 we discussed the difficult period that most of 1999 represented, despite being considered a "bubble" market as it went parabolic at the end of the year. But there were plenty of cross-currents that could throw you off. We remember buying a pretty large position in WorldCom, Inc. which gained infamy during the bear market when the company went bankrupt and its CEO, Bernie Ebbers, was sent to prison. This all occurred right around the bear market bottom in 2002, but the hints of trouble brewing for WorldCom were evident even in June of 1999. We noticed that as we were buying WorldCom the stock was actually moving lower (Figure 9.16), something that O'Neil insisted should never happen to any stock while you are buying a large position in it. Buying more than just a few thousand shares of any stock should never be easy, but somebody was pelting our order with stock they wanted to sell, and the stock kept going down in earnest. About half-an-hour later we called our trading desk to dump the stock, which was down about half-a-point from where we had bought the shares, and exited the position in its entirety. O'Neil later called up to ask, "What's up with WorldCom?" We told him of the experience we had

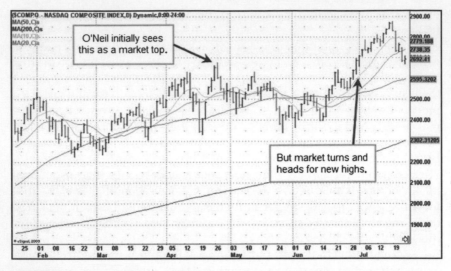

FIGURE 9.15 NASDAQ Composite Index daily chart, 1999—a top that wasn't.
Chart courtesy of eSignal, Copyright 2010.

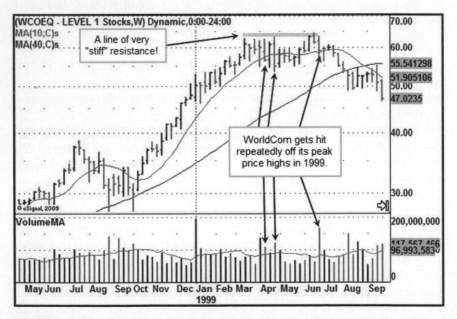

FIGURE 9.16 WorldCom, Inc. (WCOEQ) weekly chart, 1998–1999. The "line of
stiff resistance" overcomes WorldCom.
Chart courtesy of eSignal, Copyright 2010.

trying to buy a good-sized position in the stock and that it kept coming down as we were executing the order. Perhaps, we speculated, WorldCom was simply under pressure because of news that the Federal Trust Commission was investigating undersea cable operators, of which WorldCom was one at the time. O'Neil pointed out that he had noticed that whenever WorldCom tried to break out of its base, a seller would show up and hammer the stock. O'Neil wanted no part of it as he surmised, "Maybe Janus or someone big is dumping their stock. What I want to know is, 'Why?'"

By 2002, we had our answer, but the price/volume action of the stock was telling you that something was very wrong well in advance. In this case we were lucky, since using O'Neil's "50,000 share rule," whereby any stock you are buying 50,000 shares of or more should be difficult to buy, got us out of WorldCom immediately. This was typical of O'Neil's understanding of the "line of least resistance." In WorldCom's case, the different points at which it tried to break out to new highs in 1999 were not lines of least resistance, but rather lines of very stiff resistance!

"Watch Out, It's Billy O.!"

Most investors who follow O'Neil know of the "ascending base," but most do not know that there are a number of corollaries to the ascending base, which is a jagged sort of formation where the stock has three sharp pullbacks in an overall ascending formation of 9 to 18 weeks long with each pullback ending just above the low of the previous pullback, such as Home Depot, which formed an ascending base in the second quarter of 1998 (Figure 9.17). We recall going down to the floor of the New York Stock Exchange when O'Neil was playing Home Depot very heavily. At the time, O'Neil owned one seat on the floor and leased the other. O'Neil once grumbled that he hired some consultants to review his business, and they advised selling one of the seats and leasing one instead. This turned out to be a big mistake, as the value of the seat went up quite a bit after that, leading to O'Neil's subsequent distrust of "consultants" of any kind.

Running around the floor of the exchange with Lou Sulsenti, O'Neil floor broker at the time, was always an interesting and educational experience. In this case, we recall Lou telling the story of getting a "G" order to execute in Home Depot, which means an order that a member firm is making on its own behalf, so when he went up to the post Louie yells out, "50,000 HD to buy, G!" The Home Depot specialist, in testimony to O'Neil's recognized prowess on the floor, rolls his eyes, "Back again? Don't tell me this thing is going higher again?!?" Short-sellers in Home Depot who were in the crowd see O'Neil's "G" orders coming in to buy the stock, prompting them to warn each other, "Watch out, [it's] Billy O.! Watch out [it's] Billy O.!" Such was O'Neil's reputation on the floor, and it was not limited to

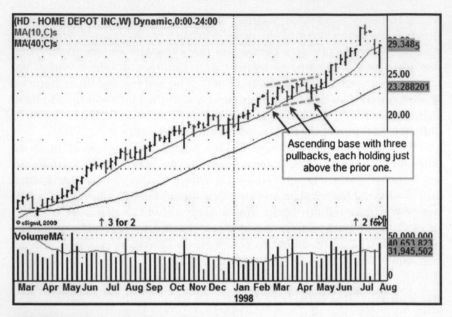

FIGURE 9.17 Home Depot (HD) weekly chart, 1998. HD forms an ascending base before pushing sharply higher in mid-1998.
Chart courtesy of eSignal, Copyright 2010.

his trading ability, but also his gestures as a human being. Way back when, a floor broker for O'Neil, whom we knew as "Bob," was working on the roof of his house one weekend and fell off, injuring himself severely and becoming paralyzed from the waist down. O'Neil brought the floor broker back to California and gave him a job at the home office in Los Angeles, making sure that he was well taken care of. Every time we went on the floor, certain floor brokers on the exchange would ask, "How's Bob?" The NYSE members and floor brokers were like a big family, and they recognized that O'Neil had taken care of one of their own. For this O'Neil was afforded great respect, perhaps even more than for his trading prowess, on the NYSE floor.

O'Neil's buying spree in Home Depot came as a result of the breakout from the ascending base in Figure 9.17 as this is a very powerful pattern to buy off of, and O'Neil knew what he was looking at. Certainly the upside action of the stock after O'Neil started buying Home Depot stock with his "G" orders on the NYSE floor was enough to impress the specialist, who probably didn't want to have to act as a seller of last resort in the face of O'Neil's relentless buying of the stock. In such case, the specialist was more likely to turn and start buying the stock for his own firm's account.

A Boring Base Is Not so Boring

Another "little pattern" that O'Neil discussed is one that is somewhat similar to an ascending base but simply looks like three little bases all on top
of each other instead of the more "jagged" look of the ascending base seen
in Home Depot. Overall the stock appears to be making little net progress
as it "breaks out and moves up a little bit, forms another little base, breaks
out again and moves up a little again, and forms another little base." This
is one of those patterns that lull you into thinking the stock isn't able to
make any real upside progress. As O'Neil put it, "The pattern fakes you out
into thinking that the stock is boring and won't go anywhere—but then it
moves out and takes off. Watch for it." In late 1999, Ariba, Inc. (ARBA),
part of the "dot-com sub-craze" in emerging business to business or "B2B"
e-commerce plays, was showing this type of formation as it set up in three
little "stair-step" style bases, each three to four weeks in length so that
they are not of sufficient duration to meet the definition of a "flat base"
which must be five weeks or more in length (Figure 9.18). From August to
November 1999 Ariba slowly wended its way higher, launching on a threefold price move that carried into March 2000.

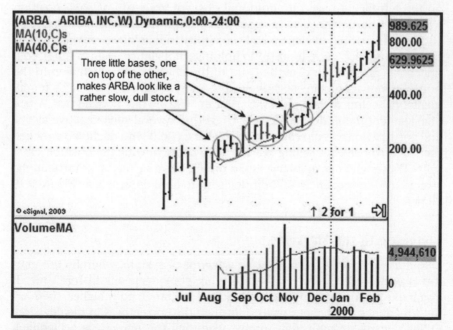

FIGURE 9.18 Ariba, Inc. (ARBA) weekly chart, 1999–2000. Three little bases form
a dull-looking stair-step formation, which then launches higher.
Chart courtesy of eSignal, Copyright 2010.

The essential force behind any of these patterns is that they indicate a stock that is "coiling" as it prepares to spring to the upside. Often, such patterns, unless you understand them and know how to look for them, can lull you into thinking that the stock can't get any kind of consistent upside movement going. In particular, if you buy a stock, say, in the first little base of a three-base stair-step type of formation, it is very likely that the stock's lack of decisive upside action will wear you out so that you sell the stock, perhaps taking a small profit, and then forget about it, missing the huge price move when it begins. Recognizing when the "line of least resistance" has been broken, however, and the stock is free to romp higher, is critical in understanding these types of patterns. In the same manner that the ascending base has three pullbacks in the formation, the "stair-step" formation has three little bases, which do not pull back down into the prior range. The basic idea is that what looks "dull" may actually be coiling up, and one should pay close attention to these types of patterns when they occur.

Before the advent of online services like William O'Neil Direct Access (WONDA), one of the best-selling and most popular institutional products offered by the firm to its institutional clients was the Data Monitor. This was a custom chart book created for each client's portfolio, containing a weekly O'Neil Data Graph®, with the option for a daily chart to be shown on the left-facing page (at additional cost, of course), for each position owned by a particular client in their respective portfolios. In this manner institutional portfolio managers had the ability to quickly reference, review, and monitor each of their portfolio holdings at a glance. Data Monitor contained an "alerts matrix" in the front of the chart book, which alerted the portfolio manager to any negative or positive changes in the stock's fundamental or technical data points. Earlier in 1999 we had noticed that Waste Management Industries (WMI) was triggering several such negative alerts, and normally this would cause us to advise a client who might have owned the stock to consider selling WMI, or at least reviewing the position carefully. Those who may not have acted on the negative alerts, unfortunately, reaped the consequences of their decision to hold the stock, as Figure 9.19 shows.

Listening to the Market

O'Neil always views the market as a feedback system, whereby the market is either confirming or disconfirming your decisions in real time. If you make the decision to buy a stock and the stock goes higher, the market's feedback mechanism was confirming the correctness of the decision. O'Neil's great strength is in totally accepting the market as a feedback mechanism, and abiding by the evidence the market offers in real time, even if it contradicts his earlier views. An example of this is seen in Best Buy (BBY) in Figure 9.20, which we were fairly bullish on as it broke out of

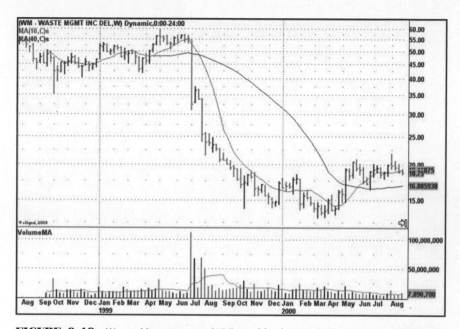

FIGURE 9.19 Waste Management (WM) weekly chart, 1999. WM splits wide open after weak sales growth flashed an early sell signal.
Chart courtesy of eSignal, Copyright 2010.

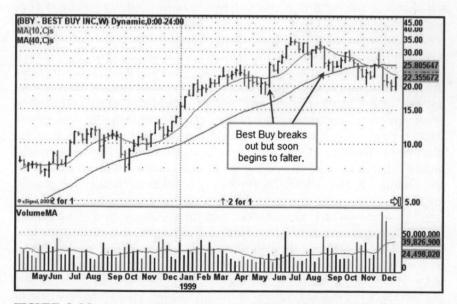

FIGURE 9.20 Best Buy (BBY) weekly chart, 1998–1999. Best Buy moves to new highs but quickly begins to falter as the general market begins to weaken.
Chart courtesy of eSignal, Copyright 2010.

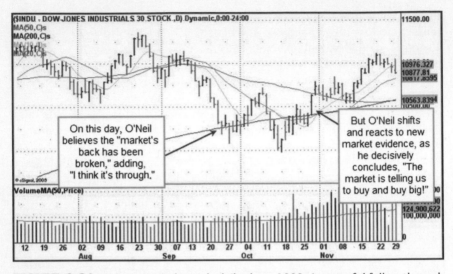

FIGURE 9.21 Dow Jones Industrials daily chart, 1999. A powerful follow-through day on October 28, 1999 leads O'Neil to buy, and buy big.
Chart courtesy of eSignal, Copyright 2010.

a seven-week base, paused for one week, and then continued higher over the next four weeks. BBY began to falter, however, and as the market began to mistreat him, O'Neil became suspicious of the overall environment.

On September 24, O'Neil was fairly certain that "the market's back has been broken." He summed it up tersely, "I think it's through." Indeed, the market looked quite weak (Figure 9.21) as the Fed began to raise interest rates, and enough feedback was provided by both leading stocks and the general market to validate this view. However, O'Neil recognizes at all times that market conditions can change very rapidly, and this is why he never, ever assumed a rigid position, no matter how certain he was about the state of the market at any given time. This is a critical lesson for investors of all stripes. In the market there are no constants, and changes in the market environment, some more rapid than others, are part and parcel of the game. Modern civil engineers understand that large structures which are subject to the more intense forces of nature, such as hurricane-force winds or earthquakes, must have certain features built into the design that allow the structure to sway, move, and bend with these forces, which decreases the chance that they will be toppled instead. In the same way, investors who cling to rigid opinions, and thereby resist the forces of the market as they shift and change, risk being snapped in half like a brittle little twig.

The market continued to plumb new lows going into mid-October, and there was still no concrete evidence that the market decline was ending, until it finally undercut the September lows and began to rally, posting a massive follow-through day on the ninth day off the bottom (Figure 9.21). Reacting to new evidence, O'Neil was no less than decisive as he adamantly declared, "The market is telling us to buy and buy big!" There were plenty of stocks to buy, and the ensuing price runs in many of these stocks made us a fortune.

On the way up, however, given the sharpness and steepness of the rally, some leading stocks would exhibit a great deal of volatility as they ran up sharply, pulled back sharply for a few days, and then turned and charged to new price highs. During one of our "market school" sessions, Bill talked about handling volatility in a high-flying stock, using the example of Immunex (IMNX) as he advised, "It is wise to go back and map out all the pullbacks the stock had during a rally phase. Check the percentage decline off the top and the number of days over which the decline occurs. This gives you some idea of where the stock can trade within a normal uptrend and will keep you in when it corrects sharply." This basic idea kept us in some of the volatile leaders we were playing, and IMNX's weekly chart (Figure 9.22) shows the typical one-week pullbacks that the stock put in as it moved higher. Once the duration of the stock's pullback in early March 2000 exceeded those seen on the way up from December through February, it was clear that at the very least the uptrend was starting to run out of gas, and at the very least would have to build a new base and set up again if it had any chance of pushing into new high price ground again.

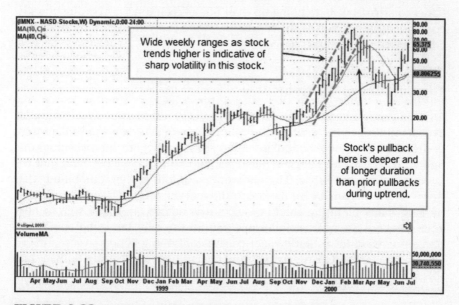

FIGURE 9.22 Immunex (IMNX) weekly chart, 1999–2000.
Chart courtesy of eSignal, Copyright 2010.

"You Screwed Up!"

In February of 2000 it was time for Bill O'Neil to pass out the "commission checks" for all the internal portfolio managers who had made money that year. As is standard at most proprietary trading outfits, the portfolio managers were paid a percentage of the gross profits they made in their internal account. You might think that clocking performance numbers in the low 500 percent range in 1999, as we both did, would merit some heavy praise from O'Neil, but far from it. He brought in your check and handed it to you, and then started flipping through what we used to call the famous O'Neil Personal Data Assistant, which was essentially a very fat legal pad on which he wrote endless notes, folding back the pages that already had notes scribbled in every available square millimeter of their cellulose surface.

O'Neil kept track of his portfolio managers, particularly their mistakes, and these often found their way onto his non-electronic, legal pad PDA. O'Neil respected those who could perform well in the market, and you only gained credibility with him as a portfolio manager if you could keep up with the group and its high performance standards. He was always happy if you were making big money for the firm, but he just didn't gush over it, or waste time allowing you to bask in the warm afterglow of a very profitable trading year. He preferred to go over mistakes, which is what he would do as he flipped through 30 pages of his legal pad and found the exact page where he had his notes on your trading mistakes. After reviewing critical mistakes you made, despite being up over 500 percent on the year, he quickly concluded, "You screwed up. If you had done everything exactly right you could have been up 1,000 percent."

The Bursting of the Bubble

As we moved into the end of February 2000, the market was becoming even frothier as many leading stocks burst into climax runs. As well, money poured into ever more speculative stocks, in particular the mass dot-com bubble IPOs with no sales, no earnings, and no real business plan that related to generating either. The climactic action in leaders combined with this increased "speculative flavor" to the market was to O'Neil a clear sign of danger lurking in the shadows. This was not necessarily a sign to hurl your stocks at the nearest seller and run for the hills, but to be on a Code Red alert ready to instantly react to the confirming action of a technical top in the market. Obviously, sentiment had become frothily bullish, but this was merely one lesser, but still key, piece of the puzzle, and in and of itself was not sufficient to call a top. When the associated technical evidence began showing up as climax runs turned into climax tops and heavy distribution began to beset the market, it simply added conviction to the conclusion that it was time to begin exiting the market in earnest.

After the top on March 17th, O'Neil wisely counseled us to stay out of the market for at least three months. O'Neil told us, "Watch stocks that were big winners—they will break once and then try to rally sharply and then they break again, at which point you can put a fork in 'em." O'Neil recalled that in prior market cycles "you might have two or three 'story stocks' going nuts, but to see 200 to 300 like you have the past several months means we've seen a tulip craze or 'bubble,' if you want to call it that. The magnitude of this tulip craze indicates that it needs time to work out of the system."

The steepness of the market's decline caused O'Neil to begin seeing some similarities to the bear market of 1962, which finally culminated in a climactic low during the Cuban Missile Crisis of October 1962. As we all flew to New York in early June of 2000 to present at the *Investor's Business Daily* workshop to be held at the Hyatt Regency Central Station on Saturday the 3rd, we did not realize just how eventful this trip would be.

Overpaid Analysts

We were both tagged to participate in the workshop by making a presentation on the Daily Graphs investment tool after lunch, so along with our faithful assistant Mike Webster, one of the newest internal portfolio managers at O'Neil at the time, the three of us landed in New York that Wednesday night. Holing up at the Peninsula Hotel on Fifth Avenue we began preparations for the weekend event as well as the next day's full slate of appointments we had scheduled with several O'Neil institutional clients with offices in the city. On Thursday, June 1st, we went in to see one client firm which had just hired a hot-shot "million-dollar" Internet analyst who allegedly "knew everything" about the Internet "space." Hiring a high-priced Internet analyst after the dot-com bubble market had topped didn't seem too smart to us, but we went into the meeting with the best of intentions.

This particular client firm gave us a very gracious reception when we showed up at their offices on Park Avenue. After a bit of bantering about the current state of the market, we were all ushered into their conference room to begin a meeting during which we were to review their current portfolio holdings. The three of us, along with several staff, including the "million-dollar" Internet analyst, began viewing WONDA charts that were being projected up onto a screen on the wall at the end of the long conference table. Mike Webster sat in the back, since he could only act as an observer, and as we went through the stocks, an almost surreal, yet comical repartee began to take form as Mike kept instinctively reacting to each new chart that he saw by softly saying to himself the same phrase, over

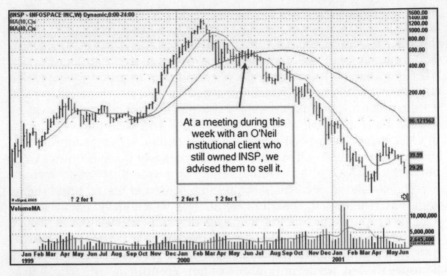

FIGURE 9.23 Infospace (INSP) weekly chart, 2000. The top is in.
Chart courtesy of eSignal, Copyright 2010.

and over again: "That's a top. That's a top. That's a top." While he was actually saying this quietly to himself, the room was quiet enough so that everyone could hear him, and each time he uttered this simple but accurate phrase the million-dollar Internet analyst harrumphed and laughed quietly at the "naïve" upstart calling tops in his beloved Internet holdings. Among the stocks that they owned was Infospace (INSP), shown on a weekly chart in Figure 9.23. We advised them to sell the position, but their analyst began a long-winded discourse on why INSP was "undervalued."

At the time, Mike Webster was a rookie portfolio manager at O'Neil, and the spectacle of him outanalyzing a hot-shot "million-dollar" analyst without even trying was something that was truly, as the famous credit card commercial puts it, "priceless." We should note that while the analyst was both arrogant and ignorant, the CEO of the client firm was himself extremely gracious and grateful for the meeting. At one point we had told this client that we expected the NASDAQ Composite Index to push below 2500 at its nadir. In 2001, when it finally did, the CEO sent our entire institutional services department a case of very fine Dom Perignon, congratulating us for accurately making what he had originally thought to be an "unbelievable" prediction.

Avoiding the Nokia Trade

Friday morning, June 2nd, we found ourselves at breakfast in the Luncheon Club of the New York Stock Exchange, where our firm of William

O'Neil + Company, Inc. was a member. We met up with O'Neil NYSE floor broker Lou Sulsenti when we first arrived at the exchange and headed upstairs to eat, where we were joined shortly thereafter by Steve Porpora, the second floor broker whom many readers may recognize as a former NYSE floor commentator on CNBC throughout a good part of the 2000s until O'Neil shut down his floor operations in 2008.

At 8:30 A.M., just as we were settling in and enjoying our blintzes, omelets, and Canadian bacon, the monthly jobs number hit the newswires: 131,855 jobs had been added in May when many feared that the brutal market top and bubble-bursting in March might have severe economic consequences. Employment tends to lag market turns, but the futures were reacting big to the upside. The room began to clear out very quickly as most of the floor brokers in the room headed downstairs. An avalanche of buy orders was expected at the opening, so Steve Porpora, who functioned as Director of Floor Operations for O'Neil headed downstairs while we finished up with breakfast. It was somewhat surreal to be sitting in an almost empty room that just a few minutes before had been filled with a multitude of floor brokers devouring their healthy start to the day. A lot of very fine breakfast fare was left uneaten on those NYSE Luncheon Club tables that morning. In some cases, you had to admire the dedication of the NYSE members as duty took precedence over sustenance. When you run all over a floor the size of perhaps half a football field, racing from post to post throughout the day, all those carbs come in very handy. On the other hand, we don't recall ever seeing a skinny NYSE floor broker.

Either way, once we had finished eating, it was down the elevator to the floor, but not before stopping in the men's room to snare a "souvenir" comb. Trays of black combs with New York Stock Exchange stamped on the side in gold letters could always be found in the Luncheon Club restroom, and it became a custom to take one each time we showed up at the exchange and stuffed our faces. We are not telling how many of these combs we have. Once we were on the floor, the excitement began to build. In those days, before traders began letting electrons run their orders around for execution, nothing would get the floor in a good mood faster than a busy morning, because when the floor brokers are busy executing orders that means they are making commissions, while the specialists are ringing the cash register as they work the spreads, providing supply and taking stock for their own account as supply and demand shifted throughout the day.

Once the bell rang, what had been a steady, low-volume drone rose sharply to a roar as the flood of orders hitting the floor translated into a flood of sound. Standing in the O'Neil floor booth, we decided to check out Nokia (NOK). Using the phone in the booth, we called the trading desk at O'Neil's home offices, yelling to our trader over the phone, "Jack, buy 50,000 Nokia." We then handed the phone over to O'Neil floor broker Louie

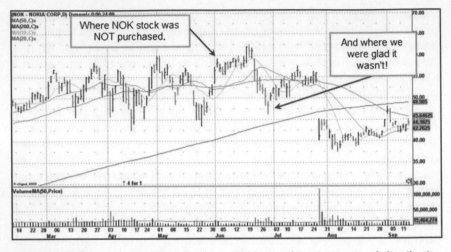

FIGURE 9.24 Nokia (NOK) daily chart, 2000. Watching institutional distribution in action on the floor of the NYSE.
Chart courtesy of eSignal, Copyright 2010.

Sulsenti so that Jack Hodges, the O'Neil desk trader back in Los Angeles to whom we had just given the order, could in turn give the order to Louie. A bit circuitous, as one might wonder why we couldn't just tell Louie to buy the 50,000 NOK ourselves. After all, we were on the floor, in the O'Neil floor booth, standing right next to him. But those were the rules for giving an order, and we had to follow them. Order in hand, and correctly "routed," off to the NOK trading post we went (Figure 9.24).

As we approached the NOK post, a small group of three or four floor brokers was standing around with orders to buy, but they were all sitting on the bid side of the market waiting for the stock to come to them. Louie, a street-smart floor broker if there ever was one, noticed a guy standing off to the left, away from the crowd. As we said to Louie, "Let's go in and take stock," he waved us off, barking, "Wait a minute. See that guy over there? Watch him." The "guy" we were to watch was a floor broker from Donaldson Lufkin and Jenrette, or DLJ. Louie's instincts proved to be correct, as the DLJ guy suddenly leapt into the crowd and took the offer price for 50,000 shares. The other brokers in the crowd who had been lying back, waiting for a seller to show up, suddenly had to execute their orders or risk being left behind. When they all stepped up to buy stock at the offer price, the DLJ floor broker turned around and yelled out, "Sold, sold, sold!" pointing to each buyer in succession. Louie curtly ordered, "Let's get outta here." We did not argue and left NOK for someone else to buy. In this case, Louie saved us from making a dumb stock purchase. In hindsight, the pattern was never really right, but NOK had actually bucked the March market top in 2000 and remained only 3 percent off its all-time high. It was an interesting lesson in the truism that faulty chart patterns are often indications of institutional distribution, and in this case we witnessed such distribution in action, right on the NYSE floor, where the rubber meets the road. June 2, 2000, was a follow-through day for the market, signaling that it was now in a rally phase. O'Neil immediately grasped onto the bear market bottom of October 1962 as a precedent for the market bottom in June 2000. In his experience, the sustained velocity of the 1962 bear market decline was the only thing he had seen that was similar to the NASDAQ's decline off the March 2000 top. Because the NASDAQ Composite was also the index in which the dot-com bubble phenomenon was centered, it bounced the hardest off the late May lows (Figure 9.25). These lows had in turn undercut the April lows, constituting a shakeout that faked out short-sellers as the market turned and began to rally. Seven days after that May 24th bottom, the huge gap-up move on June 2nd constituted a clear follow-through day, given that it came on heavier trading volume than the prior day.

Despite the follow-through, there were very few stocks breaking out from proper bases and into new high price ground. Most of the movement was occurring in former leaders that had topped with the market in March 2000 and that were now bouncing sharply off lows. Groping around for something to buy on that June 2nd follow-through took us to Nokia (NOK), which we decided not to buy, but in the process we missed Corning, Inc.

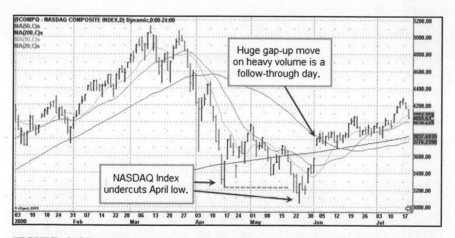

FIGURE 9.25 NASDAQ Composite Index daily chart, 2000. After undercutting the April lows, the NASDAQ bottoms and then posts a follow-through day on June 2nd, 2000, signaling the start of a new rally phase.
Chart courtesy of eSignal, Copyright 2010.

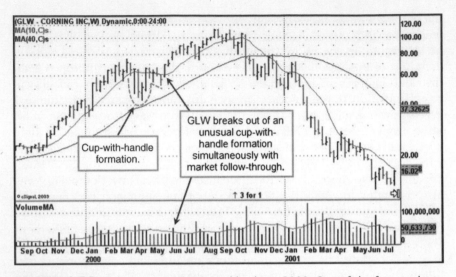

FIGURE 9.26 Corning, Inc. (GLW) weekly chart, 2000. One of the few stocks to break out with the June 2nd follow-through day.
Chart courtesy of eSignal, Copyright 2010.

(GLW), a glassmaker that was spinning fiberoptic cable for the new high-speed Internet age. While we were getting lessons in institutional distribution at the NOK post, O'Neil zeroed in on GLW's clean breakout from a slightly "udder-like" cup-with-handle formation, seen in Figure 9.26.

"Bill the Rock Star"

Saturday morning, on June 3rd, we woke up bright and early to get ready for the Advanced Investment Workshop. Arriving at the Hyatt Regency Central Station, we noted that a crowd was already starting to gather. Previous workshops had been a one-stage affair with perhaps 200–300 attendees at most, but this place was packed with what was later estimated to be around 800 attendees, the largest O'Neil investment workshop in history. In hindsight, it makes complete sense, considering the tulip craze of the market that had topped in March 2000. On that Saturday, the crowd was quite bubbly and excited about the previous day's follow-through, and there was tremendous electricity in the air. Steve Porpora, O'Neil's Director of NYSE Floor Operations, proclaimed, "Bill's a rock star!"

Because of the tremendous size of the audience, instead of the usual single-stage set-up we were used to dealing with, we had two stages stretching across the front of the room. Looking back on it all now, the mass ebullience in that room that day was clearly a sign that the bear market of 2000 was far from over. Leaving the hotel conference area that evening as we departed the workshop, attendees tried to follow us as some ran down the up escalator adjacent to the down escalator on which we were descending to continue asking us questions. As we tried to get into our cab, some attendees tried to get into our cab with us, but since we were headed off to dinner with O'Neil NYSE floor broker Lou Sulsenti, a street-smart, tough Italian boy from "Jersey," who was also in the cab with us, he played the role of bodyguard as he kept our would-be taxi-cab-mates at bay. All we could do was look at each other and say, "Major market top!"

THE GREAT BEAR OF 2001–2002

By September 2001 the market was rolling over again, and the second leg of the great post-bubble bear market of 2000–2002 set in with a vengeance. The general market and leading stocks broke down steadily through the last quarter of 2000 and the first quarter of 2001, until the market put in a follow-through day on March 27, 2000, as the daily chart of the Dow Jones Industrials in Figure 9.27 shows.

The March 27th follow-through came on the fourth day off the bottom, hence a "fourth-day follow-through," which is normally a sign of strength.

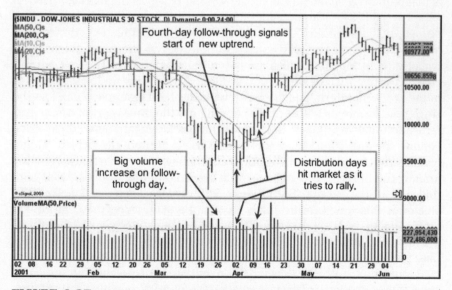

FIGURE 9.27 Dow Jones Industrials daily chart, 2001. A fourth-day follow backs and fills at first before turning to higher highs.
Chart courtesy of eSignal, Copyright 2010.

The market, however, began to roll over again over the next few days, and began to break as volume picked up, marking an initial distribution day, which can normally signal an end to the rally attempt. However, the understanding of follow-through days is very subtle, and O'Neil would articulate certain ideas about how any follow-through, as well as the general price/volume action of the major market indexes, must be seen in the context of the overall market position within the bull/bear cycle. With respect to some of the weakness seen in April of 2001, he pointed out, "Generally, you should see, as the market is coming off a strong follow-through day and is rallying, what look like distribution days but are then followed by up days, so that the pattern of distribution days does not really build on weakness—it forms as a result of bearish psychology reacting to a rally in the market, and then the market shakes it off and moves up for a day or two." In Figure 9.27 we have pointed out the two distribution days that hit the market just as it was coming up, distribution days that came on heavier, above-average volume and that looked quite negative at the time.

A Walking Encyclopedia of Historical Chart Patterns

Often such distribution days that are so early after a follow-through will be accompanied by shakeouts along the lows of bases as the market turns. As O'Neil would say, "The potential for heavy selling in some stocks is also normal at this juncture." At the time, O'Neil recalled his experience with McDonald's (MCD) in 1970 as an example. O'Neil was very much like a walking encyclopedia of historical stock chart patterns. He would recall chart patterns of stocks from the past, quickly reciting the characteristics of the stock's pattern, and he did so with the 1970 example MCD: "As the stock was forming a bottom and rounding out the lower part of a 'cup' pattern, about half-way up off the bottom the stock got hammered on massive volume for one week. The stock then turned around and tripled." Going back to check the old copies of MCD charts from the 1970s that were lying around the office, we could see what he was talking about. O'Neil continued with the lesson, "So the point is that ugly, hammering sell-offs in stocks at this juncture are likely to be fake-outs, since they can be exacerbated by bearish psychology caused by negative news at the turn." This is often why potential leading stocks have quick, very sharp shakeouts through the lows of their bases, such as Cisco Systems (CSCO) in 1991. News of the Iraqi invasion of Kuwait at that time marked the panic lows of the October 1990 bear market bottom, and the ensuing and extreme washout of bearish psychology is reflected in the chart of CSCO at that time (Figure 9.28).

FIGURE 9.28 Cisco Systems (CSCO) weekly chart 1990–1991.
Chart courtesy of eSignal, Copyright 2010.

From Chop and Slop to Doughnuts and Milk

The market action after the March 2001 follow-through was tepid. O'Neil lamented the fact that there was no power or momentum in the market. "Nothing works. Lots of funds are loaded up with techs and are "muscle-bound." Stocks run up and then run down, like Sun [Microsystems] on news alone (Figure 9.29).

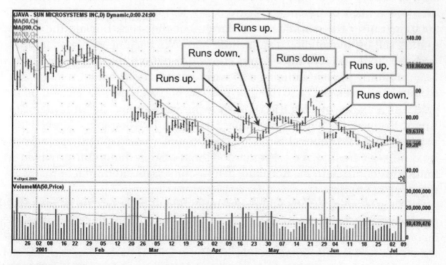

FIGURE 9.29 Sun Microsystems (JAVA) daily chart, 2001.
Chart courtesy of eSignal, Copyright 2010.

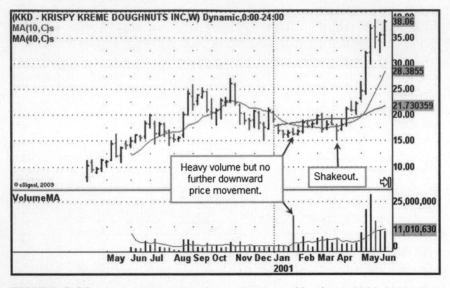

FIGURE 9.30 Krispy Kreme Doughnuts (KKD) weekly chart, 2000–2001. New merchandise in an otherwise short and lackluster market rally.
Chart courtesy of eSignal, Copyright 2010.

With so little that looked correct to buy from an O'Neil perspective in 2001, the emergence of Krispy Kreme Doughnuts (KKD) as it broke out approximately one month after the late March follow-through and market turn was a blast of fresh air (Figure 9.30). KKD had come public in April 2000 right after the market top in March, but the stock bucked the initial market sell-off by building a short little base. We became rather enamored with the stock as it continued to perform throughout the summer of 2000, finally topping out and building a 26-week base from which it broke in May of 2001. This was the only time we ever owned a stock that caused us to gain weight, since owning KKD somehow became an excuse for bringing in Krispy Kreme Doughnuts at the time. The closet-like employee kitchenette in the O'Neil Institutional Services department was frequently populated by dozens of fresh, Krispy Kreme doughnuts, something that provided a humorous contrast to the normally health-conscious environment that was the rule at O'Neil.

Trying to ward off the subjective influence of our taste buds, we tried to assess the prospects for KKD once it emerged from its 26-week base as objectively as we could. There were some bullish reasons for owning the stock, and it gave some insight into how O'Neil places importance on certain characteristics that are specific to retail-oriented stocks like Krispy Kreme Doughnuts, Inc. At the time, O'Neil boiled it down like so, "This is a real business with a strong brand, strong products that have barely touched their markets. Look at TCBY and Snapple—they had huge moves even though they turned out to be fads. Krispy Kreme could also be a fad, but it could have a huge move first. Krispy Kreme creates 'scarcity' before they move into a market. First they open one or two stores and people see the long lines and hear the rave reviews, thus setting up strong demand for the next stores they open. You must try and maintain your position—do not cut back excessively as this is a winner. Calculate how much they can expand. Charles Tandy once told me [O'Neil] that their strategy was to experiment in each city to see how many stores they could open up before saturating the market. They found that Radio Shack could open 25 stores per major city before saturating. Eventually they had 5,000 stores. Krispy Kreme has 174 stores. There could be huge expansion, and if the company is able to produce a solid 20 to 25 percent growth rate over three to five years, a high P/E here is not unreasonable."

KKD is also a lesson in how the crowd can often be fooled. In late March of 2001 many were shorting the stock on the basis that it was "just a fad" and that insiders would be tossing stock out the window once the stocks IPO "lock-up" period was over, during which insiders were finally allowed to sell stock following the initial public offering. Once the lock-up period ended, insiders didn't sell, and shorts had to scramble to cover their positions as natural buyers also showed up, given the company's strong sales growth and product recognition. The stock soared, and KKD ended up doubling from the pocket pivot buy point (Figure 9.31). While Krispy

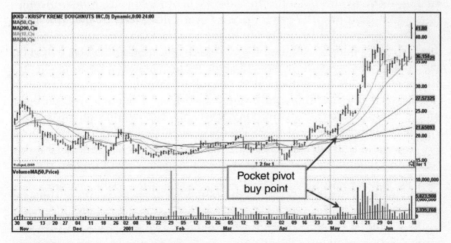

FIGURE 9.31 Krispy Kreme Doughnuts (KKD), daily chart, 2001. A pocket pivot buy point gives an early entry point.
Chart courtesy of eSignal, Copyright 2010.

Kreme never got too far past the $40 price level after doubling in price off the early May 2001 breakout, it still illustrates how O'Neil looked at retail stocks, and how Krispy Kreme, while it worked, worked reasonably well, and while we did not exploit the move in the stock as fully as we may have liked, it was still grist for the mill in otherwise bleak times for bull-trend-followers as we were at O'Neil.

Adjusting the "Follow-Through Day" Threshold Level

It was around June of 2001 that O'Neil began to believe that his 1 percent upside move requirement as one of the vital parameters of a market follow-through day signal was insufficient. A "follow-through day," or "FTD," is a signal generated when the indexes are up 1 percent or more on heavier volume than the prior day, and this must occur on the fourth through seventh days, optimally, or suboptimally a few days later, following an initial low in the general market averages. When the market posts a follow-through day, it is, according to O'Neil methodologies, at that point technically in a "rally phase." Not all follow-throughs lead to a bull market, but no bull market has started without one, as O'Neil was always quick to point out.

Understanding that the markets had become far too volatile following the March 2000 top meant changing the 1 percent index move requirement to 2 percent. At the time, however, this 2 percent follow-through requirement was based solely on observation. The fact is that optimization studies we had already done on our own showed the most statistically reliable percentage move requirement for the indexes, in order to call a follow-through day at that time, was 1.7 percent. We never told O'Neil of this, but were not surprised that he instinctively began to sense that the number had to change, and 2 percent seemed like a reasonable number to him based on the number of observations he had made in the 2000–2001 period.

In making his assessment that the follow-through day percentage index move requirement should be increased from 1 percent to 2 percent, one of the examples he was looking at was the follow-through day of July 25, 2001, shown in Figure 9.32. This was an 11th-day follow-through on the Dow Jones Industrials and NASDAQ Composite Index, and a 10th-day follow-through on the S&P 500. However, the index moves on that day for each of these three indexes was 1.6 percent, 1.28 percent, and 1.61 percent, respectively. At the time O'Neil expressed great skepticism about this late follow-through. "The concept of a follow-through is overwhelming power to the upside. We ran a screen on the 200 new highs that were made yesterday and found only 16 of the stocks had EPS greater than or equal to 72 and Relative Strength greater than or equal to 80. So it was a laggard rally. This is NOT powerful upside action!" A few days later the market began

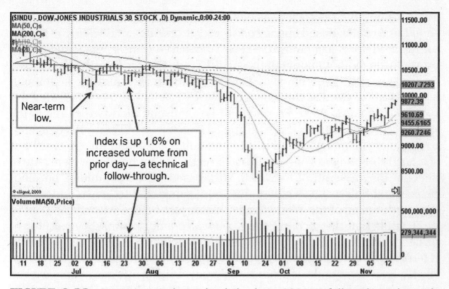

FIGURE 9.32 Dow Jones Industrials, daily chart, 2001. A follow-through in July lacks power, and soon fails as the market breaks again to the downside by the end of summer.
Chart courtesy of eSignal, Copyright 2010.

to roll over again, negating the follow-through day as the market broke to fresh lows and the bear market of 2000–2001, so far, continued.

Steadfast on 9/11

The morning of September 11, 2001, started like any other day at William O'Neil + Company. We were in our offices well before 5:30 A.M., 8:30 A.M. New York Stock Exchange Time, getting ready for the market day and working out how to handle our short positions. One of us was 200 percent short coming into the market opening that day, the other 100 percent in cash. When the first jet hit the World Trade Center, the images of the north tower with a gaping hole in it was described as a "small plane, perhaps a Cessna" that had errantly flown into one of the two tallest buildings in New York City. Knowing the size of the buildings at the World Trade Center, we quickly surmised that the hole in that building could not have possibly been made by a little Cessna 172, or even a Cessna 372, if they had made one that big! The futures began to hurtle to the downside, and it was a strange feeling to be 200 percent short that morning knowing that a huge gap-down in the markets was going to result in a very profitable trading day when the markets re-opened as you watched images of people jumping out of broken windows in the upper floors of the north tower.

At about that time, the O'Neil trading desk had been on the phone with their Los Angeles-based counterparts at Cantor-Fitzgerald when the first jet hit the 93rd floor, just below the New York-based Cantor-Fitzgerald offices on the 101st to 105th floors of the World Trade Center's north tower.

At that point we immediately began to try to account for O'Neil personnel who worked at the New York Stock Exchange. They included our two floor brokers, Steve Porpora and Lou Sulsenti, and two clerks in the booth. Steve, who had been depositing a check at an ATM for his daughter, saw one of the jets when it hit, and immediately headed for the shelter of the NYSE building at Wall and Broad streets. At that point, we were able to account for three out of four New York-based O'Neil personnel, but floor broker Lou Sulsenti was still on his train, scheduled to arrive underneath the south tower of the World Trade Center just before what turned out to be the time that the second jet hit. Lou was coming out of the south tower as debris rained down around him, and he was finally able to find his way to a ferry boat at the southwest end of Manhattan Island that took him across the Hudson River and back into New Jersey. During this entire time we had no idea where Lou was until we finally heard from him at 11:30 A.M., New York Time.

O'Neil's reaction to the events of that day was steadfast and typically optimistic. He believed that these troubles had been brewing for a while, so 9/11 was simply the culmination of the flawed antiterrorist policies of the Clinton administration, and that the attacks of 9/11 would provide a catalyst for taking decisive action to address the growing threat of terrorism. He believed that 9/11 would ultimately be transmuted into a positive by the country and the markets. He felt that this was about as bad as it could get, and hence when the markets re-opened, the market would initially sell-off and then quickly bottom, setting off a new rally phase in the market. O'Neil's calmness during those times also had a calming effect on those of us who worked with him, so we were able to keep our heads and think through what would happen when the market re-opened a few days later. When the markets finally did re-open on September 17th, we began to cover our shorts as we turned with the market and went long defense stocks like Lockheed Martin (LMT), shown in Figure 9.33. The United States was now on a war footing, and as was the case in prior periods where the country was at war, whether it said so or not, the defense industry and its associated stocks would be the place to look for "big stocks."

Initially, the defense stocks did not have the typical earnings growth numbers one might expect to see in a "CAN SLIM" stock, but in certain environments we relied on O'Neil's model book studies when it came to identifying the stocks that institutions would have to own in any given market cycle. Given that most growth stocks were still reeling from the

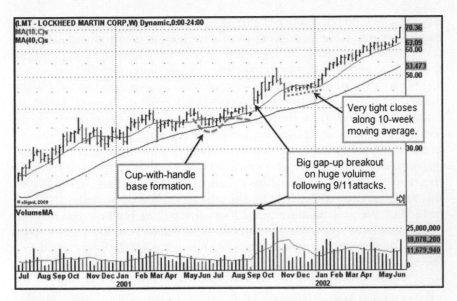

FIGURE 9.33 Lockheed Martin Corp. (LMT) weekly chart, 2001–2002.
Chart courtesy of eSignal, Copyright 2010.

deleterious economic and wealth effects of the dot-com bubble-popping in March of 2000, 9/11 did little to embolden or even encourage consumers to spend as they simply became more cautious, drawing like turtles into their shells. Understanding which of the defense stocks institutions would turn to as a big stock holding in the sector was critical in optimizing the group move.

Defense stocks launched higher when the markets re-opened on September 17th, and Lockheed Martin gapped out of a 14-week cup-with-handle base on huge volume. It is quite interesting to note that going into the events of 9/11 Lockheed Martin had been quietly building a rather well-formed cup-with-handle formation, almost as if it knew what was coming as it coiled up for its big breakout. Lockheed Martin ran up for six more weeks before pulling back to a point just above its breakout point, as Figure 9.33 shows, and then building a series of very tight weekly closes as it slowly moved up along its 10-week (50-day) moving average. This was very tight, constructive price action, and Lockheed broke out again in early January 2002 as it continued higher, even as the general market began to wobble and roll over again to fresh new lows.

Back in those uncertain days it was easy to get depressed about all that was going on after 9/11, including the Anthrax attacks that were making the news. The administrative assistant in the O'Neil Institutional Services

Department who passed out the day's mail wore plastic gloves and a surgical mask while she opened up each envelope or package and checked for unusual substances. During this time one could always depend on Bill O'Neil for a pep talk. His optimism was tireless, and after a while you realize that this is one the primary secrets to his success. He proved the old adage that you will never see a "successful pessimist." He would call up, citing an article about a study regarding the main causes of death. He informed us that the #1 cause of death was smoking, and the #2 cause of death was "simply how one reacts to daily stresses and their emotional consequences—a very key concept!" O'Neil knew that reacting badly to the emotional stresses of trading was deadly in the markets, which is why he always advised to "sell to the sleeping point." As in trading, O'Neil believed that life was not about what happened to you, but how you react to what happens to you in life. In this manner, "keeping your head screwed on right," whether in the markets or in life following a frightening event like the attacks of 9/11, was paramount to survival.

The Market Cleans House

As 2002 wore on, the move in defense stocks ended, and a general malaise began to set in as the debate over whether to go to war with Iraq was the main topic of the day. The bear market was breaking to new lows, and the financial services industry, particularly in the investment arena, was contracting rapidly. Hedge fund clients of O'Neil's were closing left and right, and some of the bigger client firms were beset by mutual fund timing scandals or swallowed up by larger financial entities. The bear market was putting everyone in their places, and every corner of excess was being rooted out. O'Neil would muse at the time, "The market is the only thing in life that is the 'great leveler.' You can argue with your wife, your family, your co-workers, the IRS, and so on, but you can't argue with the market because it will clean you out. It doesn't care who you are!" By late October 2002, everyone was pretty well cleaned out as the NASDAQ finally bottomed out after plummeting 78.4 percent from its bull market peak in early 2000.

Shorting Cisco Systems Near the Bottom

There is no greater example of Bill O'Neil's optimism than when he turns pessimistic. In October 2002, he became so pessimistic that he decided to short Cisco Systems (CSCO) right near its bear market lows (Figure 9.34). We know this because Bill O'Neil called us to tell us he had done so. When the last bull in the market throws in the towel and starts shorting CSCO at around $10 a share, more than 90 percent from its bull market peak,

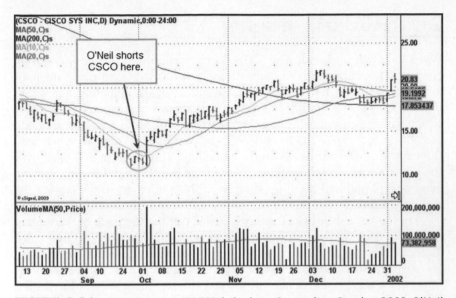

FIGURE 9.34 Cisco Systems (CSCO) daily chart. September–October 2002. O'Neil shorts CSCO at the lows.
Chart courtesy of eSignal, Copyright 2010.

then that has to be the bottom! We had heard this from other old-timers in the firm, but it was interesting to see O'Neil actually do this. Notice, however, how CSCO turns up off its lows on huge volume. Most traders, having shorted CSCO a few days earlier, might have added to their short position in response, or simply and stubbornly sat with the position. Not O'Neil. He could care less what he thought two days earlier as he quickly covered the Cisco short position and went long eBay, Inc. (EBAY), something we discussed in Chapter 3.

As the nation prepared to go to war in Iraq, the market corrected 17.6 percent off its December 2002 peak as measured on the NASDAQ Composite Index, and many were expecting the worst. At the very least it was expected to be a protracted war that would involve Saddam Hussein retaliating with chemical or biological weapons. Other fears grew around the idea that attacking Iraq would provoke radical Islamic terrorists into conducting additional terror attacks on American soil. There was, in fact, a very large wall of worry building, and O'Neil, having seen the market rally sharply in January 1991 when allied forces launched the attack that ejected invading Iraqi military forces from Kuwait in the Persian Gulf War, saw a similar potentiality evolving as U.S. forces moved into their final positions in early March 2003.

2003–2005 BULL MARKET

When the swiftness with which U.S. forces penetrated into Iraq and took control of the capital city of Baghdad took the crowd by surprise, the market followed through to the upside on March 17, 2003, launching a new bull market. One of the first stocks out of the gate was Amazon.com (AMZN), which we began to play heavily (Figure 9.35). AMZN did not show immediate power as it broke out to new highs on March 17th, right in synch with the market's follow-through on the same day. The stock pulled back over the next four weeks before finding support at the 10-week (50-day) moving average. Volume had dried up sharply on this pullback, so we bought the stock right there.

For the next six weeks the stock closed right at the peak of the weekly ranges for each of those weeks; five of those six weeks closed at new price highs. O'Neil was quick to point out just how constructive this action was, and that he had calculated an upside price target for AMZN of $60 a share. In an interesting coincidence, we owned the stock as well and had used Point & Figure charting techniques to calculate an upside price target of $61 based on the upside thrust of those six weeks where the stock closed right at the peak of each weekly range. AMZN finally peaked at 61.15, with

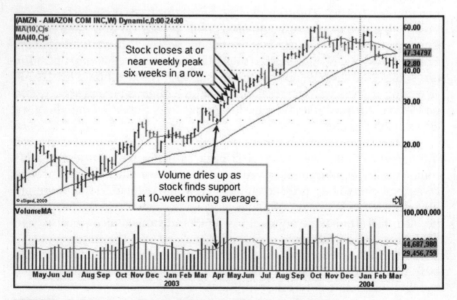

FIGURE 9.35 Amazon.com (AMZN) weekly chart, 2003–2004.
Chart courtesy of eSignal, Copyright 2010.

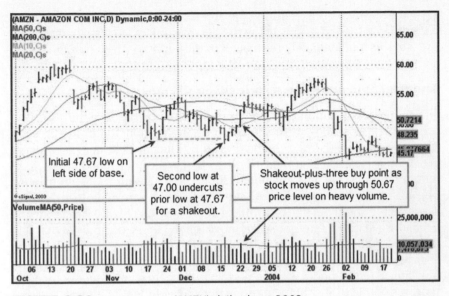

FIGURE 9.36 Amazon.com (AMZN) daily chart, 2003.
Chart courtesy of eSignal, Copyright 2010.

a little climax top type of move in October 2003, and then began building a big, ugly base (Figure 9.36).

As AMZN continued to build its base, it put in an initial low of 47.67 on the left side of the base on November 19, 2003. The stock rallied for a few days and then spent the next two to three weeks drifting back downward before undercutting the initial 47.67 low at an even 47.00 on December 17th. This was the only time we ever saw O'Neil implement the old Livermore trick of buying off the bottom on a "shakeout-plus-three" situation in real time. On December 23rd, he called to declare that AMZN was a shakeout-plus-three buy based on adding three points to the 47.67 low of November 19th in order to come up with a new buy point of 50.67. On that day, as Figure 9.36 shows, AMZN pierced the 50.67 buy point with volume up sharply on the day. In this particular case, the "shakeout-plus-three" or "SO+3" buy signal on AMZN resulted in a tepid rally, and the stock eventually rolled over and failed, gapping down hard in late January 2004.

One significant takeaway from O'Neil's implementation of the SO+3 buy rule that Livermore would make use of from time to time is that the shakeout in the pattern should be exactly that—a quick and sharp shakeout that immediately turns and begins rallying to the upside, as AMZN did over the next four days following the 47.00 low on November 17th. The stock should not have undercut the prior low at 47.67 and drifted lower or sideways for a few days. The turn off the lows following the undercut should be swift, as this confirms the stock's ability to recover quickly and with some authority, hence giving the SO+3 a look of extreme buoyancy in the stock as it immediately rises back to the surface—the top of the base.

The Past Doesn't Repeat, but Often Rhymes

O'Neil frequently had interesting stories to tell about stocks he played in the past and how they were similar to what was going on in the present. When Netflix, Inc. (NFLX) emerged as an IPO in May 2002 at $7.50 a share, the market was still in a bear trend so the stock immediately tanked, finally bottoming out in December 2002 at $2.42 a share. The stock then began working its way higher. Along with Amazon.com and other dot-com e-commerce survivors like eBay, Inc. (EBAY), NFLX (Figure 9.37) rode the second wave in the Internet stock move among those companies that had actually figured out how to make money running a business on the Internet. This new wave began in late 2002 and into early 2003, and NFLX's DVD-by-mail movie rental model was the perfect service for a consumer population that was opting to stay home more in the wake of the 9/11 attacks.

After a long price run, Netflix began to shows signs of topping as it failed from a late-stage base in April of 2004. Note how this move occurred on low volume, as Figure 9.37 shows. The two weeks just before the week

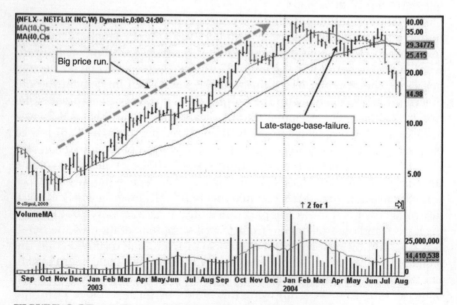

FIGURE 9.37   Netflix, Inc. (NFLX) weekly chart, 2003–2004.
Chart courtesy of eSignal, Copyright 2010.

of the late-stage-base-failure it moved up straight from the bottom of the stock's chart base on below-average volume, with the second week occurring on extremely light volume, a sign that buying demand was beginning to wane. Talk of Blockbuster, Inc., the grandfather of movie rental chains, moving into the DVD-by-mail business in early 2004 was weighing on NFLX stock. The stock had, by this time, had quite a price run, so it was obviously late in its "cycle" when this news hit, and O'Neil made an interesting observation at the time, comparing Netflix and Blockbuster to motor-home maker Winnebago and car maker General Motors back in the 1960s and 1970s: "Years ago when Winnebago was making RVs and selling them like gangbusters, their stock was a huge winner. General Motors came along and announced they were going to build these RVs also, but they never made much money in that line of business. This is similar to Blockbuster announcing they are going to compete with Netflix."

As it turned out, Blockbuster never made a go of the DVD-by-mail business and never became a competitor to Netflix. At the time of this writing, in early 2010, Netflix is still in business while Blockbuster has declared bankruptcy. It is also interesting to note that in 2010 Winnebago is still in business, and General Motors has been taken over by the U.S. government, garnering the nickname Government Motors—proof that some individuals know how to run a business correctly, and some don't, and it is usually the early innovators that prevail over time.

O'Neil viewed 2003 as the first year of an economic cycle, and in February 2004 he was keeping an eye on where we were in the cycle. As he put it, "There is a certain order to a bull cycle. In the first year or initial phase of the bull market the hot, newer names will have their move. Sometime later, 8–12 months or so, big business starts to participate in the new economic cycle and you will see cyclical growth stocks come on. Later on, the capital spending stocks will come on as businesses are flush with cash and start spending on capital equipment. In the old days, capital equipment stocks were the machinery stocks; today they are technology stocks." The tone of the market in 2003 going into 2004 was also much different from the heady days of the 1990s when markets were in a grand, parabolic upside move that ended in the March 2000 market top and bubble-bursting. O'Neil, however, was familiar with how this could cross us up, and he warned, "When I made a lot of money in Syntex many years ago I had trouble making money right after that big success. I would sell stocks too soon, since I figured if they weren't up six points a day there was something wrong—I had gotten acclimated to SYN's strong uptrend and couldn't adjust to slower, yet still profitable stocks." In 2004 we had to adjust from an environment that was simply slower and less parabolic than that of the late 1990s.

In early 2004 there were several textbook examples of topping action that O'Neil called to our attention. Often the phone would ring, and O'Neil

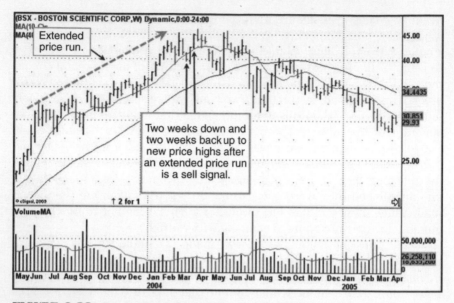

FIGURE 9.38 Boston Scientific (BSX) weekly chart, 2003–2005.
Chart courtesy of eSignal, Copyright 2010.

would be on the line wanting to discuss a particular stock, making note of its characteristics in real time. In March of 2004, O'Neil pointed out the two-weeks-down-and-two-weeks-up sell signal in Boston Scientific (BSX), a leading stock at the time (Figure 9.38). This occurs after an extended price run when a stock makes a new price high and then immediately pulls back two weeks before shooting back to new highs over the next two weeks, creating a "two-up-and-two-down" formation on the weekly chart. This was an old sell rule of O'Neil's, which is often misinterpreted, but in this case the two-down-and-two-up rule was a textbook sell signal, and the action in BSX here illustrates it well.

A number of biotech stocks had big moves in 2003, including Gilead Sciences (GILD) and Celgene (CELG). Joining in on the group move was Martek Biosciences (MATK), which had found a way to turn microalgae into two fatty acids, DHA and ARA, essential to brain and eye development. These in turn were added to baby formula, producing a "super formula" for infants. Martek Biosciences formed a late-stage double-bottom base in the first four months of 2004. The major flaw in the pattern, as shown in Figure 9.39, is the mid-point of the "W" formation. Normally, in a proper double-bottom base this should close below the left sides of the "W," but in this case the mid-point exceeds that high. As Martek Biosciences attempted to break out on the right side, O'Neil pointed out this flaw. As it turned

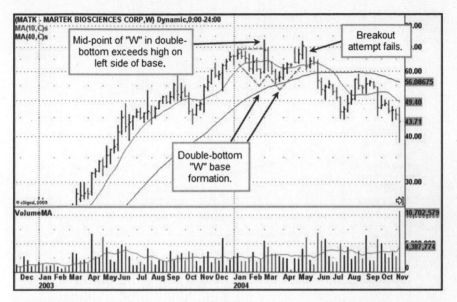

FIGURE 9.39 Martek Biosciences (MATK) weekly chart, 2003–2004. Chart courtesy of eSignal, Copyright 2010.

out, the breakout failed, and the stock broke down altogether over the ensuing months.

The IPO "U-Turn" Base

In the Institutional Services department of William O'Neil + Company, Inc., there was never any shortage of banter and debate about the market and leading stocks. As well, there was always somebody coming up with some new "concept" to which they had given a clever name. During 1999 the moves in stocks were so crazy that we would give some of their strange, short consolidations as they dashed to the upside descriptive names like Double-Flying-Eagle or IPO U-Turn. The only one that survived was the one that Michael Lowrey, an institutional salesman at O'Neil, first dubbed the IPO U-Turn. Two of the biggest IPO U-turn set-ups at the time were eBay, Inc. (EBAY) in October of 1998 and Ubid, Inc. (UBID) in December of 1998. The infamous IPO U-Turn was not only a first-stage base set-up that we observed during that dot-com bubble period, but would also serve as a later-stage base as hot Internet IPOs would run up rapidly, then correct very sharply before making a sharp U-turn right back up to new highs. In August of 2004, another Internet IPO, Google, Inc. (GOOG) formed its own first-stage IPO U-turn (Figure 9.40).

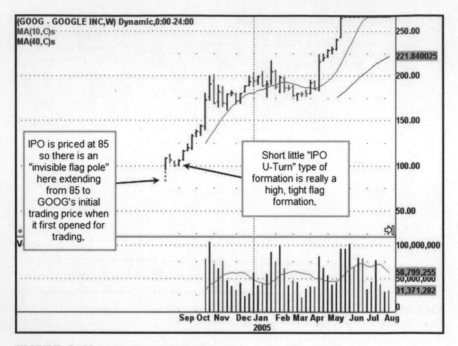

FIGURE 9.40 Google, Inc. (GOOG) weekly chart, 2004–2005.
Chart courtesy of eSignal, Copyright 2010.

When we first mentioned GOOG's IPO U-Turn formation to Bill O'Neil, he wasn't buying it. However, once it was explained in terms he could understand, he took another look at it. The primary characteristic of an IPO U-Turn is not the "U" in the formation, it is actually the "invisible flag pole" that forms when the stock opens up for trading on the first day at a price far above its initial offering price. In GOOG's case, it had come public via a Dutch auction, which priced the stock's initial public offering at $85. GOOG opened up for trading on August 19, 2004, at exactly $100 a share, pulled down a couple of bucks, and closed at 100.33. Over the next two days, the stock ran up to an intraday high of 113.48 before pulling back down to the 100 price level and then pulled a U-turn back to the upside. By including the "invisible flag pole" that GOOG formed by opening up at $100 a share on its first day of trading, a full 15 points higher than its $85 a share IPO price, we can see that GOOG's pattern was actually a "high, tight flag." In this manner, one of the primary requirements of an IPO U-turn formation is that it should generally form well above the stock's initial public offering price.

Institutional Sponsorship Is Key

Another characteristic of GOOG at the time that also influenced our decision to purchase the stock at around the $111–$112 price level, initially,
was the fact that a 13-D filing had been released and was reported by news
service Briefing.com as indicating that Fidelity Management & Research
had taken a 13 percent position in GOOG stock. In most cases, when a
large mutual fund known to have outstanding research capabilities buys a
stock like GOOG in such size, they are not planning to flip the IPO, but are
in fact accumulating stock with the idea of holding it for three to five years.
This made GOOG a "big stock" right out of the gate, and its IPO U-Turn
base worked quite well.

The Short Stroke

Occasionally we might witness the genesis of a new base pattern, such as
was the case with the "short-stroke" formation, although we didn't know it
at the time. Three days before Christmas, December 22, 2003, O'Neil called
to ask what we think about Research in Motion (RIMM). We noted that the
base was very tight, and that the company would be reporting earnings that
day after the close. We debated whether to put the stock on our institutional stock ideas list. We ourselves could not buy it for 48 hours once it
was put on the ideas list, so that our institutional clients were able to act
on the information first. We decided to wait for the earnings to come out
that afternoon, and once the news was out that RIMM had handily beaten
the estimates, the stock gapped up out of a very tight, six-week flat base,
shown in Figure 9.41. This was a very powerful move, but the stock was immediately extended from its buy point by over 20 percent, hence the idea
of trying to buy the stock up that far away from a proper buy point carried
a great deal of risk with it.

The quandary here was where to jump on what we thought was likely
to become a very hot-moving stock. The next week, the stock traded in a
very tight price range, as Figure 9.41 shows, with the stock closing at the
peak of the weekly range as trading volume dried up precipitously. This
sort of action indicated that the story here was simply too big from a fundamental perspective, and institutions were not interested in selling any
RIMM stock that they may have held. This stinginess with the stock shows
up in the very tight weekly range, the close right at the weekly peak, and
the lack of trading volume as sellers fail to show up. Later this chart pattern began to appear as the "short-stroke" formation in O'Neil's workshops.
The term "short-stroke" comes from the musical notation that indicates
where the bow of a string instrument is to briefly touch the strings in a

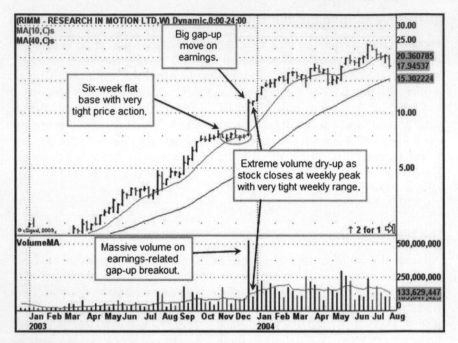

FIGURE 9.41   Research in Motion (RIMM) weekly chart, 2003–2004.
Chart courtesy of eSignal, Copyright 2010.

short stroke. This makes complete sense when you understand that O'Neil was a trumpet player in his youth and likely played in orchestras with string instruments. Statistically, it is not clear whether this pattern has any real validity, but it is something of a corollary to a high, tight flag formation where the flag is a single, very tight and "short" one-week flag.

Labels Can Be Misleading; Context Is Key

One of the drawbacks to trying to label every type of base formation is that it puts one in the position of assessing bases or chart formations on the basis of their "fit" to these base "templates." In the process, many of the chart phenomena that O'Neil goes to great lengths to measure, label, and categorize are easily misinterpreted. For example, in October of 2004 we were playing very heavily in Apple, Inc. (AAPL), which was riding a wave of iPod sales. On October 15th, Apple announced earnings and the stock gapped up through the 20 price level on the chart in Figure 9.42. The huge-volume breakaway gap to the upside had many thinking that the stock was putting in a "climax top," failing to understand that the position of the stock within its overall move and the market cycle is critical in determining when

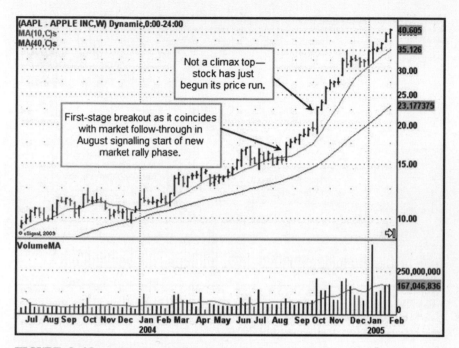

FIGURE 9.42 Apple, Inc. (AAPL) weekly chart, 2004–2005.
Chart courtesy of eSignal, Copyright 2010.

a stock is making a climactic topping move. Because the general market had only begun a new rally phase by follow-through to the upside in August of 2004, Apple's breakout in the last week of August was a breakout from a first-stage base. During their price moves, stocks will generally put in three to four later-stage bases after initially breaking out at or around the same time as the general market also begins an upside rally phase. The first breakout that coincides with the market's recovery and follow-through to the upside is the first-stage base. Climax tops generally occur after a third-stage or fourth-stage or later base is formed in a stock's overall price run.

The interesting thing about this was that at the same time a lot of individuals at the firm were thinking Apple was putting in a climax top, we were buying the stock aggressively for our own accounts. We had actually bought most of our position on the earnings gap-up on October 16, 2004, recognizing that the "line of least resistance" had been broken (Figure 9.43). In Chapter 4, we discussed buying gap-ups like this, because they are buyable, particularly when they have a "volume signature" as Apple did on that day, which is clearly visible on the daily chart in Figure 9.43 as a big upside volume spike.

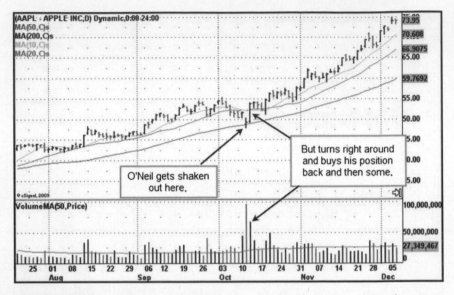

FIGURE 9.43 Apple, Inc. (AAPL) daily chart, 2004. The gap up in October was a clearly buyable move.
Chart courtesy of eSignal, Copyright 2010.

Apple was the last big, winning stock we played as internal portfolio managers at William O'Neil + Company, Inc., and O'Neil was in it very heavily at the time as well. The last classic maneuver we saw him pull occurred in our last month at the firm, when Apple announced earnings in October 2005. By that time Apple had already had a huge price run, and following this October 2005 earnings announcement the stock began to sell off, finally gapping down and dipping just below its 50-day moving average. O'Neil was shaken out of a lot of Apple stock at that point, and the stock ended up closing just above its 50-day moving average, as we see in Figure 9.44. The next day saw Apple lift off the 50-day moving average on huge volume, something that we know today as a pocket pivot buy point. O'Neil saw this action and, forgetting about whatever stock he had sold at lower prices, immediately began buying the stock back, most likely buying back even more, as this was often his policy. He would often urge us that if we found ourselves shaken out of a big, winning stock, and the stock then showed overwhelming power as it recovered and turned back to the upside, we should consider buying back our entire position and then some. This was the type of decisive and flexible reaction that O'Neil displayed which is very uncommon among average investors. O'Neil was not price-sensitive; he did not care what price he had sold a stock at and whether he was buying it back a few points higher. The point in buying the stock

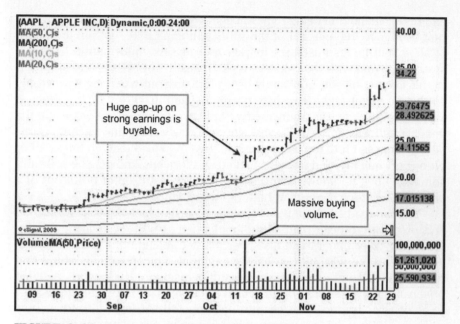

FIGURE 9.44 Apple, Inc. (AAPL) daily chart, 2005.
Chart courtesy of eSignal, Copyright 2010.

is to catch the "fat" part of the price move—whether one bought it a few points higher or lower, or sold it lower before buying it higher, is simply not a factor. The key is whether the stock is signaling that the line of least resistance has been broken, and a big move is now starting.

Buying back Apple in this manner is typical of O'Neil's aggressive style in correcting mistakes in a decisive manner that quickly compensates for the prior mistake of being shaken out of the stock. As Figure 9.44 clearly shows, had O'Neil worried about having to buy Apple stock a few points higher than where he was shaken out around the 50-day moving average he would have missed the parabolic move in Apple that ensued. Notice also that AAPL gave investors two pocket pivots.

CONCLUSION

If you ever have the opportunity to work side-by-side with Bill O'Neil, experiencing and operating in the market in real time, you might begin to understand that being one of the greatest stock market investors in history isn't about being right all the time. In fact, O'Neil was often wrong, but he never had his ego staked in being right to begin with. He constantly reminded us that "You miss 100 percent of the shots you don't take." O'Neil took a lot of shots, but he also used the market as a massive information feedback system, moving with the evidence as it changed, not before, and not after. In this manner he was constantly trying to figure out where he was wrong, so that he might take immediate corrective action. O'Neil often preaches that in the stock market there are two kinds of investors: the quick and the dead. O'Neil was quick to discern when he was wrong, and to shift course before it caused him too much damage. He could also pick up the scent of blood very quickly, and when he picked up the scent, knowing he was onto something big, he knew how to squeeze every last drop of profit out of a big, winning stock. Nobody is better at this than Bill O'Neil.

You can read all about Bill O'Neil in books like Jack Schwager's *Market Wizards,* and you can read all the books he has written himself, but you can never truly understand his sheer market genius until you see him in action. Working with him in real time, you also begin to understand that what he does is not magic. It is the result of discipline, hard work, detailed observation, tireless study, and decisive action; in this way, it is accessible to all of us as traders. This chapter has hopefully brought into focus how someone with such immense experience as an investor engages the market with his own methods in a manner that is simultaneously fluid and decisive.

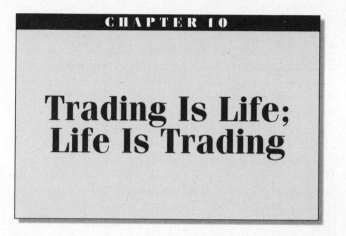

CHAPTER 10

Trading Is Life; Life Is Trading

The material covered so far can be used to optimize your own trading, but this form of learning is only half the story. If there are "misalignments" within yourself, this implies that your personal psychology is not fully optimized, and as Ed Seykota, the legendary futures trader who was interviewed in Jack Schwager's book *Market Wizards* says, you will not reach your full potential, or in the worst case, you are setting yourself up for a big fall.

Much as athletes psych themselves up for an event, traders should be sure they too have optimized themselves psychologically. As O'Neil always told us, never operate from a position of fear, or put into the positive, always operate from a position of strength. Psychological strength is paramount, and, as we all know, one of the biggest challenges when it comes to successful investing is in mastering one's own psychology. Richard Dennis and William Eckhardt selected individuals for their Turtles program, briefly mentioned in Chapter 7, section 2009 Commentary, who had the necessary psychological characteristics so that they could be taught to trade profitably.

It should then come as no surprise that many traders see trading as a looking glass into oneself. We would add that trading is like looking into the abyss and seeing yourself magnified a thousand times, where all your best and worst traits are shown in full measure. As we discussed earlier, an oversized ego is often the downfall to successful trading, especially when such an ego can shield the trader from hearing what the market is saying because the ego wants to be right, and since it has been right before, it thinks it must be right again.

ED SEYKOTA: TEACHING A TECHNIQUE THAT HAS HELPED TRADERS AROUND THE WORLD

Ed Seykota has made a lifelong study of how personal psychology affects one's trading. His interview in Jack Schwager's *Market Wizards* is still considered to be one of the best interviews ever given by a top trader. Seykota says that trading amplifies everything that is going on within a person. One of the first questions that Seykota has been known to ask traders who seek his coaching is: Do you ever cheat on your significant other? Seykota considers it important to know whether traders are willing to compromise their ethics since behavior and other tendencies in daily life outside of trading can bleed into one's trading and have an effect thereby. The two are inextricably, psychologically linked. Thus, the beauty about trading, and the beauty about life as well, is that there is no cheating. Or, as free-market economist Milton Friedman said, "There is no such thing as a free lunch." When people cheat others, they effectively cheat themselves; it will show up in their trading and performance will suffer.

For well over a quarter century, Seykota has been known to take on one student at a time to teach how to be an effective investor. He screens applicants by psychoanalyzing them to see if they have the character traits that will enable them to succeed. While Seykota might not take on a student who lacked the necessary character traits, he created a practice called the Trading Tribe Process (TTP), which teaches traders to overcome any weakness by optimizing their own psychology. Not surprisingly, Seykota's TTP (www.tradingtribe.com) has become hugely popular worldwide as trading tribes across the world have sprung up like mushrooms among traders who meet regularly to practice Seykota's philosophy. This philosophy can be summed up in two words: Right livelihood. This parallels Wallace D. Wattles' book *The Science of Getting Rich* (Top of the Mountain Publishing, 2002) where Wattles gives the reader the road map to developing the right mind-set so they can live a rich life. The term "rich," of course, does not just mean financial wealth but a wealth of beautiful friendships and relationships, strong family bonds, and worthwhile accomplishments.

TTP (explained in detail at www.seykota.com/tribe/TT_Process/index. htm) can be broken down into three phases:

Phase 1: A person gets upset and identifies why. Even though the person may understand why, he may resist the why in the form of denial by the conscious mind (CM). This can take many forms such as making excuses, or shifting blame onto others, since the ego will do what it takes to protect itself. The person will feel a general discomfort as a consequence. Over time, this general discomfort may grow if the matter is not dealt with effectively as the ego continues to mask the problem.

Phase 2: The subconscious mind (what Seykota calls "Fred") communicates with the conscious mind (CM). In a healthy person, Fred sends signals to the CM that are fully acknowledged. Wisdom is the final result. Those who resist the signals Fred is sending from one's unconscious mind to one's conscious mind end up repeating the same negative patterns and making the same mistakes. This is known as drama. And we all know certain people who nicely fit the label "drama-queen." They seem to attract drama wherever they go.

The trouble stems from suppressing, masking, or hiding one's feelings. Maybe one was told long ago by a parent, peer, or teacher that having such feelings is wrong or bad. Or perhaps one's CM may see the feeling as dangerous and block it out. Knots can then form within one's subconscious mind. Fred will raise the intensity as it attempts to get its message to the CM. Similar dramas can thus be repeated at higher and higher levels. Certain images and nightmares may reoccur as Fred attempts to get its message to the CM.

Ultimately, Fred will continue to send its message by reenacting the experience; thus the person will repeat the same drama over and over again. Further, the behavior is reinforced by neural pathways that are strengthened in the brain each time this behavior is repeated. Strong neural pathways lead to repeat behavior as the brain is comfortable travelling on a well-paved neural track. However, once one's CM fully acknowledges Fred's message, this is often experienced as an "Aha!" moment within the person, which is accompanied by the great feeling where things suddenly make sense. Some have said this wonderful moment is akin to the feeling of things just clicking into place. This feeling is usually accompanied by a physical release of tension and an outpouring of pent-up emotion.

Seykota's TTP facilitates the flow of experience between Fred and the CM. It is essential that one does not try to go it alone as the process requires a group effort to be fully effective. The problem is that many people, especially traders, tend to be fiercely self-reliant. The do-it-yourself culture can prevent one from realizing your fullest potential by not interacting in a group or a "tribe," but group participation can still mean being self-reliant. If one wishes to get the most out of TTP, then group participation will provide the highest quality experience as opposed to going it alone. No entrepreneur ever built an empire without the help of others.

The philosophy of the TTP is akin to other teachings discussed in this chapter in that we are all interconnected and we are all one. There are no boundaries, and acknowledgment of this beautiful and deep interconnectedness is the first step toward self-actualization and enlightenment. This state of enlightenment is what Seykota calls "Getting to the Zero Point." The Zero Point is the state of being in the now, of being in the present, of being "in the zone," a state the writer and philosopher Eckhart Tolle discusses fully in his seminal works *The Power of Now* (New World Library, 2004) and *A New Earth* (Penguin, 2005). As Ed Seykota writes, "It is dancing joyously, with abandon. It is splashing your hand in a mud puddle and just being there with the experience. It is putting on a trade and succumbing to the enchantment of the whole process including the market, yourself, the prices, the plusses and minuses and the pretty colors on the monitor screen" (www.seykota.com/tribe/TT_Process/index.htm).

Phase 3: As individuals continue to untie their psychological knots, long-standing, recurring, and destructive dramas disappear. One will notice a decrease in obsessive defensive anxiety, and an increase in a healthy anticipatory expectation of the future. A feeling of balance between emotion and logic, of being in the zone, an increase in creativity, an increase in physical health, improvement in friendships and relationships, and successful trading are the result.

ECKHART TOLLE: HELPING PEOPLE ACHIEVE INNER PEACE AND GREATER FULFILLMENT, A PREREQUISITE TO OPTIMIZED TRADING AND LIVING

Eckhart Tolle has become one of the great spiritual teachers of our time. *The Power of Now* has had a hugely positive impact on the planet and has been translated into fifteen different languages. The essence of his teaching is simple: Remain in the present, for that is all we have. But so many people find this challenging as they obsess about the past on some wrong that was done to them or some mistake they made.

Here are some examples of the mental games traders can play:

- *"I can't believe I sold that stock under what I paid, so even though it's set up to buy again, I won't touch it. Fool me once, shame on you. Fool me twice, shame on me."*

So this trader lets his emotions get in the way of his rational thinking. He got burned once by this stock, so now he has a negative bias against it, even though it may still be a perfectly good stock with a great buy point.

- *"I am so upset I held onto this position too long, so I'll just wait until it gets back to where I paid so I can at least break even on the trade."*

  Meanwhile, their focus is often taken away from new stocks that are buyable so they miss out on new profitable opportunities.

Just as with obsessing about the past, many people worry about the future. For example:

- *"I hope the stock I bought goes higher even though it's well under what I paid for it."*

  Instead of hoping, they should fear instead the possibility that the stock will go lower and so it should be sold.

- *"I'm afraid the stock will drop since it has risen so much, so I had better sell it up here to lock in profits, and you can't go broke taking profits."*

  Selling a stock because one is fearful that it has risen "too much" is not a reason to sell a stock if the stock has done nothing wrong and continues to act properly. Instead, traders should be hoping it continues to act well and move to a higher price, and thereby hold onto the stock.

- *"How will I pay my bills if that stock doesn't get back to my breakeven point?"*

  As O'Neil has said, never trade from a position of fear. Scared money never wins.

So while obsessing about the past or worrying about the future can take one's focus away from the present, that is not to say that there is no place for what Tolle calls "clock time" where one strategizes and plans for the future. What Tolle tells us to guard against is "psychological time" where the person gets stuck in the past or continuously worries about the future. Such distraction can derail a person from staying focused in the present. If people spend too much time thinking about their circumstances, rather than simply doing something in the present to make incremental progress, they are more likely to fail. To use an American football analogy, the player found "small holes," but he ran through every one of them, finally getting to the goal line. O'Neil would tell us to always work hard and to understand that progress is often incremental, and to just keep "running for daylight, wherever you see it."

Life is rarely still, but we can maintain a state of peace and harmony by staying in the present and dealing with whatever challenges life throws at us. An analogy we have always loved is that every person is like an ocean. Life is the stuff on the surface that happens. Sometimes, the surface can be quite turbulent and volatile, but it is still only on or near the surface. The real you is all the depth under the surface, which cannot be disturbed and is connected to all other oceans. So whatever challenges or setbacks may occur, know that this depth is the real you, and acknowledging and focusing on this depth will keep you grounded, so that when life's challenges arise, you will be best equipped to handle the situation. Like the great redwoods that live for thousands of years, they let life unfold naturally, absent of worry.

Worry and unhealthy obsession are rooted in the ego, and the ego often fuels the mind with obsessive thoughts that can dominate one's focus and take them out of the present. Leaving your ego behind can be the best prescription for staying in the present. Tolle says that the next time something bad happens, instead of going into mental overdrive, observe yourself thinking, as if you were an outside observer observing you. When you do this, you may see that all this thinking noise that goes on inside your head is not really you, and any tough times that arise are also not you, but just stuff that passes through. Keep a comfortable space, an "inner stillness," between you and whatever is happening. Whenever the market does something completely unexpected and which could cause big losses in one's trading account, one market wizard we knew was famous for addressing the situation by calmly saying to himself, "Isn't this interesting," and then proceed to quietly observe the situation unfolding, taking any needed action in the present. This inner stillness will keep you in the present so that you can take the best possible course of action since you will be able to maintain your focus. This inner stillness is your true self-esteem. Do not let your ego disconnect you from this. Also, once you can let go of your ego, you will no longer be attached to labels nor hurt by criticism.

Inner stillness is the true you which is analogous to the depth of the ocean. Your words and actions that flow from this spaciousness, this inner stillness, will be helped by universal forces, since you attract and manifest according to what is going on inside of you. Like radio waves that are emitted through the atmosphere, you send out various levels of energy based on how you feel, and how you feel is referred to as your "vibrational state." A high vibrational state corresponds to feelings of joy, euphoria, and passion while a low vibrational state corresponds to boredom, depression, anger, and self-pity. This is discussed in more detail in the following section on Esther Hicks who writes that the higher the frequency of your vibrational state, the more positive the circumstances you will attract into your life. It is therefore important to accept and embrace whatever happens to you, because you are then in the strongest state and therefore best equipped to deal with the situation. In a sense, after tragedy occurs, true acceptance of what has happened is when the healing begins. This is akin to Seykota's TTP where traders emotionally embrace what Fred is telling their CM, which simply means that their CM fully acknowledges Fred's message, and this leads them to their Aha! moment. TTP essentially short-circuits and bypasses the stages of denial, anger, bargaining, and depression that occur when tragedy strikes. That said, as Tolle writes in *Practicing the Power of Now* (Novato: New World Library, 2001, 135), "Don't let the mind use the pain to create a victim identity for yourself out of it. Feeling sorry for yourself and telling others your story will keep you stuck in suffering. Since it is impossible to get away from the feeling, the only possibility of change is to move into it; otherwise, nothing will shift." Tolle advocates moving into the painful emotion, embracing it, surrendering to it just as Ed Seykota's TTP would advise; otherwise you will be likely to repeat it by way of the subconscious mind, re-creating the same situations over and over again. True acceptance of what has occurred is akin to the CM fully acknowledging Fred's message.

True acceptance of any negative news or tragedy should not be confused with negative mind-sets or negative attitudes, both of which are poison. O'Neil used to tell his employees that anyone with a persistently negative attitude would be fired. A negative state of mind can be caused by letting one's ego rule one's thinking, and such thinking often leads to negative, worrying, and often obsessive thoughts. When asked how one drops negativity, Tolle simply answers in *The Power of Now: A Guide to Spiritual Enlightenment* (Novato: New World Library, Vancouver: Namaste Publishing, 2004, 79), "By dropping it. How do you drop a piece of hot coal that you are holding in your hand? How do you drop some heavy and useless baggage that you are carrying? By recognizing that you don't want to suffer the pain or carry the burden anymore and letting go of it."

Practicing the Power of Now includes several exercises we have found useful:

- Watch your thoughts and emotions as well as your reactions to various situations. Notice if your attention is in the past or future. Like darkness that cannot escape the light, such attention dissolves when you shine the light of consciousness on it. Whenever you feel negativity rising within you, tell yourself to get out of your mind and be present. Keep a trading diary where you note your thoughts and feelings as your react to the daily twists and turns of the stock market.
- Stay focused on whatever you are doing. Do not get sidetracked by wondering when the gains will come or by the gains that have come. This is akin to counting the money in your trading account or making the market pay for luxuries you don't yet have. Focus on making

decisions in real time and reacting to what the market is actually doing, rather than what you think it should be doing, or what you fear or
hope it might do.

- Monitor your mental and emotional state through self-observation.
Your interest should be more on what goes on inside you than on what
happens outside. If your inside is in alignment, the outside falls into
place. Do you ever feel guilt, pride, resentment, anger, regret, or self-
pity? If so, you are reinforcing a false sense of self and accelerating the
aging process by building up a storehouse of the past in your psyche.
These negative feelings can take away your focus from the matter at
hand, namely trading, which requires being fully in the now.

- Give up waiting as a state of mind. Just be, and enjoy being. If you are
in the now, you never have to wait for anything. Don't say to yourself,
"Someday, I will have made enough money in the market to own that
big house." Life is in the now.

- Become aware of your breathing as you trade. This can help restore
focus. This is a particularly powerful technique for anyone, and especially for those who meditate. "Blanking" the mind will paradoxically
lead to answers because it enables a person to access inner stillness.
One can also focus attention on the body, a technique that can take
one's attention away from one's thinking. Ask yourself, "Is my body
alive? Can I feel life and energy in my hands, arms, legs, and feet?"
As you breathe, observe how your lower abdomen gently expands and
contracts. When you can feel your inner body's energy, let go of any visual image and focus exclusively on the feeling. Become one with it, so
that there is no boundary between you and your body, no boundary between your inner and outer self, and no boundary between you and all
that is—as you become one with all that is. The more consciousness
you direct into your inner body, the higher its vibrational frequency,
much like a light that grows brighter as you turn up the dimmer. In this
state, you tend to attract positivity that reflects this higher frequency.
You are anchored in the now, where the external world and your egoic
mind cannot overtake you.

- Whenever you need to find an answer to a problem or are looking for
a creative solution, stop thinking. Focus your attention on your inner
self for at least a few minutes. While doing this, the answers may come.
If not, at least your thinking will be fresh and creative when you re-
sume your task. We have come up with some of our more creative
trading ideas and research ideas in this manner, and sometimes will
even "dream" on it.

- Offer no resistance to life. This means being in a state of ease and light-
ness. Should the market go against your positions, you are relaxed and

can take the best course of action. You maintain clarity. You lose the need for things to be in a certain way. Your dependence on outer form is gone. Paradoxically, when you reach this state, the general conditions of your life, that is, the outer forms, tend to improve greatly. All good things, of course, will still eventually come to an end, but with your dependence on form gone, you have no fear, and life easily flows.

- Should someone say or do something that is rude or hurtful, instead of unconsciously reacting by attacking or defending or withdrawing, let it pass right through you. Do not resist. You can still tell people their behavior is unacceptable, but you are in control of your inner state. You are then in your power, not someone else's, nor are you controlled by your ego. Watch out for any kind of defensiveness within yourself. Is your ego trying to protect itself? By identifying your defensiveness, you remove your identification with it. In the light of your conscious awareness of it, this defensiveness will dissolve. Arguments and power mind games, which are destructive to relationships, also dissolve. While this relates to dealing with others, it can spill over into one's trading if one's focus is temporarily derailed due to some prior disagreement that is festering in one's mind.

- Paradoxically, do not look for peace. Forgive yourself if you are not at peace, namely, if you find yourself obsessing about the past or worrying about the future. As you accept and surrender to not being at peace, you are accepting what is, which is essential to being in the now, and every moment can become the best moment, which, in its purest essence, is enlightenment. Surrendering brings about important change. By surrendering, Tolle does not mean giving up or failing to rise to the challenges of life. Instead, you see clearly what needs to be done, doing one thing at a time, focusing on one thing at a time. As Tolle writes in *Practicing the Power of Now* (Novato: New World Library, 2001, 115), "Surrender is the simple but profound wisdom of yielding to rather than opposing the flow of life. The only place where you can experience the flow of life is the Now, so to surrender is to accept the present moment unconditionally and without reservation. It is to relinquish inner resistance to what is." Thus, should your positions in the market take a nosedive, you don't need to deceive yourself by hoping they will bounce back, or worse, by denial or by blocking out the situation, as some traders have been known to bury their trades in such dire situations. You accept the situation fully; then you take action by doing everything you can to repair the situation. That might mean taking a loss on multiple positions. But losses, whether big or small, can always become bigger, so deal with the issue now.

We conclude Tolle with a powerful passage from his seminal bestseller *A New Earth* (New York: Penguin Group, 2005):

> *There are many accounts of people who experienced that emerging new dimension of consciousness as a result of tragic loss at some point in their lives. Some lost all of their possessions, others their children or spouse, their social position, reputation, or physical abilities. Whatever they had identified with, whatever gave them their sense of self, had been taken away. Then suddenly and inexplicably the anguish or intense fear they initially felt gave way to a sacred sense of Presence, a deep peace and serenity and complete freedom from fear. When forms that you had identified with, that gave you your sense of self, collapse or are taken away, it can lead to a collapse of the ego, since ego is identification with form. When there is nothing to identify with anymore, who are you? When forms around you die or death approaches, your sense of Beingness, of I Am, is freed from its entanglement with form: Spirit is released from its imprisonment in matter.*
>
> *You realize your essential identity as formless, as an all-pervasive Presence, of Being prior to all forms, all identifications. You realize your true identity as consciousness itself, rather than what consciousness had identified with. The ultimate truth of who you are is not I am this or I am that, but I Am.*
>
> *When you yield internally, when you surrender, a new dimension of consciousness opens up. If action is possible or necessary, your action will be in alignment with the whole and supported by creative intelligence, the unconditioned consciousness which in a state of inner openness you become one with. Circumstances and people then become helpful, cooperative. Coincidences happen. If no action is possible, you rest in the peace and inner stillness that come with surrender (56–58).*

ESTHER HICKS: TEACHER OF THE LAW OF ATTRACTION

Esther Hicks defines true success as the amount of joy you feel as you live your life. She writes that the universal law, like the physical law of gravity, is that the more joy you feel, the higher your vibrational frequency. The higher your vibrational frequency, the faster you will manifest what you desire. When we feel good, we are enabling the universe to deliver our desires. When we feel bad, we are closing ourselves off to our connection with the universe. Anyone can walk the path that leads to this higher vibrational frequency. We have all heard of the power of positive thinking. Hicks says it is rather the power of positive feeling and the power of positive doing that serve as far more potent methods to raise one's vibrational frequency. In her books, *The Law of Attraction* (Hay House, 2006) and *Ask and It Is Given* (Hay House, 2004), she gives many mental exercises readers can practice to raise their vibrational frequency. In more challenging circumstances, such as the death of a loved one, or the loss of a job, feeling positive in the face of such loss or disaster can be nearly impossible, but the power of positive doing often will change people's mind-set so they can begin the healing process and eventually come to terms with the situation. But before one is even willing to take action and do, one must accept and embrace the loss or the tragedy as prescribed by Tolle, and this means accepting and embracing the sadness, the depression, and the loss; otherwise, one may remain in a prolonged state of deep depression where one does nothing and only thinks and feels negative thoughts. Remember, it is how you react to what happens that matters.

Using a real-life analogy where tragedy can strike at any moment, Mario Andretti said he rarely crashes because while most drivers panic and focus on the wall when going into an out-of-control skid, he focuses on the road, on where he wants to go. This is a great metaphor for achieving one's goals, even in the face of great hardship and potential disaster.

Putting together the teachings of Tolle and Hicks, we have the following strategy when bad news hits, whenever we suffer a loss, or when major disaster strikes:

Phase 1: Accept and embrace loss/surrender to tragedy, which leads to ...

Phase 2: The power of positive doing, which leads to ...

Phase 3: The power of positive feeling, which leads to ...

Phase 4: The power of positive thinking.

All four phases immediately produce a higher vibrational state within people, so they can immediately begin to attract what they want into their life, but the key is in raising ones vibrational state. Phases 1, 2, and 4 all can lead to Phase 3 which directly raises one's vibrational frequency, and in turn positively impacts one's trading.

JACK CANFIELD: SEMINAL WORKS ON PERSONAL OPTIMIZATION

According to the results of a famous NASA experiment, it takes 30 days to permanently rewire your brain. Astronauts had to wear goggles that turned everything in their view upside down. After a few days, they were able to learn their new "upside down" environment so they could effectively move about. After 30 days, the rewiring in their brains became permanent so they could go back to a normal view, but then be able to put on the "upside down" goggles and still move about with ease. The astronauts who took their "upside down" goggles off after 15 days and then put them back on after a few days had to relearn how to move in their upside-down world. They could not just move about with the same ease that the astronauts who had worn the goggles for 30 days were able to. This proved that it took 30 days to rewire the brain permanently. The findings carry a broader message, which is that we are capable of massive change in any area we choose, but we must practice this change for 30 uninterrupted days to make it permanent. Most people do not consistently practice something they wish to change about themselves for 30 days straight, but that is what it takes. Anyone can make positive changes within themselves if they institute whatever it is they wish to change about themselves into their lives for 30 days.

Jack Canfield, author of *Chicken Soup for the Soul* (HCI, 2001), among many other noteworthy books, suggests focusing on your goals for 30 days by first writing them down on 3×5 index cards, visualizing the goal, going forward in time and stepping into the goal, "feeling" what it's like to have already achieved the goal, which has the effect of emotionally engaging yourself, and then looking back to see the things you had to do to make it happen. This is an effective way of programming your subconscious, which represents 85 percent of your brainpower. And since your brain sends out brainwaves just like radio signals, know that when you think a thought, others may be picking up those thoughts perhaps on a subconscious level. In this way, you can draw people into your focus by sending out your positive thoughts. This is why the message from the documentary, *The Secret* is so powerful. When you visualize your goals, and feel what it is like to have achieved those goals, you send out a powerful message to the world. The "how" will show up in various ways that provide the path upon which you will travel to achieve your goals. For example, not only will others pick up your positive thoughts on a subconscious level, but they will also see the change in you in your body language, your mannerisms, your energy, and your attitude, and perhaps be more likely to assist. So it is imperative that you optimize the thoughts you hold in your head. Change your thinking from negative to positive. Stop looking at negative news, and drop out of the "ain't it awful" club. If you are around people who are negative or who constantly complain, keep your distance. Read uplifting books, biographies, and books on leadership mind-sets. And don't let fear stop you from achieving your goals. Embrace the fear and do it anyway.

Interestingly, Dean Radin, a well-regarded scientist who was interviewed in the documentary *What the Bleep?* spoke of how he has observed that people's thoughts could affect the outcomes of computerized random number generators to a statistically significant degree. In his experiments, a group of people in a room together focused at once and in unison on either of two numbers, a "zero" and a "one," that would be randomly spit out by a computer. If the group focused on zeroes, the computer would spit out zeroes with greater frequency, and in a manner that was statistically significant. Thus if people's thoughts can have an outward effect, much like radio waves permeating the atmosphere even though we cannot see them, and influence the numbers being spit out "randomly" by a computer, this is further evidence for always keeping one's thoughts positive. Beware of negative thinkers and the energy they emit!

PSYCHOLOGICAL CHECKLIST: QUESTIONS TO ASK YOURSELF

As we continue to move ahead, it can be instructive to create psychological checkpoints to insure progress. Certain questions should be asked, and even creating a daily or weekly "to do" list can be beneficial. Here are some questions and daily exercises that can help one stay on track and remain in an optimized state.

Abundance versus Scarcity

Those who smile inwardly at the misfortune of others come from a mental state of lack. Envy is born from this state of scarcity. Renowned philosopher Ayn Rand wrote in her essay "The Age of Envy" (*The Objectivist*, 1971) that the culture in the United States is one of envy where people love to marry the rich and famous to scandal. The misery encountered often gives such people a feeling of comfort and satisfaction.

People should honestly ask themselves if they come from a state of scarcity or "lack," or a state of abundance. To find the answer, people should ask themselves if they feel even a hint of satisfaction when someone more successful or wealthy than they takes a fall. This is not to be confused with a healthy drive against a competitor. If you come from a state of abundance, you should honestly feel happy at other people's success, wealth, and riches. If you look up to their achievements in your own goal setting, and set your goals accordingly, then this is a healthy indication that you are coming from a state of abundance. You see the world as providing limitless opportunities for yourself, so that the world is indeed yours, whether you are seeking adventure, accomplishments, wealth, or rewarding and mutually supportive personal relationships.

Confidence versus Insecurity

It is a commonly held belief that being smart, being right, or displaying wealth means commanding respect and influence. Others strive to look as good as possible by wearing the best clothes, obsessing about their bodies, and undergoing cosmetic surgery. While there is nothing wrong with looking good and being proud of one's accomplishments or sharing the news of these accomplishments with others, people must ask themselves if they are crossing over the line by doing any of the above to show off or so that they can secure bragging rights. All of this is nothing less than a form of an unhealthy, oversized ego or superiority complex. Bragging about one's car, one's house, one's bank account, the number of shares bought, one's grades, one's clothes, or one's physical beauty all could imply insecurity and a lack of confidence. Likewise, an inferiority complex is just the reverse of this but also presupposes a person who lacks confidence.

Truly enlightened people do not need to be respected or loved, or need to practice such bragging rights, as they know that on a cellular level everyone is one, everyone is connected, and they are connected to their infinite potential and stillness and infinite depth at all times.

Life's Purpose

On a daily basis, affirm your goals, affirm your talents, practice giving thanks for all that is good in your life, meditate to clear your mind, focus on how you can both evolve yourself and evolve others, focus on the good you can do, have fun with everything you do, even if it may be a task that is normally dull or unpleasant by reframing your perspective of the task, and get into the habit of asking yourself the questions, "How can I help?" "How can I be a positive influence on others?" and "How can I use part of the money I make in the market to help others and help my favorite charities?" Even a word of appreciation or a devoted glance is often all it takes to lift another person's spirits. This is real power. Real power is power than cannot be taken away from you. Wealth, status, physical beauty—these can quickly vanish. Spiritual beauty, on the other hand, is yours and yours to share forever. All of these practices will not only serve to raise your vibrational frequency, but will also create strong positive, empowering neural connections within your mind, so that you can achieve your goals as you uplift others around you.

When you encounter a negative event, especially if it is one of great loss or tragedy, use the event to surrender as prescribed by Tolle so you gain inner peace, that quiet comfortable space around you, that inner stillness. Inner peace is far greater and deeper than happiness which is just a temporary state. Your inner peace manifests by your connecting deeply with your deep pool of radiant energy and will result in being your most effective so that you can create the best outcome as the universal energies work in your favor.

PARALLELS BETWEEN TEACHINGS

There are beautiful parallels between Ed Seykota's teachings and the teachings of those who are not necessarily focused in the world of investments, including notable authors like Eckhart Tolle, Esther Hicks, Jack Canfield, Bob Proctor, and Wallace D. Wattles, whose books we have read and put into practice. Documentaries such as *The Secret*, *What the Bleep?* and *Moses Code* also make excellent resources. These teachings are not about proselytizing others to your world view or your way of doing things. In fact, proselytizing has no place here, since that would be about converting someone to your belief system or faith, and telling people what they should believe. These teachings are not a belief system but a process to help people reach their highest potential and to develop their own beliefs. To the extent that the teachings themselves become a belief system, and people try to convert others to it, these teachings no longer serve their original intention.

That said, we have all seen ludicrous amounts of advertisements and spam that promise to make people rich or fulfilled through various techniques. The best techniques give honest, useful advice. So if readers have not read any of the books or visited any of the web sites mentioned in this chapter before, then they should read works by some of the authors mentioned in this chapter. The key is to put the learning into practice. Don't fall into the trap of becoming a book and seminar junkie. Some people love buying and reading these books because they make them feel good, and they love going to the seminars where they can be inspired, yet for some reason, they are often not much better off in the future, financially, emotionally, or spiritually.

We remember a William O'Neil + Company, Inc workshop that we were conducting with Bill O'Neil in New York City back in 2001. We thought to ourselves as we scanned the audience, which numbered about 800, that probably only a tiny handful would make consistent and diligent use of this information. To make proper use of the information we were teaching, required learning, doing, having discipline, and being diligent, not just for a few months, but indefinitely. Most people fall short of this. The key is to take consistent action permanently, not just over the short or long term, by putting the knowledge to good use. It can be easy to make big commitments at these seminars when energy levels are running high, but the real test is in the months and years that lie ahead.

IN CONCLUSION

We are all on an evolutionary path not just as traders but in a larger sense as human beings. Even though most of us may not be truly 100 percent enlightened, just as it may be close to impossible to trade flawlessly, life is a learning and growing process where we evolve and help others to evolve. The benefit is twofold since by elevating others, we raise our own vibrational state, which, in turn, brings us closer to our goals.

In our own experiences, there were times we have learned more by teaching others than by learning directly from the masters such as O'Neil. We found that teaching was often a way to solidify the concepts in addition to the benefit of feeling good about helping another person understand and make profitable use of a concept. In a larger sense, just as finding one's true passion in life is paramount, those who also find a cause that resonates deeply within themselves where they can take action and make a difference, generally leading more fulfilled lives.

Trading is life, and life is trading. Like life, the markets will throw a variety of situations at you. Like life, the markets will try to "throw" you. What can make the difference between fulfillment and emptiness, success and failure, joy or frustration, will be your ability to remain in the present as you calmly assess the situation, free of the egoic mind, and effortlessly react to the situation at hand as it is unfolding. In this way, you will grow and evolve, not only to help yourself, but to become a positive influence and shining example to everyone you encounter.

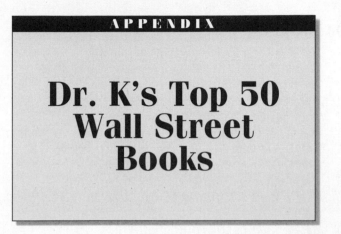

Dr. K's Top 50 Wall Street Books

T he following is a list of books that I feel deserve mention. In terms of the Top 50 list, these are books that helped broaden or deepen my understanding of how markets function, helped me understand my own personal investment psychology as a trader, or helped further develop and fine-tune my investment methodology. The number next to each title is its rank (on a scale of 1 to 10) in terms of quality and relevance. In terms of the Top Non–Investment-Related Books list, these are books that helped me align my personal psychology, which helped pave the way to success.

The copyright dates of books written before 1960 are in boldface. It is interesting to read books written in entirely different eras to understand that human nature has not changed. This is why a sound methodology can endure over decades if not centuries.

The Top 50

9.9 *How to Make Money in Stocks* by William O'Neil
9.9 *How to Make Money Selling Stocks Short* by William O'Neil and Gil Morales
9.9 *Trend Following* by Michael Covel
9.8 *The Battle for Investment Survival* by Gerald Loeb **1935**
9.8 *Reminiscences of a Stock Operator* by Edwin Lefèvre **1923**
9.7 *Lessons from the Greatest Stock Traders of All Time* by John Boik
9.7 *The Best: Tradingmarkets.com Conversations with Top Traders* by Kevin Marder
9.7 *The New Market Wizards* by Jack Schwager

9.7   *Market Wizards* by Jack Schwager
9.7   *Bulls Bears & Millionaires* by Robert Koppel
9.7   *The Mind of a Trader* by Alpesh B. Patel
9.7   *How to Trade in Stocks* by Jesse Livermore **1940**
9.7   *The Winning Edge* by Jake Bernstein and Nancy Toghraie
9.6   *Zen in the Markets* by Edward Allen Toppel
9.6   *Stock Market Logic* by Norman Fosback
9.5   *The Art of Contrary Thinking* by Humphrey B. Neill **1954**
9.5   *Wall Street Ventures and Adventures* by Richard Wyckoff **1930**
9.5   *The Wall Street Waltz* by Kenneth Fisher
9.5   *The Momentum-Gap Method* by Robert Cable
9.5   *How I Made $2 Million in the Stock Market* by Nicolas Darvas **1960**
9.5   *Money Talks* by Robert Koppel
9.5   *The Roaring 2000s* by Harry Dent, Jr.
9   *Tape Reading and Market Timing* by Humphrey B. Neill **1931**
9   *Only Yesterday–An Informal History of the 1920s* by Frederick Allen **1931**
9   *Liar's Poker* by Michael Lewis
9   *The Amazing Life of Jesse Livermore* by Richard Smitten
9   *Jesse Livermore Speculator King* by Paul Sarnoff
9   *How to Be a Billionaire* by Martin Fridson
9   *One-Way Pockets: The Book of Books on Wall Street Speculation* by Don Guyon **1917**
9   *Twenty-Eight Years in Wall Street* by Henry Clews **1888**
9   *Secrets of the Investment All-Stars* by Kenneth Stern
8.8   *Causes of the 1929 Stock Market Crash* by Harold Biermann, Jr.
8   *Trader Vic—Methods of a Wall Street Master* by Victor Sperandeo
8   *Trader Vic II—Principles of Professional Speculation* by Victor Sperandeo
8   *Winning on Wall Street* by Martin Zweig
8   *Trading for a Living* by Dr. Alexander Elder (with study guide)
8   *The Ups and Downs of a Wall St. Trader during the Depths of the Great Depression of the 1930s* by David Feldman
8   *Statistical Reasoning* by Gary Smith
8   *Wall Street: A Pictorial History* by Leonard Levinson
8   *Oh Yeah?* By Edward Angly **1931**
8   *Market Timing for the Nineties* by Stephen Leeb
8   *Intermarket Technical Analysis* by John Murphy
8   *Extraordinary Popular Delusions & the Madness of Crowds* by Charles Mackay **1841**

8 *Encyclopedia of Technical Market Indicators* by Robert Colby & Tom Meyers
8 *The New Money Masters* by John Train
7 *The Technical Analysis Course* by Thomas Meyers
7 *The Tao Jones Averages* by Bennett Goodspeed
7 *The Money Culture* by Michael Lewis
7 *The Hulbert Guide to Financial Newsletters* by Mark Hulbert

Best of the Rest

7 *The Education of a Speculator* by Victor Niederhoffer (imploded October 1997)
7 *Secrets of Profiting in Bull and Bear Markets* by Stan Weinstein
7 *One Up on Wall Street* by Peter Lynch
7 *Investments* (Text used in MBA Investments 233 course at UC Berkeley)
7 *Inside Wall Street* by S. Marshall Kemper **1920–1942**
7 *Dun & Bradstreet's Guide To Your Investments 1991* by Nancy Dunnan
7 *Confusion de Confusiones* by Joseph de La Vega **1800s**
7 *Confessions of a Stock Broker* by Andrew Lanyi
7 *Classics II* by Charles D. Ellis
7 *Bernard Baruch: My Own Story* by Bernard Baruch
7 *What Works on Wall Street* by James O'Shaunessy
7 *The Super Traders* by Alan Rubenfeld
7 *The Nature of Risk* by Justin Mamis
6 *The Mathematics of Money Management* by Ralph Vince
6 *Men and Mysteries of Wall Street* by James Medbery **1878**
6 *Market Movers* by Nancy Dunnan and Jay Pack
6 *Economics* by Paul Samuelson and William Nordhaus (text)
5 *The New Technical Trader* by Tushar Chande and Stanley Kroll
5 *The Merchant Bankers* by Joseph Wechsberg
5 *The Five-Day Momentum Method* by Jeff Cooper
5 *The New Stock Market* by Diana Harrington, Frank Fabozzi, and H. Russell Fogler
5 *How to Buy Stocks*, 7th edition, by Louis Engel and Brendan Boyd
5 *Handbook of Financial Markets* by Frank Fabozzi
5 *The Corporate Alchemists* by Lee Davis
5 *Portfolio Management Formulas* by Ralph Vince
5 *Hit and Run Trading* by Jeff Cooper

Top Non-Investment Related Books

The Power of Now by Eckhart Tolle
A New Earth by Eckhart Tolle

The Science of Getting Rich by Wallace D. Wattles
Ask and It Is Given by Esther Hicks
The Law of Attraction by Esther Hicks
Chicken Soup for the Soul by Jack Canfield
Sacred Hoops by Phil Jackson
Narrative of the Life of Frederick Douglas
The World As I See It by Albert Einstein
Wooden by John Wooden
Autobiography by Benjamin Franklin
Right Reason by William F. Buckley, Jr.
The Art of the Deal by Donald Trump
Leaders by Richard Nixon
Malcolm Forbes—The Man Who Had Everything by Christopher Winans
The Elements Beyond Uranium by Glenn Seaborg

About the Authors

GIL MORALES

Mr. Morales began his investment career in 1991 as a stockbroker in the Beverly Hills branch of Merrill Lynch. In 1994 he joined PaineWebber, Inc., where he quickly achieved Chairman's Club status as a top producer. In 1997, William O'Neil personally recruited Mr. Morales to join William O'Neil + Company, Inc. where he spent the next eight years as a vice-president, a top performing internal portfolio manager responsible for managing a portion of the firm's proprietary assets, and manager of the O'Neil Institutional Services group responsible for advising over 500 of the largest and most successful institutional investors in the world, including mutual fund, pension fund, and hedge fund clients. Mr. Morales also co-authored with William J. O'Neil a book on short-selling, *How to Make Money Selling Stocks Short*, published by John Wiley & Sons in 2004. In 2004, Mr. Morales was appointed Chief Market Strategist for William O'Neil + Company, Inc. Mr. Morales is the author and publisher of The Gilmo Report (www.gilmoreport.com) and co-author and publisher of *The Virtue of Selfish Investing* (www.virtueofselfishinvesting.com). Along with Dr. Kacher, Mr. Morales is currently a managing director of MoKa Investors, LLC, a Registered Investment Advisory firm. Mr. Morales received his B.A. in economics from Stanford University.

DR. CHRIS KACHER

In 1995, Dr. Kacher operated one of the first Internet-based stock advisory services. He then went on to generate triple digit percentage returns for six years in a row during the 1995–2000 period before moving to cash for most of the 2000–2002 bear market, one of the worst in history. From 1996–2001, Dr. Kacher served as stock market research analyst for William O'Neil + Company, the New York Stock Exchange member firm, institutional research provider, and publisher of *Investor's Business Daily* newspaper.

During this period, William O'Neil hand-picked Dr. Kacher to manage a portion of the firm's proprietary capital, whereupon Dr. Kacher became a top-performing internal portfolio manager at the company. Dr. Kacher is a frequent contributor to The Gilmo Report and the co-author and publisher of *The Virtue of Selfish Investing* (www.virtueofselfishinvesting.com). Along with Mr. Morales, Dr. Kacher is currently a Managing Director of MoKa Investors, LLC, a Registered Investment Advisory firm.

Musically gifted, Dr. Kacher was classically trained on the piano beginning at age 3, composing his first song at age 5, which he called "Night Fog," and performing as a concert pianist from ages 5 to 12 in high-profile cities in the United States and Japan. Dr. Kacher received his B.S. in Chemistry and Ph.D. in Nuclear Physics from University of California at Berkeley, where he was awarded the Berkeley Graduate Fellowship Award and the American Chemical Society award for excellence in undergraduate research. He co-discovered Element 110 on the Periodic Table of Elements and confirmed the existence of Element 106. Dr. Glenn Seaborg, the discoverer of plutonium and nine other elements, supervised Dr. Kacher's work as a doctoral student at U.C. Berkeley.

Index